MW01012073

THE SOUL'S UPWARD YEARNING

Robert J. Spitzer, S.J., Ph.D.

THE SOUL'S UPWARD YEARNING

Clues to Our Transcendent Nature
from Experience and Reason

Volume Two of the Quartet:
Happiness, Suffering, and Transcendence

IGNATIUS PRESS   SAN FRANCISCO

Nihil obstat: David J. Leigh, S.J.
                  Censor Librorum

Imprimatur: +The Most Reverend Kevin J. Vann, J.C.D., D.D.
                  Bishop, Diocese of Orange
                  June 29, 2015

Unless otherwise noted, Scripture quotations (except those within citations) are from the Revised Standard Version of the Bible—Second Catholic Edition, © 2006 by the National Council of the Churches of Christ in the United States of America. All rights reserved.

Cover design by John Herreid

© 2015 by Ignatius Press, San Francisco
All rights reserved
ISBN 978-1-58617-955-7
Library of Congress Control Number 2015939069
Printed in the United States of America ∞

In loving memory of my father and mother, who showed me a path to the transcendent through the connection between mind and heart. And to my brothers and sisters—John, Louise, Allan, and Lynne, and their families—who sustained me with their love and faith.

Love is like a fire. It rises perpetually upward, yearning to be absorbed at its very center.... And so the soul will be called, and so shall she be, God by participation.

—Saint John of the Cross,
Dark Night of the Soul

CONTENTS

ACKNOWLEDGMENTS

I am most grateful to Joan Jacoby—whose invaluable work transformed my thoughts once again into a full manuscript—for typing multiple copies of each chapter, making helpful editing suggestions, and helping with research. I am particularly grateful for her appreciation of the subject, and her undying patience.

I am also grateful to Joe Miller and Karlo Broussard for their important input and assistance on the manuscript, and Juliana Gerace for her help in preparing it.

I would also like to express my appreciation to the board and friends of the Magis Institute who gave me the time and resources to complete this Quartet.

INTRODUCTION

We live in paradoxical times—experiencing an increase in skepticism and antagonism toward the transcendent in the very era in which we have the greatest clarity about our interior awareness of the numinous, our ability to transcend artificial intelligence, our capacity to survive bodily death, evidence for a Creator from contemporary physics, and proof of God from contemporary metaphysics. Part of this paradox may be attributed to ignorance of these new discoveries as well as the popular culture's increased fascination with materialism. Yet, there is something still more fundamental underlying this trend—a kind of malaise, a superapathy that has distracted and even prevented people from asking the most important questions about true meaning and purpose in life. It is almost as if we have regressed to a pre-Platonic state in which many really don't care whether they are living for the fullest possible purpose, dignity, and destiny. It is as if some huge cultural propaganda machine has talked us out of believing that such an ideal is possible—and we really believe it and submit to a life that is second, third, or fourth rate by Platonic standards, settling for entertainment rather than enlightenment, for "good times" instead of contribution, for being admired instead of loving and being loved, and for image instead of reality.

The Rationale for This Book

As we shall see throughout this volume, there is considerable evidence to support the fact that we are transcendent beings and that an ultimate transcendent reality exists. For the moment, suffice it to say that there are some easily recognizable clues to our transcendent nature that should be considered before consigning ourselves to naïve materialism. A little over a century ago, the vast majority of people in every culture were religious,[1] and despite skepticism toward religion in contemporary Western culture, 84 percent of the world's population still remains religious today.[2] A cursory examination of this phenomenon indicates that the virtually universal propensity toward religion is more than mere group conformity. It seems to arise from within every individual person.[3]

This is further corroborated by a recent study published in the *American Journal of Psychiatry* that indicates that nonreligious affiliation leads to marked increases in suicide rates, familial tensions, drug use, and a sense of meaninglessness and despondency.[4] It seems that rejection of the transcendent leads to alienation from reality, others, and especially ourselves. Why would this occur if transcendence is not integral to our nature and consciousness?

There is another dimension to the loss of transcendence in our culture—prayer appears to be efficacious not only in healing our minds and hearts, but also our bodies. Though studies of the efficaciousness of intercessory prayer *at a distance* are inconclusive, there is considerable evidence that *proximal* intercessory prayer is effective in healing illnesses, even beyond the scope of medicine.[5] Furthermore, faith and prayer can be remarkably helpful in contending with suffering. Faith and loving friendships are the two most important factors for positively contending with daunting challenges, pain, deprivation, and grief.

---

[1] See Mircea Eliade, *The Sacred and the Profane: The Nature of Religion* (New York: Harcourt Brace Jovanovich, 1987), p. 211.

[2] See Pew Research Center, "The Global Religious Landscape", December 18, 2012, http://www.pewforum.org/2012/12/18/global-religious-landscape-exec.

[3] The important studies of Rudolf Otto and Mircea Eliade will be discussed in detail, along with the analysis of Immanuel Kant and John Henry Newman on conscience, in Chapters 1 and 2. See Rudolf Otto, *The Idea of the Holy: An Inquiry into the Non-Rational Factor in the Idea of the Divine and Its Relation to the Rational* (New York: Oxford University Press, 1958), and Eliade, *Sacred and the Profane*.

[4] See Kanita Dervic et al., "Religious Affiliation and Suicide Attempt", *American Journal of Psychiatry* 161, no. 12 (December 2004): 2303–8, http://ajp.psychiatryonline.org/article.aspx?articleid=177228, which indicates that a lack of religious belief increases suicide rates, drug addiction, tensions among family and friends, as well as decreased sense of meaning and destiny. See a summary of the study in this volume, Chapter 2.

[5] See Dale Matthew, M.D., and Connie Clark, *The Faith Factor: Proof of the Healing Power of Prayer* (New York: Viking Books, 1998) and Cindy Gunther Brown, Stephen Mory, Rebecca Williams, and Michael McClymond, "Study of the Therapeutic Effects of Proximal Intercessory Prayer (STEPP) on Auditory and Visual Impairments in Rural Mozambique", *Southern Medical Journal* 103(9) (September 2010): 864–69.

The loss of transcendence in our culture has led and will likely continue to lead to a decline in ethical motivation and conduct. The empirical study of K. Praveen Parboteeah[6] used the religious typology of Marie Cornwall[7] to confirm the findings of previous studies,[8] showing that "belief in church authority, religiosity's affective component, and the behavioral component are negatively related to individuals' willingness to justify unethical behaviors."[9] Thus, religion influences—and frequently strongly influences—people's unwillingness to be unethical. In view of these findings, the decline of religion is likely to lead to the continued decline of ethics in our culture.

In sum, the loss of transcendence in our culture has four negative consequences:

1. It causes us to underestimate and depreciate our nature, dignity, destiny, and meaning in life.
2. It takes away an important source of healing and consolation for those who are suffering and sick.
3. It causes alienation from reality, others, and ourselves, negatively impacting suicide rates, familial relations, substance use, and sense of fulfillment and hope.
4. It leads to a decline in ethical motivation within individuals and ethical conduct within culture.

If we do not try to help our culture overcome this self-limiting, self-depreciating, and self-destructive belief in "mere materialism", we consign ourselves to be a part of it, for its very negativity demands that those not controlled by it *do* something. What can we do? We might begin by being Socratic gadflies—irritants who unveil the

---

[6]See K. Praveen Parboteeah, Martin Hoegl, and John B. Cullen, "Ethics and Religion: An Empirical Test of a Multidimensional Model", *Journal of Business Ethics* 80, no. 2 (June 1, 2008): 387–98.

[7]See Marie Cornwall et al., "The Dimensions of Religiosity: A Conceptual Model with an Empirical Test", *Review of Religious Research* 27, no. 3 (March 1986): 226–44.

[8]See Charles R. Tittle and Michael R. Welch, "Religiosity and Deviance: Toward a Contingency Theory of Constraining Effects", *Social Forces* 61, no. 3 (March 1983): 653–82; Gary R. Weaver and Bradley R. Agle, "Religiosity and Ethical Behavior in Organizations: A Symbolic Interactionist Perspective", *Academy of Management Review* 27, no. 1 (January 2002): 77–97; Jonathan H. Turner, *The Institutional Order* (New York: Addison-Wesley Educational Publishers, 1997); and Thomas J. Fararo and John Skvoretz, "Action and Institution, Network and Function: The Cybernetic Concept of Social Structure", *Sociological Forum* 1, no. 2 (March 1, 1986): 219–50.

[9]Paraboteeah, Hoegl, and Cullen, "Ethics and Religion", p. 393.

truth, mystery, and transcendence of every person—by pointing to little clues, like cosmic emptiness, alienation, loneliness, and guilt.[10] We can show how these feelings reveal an incipient awareness of "something missing" in life, something profoundly unfulfilled, undiscovered, and unlived.

Since these feelings are only indications *that* something is missing in our lives, we will want to go further and reveal *what* is missing. Some people will intuitively know that cosmic emptiness, alienation, and loneliness is a yearning for a supreme transcendent reality, and they will readily acknowledge their need for such a reality and move toward faith. These individuals will probably not require much intellectual support, because they have a strong sense of their own transcendence, the presence of a higher transcendent reality, and the transcendent mystery of others. These individuals feel the presence of the spiritual and sacred, have an affinity for religious belief, and have a proclivity toward prayer. However, others, particularly in Western Europe and other parts of the world influenced by materialist assumptions, do not have this strong intuition of transcendence and the sacred. Their presumption that the physical world is the "really real" makes transcendence seem vague at best—and probably mere fantasy. A large percentage of these individuals do this a priori without examining, let alone challenging, their materialistic assumptions. This is astonishing, because if we really are transcendent beings, and there really is a transcendent reality calling us to an eternity of unconditional truth, love, goodness, beauty, and being, then this group will have literally abandoned their ultimate meaning, dignity, and destiny without a single reflective thought!

I believe we owe it to these individuals—as much as they owe it to themselves—to provide extensive evidence and deep insight into the possibility and plausibility of their transcendent nature and destiny. Failure to do so would amount to being a guilty bystander who watches a person harm himself without attempting to intervene. Herein lies the rationale for this book.

First and foremost, this book was written to help *readers* to redress objections to transcendence and Christianity, and to show the probative nature of the newest discoveries and studies in science, philosophy,

[10]See Volume I, Chapter 5, Section I.

psychology, and the New Testament. Though faith is ultimately grounded in the heart—in our affinity and need for God—we must also believe that the reality of God is not only credible, but worthy of certainty and conviction. The heart's reasons are essential, but without the mind's reasons, they might seem to be ungrounded idealism that can undermine conviction and openness to God and grace.

My hope is not only to help readers understand the mind's reasons, but also to provide a tool for them to communicate these reasons to others. Readers need not master the contents of this multifaceted justification of transcendence, but only familiarize themselves with the basic contents of it, so that they can point out chapters or pages that respond to people's questions, criticisms, and doubts with the latest findings from contemporary philosophy, science, psychology, and theology. The purpose for doing this is to *remove rational obstacles* to faith that are based on incomplete or sophistical argumentation.

This book does not provide the heart's reasons for faith, because these come from our interior desires and choices. So, for example, if someone feels no affinity for love or God, or believes that each of us can be our own ultimate purpose, fulfillment, and authority, or sees no need to be redeemed from darkness, decline, and self-centeredness, he will probably be disinclined to faith—if not antagonistic to it. All the mind's reasons will not convince him to move toward God or redemption. However, if the "heart's reasons" are acknowledged, then the "mind's reasons" can solidify belief and trust in God while providing conviction and motivation to pursue the path to salvation.

The Method and Plan of This Book

I decided to write this book from the *inside out*—from the interior awareness of transcendence to rational proof of God, as well as to the data of near-death experiences and to the data from contemporary physics and cosmology. This was prompted by my belief that most people begin their religious journey with an interior sense of the transcendent, which frequently becomes thematized through religious symbols, rituals, and practice—but not always. This is confirmed by the observations and studies of the numinous experience, religious desires, conscience, and religious myth discussed in Chapters 1 and 2. These studies strongly suggest that a transcendent reality comes to all of us interiorly—in the numinous experience (the interior presence of a mysterious, powerful, fascinating, daunting, and desirable "wholly Other"), our sense of the sacred (in religious community, tradition, ritual, and holy places and times), our consciences' informing us of good and evil, and our interior awareness of an archetypal myth calling us to be heroic in a cosmic struggle between good and evil. The transcendent not only makes itself present to us; it invites us to come closer to it, learn from it, and seek our ultimate destiny through it. This presence (and invitation) is the origin of faith, because it not only tells us about the reality of transcendence, but incites us to desire knowledge of and communion with it. It seems that we are imbued with this awareness and desire from a very early age, leading us to pursue religious revelation, community, ritual, and story, and eventually to seek rational justification for it. Is there additional evidence that can help us understand the source of this interior awareness of and desire for the transcendent?

In Chapter 3 we investigate our desire for perfect truth—the knowledge of everything about everything. The recognition of this desire goes back to the time of Plato, who revealed its extraordinary and mysterious nature. We turn to Bernard Lonergan's contemporary work *Insight: A Study of Human Understanding*[11] to delve more deeply into Plato's insight, and there encounter our tacit awareness of complete intelligibility. This leads Lonergan to his proof of God's existence (see Chapter 3, Sections III and IV). Lonergan shows that a "unique unrestricted act of thinking which is the Creator of all else" must exist and is the only possible source of our tacit awareness of complete intelligibility. God not only exists—He must be present to us.

This leads us to an exploration of the other three transcendental desires: for perfect love, for justice or goodness, and for beauty (Chapter 4). We make the discovery that perfect love must be the source of our desire for it, that perfect justice or goodness must be the source of its desire, and so also perfect beauty. We then show that perfect

[11] Bernard Lonergan, *Insight: A Study of Human Understanding*, in *Collected Works of Bernard Lonergan* 3, ed. Frederick E. Crowe and Robert M. Doran (Toronto: University of Toronto Press, 1992).

love, justice or goodness, and beauty must be the same reality as
perfect truth, that is, the unique unrestricted act of thinking. At this
point we no longer rely solely on our experience and intuition of the
transcendent within us; we also have rational verification of God's
existence and presence to us. The qualities of perfect truth, love,
justice or goodness, and beauty correlate with many of the characteristics of the numinous experience and our awareness of the sacred,
causing us to conclude that God is actively inviting us into His loving, fascinating, mysterious, awe-inspiring, majestic, sacred presence.

Is there other evidence for our transcendental nature and God's
presence to us? In Chapter 5, we explore a new kind of evidence
for our transphysical nature: near-death experiences. Contemporary medical studies of patients' experiences of transphysical existence after clinical death yield surprising results that cannot be easily
explained by hallucinatory theories and other hypothesized physical
causes. In literally thousands of cases, independent researchers have
verified patients' accounts of data occurring during the time of clinical death. Much of this data is quite unusual and could not have been
"guessed". Furthermore, 80 percent of blind people, most of whom
are blind from birth, experience sight during clinical death. Such
findings strongly suggest that we have a transphysical component that
is conscious, capable of vision, hearing, memory, recall, and motion.
These data not only suggest our transphysical nature but also the presence of a higher power, frequently described as an intensely loving
white light, that relates to us during clinical death. This combines
well with the previous analysis of our awareness of perfect truth-
love-justice or goodness-beauty as well as the numinous experience
and our desire for the sacred.

Chapter 6, "The Soul and Its Brain: Toward a Theory of Transphysical Self-Consciousness", endeavors to make a strong case for
our transcendental nature ("soul") within the contemporary debate
on consciousness and philosophy of mind. This is one of the major
grounds upon which the battle between materialism, panpsychism,
and transcendentalism is being waged. Unfortunately, the prevailing materialism within our academic and scientific culture is causing
many analytically oriented people to ignore the case for the transcendental soul, and to replace it with less explanatory philosophies—
such as quantum physicalism (a new form of materialism) and

protomentalism (panpsychism). The objective of the chapter is to help readers know how to respond to these partially explanatory views of consciousness so that they can live according to the fullness of their nature, dignity, and destiny. Reducing ourselves to mere atoms, molecules, or quantum systems—or to a mere dimension of a universal consciousness embedded in physical processes—causes us to "underlive" our lives, undervalue our dignity, and underestimate our nature and destiny, which is a completely avoidable self-imposed waste and travesty. Hopefully, this book can provide the experiential and rational ground to avert this tragic end.

In Appendix 1, we give a summary of recent evidence from physics and cosmology, pointing to a creation of physical reality by an intelligent transcendent cause. We explore the Borde-Vilenkin-Guth theorem for a beginning of any universe (or multiverse) with an average rate of expansion greater than zero,[12] the evidence for a beginning of the universe from entropy, and the implications of supernatural design in the occurrence of low entropy and the values of our universal constants at the Big Bang (13.8 billion years ago). This strongly implies the presence of a transcendent intelligent Creator, which correlates well with the conclusion of Lonergan's proof of God—the existence of a unique unrestricted act of thinking that is the Creator of all else that exists. In Appendix 2, we provide an additional proof of God's existence on the basis of the Thomistic insight that "existence precedes essence", which also correlates with Lonergan's proof of God and the evidence of contemporary physics and cosmology. This concludes our examination of the evidence for the transcendent from experience and reason.

Since the evidence in this book comes from a variety of sources and methods, it forms what John Henry Newman termed an "informal inference"[13] in which multiple antecedently and independently probable sources of data corroborate and complement one another. This allows for modifications of data in one or more sources, without affecting the probative force of the combined data in their mutual

---

[12] A "theorem" is a proof and should be distinguished from a "theory", which unifies particular observations within a consistent explanation. For this reason, the Borde-Vilenkin-Guth theorem is frequently referred to as a proof.

[13] See John Henry Newman, *An Essay in Aid of a Grammar of Assent* (Worcester, Mass.: Assumption Press, 2013), pp. 189–215.

corroboration. These data sets originate from four distinct evidential and methodological frameworks. First, the numinous experience, the desire for the sacred, and our four transcendental desires are based on our *interior experience* and intuition. Second, Lonergan's proof of God and the Thomistic proof of God are based on *logical proofs* applied to objective experience. Third, near-death experiences are based on *verified empirical data* reported by patients during clinical death. Fourth, the evidence of a transcendent intelligent cause beyond physical reality proceeds from theorems and theories based on scientific method applied to observational data.

This remarkable confluence of sources and methods forms a strong probative case for the existence of an ultimate transcendent Being as well as our transcendental and transphysical nature. At this juncture experience and reason (natural explanation) can go no further. Yet, questions about our transcendent destiny still abound. Does God grant eternal life? If so, what is that life like? Does God redeem suffering? If so, how? Does God answer prayers? Does He heal us interiorly? Is He unconditionally good and loving? Does He inspire and guide us? Can we be eternally separated from God? What is our path to salvation? Since these questions are beyond reason, we must look to the only available other source of answers: God Himself. We must seek the possibility and reality of God's self-revelation. This will be the content of Volume III of the Quartet—*God So Loved the World: Clues to Our Transcendent Destiny from the Revelation of Jesus.*

The Perspective of This Volume

We begin our exploration of transcendence (from experience and reason) with the *subjective* domain: our *interior* experience. Some readers may think this peculiar because convention dictates that we begin with our strongest *objective* (publicly corroborateable) evidence— evidence from logical proofs, physics and cosmology, or perhaps near-death experiences. This would make sense if we wanted to focus on the "mind's reasons" for transcendence, but the "mind's reasons" are not directly involved in the intuitive, emotional, and interpersonal dimensions of consciousness. However, transcendence *is* directly involved in these three dimensions of consciousness, so much so that it is hard to escape the thought that the transcendent is in a relationship with us from our very inception, inviting us evermore deeply into itself as the culmination of our purpose and destiny.

Thus we do not begin with the provable fact of the existence of God (the one unconditional and unrestricted act of thinking that creates all else that exists), but rather with the interior presence of a transcendent, mysterious, fascinating "wholly Other" who is concerned for us individually and collectively. Though objective evidence has the advantages of public corroboration and standards of clarity and certitude, its conclusions stand at a distance, leaving open the possibility that the transcendent might be dispassionate, uncaring, disinterested, and cold.

When we begin with four dimensions of our interior awareness of the transcendent—the numinous experience, the presence of the sacred, conscience, and the interior myth of cosmic struggle—we give primacy to the Transcendent Reality's passionate, interpersonal, dialogical, and concerned character. When the Transcendent Reality interacts with us interiorly, it reveals its desire and plan to bring us to fulfillment in itself. By starting with our interpersonal relationship with the transcendent, we will not be left with an "impersonal conclusion to a syllogism", but rather with the presence of a passionately interested transcendent reality whose omnipotence, omniscience, and creativity can be substantiated through logical proof, scientific evidence, and corroborated accounts of transphysical existence (during near-death experiences).

The reader may be wondering why I do not accentuate the passionate and interpersonal accounts of a particular mystical tradition, such as those of Saint Teresa of Avila, Saint John of the Cross, Julian of Norwich, or Evelyn Underhill in the Christian tradition. Though we discuss these accounts in other parts of this Quartet, I believe it is important to focus on well-documented, well-researched, transcultural, and interreligious scholarly studies of religious experience, because these will be less subject to the problems of personal, cultural, and religious perspectives, which we will want to consider seriously *after* exploring the more common features of religion and religious experience. For this reason, I focus first on the seminal and foundational studies of the American empirical philosopher and psychologist William James and the eminent German scholar of comparative religion Rudolf Otto (Chapter 1), and then turn to the most comprehensive scholar of the history of religion, Mircea Eliade (Chapter 2). These studies are complemented by the work of Immanuel Kant and John Henry Newman on moral obligation and conscience, and the work of Carl Jung on universal archetypes and the myth of cosmic struggle. Using these as a foundation, readers can add the accounts of mysticism in various religious traditions, noting how those traditions fit into the general descriptions provided by James, Otto, Eliade, and Jung.

The Christian mystical tradition is particularly enlightening and very well studied. Readers may want to begin with Benedict Groeschel's *Spiritual Passages: The Psychology of Spiritual Development*,[14] Saint Teresa of Avila's *Book of Her Life*,[15] and Saint John of the Cross' "The Living Flame of Love".[16] Readers interested in a deeper and more comprehensive study may want to consult Evelyn Underhill's *Mysticism: A Study in the Nature and Development of Spiritual Consciousness*,[17] and Adolphe Tanqueray's *The Spiritual Life: A Treatise on Ascetical and Mystical Theology*.[18]

[14]Benedict Groeschel, *Spiritual Passages: The Psychology of Spiritual Development* (New York: Crossroads Publishing, 1984).

[15]Teresa of Avila, *The Book of Her Life*, in *The Collected Works of St. Teresa of Avila*, vol. 1, trans. Kieran Kavanaugh and Otilio Rodriguez (Washington, D.C.: ICS Publications, 1976).

[16]John of the Cross, "The Living Flame of Love", in *The Collected Works of St. John of the Cross*, trans. Kieran Kavanaugh and Otilio Rodriguez (Washington, D.C.: ICS Publications, 1979).

[17]Evelyn Underhill, *Mysticism: A Study in the Nature and Development of Spiritual Consciousness* (New York: Renaissance Classics, 2012).

[18]Adolphe Tanqueray, *The Spiritual Life: A Treatise on Ascetical and Mystical Theology* (Rockford, Ill.: Tan Books and Publishers, 2013).

Chapter One

The Numinous Experience

Introduction

The evidence for our interior awareness of a transcendent reality is primarily subjective, though it is not limited to *our* personal subjective experience alone. It can be correlated with the subjective experience of thousands of others in different cultures and religions to detect similarities and patterns that show their virtually universal presence in both history and the contemporary age. Though this is not strictly speaking objective evidence (grounded in a similar extrinsic publically accessible data source), it is persuasive because of its multiple occurrences. This evidence, as William James notes, is not dissimilar from much of the evidence for neurosis, psychosis, and other mental disorders described in the annals of contemporary psychology. As we shall see, the evidence strongly indicates that individuals have religious experiences that have a common root. But does this common root indicate the presence of a *transcendent other* or only a manifestation of hyperimagination or hyperemotion arising out of merely natural causes? If one contends that the cause of the numinous is merely natural, then we will have to find *completely* naturalistic answers to the following questions: Why is 84 percent of the world religious?[1] Why do most world religions share seven common beliefs amid many differences?[2] Why do people from every culture throughout history

---

[1] As stated previously in the Introduction, according to a study by the Pew Research Center *84 percent* of the world's population (in 230 countries and territories) identify with a religious group. This encompasses 5.8 billion religiously affiliated adults and children out of a world population of 6.9 billion. See Pew Research Center, "The Global Religious Landscape", December 18, 2012, http://www.pewforum.org/2012/12/18/global-religious-landscape-exec.

[2] Freidrich Heiler enumerates seven major similarities among the seven major contemporary religions. See Freidrich Heiler, "The History of Religions as a Preparation for the Cooperation of Religions", in *The History of Religions*, ed. Mircea Eliade and J. Kitagawa (Chicago: Chicago University Press, 1959), pp. 142–53.

believe that something "wholly Other" is present to them and inviting them into itself?[3] Why do people from every culture throughout
history believe that this wholly Other is fascinating, wonderful, and
desirable amid its mystery and overpowering energy?[4] Why do the
vast majority of people from every culture feel a call to worship, both
privately and publicly?[5] Why do people of virtually every culture
naturally connect with symbols of transcendent mystery, power, and
glory?[6] Why do people of every culture throughout history have a
sense of sacred origins, places, times, and history?[7] Why does religious belief come so naturally to children of every culture?[8] Why
do divine goodness, divine power, personified evil, and evil power
appear in the dreams of virtually every religion and culture with similar symbols?[9]

Religious believers and mystics assert with certainty that our interior awareness of the absolute, the transcendent, the spiritual, and the
sacred comes from a divine source because this interior awareness is
of something other, something higher, something not controllable
by us. Though we sense this presence within us, we are aware that
it is outside of us, and if we allow it, it can sweep us into its energy,
mystery, and love.

Secular psychologists and anthropologists contend the opposite.
Some think that they have never had an experience of a divine other

---

[3] See Rudolf Otto, *The Idea of the Holy: An Inquiry into the Non-Rational Factor in the Idea of
the Divine and Its Relation to the Rational* (New York: Oxford University Press, 1958). This is
discussed explicitly below in Section I.

[4] See ibid.

[5] See Mircea Eliade, *The Sacred and the Profane: The Nature of Religion* (New York: Harcourt
Brace Jovanovich, 1987); discussed explicitly in Chapter 2.

[6] See ibid.

[7] See ibid.

[8] Harvard psychiatrist Robert Coles interviewed in depth over five hundred Catholic, Protestant, Jewish, Islamic, Native American, and agnostic children, ages eight through twelve,
living in North and South America, Europe, Africa, and the Middle East. He found that the
vast majority of children had a strong belief in a transcendent Deity who was in a relationship
with them personally and with others. Since they felt that God cared for them and had expectations of them, they had strong convictions about theological matters and wanted answers
to perceived contradictions between their spiritual experience and theological doctrines. The
children were earnest and sincere about their beliefs and theological viewpoints. See Robert
Coles, *The Spiritual Life of Children* (New York: Mariner Books, 1991).

[9] See Carl Jung, *The Archetypes and the Collective Unconscious*, in *Collected Works of C. G. Jung*,
vol. 9, pt. 1, trans. R. F. C. Hull (Princeton: Princeton University Press, 1981).

that incites humility, excitement, fascination, and worship. Others contend that they have such feelings, but are certain that their origin is from their unconscious minds and their free-floating imagination.

It is interesting to note that both groups come to the investigation of religious experience with a considerable number of presuppositions. Religious people not only come with openness to faith, but also with a desire not to reduce spiritual or transcendent data to materialistic or physical categories (they are methodologically nonreductionistic). Alternatively, secular psychologists and anthropologists tend to be closed to the possibility of transcendence and faith and feel the need to be reductionistic in order to be "honestly scientific".

There is a problem from the outset with attempting to reduce and explain transcendent and transphysical realities in terms of physical and material categories. Transcendent categories, by definition, go *beyond* the physical, and so we can never be sure whether physical categories are capable of explaining what lies beyond them. Scientific honesty does not require forcing square pegs into round holes. Should scientists ask whether transcendent experience is reducible to physical processes, or should they ask whether transcendent experience can*not* be adequately explained by physical processes? Should science be focused on how to make transcendent experience explicable by physical categories, or should it ask if transcendent experience has a dimension of the transphysical in it? Should people's experience of an absolute spiritual Other be respected as having a quality of genuine *otherness*? The enterprise of honest scientific inquiry is a matter of interpretation, but we should bear in mind that every reductionistic system falls prey to one of logic's most fundamental precepts (discussed earlier): that there are far more errors of omission than commission. These errors of omission can come from innocent ignorance or from willful aprioristic assumptions. But whatever the case, they generally produce history's most egregious intellectual and methodological blunders.

For this reason, I have chosen to discuss the topic of our interior awareness of the transcendent from two authors who are open to the transcendent, are not governed by reductionistic, methodological assumptions, are acquainted with a vast number of transcendent experiences from virtually every culture and religion, have understanding and respect for the symbols and expressions of those cultures and religions, and draw their conclusions from their vast empirical and historical studies: Rudolf Otto (Chapter 1) and Mircea Eliade (Chapter 2, Section I).[10]

I. The Numinous Experience

No one has influenced the study of the interior awareness of transcendence more than the great scholar of comparative religion Rudolf Otto in his classic work *The Idea of the Holy*. Though Otto borrowed from the American psychologist William James (*The Varieties of Religious Experience*)[11] and the liberal German theologian Friedrich Schleiermacher, he nuances and goes beyond them in many significant respects. His seminal work influenced the great historian of religion Mircea Eliade (see Chapter 2) and most major Protestant theologians of the twentieth century (including Karl Barth, Paul Tillich, and C.S. Lewis), as well as Catholic philosophers and theologians (e.g., Max Scheler and Karl Rahner).

After a comprehensive study of historical and contemporary religion, Otto concludes that most individuals have an irreducibly, nonrational experience of the numinous (the interior presence of the transcendent or divine).[12] The "numen" (that which is experienced as transcendent) presents itself fundamentally as "wholly Other",[13] having two distinct poles of *feeling*-content":

1. A sense of something mysterious, overwhelming, and daunting that elicits from us a sense of diminution, humility, submission, and creatureliness

[10] I will complement these studies with an analysis of how our awareness of the transcendent blends with our sense of *good and evil* from three points of view: Kant's and Newman's sense of the divine origin of moral duty and conscience (Chapter 2, Section II), Carl Jung's archetypes of God, devil, wise old man, and hero as indicative of a cosmic struggle between good and evil (Chapter 2, Section III), and J. R. R. Tolkien's belief that myth is explicitization of a deeply believed metaphysical (spiritual) reality in which individuals participate on their highest level (Chapter 2, Section III).

[11] See William James, *The Varieties of Religious Experience* (New York: Modern Library, 1929).

[12] See Otto, *Idea of the Holy*, pp. 6–7.

[13] As will be explained in Section II below, the numinous experience at base is one of mysteriousness in which the numinous object is felt to be completely different from the experiencing subject—"wholly Other". Otto describes it as follows: "Taken in the religious sense, that which is 'mysterious' is—to give it perhaps the most striking expression—the 'wholly other' ... that which is quite beyond the sphere of the usual, the intelligible, and the familiar" (ibid., p. 26).

2. A sense of something fascinating, desirable, good, caring, and comforting that invites us into its fullness, fulfills us, and in so doing produces a unique kind of spiritual joy (bliss)

Otto nuances the elements of these two poles in considerable detail, careful to show their nonrational (i.e., prerational, prereflective, prethematic) feeling-content that is intrinsic to the numen present to us. Before discussing these nuances, it must be emphasized that these different (virtually opposing) poles of feeling-content are not synthesized in *our* consciousness, but rather in the wholly-Other *numen* present to us. The wholly-Other numen is immediately present to us, and the two poles of feeling are synthesized in *it* (not in us). Otto asserts strongly that the presence of the numen to individuals is the foundation of religion throughout history and the world: "There is no religion in which [the numen present to individuals] does not live as the real innermost core, and without it no religion would be worthy of the name."[14]

It now remains to give a nuanced description of each of the poles, an explanation of their recognition in history, and their synthesis in both the numen itself and individual experience. This will be done in three sections:

1. The First Pole: *Mysterium Tremendum* in the Numen (Section II)
2. The Second Pole: Fascination, Desire, Love, and Bliss in Our Experience of the Numen (Section III)
3. The Unity and Opposition of Both Poles in Our Experience of the Numen (Section IV)

We will then consider the distinctive contribution of Christianity to the awareness of the transcendent: the *unconditional* love of God (Section V).

II. The First Pole: *Mysterium Tremendum* in the Numen

The elements of dread, awe, dauntingness, and creatureliness are the most evident dimensions of the numen in the early stages of the

---

[14] Ibid., p. 6.

development of individual and cultural religious consciousness.[15] Since this pole of feeling-content is manifest earlier in history than the elements of the second pole, it makes sense to address it first (as Otto does). However, by putting this pole in a primary position, we do not mean to imply that it is more important or powerful than the elements of the second (more positive) pole in a mature person or culture (see below, Section III).

Otto is in fundamental agreement with William James about the most basic appearance of the numen (though he thinks that James' analysis is somewhat unnuanced), and so he quotes James as follows:

> It is as if there were in the human consciousness a *sense of reality, a feeling of objective presence, a perception of* what we may call *"something there"*, more deep and more general than any of the special and particular "senses" by which the current psychology supposes existent realities to be originally revealed.[16]

Otto concurs with James that the numen appears as an objective presence, and that it is distinguishable from every other object we experience, because it is more deep and more general (all-encompassing) than all other objects. However, Otto goes further than James noting that this deep and all-encompassing objective reality appears to be very *powerful* and *spiritual*, causing us to be respectful, humble, and submissive before its presence. Otto calls this reaction "creature consciousness" and distinguishes himself from Friedrich Schleiermacher, who implies that the self-conscious act of being a creature is primary. Otto contends that the presence of the powerful and overwhelming numen is primary, and this causes us to react to it with a sense of reverence, humility, and creatureliness.[17]

There are two special characteristics of this first pole of experience: overwhelming power and spiritual presence. Notice that these two characteristics are categories of *thought*, and Otto insists that such categories are not primary to the experiencing subject, but rather are derived from more primary *feeling-contents*. So what are the feeling-contents that give rise to these categories of overwhelming power and spiritual presence?

---

[15] See ibid., pp. 32–33, and the explanation of it in Section III below.
[16] James, *Varieties of Religious Experience*, p. 58 (emphasis in original).
[17] Otto, *Idea of the Holy*, p. 10.

For Otto, the first response we have when the numen becomes present to our consciousness is fear—but not the fear we might have toward a natural object. Rather, it is the fear we have toward spiritual presence, such as ghosts. The fear of natural objects (that can threaten survival or safety) tends to produce a hyperactive state (induced by adrenaline), raising blood pressure, inciting panic, making us feel warm, and causing the face to flush. The fear we feel when confronted by a ghost or spirit (or hearing a ghost story) is quite different; it makes us feel cold and causes our blood pressure to drop, the blood to drain from our face, and our flesh to creep or crawl.

Otto terms this special kind of fear toward a spiritual presence "daemonic dread".[18] "Daemon" here does not mean "demon" in the sense of a malignant or evil spirit, but only "spirit" in a general sense that can refer to a benign or good spirit. When we feel the presence of a benign or good spirit, it evokes a sense of uncanniness, of being beyond our control or power. Its otherworldly character makes it unpredictable and feels *daunting*.[19] Though the numen does not present itself as evil, it does present itself as "beyond us" and capable of overpowering us.[20] We sense its overwhelming or superior power even if it is manifest in a "gentle tide, pervading the mind with a tranquil mood of deepest worship".[21] William James recounts a case study in which the superior power of the numen manifested itself gently and sublimely:

> The perfect stillness of the night was thrilled by a more solemn silence. The darkness held a presence that was all the more felt because it was not seen. I could not any more have doubted that *He* was there than that I was. Indeed, I felt myself to be, if possible, the less real of the two.[22]

This higher power carries with it a profound sense of mystery and incomprehensibility. Otto describes our experience of this incomprehensible mystery as "stupor", which he distinguishes from "tremor": "*Stupor* is plainly a different thing from *tremor*; it signifies

---

[18] Ibid., pp. 14, 16–17.
[19] See ibid., p. 14.
[20] See ibid., p. 19.
[21] Ibid., p. 12.
[22] James, *Varieties of Religious Experience*, p. 66.

blank wonder, an astonishment that strikes us dumb, amazement absolute."[23] We are tacitly aware that we cannot comprehend this higher power, and so we view it as *wholly Other*. In its overwhelming presence, we sense our creatureliness, what Otto and Schleiermacher term "creature consciousness".

There is one additional element in the feeling-content of the first pole; Otto describes it as "energy or urgency",[24] which betokens passion or will within the numen. The felt presence of the numen not only indicates spiritual presence, overwhelming power, and incomprehensible mystery, but also something personal and passionate in its energy. Otto states: "It everywhere clothes itself in symbolical expressions—vitality, passion, emotional temper, will, force, movement, excitement, activity, impetus."[25] Terms like "vitality", "passion", "emotional temper", and "will" are concepts—what Otto terms "symbolical expressions"— representing our experience of the more fundamental feeling-contents within the numen. So how does the numen appear to us through the feeling-contents of spiritual fear, dauntingness, overpoweringness, mysteriousness, and vitality-energy? It appears as a wholly-Other, superior, incomprehensible, and mysterious power with passion, emotion, and will that elicits from us a sense of creatureliness, humility, submission, respect, reverence, and worship.

From Otto's descriptions, we can infer four layers in our encounter with the numen: (1) a fundamental layer of *feeling-contents*—spiritual fear, tremor, dauntingness, overwhelmingness, stupor, mysteriousness, and energy-vitality; (2) a layer of *intuited appearance* of the numen—as a wholly-Other, spiritual, superior, incomprehensible power with passion and will; (3) a layer of *reaction* to the presence of this mysterious higher power—a sense of diminution, humility, respect, and creatureliness; and (4) a layer of action following our reaction—reverence and worship. This constitutes our initial or primary response to the numen. Some people, religions, and cultures do not move beyond this initial encounter with the numen (which Otto terms "the first pole"),[26] but most major religions do move beyond it to the second more positive pole of feeling-contents. This is borne

[23] Otto, *Idea of the Holy*, p. 26.
[24] Ibid., pp. 23–24.
[25] Ibid., p. 23.
[26] Ibid., pp. 6, 14, 32, 199, and 201.

out by the fact that most contemporary religions today share seven common characteristics, four of which are derived from the second pole (see below, Section III).

III. The Second Pole: Fascination, Desire, Love, and Bliss in Our Experience of the Numen

Just as the first pole is marked by feeling-contents of dauntingness, overwhelmingness, mysteriousness, and energy-vitality, so the second pole elicits another set of feelings: we find the numen attractive, alluring, charming, fascinating, and enchanting. Otto phrases it as follows:

> The mystery is for [the person experiencing the numen] not merely something to be wondered at but something that entrances him; and beside that in it which bewilders and confounds, he feels a something that captivates and transports him with a strange ravishment, rising often enough to the pitch of dizzy intoxication.[27]

So what is so fascinating, alluring, enchanting, and even intoxicating in the numen? It resembles what is fascinating and enchanting in the natural world: love, goodness, beauty, home, and the joy that arises out of them. These qualities are attributed to God in all major religions,[28] and they are attributed to the *experience* of God in all major mystical traditions.[29] When they are experienced in the numen, they have a purer and more integrated reality than when they are experienced in the natural world. Otto states it as follows:

> The ideas and concepts which are the parallels or "schemata" on the rational side of this non-rational element of "fascination" are love, mercy, pity, comfort; these are all "natural" elements of the common psychical life, only they are here thought as absolute and in completeness.[30]

[27] Ibid., p. 31.
[28] See below, Section III, regarding Heiler's seven common characteristics of major religions. See also Heiler, "History of Religions as a Preparation", pp. 142–44.
[29] See ibid. and pp. 150–52. See also Otto, *Idea of the Holy*, pp. 36–39.
[30] Otto, *Idea of the Holy*, p. 31.

In heightened experiences of the numen (such as mystical experiences), the characteristics of the second pole have an absolute or perfect quality that elicits ecstatic joy.

Interestingly, these characteristics are attributed to the transcendent or Divine Being by Platonists and other rational monotheists. Plato not only attempts to prove the absolute and perfect one true good love, and the beautiful, but implies that he and others can experience it through the contemplation of love and the beautiful in its highest form:

> He who has been instructed thus far in the things of love, and who has learned to see the beautiful in due order and succession, when he comes towards the end will suddenly perceive a nature of wondrous beauty ... a nature which in the first place is everlasting, not growing and decaying ... but beauty absolute, separate, simple, and everlasting, which without diminution and without increase, or any change, is imparted to the ever-growing and perishing beauties of all other things.[31]

Though Plato does not attribute this experience specifically to the numen (the presence of the divine within him), he associates perfect love, beauty, and goodness with the one God, and implies (in the above passage) that he and others have experienced it.

One of Plato's most ardent followers, Plotinus (A.D. 204–270), sees the mystical experience of the numen flowing directly out of contemplation of the One, which is good, loving, and beautiful. His disciple Porphyry indicated that Plotinus had reached "ecstatic union with the One"[32] on four separate occasions.

Evidently, Plotinus and other Neo-Platonic philosophers went far beyond the domain of rational philosophy into their inward experience of the One. This led to an experience of the One's absolute goodness, love, and beauty, which they identify as "ecstatic union with it".

Inasmuch as this supreme Being has the qualities of absolute love and goodness, it must in some sense be interrelational, and this implies personal qualities. Just as numinous energy and vitality (first pole)

---

[31] Plato, *Symposium*, in *Symposium and Phaedrus*, trans. Benjamin Jowett (New York: Classic Books America, 1993), 210a–211b, p. 43.

[32] Plotinus, *The Enneads* (Abridged Edition), ed. John Dillon (New York: Penguin Classics, 1991), p. lxxix.

suggests *personal* attributes such as will and passion in the numen, so also the alluring, enchanting, and fascinating elements of the numen (second pole) suggests positive *personal* attributes of openness, love, and goodness. The first pole elicits a relationship of humility, submission, and reverence, while the second pole elicits a relationship of closeness, familiarity, and friendship.

Both James and Otto pay close attention to the heightened or mystical dimension of the numinous experience. James describes several cases in which ordinary people (not monks or sisters in a monastery) experienced the numen in a heightened state. One case study described it as follows:

> For the moment nothing but an ineffable joy and exaltation remained. It is impossible fully to describe the experience. It was like the effect of some great orchestra, when all the separate notes have melted into one swelling harmony, that leaves the listener conscious of nothing save that his soul is being wafted upwards and almost bursting with its own emotion.[33]

One can see in James' case study the contrary elements of both calm and transport: a sense of peace and propulsion. Otto notes that this peace-propulsion can be induced by the presence of the numen through many gateways. It can come from reading a passage of Scripture, reflecting on a supreme truth (e.g., perfect goodness or perfect love), taking a walk in a natural setting, hearing a bird's song, looking at religious art or architecture, hearing a religious hymn or glorious symphony, or simply sitting at one's dinner table or desk. In my case, it once occurred while giving a physics lecture (see Volume I, Chapter 8, Section II). When the feeling of peace-propulsion occurs, it is generally accompanied by a profound sense of unity with everything, which takes away alienation and causes us to feel like we are perfectly at home with the totality. This sense of being "perfectly at home with the totality" is frequently connected with spiritual joy. Otto puts it this way:

> In all these forms, outwardly diverse but inwardly akin, it appears as a strange and mighty propulsion towards an *ideal good known only to*

---

[33] James, *Varieties of Religious Experience*, p. 66.

religion and in its nature fundamentally non-rational, which the mind knows of in yearning and presentiment, recognizing it for what it is behind the obscure and inadequate symbols which are its only expression. And this shows that *above and beyond our rational being* lies hidden the ultimate and *highest part of our nature*, which can find no satisfaction in the mere allaying of the needs of our sensuous, psychical, or intellectual impulses and cravings. The mystics called it the basis or *ground of the soul*.[34]

In this remarkable passage, Otto describes three key characteristics constituting a *heightened* experience of the numen:

1. The numen causes a sense of propulsion into itself.
2. In this propulsion, we sense the numen as perfect goodness and a supreme Being (known only to religion).
3. Our temporary connection or unity with this supreme perfect goodness reveals to us our highest transcendent nature—our soul, which can only be satisfied by the supreme goodness.

For James and Otto, many individuals from virtually every major religion and culture have heightened experiences of the numen. Embedded in that experience is an awareness that our propulsion toward it (being swept into it) is not caused by ourselves, but induced by the divine "wholly Other" present to us. As we are swept into it, we become aware at once of its supremeness and goodness (including elements of both the first and second poles), and when this happens we are transformed—we no longer think that we are merely physical or material, but that we are transcendent, having a soul that can only be satisfied by supreme goodness itself. This puts all material things into perspective, as merely partial, temporary satisfactions of our sensuous and psychical nature.

Though these *heightened* experiences are important, it should not be thought that incisive encounters with the numen are limited only to people who have experienced them. "Average people" can enjoy sparks of divine love-goodness-beauty-joy, but it might occur so gently, subtly, and quickly that they fail to recognize what is happening to them until they encounter a book or a conversation that

[34] Otto, *Idea of the Holy*, p. 36 (emphasis mine).

describes the numinous experience. After hearing these descriptions, they might say, "Well, I've never had a heightened experience of the numen, but I think I have had an experience of connecting with God that has His distinctive signature in it—some sense of supremeness, specialness, holiness, and goodness that is different from other interior experiences."

Sometimes average people can be praying an ordinary prayer like the Our Father or a well-known Psalm, and sometimes a few of the words will, as it were, leap off the page—leaving in its wake a feeling of supremeness-holiness-goodness-peace. Sometimes the average people can look at the simplest religious object, such as a little picture or statue, and it will incite the same special interior experience. Sometimes these same stimuli can cause us to recall a hazy experience of something that happened to us as children or young adults. Frequently young people do not reflect on the specialness of their experiences and therefore have no *rational* memory of them. Nevertheless, they have a *prerational* memory of them, and when the numen presents itself in a gentle way (say, looking at a picture), it brings to mind the feeling embedded in their prerational memory, causing them to say, "That was really strange; I feel like I remembered something profound and good from my past."

We should not underestimate our proclivity to put prerational memories into the recesses of our mind. When we don't reflect on the specialness of an experience, we don't remember it *as special*. It simply gets remembered as a set of intense feelings that can be reawakened when it happens to us again. When C. S. Lewis was a child, he had *heightened* experiences of the numen, but because he did not reflect on them as special, he simply put this peculiar set of feelings into the recesses of his mind, which he only remembered after having religious conversations and subtler experiences of the same feelings as an adult.[35]

These seemingly strange but subtle experiences should not be discounted, for even though the experience can be gentle, subtle, and brief, it will retain traces of the distinctive signature of the numen (supremeness, mystery, and holiness combined with some sense of

---

[35] See C. S. Lewis, *Surprised by Joy: The Shape of My Early Life* (New York: Harcourt, Brace, Jovanovich, 1966).

goodness, love, and joy). The most subtle of these experiences com-
municates a sense of our true home in the supreme and holy goodness that elicits a sense of peace (absence of alienation) and unity with
everything in which time stands still.

Though it seems like a contradiction to suggest that the numinous
experience can be subtle or gentle, the numen can relieve alienation
gently, can reveal its superior power and incomprehensibility softly,
and can overwhelm us with deep beauty and goodness like Elijah's
"still small voice":[36]

> [The Lord said to Elijah,] "Go forth, and stand upon the mount
> before the LORD." And behold, the LORD passed by, and a great and
> strong wind tore the mountains, and broke in pieces the rocks before
> the LORD, but the LORD was not in the wind; and after the wind
> an earthquake, but the LORD was not in the earthquake; and after the
> earthquake a fire, but the LORD was not in the fire; and after the fire a
> still small voice. And when Elijah heard it, he wrapped his face in his
> mantle. (1 Kings 19:11–13)

As noted above, when the numen presents itself in a gentle or
subtle way, and we do not reflect upon the specialness of the experience, we put the experience in the recesses of our mind. We might
say that it becomes subconscious or unconscious. Sometimes we will
have stronger experiences of the numen later in our lives, and then
we frequently bring our subconscious or recessed memory to our
conscious mind, enabling us to see a pattern of interaction with the
Divine One throughout life. However, if we don't have a strong
experience later in life, does that mean that the gentle presence of
the numen is completely ineffective in our lives? Absolutely not. As
will be seen with respect to Mircea Eliade's analysis of sacred symbols
and the transconscious, multiple, subtle, unreflective experiences of
the numen create a strong *unconscious* impression that becomes part
of our general frame of mind, causing us to desire, seek, and value
sacred and religious symbols, community, worship, and revelation.

---

[36] The Hebrew *qoi D'mämäh daQäh* can have two meanings because the noun *qoi* can mean
either "a voice" or "a sound". *D'mämäh* generally means "quiet". *daQäh* generally means
"small or weak". Thus the expression could refer to a natural phenomenon "a soft weak
sound" or "a soft gentle voice". These can be combined to mean that Elijah heard the voice
of Yahweh in a gentle sound.

The numen's subtle and persistent appearance causes us to be naturally spiritual and religious, inciting us to find outward communal expressions of what we interiorly sense and desire. This may explain why the vast majority of people throughout history have had a sense of the spiritual and transcendent, have sought religious communities, were moved by sacred symbols, liturgy, and music, and found their highest sense of fulfillment through these outward expressions and connections to the transcendent and spiritual domain.

IV. The Unity and Opposition of Both Poles in Our Experience of the Numen

The two poles of the numinous experience might be compared to the double helix characterizing DNA—they are not really separated in the numen, but rather fully integrated, complementing each other, presenting a good and even loving Deity. As Heiler indicates in his seven common characteristics of major religions, the Supreme Transcendent Reality for all major religions is loving, and the Deity reveals this love within individuals.[37] When we combine the studies of Otto and Heiler, it is difficult to imagine that the numen is not in some sense *personal*. Even if we concentrate on the mysterious, incomprehensible, and wholly-Other characteristics (of the first pole) associated with some Eastern religions, we still sense that the numen is making itself felt—inviting us more deeply into itself—and is not simply a passive depersonalized reality (like a metaphysical substrate) into which we are merely and ultimately assimilated. When the second pole (which includes a sense of goodness, love, comfort, peace, and joy) is considered along with the characteristics of the first pole, the *personal* element of the "wholly Other" becomes more clear, because the characteristics of the second pole are oriented toward relationship—and specifically, fulfillment and joy in relationship. Understating the characteristics of the second pole generally leads to a diminution of the personal qualities of the numen.

[37] See Heiler, "History of Religions as a Preparation", p. 143 (the fourth characteristic of all major religions).

There is one other observation that should be made before nuancing the feeling-content of both poles. Otto believes that the first pole (the mysterious, powerful, and daunting pole) is the primary manifestation of the numen in the development of religious consciousness, and the second pole (which is always present but deemphasized in early cultures) becomes gradually manifest as history progresses. The gradual manifestation of this second pole may be a major influence in the progress of culture throughout the world. It seems to come to light with specially inspired prophets, wise men, and enlightened individuals. These enlightened individuals—these external sources of inspiration—do not invent these positive characteristics of the Transcendent Reality, but rather point to It as the origin of their enlightenment. Thus if Buddha, Ezekiel, or Jesus speaks about the love of the Transcendent Reality, they are speaking about their *experience* of that reality, and not about their theological speculations. We assent to their teachings, not out of blind faith in their authority, but out of an interior conviction that what they are saying resonates deeply with what we know to be intuitively true. They are saying something that we recognize from our experience of the numen, and for this reason, people (both individually and collectively) are willing to allow their thoughts about the numen (at first sensed to be daunting) to evolve toward a fascinating, caring, and joy-filled Being. Otto puts it this way:

> It may well be possible, it is even probable, that in the first stage of its development the religious consciousness started with only one of its poles—the "daunting" aspect of the numen—and so at first took shape only as "daemonic dread."[38] But if this did not point to something beyond itself, if it were not but one "moment" of a completer experience, pressing up gradually into consciousness, then no transition would be possible to the feelings of positive self-surrender to the numen. The only type of worship that could result from this "dread" alone would be that of ... expiation and propitiation, the averting or the appeasement of the "wrath" of the numen.[39]

[38] Recall that "daemonic" does not mean "demonic" in the sense of an evil or malignant spirit. It only refers to the other-worldly reality of the spiritual, which like sensing a ghost (or hearing a ghost story) can elicit uncanniness, a shudder, or "creeping flesh", which points to an uncontrollable spiritual presence near us or in us.

[39] Otto, *Idea of the Holy*, p. 32.

The emergence of the second pole in the evolution of religious consciousness is corroborated by the work of Friedrich Heiler's seven common characteristics among the world's major religions:

1. The transcendent, the holy, the divine, the Other is real (from the first pole).
2. The transcendent reality is immanent in human awareness (from the first pole).
3. This transcendent reality is the highest truth, highest good, and highest beauty (from the second pole).
4. This transcendent reality is loving and compassionate—and seeks to reveal its love to all of us (from the second pole).
5. The way to God requires prayer, ethical self-discipline, purgation of self-centeredness, asceticism, and redressing of offenses (from mostly the first pole).
6. The way to God also includes service and responsibility to people (from the second pole).
7. The highest way to eternal bliss in the Transcendent Reality is through love (from the second pole).

The world's major religions differ considerably on the interpretation of the above seven common characteristics, and, in several cases, some of the characteristics are elevated above others or even mitigate others. However, if one accepts at least traces or fragments of the above seven characteristics in all major religions, it reveals the presence of Otto's second pole in the gradual evolution of religious consciousness, suggesting strongly that this pole is intrinsic to our common experience of the numen. If the second pole were not present in our common experience of the numen, it would be difficult to explain how the third, fourth, sixth, and seventh characteristics became universally recognized and accepted.

The probable reason why early religious consciousness emphasized the first pole was because its characteristics are powerful and fearful, and, like children, we pay most attention to what can harm or overpower us. As we mature and become less daunted by the overpowering and uncontrollable Other, we allow the *Other's* more benign and compassionate qualities to be recognized—typifying Maslow's need hierarchy.

In that theory, Maslow ranks basic personal needs according to five levels: (1) physical needs, (2) safety and security needs, (3) the need for love and belonging, (4) the need for self-esteem, and (5) the need for self-actualization. Maslow contends that when needs on a more basic level are not met, we will not feel need on higher levels. However, when that more basic need is met, the next level of need emerges as important. Accordingly, when religious consciousness is preoccupied with the daunting, mysterious, and uncontrollable qualities of the numen (safety and security needs), it is unlikely to experience a need for love and belonging from the numen. However, over the course of time, it becomes apparent that the numen is not *completely* daunting in its interaction with us—and that the numen manifests graciousness and goodness—at which point, the need for security becomes much less important, and the need for love emerges.[40] At that point, the second pole of the numen's feeling-contents becomes evident and desired.

V. The Fullness of Christian Revelation

As noted above, all major world religions (according to Heiler) believe that the Supreme Transcendent Power is both good and loving. This general belief is interpreted quite differently in each of the major religions. Some subordinate love to justice and the moral law, some hold that the Deity's love is oriented toward a group rather than toward individuals, and some define love in a very restricted way.

However, Jesus' teaching on the love of God is quite distinct. First, He proclaims the *unconditional* love of God, and places it at the center of His teaching, making all other teachings and doctrines subordinate to it. He also defines love in a special way that requires Christians to find a distinct word to describe it (*agapē*).[41] In these two

---

[40] Otto believes that in the transition from emphasis on the first pole to integration of the first and second poles, there is an intervening stage of magic. As the benevolent qualities of the numen emerge, priests or shamans attempt to control or manipulate the benevolent side of the Divine Other by means of incantations, formulae, or other magical pursuits. However, this intervening stage is temporary and is corrected by specially inspired prophets or wise people—who point to the purity of goodness and love in the divine and discourage attempts to manipulate the Deity, as if it were self-seeking. See ibid., pp. 15, 33, 66.

[41] See the extensive analysis of Jesus' view of *agapē* in Volume III, Chapter 1. For an explanation of Jesus' proclamation of God as *unconditional* love, see Volume III, Chapter 2, Section III.

respects, Jesus appears to be quite distinctive in the history of religions. Jesus proclaims the unconditional love of God through several distinct teachings First, He teaches His disciples to address God as *He* does—as "Abba", which means "affectionate, understanding, trustworthy father" with connotations of childlike delight, for example, "daddy" (see Volume III, Chapter 2). Second, He identifies God the Father with the father in the Parable of the Prodigal Son, who is unconditionally forgiving, compassionate, and humble (see Volume III). Third, He says that the whole law and prophets are summed up in the commandments to love God and neighbor. Inasmuch as the Torah (the Jewish law) reflects the heart of God, love must be the essence of God's heart. Fourth, Jesus places this radical doctrine of God's unconditional love at the very center of His teaching, making all other teachings subordinate to it. The combined effect of these four proclamations is a distinctive recasting of love into the primary end or goal of every individual, and even of history and culture.

With respect to Jesus' definition of love, Jesus is primarily concerned with the *interior heart* of love. This is most manifest in the Beatitudes (interior attitudes of love), which are placed at the *beginning* of the Sermon on the Mount in the Gospel of Matthew (see Mt 5:1–12), showing the priority of the interior disposition of the heart, in care and compassion. Jesus gives several examples in His parables and actions to illustrate this love. The most notable parable, the Parable of the Good Samaritan, portrays a foreigner whose *heart* is moved with *care* and *compassion* toward a Jewish man (an enemy of the Samaritans) who has been beaten severely by robbers (see Lk 10:25–37). The most notable action in Jesus' life is His love for sinners (see Volume III, Chapter 3, Section II.C) and His self-sacrificial death on the Cross (see Volume III, Chapter 3, Section IV).

Jesus then shows how these interior attitudes should manifest themselves in exterior actions—love of enemies; prayer for those who hate us; turning the other cheek; forgiving one another seventy times seven times (an innumerable number of times); having mercy on the marginalized, ignored, and displaced; loving sinners and even criminals—which He declares is imitating God's love in its perfection (see Mt 5:43–45 and Lk 6:35–36). The combination of these teachings in a single doctrine of love is distinctive in the history of religions.

This distinctive and radical interpretation of the meaning of love and God's unconditional love has the peculiar effect of not only subordinating the first pole to the second pole (subordinating fear to love), but also of completely removing the fearful and dreadful from the first pole. This removal of the fearful and dreadful is central to the teaching of Saint Paul. For example, in the Letter to the Romans, Paul says: "[Y]ou did not receive the spirit of slavery to fall back into fear, but you have received the spirit of sonship. When we cry, 'Abba! Father!' it is the Spirit himself bearing witness with our spirit that we are children of God" (Rom 8:15–16). The Second Letter to Timothy states: "[F]or God did not give us a spirit of timidity but a spirit of power and love and self-control" (2 Tim 1:7).

This viewpoint is also central to the teaching of Saint John: "There is no fear in love, but perfect love casts out fear. For fear has to do with punishment, and he who fears is not perfected in love" (1 Jn 4:18). This subordination of fear to love (including the elimination of fear) has its origin in Jesus, and is reported in several passages of the Synoptic Gospels. Jesus tells the synagogue official whose child is about to die, "Do not fear, only believe" (Mk 5:36). He tells His disciples not to worry about any dimension of their *temporal* lives: "Therefore I tell you, do not be anxious about your life, what you shall eat or what you shall drink, nor about your body, what you shall put on.... And which of you by being anxious can add one cubit to his span of life? And why are you anxious about clothing? ... Therefore do not be anxious, saying, 'What shall we eat?' or 'What shall we drink?' or 'What shall we wear?'" (Mt 6:25, 27–28, 31).

He also exhorts His disciples not to fear anything from the *spiritual* domain: "And do not fear those who kill the body but cannot kill the soul; rather fear him who can destroy both soul and body in hell. Are not two sparrows sold for a penny? And not one of them will fall to the ground without your Father's will. But even the hairs of your head are all numbered. Fear not, therefore; you are of more value than many sparrows" (Mt 10:28–31).

Though some religions exhort their followers to control fear and to expect peace in the afterlife, Christianity seems to be distinctive in creating an antithesis between fear and *love* and asking its followers to replace fear with *trust* in the unconditionally loving God. This has a remarkable effect within the Christian mystical tradition. Christianity shares several common features with other religions' mystical traditions, for example, the dimensions of mysteriousness, unity with the totality, joy (bliss), and the beauty of the sacred. However, in the Christian mystical tradition, a loving relationship with the unconditionally loving Deity is the overriding feature that gives rise to unity, joy (ecstasy), and beauty (glory). For this reason, Christian mystics associate the experience of God with being perfectly at *home* through an unconditionally loving Divine Being.

Evelyn Underhill wrote extensively about Christian mysticism in the first half of the twentieth century. She was familiar with mysticism in non-Christian traditions, but wrote far more extensively on the personal love intrinsic to the Christian mystical tradition. She was not interested in objective approaches to religious experience (such as William James and Rudolf Otto), preferring instead to take a personal psychological approach that incorporated elements of her own religious experience with well-known Christian mystics ranging from Jan Ruysbroeck and Meister Eckhart to Saints Augustine, Teresa of Avila, and John of the Cross. In her classic work *Mysticism: A Study in the Nature and Development of Spiritual Consciousness*, she contrasts the abstract knowledge of God from metaphysicians and theologians with the personal loving connection with God in Christian mysticism:

> In mysticism that love of truth which we saw as the beginning of all philosophy leaves the merely intellectual sphere, and takes on the assured aspect of a *personal passion*. Where the philosopher guesses and argues, the mystic lives and looks; and speaks, consequently, the disconcerting language of first-hand experience, not the neat dialectic of the schools. Hence whilst the Absolute of the metaphysicians remains a diagram—impersonal and unattainable—the Absolute of the mystics is *lovable, attainable, alive.*[42]

This point is brought home through the sixteenth-century Carmelite mystic Saint Teresa of Avila, who links the personal love of the Deity with the ecstasy of mystery:

> The *loving exchange* that takes place between the soul and God is so sweet that I beg Him in His goodness to give a taste of this *love* to anyone who thinks I am lying. On the days this lasted I went about

---

[42] Evelyn Underhill, *Mysticism: A Study in the Nature and Development of Spiritual Consciousness* (New York: Renaissance Classics, 2012), p. 16 (emphasis mine).

as though stupefied. I desired neither to see nor to speak.... It seems the Lord carries the soul away and places it in *ecstasy*; thus there is no room for pain or suffering, because *joy* soon enters in.[43]

Saint John of the Cross, another Carmelite mystic and companion of Saint Teresa of Avila, writes that the unconditional love of God is manifest most profoundly in the infinite One "making us His equal"[44] by at once coming to be with us and raising us up to Him. His love is at once affectionate, humble, and gentle:

> Since He is the virtue of supreme *humility*, He *loves you* with supreme humility and esteem and *makes you His equal*, gladly revealing Himself to you in these ways of knowledge, in this His countenance filled with graces, and telling you in this His union, not without great rejoicing: '*I am yours and for you* and *delighted* to be what I am so as to be yours and give myself to you.[45]

The idea of God being supremely humble, supremely gentle and affectionate, and making us His equal (fundamental dispositions arising out of His unconditional love) is distinctive to Christianity; though some religions address these characteristics in God, they are not viewed as the central essence of God or the core of our relationship with Him.

Christian mysticism does not find its culmination away from the world. As Christian mystics move into a deeper relationship with God (including ecstatic union), they do not pull away from the world into a rarified, passive, and exclusive domain. Rather, as Underhill asserts, the Christian mystic is self-creative,[46] and above all a "doer".[47] The

---

[43] Teresa of Avila, *The Book of Her Life*, in *The Collected Works of St. Teresa of Avila*, vol. 1, trans. Kieran Kavanaugh and Otilio Rodriguez (Washington, D.C.: ICS Publications, 1976), p. 194.

[44] This expression that John uses in "Living Flame of Love"—"since He is the virtue of supreme humility, He loves you with supreme humility and esteem and *makes you his equal*"—is not to be taken literally. John is fully aware that this would be a contradiction—"an infinite-finite". He uses this expression as a *metaphor* for God's supreme humility and gentleness.

[45] John of the Cross, "The Living Flame of Love", in *The Collected Works of St. John of the Cross*, trans. Kieran Kavanaugh and Otilio Rodriguez (Washington, D.C.: ICS Publications, 1979), p. 613 (emphasis mine).

[46] See Underhill, *Mysticism*, p. 21.

[47] Ibid., p. 16.

more Christian mystics experience the love and ecstasy of the Divine Lover, the more they are inspired to serve all of God's beloveds, even to the point of trial, suffering, and death in imitation of Jesus. This is certainly evidenced in the lives of Saint Teresa of Avila and Saint John of the Cross, who reformed the Carmelite Order and, as a result, experienced considerable trial, sacrifice, and suffering. This is also evident in the lives of other mystics, such as Jan Ruys-broeck, who was involved in fighting controversial teachings in Brussels and who later became a Prior of a monastery he founded, and the life of Saint Augustine, who in addition to writing an encyclopedia of theological, spiritual, and polemical works was involved in fighting controversies and served as bishop of Hippo. The same holds true for Saints Francis of Assisi, Catherine of Siena, Hildegard of Bingen, and Ignatius Loyola, to mention just a few. The centrality of contemplation leading to action (instead of to passivity and reclusiveness) appears to be peculiar to Christian mysticism. No doubt other mystical traditions speak of mystics as being active, but not in the same central way as Christianity.

In sum, Christianity brings the second pole of the numinous experience to its fulfillment in the *unconditional* love of God, the definition of love as "*agapē*" (compassionate, forgiving, self-sacrificial love of all mankind—friends and enemies), and the completion of the mystical life through loving action in the world. As will be seen in Volume IV of this Quartet, these distinctive features of Jesus' revelation changed the course of history and culture, leading closer and closer to the recognition of the intrinsic dignity and unique goodness and lovability of *every* individual whom Jesus associates with God: "[A]s you did it to one of the least of these my brethren, you did it to me" (Mt 25:40).

VI. Is the Numen *Really* a Transcendent Other?

As we have seen, Rudolf Otto identified some *common* elements of religious experience in individuals from virtually every religion and culture. He discovered several "feeling-contents" associated with what he terms the "numen" (that which is experienced as transcendent and wholly Other). These feeling-contents have two poles:

1. A sense of something mysterious, overwhelming, and daunting that elicits from us a response of diminution, humility, submission, and creatureliness
2. A sense of something fascinating, desirable, caring, and comforting that invites us into its fullness, fulfills us, and in so doing, produces a unique kind of spiritual joy (bliss)

If these findings are accurate and our experience of the "numen as wholly Other" is not completely subjective, then it indicates the reality of a transcendent Being that makes itself present to us as overwhelming and fascinating, dreadful and loving, daunting and good, uncontrollable and caring, unreachable and inviting, mysterious and revealing, and transcendent and immanent. This synthesis of contrasting feeling-contents is not experienced in the world around us, and so we call it "holy" or "sacred", and we are inclined to worship it, praise it, pray to it, and seek our *ultimate* home in it. Since it is not to be found in this world, no combination of feelings arising out of our interaction with the world can describe it. The feeling-contents associated with the numen constitute a category unto itself ("*sui generis*"). The sense of the numen (the holy, transcendent, mysterious "wholly Other") is embedded in the above feeling-contents at their very inception, and so they are not like other feeling-contents that come from the world and lack the numinous presence.

Is there any way of showing that the numinous experience is not completely subjective? This question is important, because if it is not completely subjective, then it is quite likely that a transcendent, fascinating, loving God is present to us and inviting us to Himself. Let's begin with some methodological parameters. First, we will not be able to develop an empirical test for the transcendent, because the transcendent is transempirical. Similarly, we will not be able to develop a physical test for the transcendent, because it is transphysical. We will not be able to develop a "proof" that our experience is transcendent, because proofs are based on objective evidence and necessity, but the numinous experience is primarily subjective and gratuitous. So it looks as if we are not going to be able to show a nonsubjective component of the numinous experience by the three most rigorous, publically accessible methods: (1) an empirical test, (2) scientific method, or (3) deductive method (logical proof).

So where does that leave us? We cannot change the nature of the numinous experience to make it subject to the three most rigorous kinds of verification, for all such attempts will be incoherent—trying to describe the transphysical in physical categories, the nonempirical in empirical categories, the primarily subjective in objective categories, and the gratuitous in necessary categories. Is there any way we could avoid complete subjectivism? I believe that there is, and it comes from a combination of factors that the following reflection can help to reveal.

First, the numinous experience is quite common to a large number of people in virtually every religion and culture throughout the world. Most religious people (84 percent of the world population) believe they have a sense of something transcendent, mysterious, and sacred that is present as something wholly Other. Many people feel this presence only faintly, and sometimes only when they are in a holy place with sacred art, music, or symbols. Other people perceive the numen as overwhelming and even "enormous bliss". Some people have had both kinds of experiences—sometimes within a second of each other. Nevertheless, in virtually every case, no matter what the religion or culture, people identify similar themes that boil down to transcendence, mystery, sacredness, and home—embedded in a wholly-Other Being.

Inasmuch as a large percentage of the world population has a sense of this presence, we know that it cannot be a figment of our individual imaginations. This means either that there is something intrinsic to our *physical* nature generating feeling-contents of transcendence, mystery, holiness, and Otherness *or* that there is a transcendent, holy, mysterious Other generating these feeling-contents. For Otto and others, the evidence favors the latter, because the numinous experience has a *relational* quality, that is, as we respond to it, it seems to respond back to us—at least in some cases. Sometimes when we feel the presence of the numen, we can open ourselves to it, and it seems to accept our openness and becomes more deeply and intensely present to us. Sometimes we feel like we are being invited to draw closer to it, and when we accept the invitation, we are pulled closer and closer to it. Sometimes the experience is almost dialogical—invitation, then response, then deeper invitation, and deeper response. This relational component is not limited to mystics, but occurs spontaneously to average religious people.

This invitation-response component has an intersubjective (inter-personal quality) that is difficult to explain by typical physical paradigms. Physical systems (whether in the cosmos or in the brain) operate through deterministic laws (macroscopic physics) or through random-indeterminate spontaneity (quantum physical systems), but they don't operate interrelationally, because this feature requires subjectivity (*consciousness*) on both sides of the relationship. Macroscopic and quantum physical systems are not per se conscious—or at least not conscious enough to make a conscious response to our consciousness. Therein lies the rub. The intersubjective (invitation-response) quality of some instances of the numinous experience place it beyond the capabilities of physical systems to explain.

When Otto speaks about the feeling-contents of the numinous experience, he is referring to a *precognitive, prereflective* phenomenon. This does not mean that there is not consciousness embedded in our experience of the sacred, mysterious wholly Other. Just as we can feel (precognitively) the consciousness of another person at the moment of empathy ("in-*feeling*" from the Greek "*en-pathos*"), so also we can *feel* the presence of consciousness in the *empathetic* ("in-*feeling*") quality of the numen.

Frequently, the numinous experience does not give rise to a dialogue or even an experience of invitation-response. It comes to us fleetingly, manifesting itself to us as distinctively transcendent and holy—and then disappears, leaving us with a sense of unfulfilled desire (as Lewis' experience of "longing for the longing which had just ceased"[48]). Does this more fleeting, nondialogical experience still have an intersubjective (conscious) quality? It does. Even the most fleeting numinous feeling-contents have a quality of what Otto terms "the wholly Other" that connects with us *empathetically*. This empathetic (in-feeling) connection is filled with a sense of "another consciousness". When we experience it, it feels like a sympathetic vibration, a harmony of two distinct consciousnesses. At the moment of empathy with the numen, we feel its conscious presence in the "sympathetic vibration" without reflecting upon it or thinking about it.

The reader might be thinking, how can the wholly Other connect with us empathetically? Isn't this a contradiction in terms? It is not,

---

[48] Lewis, *Surprised by Joy*, p. 16.

because the quality of "wholly Other" does not refer to being "completely distant" (nonempathetic), but rather to the quality of being "a completely different *kind* of reality than we are", "a categorically higher reality". This completely different *kind* of being can and does convey empathy, and in so doing, embeds its consciousness in the feeling-content it engenders within us.

This intersubjective, empathetic, conscious quality embedded in our feeling-contents of mysteriousness, dauntingness, fascination, desirability, and comfort is incongruous with merely physical systems and natural laws. The numen is not simply a "wholly Other" in the sense of being "wholly higher"; it conveys its freedom, consciousness, and invitation in the empathetic and intersubjective quality of the feeling-contents it engenders within us. If this distinctive quality in our feeling-contents is not communicated by a real transcendent Being, then what is its origin? Very probably not a physical origin, an imaginative origin, or a merely intrasubjective feeling. Its double-edged quality of being at once wholly Other (wholly higher) and empathetically intersubjective seems to rule out these immanentist explanations. Absent these explanations, it is not unreasonable to believe that its origin is from a personal, intersubjective, transcendent Being—what might be called "a personal God".

VII. Conclusion

As noted above, this is the first kind of evidence for our transcendence and relationship with a transcendent Being. When we combine it with the evidence from Eliade's study of the sacred, Newman's study of conscience, and Jung's and Tolkien's thoughts about a cosmic struggle between good and evil (Chapter 2), our conclusion will gain in probative force, for it will be corroborated by four distinct kinds of data, all pointing to the same conclusion.

Chapter Two

The Sacred and the Cosmic Struggle

Introduction

In the previous chapter, I presented Otto's probative evidence for the presence of "human transcendence" within man's consciousness and indicated that this phenomenon is not only transcultural, but also transhistorical. Otto's first pole of the numinous experience (the mysterious, daunting wholly Other) was primary in the development of religious consciousness, while the second pole (the fascinating, desirable, good, and caring Other) gradually manifested itself later. Are there any other clues to the presence of a personal transcendent Other within an individual's consciousness? Several philosophers and theologians assert that there are:

1. Mircea Eliade on religious hierophany (Section I)
2. Immanuel Kant and John Henry Newman on the divine origin of conscience (Section II)
3. J.R.R. Tolkien, Mircea Eliade, and Carl Jung on the divine origin of myth (Section III)
4. Plato, Neo-Platonists (such as Plotinus and Augustine), Aquinas, Thomists (such as Étienne Gilson and Jacques Maritain), and transcendental Thomists (such as Bernard Lonergan and Karl Rahner) on the four transcendental desires (Chapters 3 and 4)

Not surprisingly, these clues to the "interior presence of personal transcendence" overlap, but they are not the same; they have their own distinctive features, manifesting the complex way the personal transcendent reality reveals itself within human consciousness.

These distinctive features allow the above four clues, as well as the numinous experience, to be mutually corroborative, increasing the probative force of the conclusion to which they all point: the presence of a personal transcendent reality to man's consciousness. Let us now examine each of these clues and draw a conclusion from their complementarity and corroboration at the end of Chapter 4.

I. Mircea Eliade—Religion as Hierophany

Mircea Eliade (1907–1986) was a philosopher and historian of religion at the University of Chicago who elaborated one of the most comprehensive transcultural and transhistorical theories of the origin of religion. Born in Romania and educated at the University of Bucharest, he became familiar with the work of Rudolf Otto on the numinous experience, which influenced his thought on the philosophy of religion.[1] He is the author of hundreds of articles, the general editor of the sixteen-volume *Encyclopedia of Religion*,[2] and the author of dozens of books including *The Sacred and the Profane: The Nature of Religion*,[3] and *Patterns in Comparative Religion*,[4] all of which proved to be highly influential in the contemporary study of comparative religion. After making an incredibly comprehensive cross-cultural study of the history of religions, Eliade concluded that religion originates from an irreducible experience of the sacred (common to most people) that seeks to find its outward cultural expression in myths and rituals. These myths and rituals become the communal gateways to connecting with the Transcendent Reality.

The reader may recognize the hand of Rudolf Otto in Eliade's use of "the irreducible experience of the sacred", but it should not be thought that Eliade blanketly based his research on Otto's studies. Instead, he found Otto's conclusions to be probative and conducive

---

[1] In addition to Otto, Eliade was influenced by Gerard van der Leeuw, the Dutch philosopher and historian of religion who wrote a seminal phenomenological approach to religion in 1933 entitled *Religion in Essence and Manifestation: A Study in Phenomenology*, and René Guenon, French philosopher of religion and metaphysics who set out a theory of cross-cultural "universals" among world religions—as well as other philosophers and historians of religion.

[2] Mircea Eliade, *Encyclopedia of Religion*, 16 vols. (New York: Macmillan, 1986).

[3] Mircea Eliade, *The Sacred and the Profane: The Nature of Religion* (New York: Harcourt Brace Jovanovich, 1987).

[4] Mircea Eliade, *Patterns in Comparative Religion* (Nebraska: University of Nebraska Press, 1996).

to explaining his own research into the cross-cultural expression of religion. Putting it the other way around, Eliade's research into myths, symbols, rituals, and the sacred led him to conclude that Otto was correct about the numinous experience because it could explain several cross-cultural common elements in religious expression. It could also explain the drive of *individuals*[5] (across cultures) to seek out and experience sacred myths, rituals, symbols, and communities. This last point enables Eliade's research to *expand* and *corroborate* Otto's findings (which are based on the data of *individual interior* experience of the holy) by adding the component of *outward community* expression of the sacred. Eliade worked in the reverse direction of Otto. Instead of moving from individual interior experience to outward expression, he moved from outward communal expression to interior experience. We will examine the significance and corroborative features of his research in three steps:

1. His findings about the common cross-cultural elements of religion (Section I.A)
2. His characterization of the religious individual, *homo religiosus* (Section I.B)
3. His contention that rejection of the sacred will produce a heightened state of existential anxiety in "modern man" (Section I.C)

A. Common Elements in Cross-Cultural Religious Expression

Eliade uses two major concepts to organize the common cross-cultural elements of religious expression: (1) "hierophany" and (2) "*homo religiosus*". A brief explanation of each from his seminal work *The Sacred and the Profane: The Nature of Religion* will help to elaborate his theory.

Hierophany (from Greek) means "appearance of the sacred". It expands the more common term *theophany* ("an appearance of God")

---

[5] Eliade distinguishes between "traditional man" and "modern man" in this regard. Up to the eighteenth-century Enlightenment, the vast majority of individuals across the globe strove to find meaning and reality in sacred places, times, myths, symbols, and rituals. However, since the modern age, "modern man" has become progressively more distanced from the perspective of "traditional man", thinking that rational (scientific and mathematical) explanations are superior to religious ones.

to include all world religions. All world religions are based on a belief that transcendent reality (whether it be God or gods or a quasi-personal force) has broken into the world, bringing with it sacredness or holiness (transcendent goodness, power, and beauty), splitting the world into two parts: "the sacred" (connected to transcendent reality) and "the profane" (not connected to transcendent reality). Eliade described this universal dimension of hierophanies as follows:

> It could be said that the history of religions—from the most primitive to the most highly developed—is constituted by a great number of hierophanies, by manifestations of sacred realties. From the most elementary hierophany—e.g., manifestation of the sacred in some ordinary object, a stone or a tree—to the supreme hierophany (which, for a Christian, is the incarnation of God in Jesus Christ) there is no solution of continuity.[6]

Every religion identifies a place and a time (or places and times) when the transcendent breaks into the world (and world history). When it does, it makes holy or sacred the place and the time of the "breakthrough". The sacred place does not simply remind (mentally) religious people about the "breakthrough"; it retains its sacredness, so that pilgrims who come to it can continue to have an experience of the transcendent that sanctifies them. Thus pilgrims actually experience the sacred at the place where the Transcendent Reality appeared. In primitive religions, villages have centers that imitate a place of sacredness and then extend out from that center. Eliade notes in this regard:

> Settling in a territory reiterates the cosmogony. Now that the cosmogonic value of the Center has become clear, we can still better understand why every human establishment repeats the creation of the world from a central point (the navel). Just as the universe unfolds from a center and stretches out toward the four cardinal points, the village comes into existence around an intersection.[7]

The creation or origin story provides an ideal model of place that when imitated sacralizes villages, temples, and homes. According to Eliade,

[6] Eliade, *Sacred and the Profane*, p. 11.
[7] Ibid., p. 45.

Religious architecture simply took over and developed the cosmological symbolism already present in the structure of primitive habitations.
In its turn, the human habitation has been chronologically preceded
by the provisionally consecrated and cosmicized.... All symbols and
rituals having to do with temples, cities, and houses are finally derived
from the primary experience of sacred space.[8]

In virtually every culture, the hierophany not only sacralizes space
and place, but also time. The time of the hierophany is the origin or
creation of reality. It is *the* sacred time, and like sacred places it has the
capacity to sacralize people who enter into it. But how can a religious
person enter into the sacred time (the time of origin or creation)?
With every elapsed moment of time, we pull further away from the
sacred time (origin), and so it would seem that we become more
and more profane as history progresses. Eliade discovered that most
religions do not have this problem because of their belief in what he
terms "the myth of eternal return".[9]

For Eliade, "the myth of eternal return" refers to the capacity to
return to the time of origin or creation by participating in religious
rituals or recounting sacred myths. Sacred rituals are not simply a
commemoration or mental remembrance of the sacred origin; they
are a *reliving* or "reactualizing" of it. As the ritual is celebrated, the
participants enter into the sacred time of origin, allowing them to
connect with the Transcendent Reality in it.

Myths have the same mystical powers as rituals. As myths are
recounted, the participant reenters the past sacred event, almost as if
the time separating it from the present moment collapsed (or did not
exist at all). This puts the participant in contact with the Transcendent Reality who was present at that time. Eliade phrases it this way:
"In *imitating* the exemplary acts of a god or of a mythical hero, or
simply by recounting their adventures, the man of an archaic society
detaches himself from profane time and magically re-enters the Great
Time, the sacred time."[10]

[8] Ibid., p. 58.
[9] Mircea Eliade, *The Myth of the Eternal Return: Or, Cosmos and History* (Princeton: Princeton University Press, 1971).
[10] Mircea Eliade, *Myths, Dreams, and Mysteries* (New York: Harper and Row, 1975), p. 23
(emphasis mine).

So what happens to the participants in sacred rituals and the re-counting of sacred myths? When the participants connect with the Transcendent Reality through the sacred passageways that collapse time, they come into contact with what Elide calls a "paradigmatic model", that is, with absolute truth and goodness toward which they will want to strive and ultimately imitate: "The myth relates a sacred history, that is, a primordial event that took place at the beginning of time, *ab initio*.... Once told, that is, revealed, the myth becomes apodictic truth; it establishes a truth that is absolute."[11] This paradig-matic model—this absolute truth—is not abstract; it is embedded in the stories of the creation and the heroes that completed the act of creation. Thus there is a call within the myth to imitate the actions and the virtues of heroes (and to shun the actions and vices of vil-lains). Rituals and myths, then, provide two functions:

1. They strengthen the participants by putting them into contact with the sacred moment of origin (and through this, the Tran-scendent Reality itself).
2. They present a paradigmatic model or action and virtue that is felt to be absolute truth.

The breakthrough of the Transcendent Reality is not neutral. It provides strength and a paradigmatic model to all participants who enter into the rituals and myths that represent it. In so doing, it tells us how to attain our true purpose (divine purpose), which in turn tells us how to live our lives and how to develop our character (by imi-tating the heroes of the great time of origin). The actions of the great heroes show us not only how to act, but why we ought to act that way; they give us clues about the end and goods for which we should be living, and show how certain actions fulfill those ends or goods.

For Eliade, religion is the key not only to connection with the Transcendent Reality, but also to purpose in life, to the ends and goods connected with that purpose, and to the virtues and actions that accomplish them. Without religion, "traditional man" (who lived in a society before the pervasiveness of the scientific and Enlighten-ment mentality—prior to the eighteenth century) would have been

[11] Eliade, *Sacred and the Profane*, p. 95.

purposeless, directionless, and virtueless. He would not only have been lost; he would have been insignificant and even reduced to nothing.

This last point deserves explanation. For traditional man, the sacred is reality, and the profane is insignificant and virtually unreal. So failure to make contact with the sacred is to be reduced to nothingness, and failure to imitate the paradigmatic model of the sacred is to be reduced to insignificance.

In sum, Eliade has made a most remarkable discovery—namely, that for more than four millennia, people from virtually every culture around the world yearned for and sought the sacred. In virtually every culture the expression and the fulfillment of that yearning is similar in four general areas:

1. There is a belief in the sacred (transcendent reality) in which there is absolute truth and goodness.

2. The sacred (transcendent reality) desires to connect with mankind and so enters into the profane world at a particular place. Its entrance into the world is the originative or creative moment. The physical world may have existed before the sacred's entrance into it, but the world was not significant or real prior to its entrance. Thus, for traditional man, true reality and meaning began when the sacred reality broke through.

3. When the sacred reality broke through, it sacralized (made holy) the place and time it entered. When individuals draw close to the place of entrance, it makes them holy. Similarly when individuals celebrate the ritual of origin and recount the myth of origin,[12] time collapses, and they reenter the sacred time of origin again, connecting them with the sacred, which strengthens them.

4. The celebration of rituals and recounting of myths not only strengthens the participants but also imparts what Eliade terms "paradigmatic models", that is, lessons about purpose in life, the goods to be pursued, the evils to be avoided, the virtues and laws that will help to achieve the good, and the vices that will undermine it. Thus traditional man receives purpose, direction, and virtue from reentering the sacred time through ritual and myth.

[12] The myth of origin is not only the precise moment at which the sacred enters the world; it includes unfolding of the originative moment through the actions and virtues of heroes, the overcoming of evil, and the teaching and development of people.

The odds of these similarities among the world's religions occurring by pure chance are exceedingly low, so we must seek an explanatory cause. What could have produced this fourfold coincidence of religious belief and expression in so many utterly diverse cultures with so many distinct histories? The sheer *variety* of communities, cultures, and histories virtually rules out *social* explanations as a cause of the four *common* features of religion. In the absence of a *social* cause, we will have to examine whether there could be a *common* cause within *individual persons* who participate in very different cultures. We have already seen one potential candidate for a common cause within a vast majority of individuals, namely, Otto's numinous experience. However, before we can turn to this *supernatural* interior explanation, we must rule out potential *natural* (physical) explanations. Though we cannot *completely* rule out a *natural* cause, we can show the vexing questions that natural causes (insofar as they are natural) will be unlikely to answer.

1. How does a *natural* (physical) cause produce an awareness of *transcendent* reality, a desire to draw close to that reality, and a passion to seek it?
2. How can a *natural* cause produce a belief that the Transcendent Reality wants to connect with the whole of humanity and will even "step down" to enter into the profane world to make it sacred for us?
3. How can a *natural* cause produce a belief that the Transcendent Reality is *absolutely* good and possesses *absolute* truth?
4. How can a natural cause produce a belief that real meaning (and reality itself) does *not* come from profane nature, but only from the sacred reality?

Eliade (and his colleagues) never found an adequate answer from the domain of natural causation. As a result, he rejects the possibility of finding such an answer from any secular scientific or social scientific discipline (psychology, sociology, anthropology, etc.). Realizing that no combination of natural phenomena could add up to a transnatural or supernatural one, he concluded that the cause must be some *irreducible* presence of the sacred transcendent reality within us:

To try to grasp the essence of such a phenomenon [hierophany—the appearance of sacred transcendent reality in the world] by means of physiology, psychology, sociology, economics, linguistics, art or any other study is false; it misses the one unique and *irreducible* element in it—the element of the sacred. Obviously there are no *purely* religious phenomena; no phenomenon can be solely and exclusively religious. Because religion is human it must for that very reason be something social, something linguistic, something economic.... But it would be hopeless to try and explain religion in terms of any one of those basic functions which are really no more than *another* [natural] way of saying what man is.[13]

Viewing this from the vantage point of an individual person, Eliade would assert that the interior cause for the awareness of, desire for, and fulfillment through the sacred cannot be fear, anxiety, biological impulse, or merely imaginary wish fulfillment. In the words of John Holt (writing the introduction to *Patterns in Comparative Religion*),

Eliade rejected every social scientific attempt to explain the totality of religious experience causally. For him, religion was more than an arena of meaning or discourse produced by an anxiety, an acquisitive disposition, political aspirations, or simply a penchant for creativity. As a phenomenologist, Eliade never tired of arguing that religion must be described and understood on its own terms, or within its own plane of reference. That is, the sacred manifests itself in "hierophanies"; it has a language and form of its own that has been recognized historically and cross-culturally.[14]

If natural causation (and the methodologies that describe and explain natural causes) cannot explain the occurrence and prevalence of the sacred throughout the world, we will have to look toward a supernatural explanation. Could Rudolf Otto's numinous experience provide the explanation for the similarities among world religions? Could it be the *supernatural* interior cause of what Eliade calls the "irreducibly sacred"[15] in all religious experience, belief, and expression? In view of the likelihood that Otto's numinous experience

---

[13] Eliade, *Patterns in Comparative Religion*, p. xvii.
[14] Ibid., p. xiii.
[15] Ibid., pp. xvii and 486.

comes from the presence of the Transcendent Reality within us (see Chapter 1, Section VI), I would submit that it is a very probable candidate. In order to give a more definite answer to this question, we will want to first examine Eliade's idea of *"homo religiosus"*.

B. Homo Religiosus

In the previous section we discussed Eliade's four similarities among world religions and how to find a reasonable explanation for this remarkable phenomenon among utterly diverse cultures throughout history. We now move into the interior domain of the people who participate in these religions (whom Eliade terms *homo religiosus*). Do the similarities among world religions indicate a concomitant similarity among religious people? Eliade is convinced that they do:

> Religious man assumes a particular and characteristic mode of existence in the world and, despite the great number of historico-religious forms, this characteristic mode is always recognizable. Whatever the historical context in which he is placed, *homo religiosus* always believes that there is an absolute reality, *the sacred*, which transcends this world but manifests itself in this world, thereby sanctifying it and making it real. He further believes that life has a sacred origin and that human existence realizes all of its potentialities in proportion as it is religious— that is, participates in reality. The gods created man and the world, the culture heroes completed Creation, and the history of all these divine and semidivine works is preserved in the myths. By reactualizing sacred history, by imitating the divine behavior, man puts and keeps himself close to the gods—that is, in the real and significant.[16]

Where did this common interior religious disposition come from? Did it come from the teaching of religious people within an already formed religious community, or rather did it come from something within *homo religiosus* himself, which he brought to the community of belief? Religious communities teach lessons and doctrines to their adherents—how their religious rituals function, the details of the myths, the meaning of various symbols, colors, and actions, the sacredness of

---

[16]Eliade, *Sacred and the Profane*, p. 202.

particular places and times, and so on. Yet, Eliade believes that this
alone cannot make a religion. There must be people who are aware
of the sacred, desire it, are passionate about it, and are fulfilled by it.
They must also be capable of understanding the significance of sacred
time, sacred place, sacred myth, sacred ritual, and sacred symbol.
If these interior dispositions were not antecedently present, traditional
man would never have sought out religion and would certainly not
have made it his center of meaning and the source of reality.

Without an awareness of and desire for the sacred (transcendent
reality), traditional man would have found a substitute for the center
of significance and source of reality—perhaps food, shelter, procreation, manhood, womanhood, knowledge, practical skills, and so on.
No intelligent being will place something unintelligible and undesired
at the center of meaning and reality. In light of this, it is likely that
homo religiosus did not acquire his awareness of and desire for the sacred
transcendent reality from a religious cult or community. If he did not
have an antecedent desire to connect with the Transcendent Reality,
he would have been indifferent to sacred cult and community, like
children who are indifferent to anything whose value they do not
comprehend. In contrast, *homo religiosus* is attracted to, fascinated by,
and fulfilled by the sacred represented in religious rituals and myths.
He seeks out and participates in sacred ritual because he is aware of the
sacred and understands its central significance in his life.

Recall how Otto described the numinous experience—the sense
of mystery, awesomeness, Otherness, uncontrollableness, and dauntingness arising out of a sense of the Transcendent Other's power,
majesty, and glory (the first pole), as well as a sense of fascination
with, desire for, and passion for the Transcendent Reality arising out
of a sense of its goodness and care (the second pole). Can this irreducible experience of the numen explain *homo religiosus'* awareness
of and desire for the sacred—his belief in the absolute goodness and
truth of the sacred reality; his belief that the sacred reality broke into
the profane world to connect with humanity; and his fascination with
sacred place, time, myth, and symbol? As noted above, the numinous experience cannot explain the fourfold *content* of the religious
intuition. However, it can explain why individuals have a sense of
transcendent reality that causes them to passionately desire and seek
it in sacred places, rituals, myths, and symbols. If Otto's numinous

experience does not provide the awareness, desire, and passionate pursuit of the sacred in religious community, places, myths, rituals, and symbols, then what does? What else could explain the common personal desire for, interest in, and passion about the sacred? What else could provoke individuals to surrender individually and collectively to a nonempirical reality? What else could provoke individuals to place such a reality at the center of their individual and collective universe? What else could ground *homo religiosus'* belief in the significance of sacred place, time, myth, ritual, and symbol when these realities are so much less obvious than the profane ones?

Merely natural explanations fall far short of what is needed to explain this most peculiar common desire to invest ultimate significance and reality in what is invisible, out of reach, wholly Other, and uncontrollable. If no alternative explanation can be found, then it is likely that our inner experience of the numen (transcendent reality) has incited our interest in, desire for, fascination with, and surrender to the sacred.

Yet, the numinous experience does not account for everything in the religious intuition of *homo religiosus.* Though it is the source of the feeling-contents of the Transcendent Reality's presence (as mysterious, daunting, fascinating, good, and wholly Other), it does not explain the common cross-cultural belief of *homo religiosus* in an appearance of the sacred (transcendent reality) in the world at a particular place and time, or the sanctification of the world and individuals through that appearance, or the power of ritual and myth to reactualize this appearance and sanctification. This additional intuition of the sacred transcendent reality's presence and sanctification provides the impetus to move from the numinous *experience* to *religion,* that is, religious community and expression that seeks the Transcendent Reality in sacred places, rituals, myths, and symbols. Thus it seems that the sacred (transcendent reality) manifests itself in an additional way (in an intuitive way), building upon the numinous manifestation of itself—to incite us to look for hierophany, to form religious community around it, and to be fulfilled by it. Henceforth I will call this additional intuitive manifestation of the Transcendent Reality the *religious intuition.*

The coincidence of Otto's and Eliade's research has a mutually corroborative effect, because they come from different data sets—Otto's from the study of the common interior spiritual experience of *individuals*, and Eliade's from the study of the common beliefs and expressions of world *religions*. When two distinct data sets connect causally, it enhances the probative force of both and provides a broader and deeper explanation of our relationship to the transcendent.

C. The Anxiety of "Nonreligious Man"

Up to now, we have been summarizing Eliade's findings about religion in what he calls "traditional man". Recall that this term signifies the mindset of people prior to the time when scientific and Enlightenment viewpoints became dominant among certain groups in Western Europe (around the eighteenth century). Recall also that virtually every person at the time of traditional man was *homo religiosus*. Though Eliade indicates the presence of some philosophical atheism or agnosticism during that time, it was so rare that it did not represent what might be termed a "cultural viewpoint".

The time of "modern man" is distinct, because a significant percentage of modern individuals are nonreligious (16 percent), and in Western Europe, the percentage is significantly higher (approximately 50 percent). Furthermore the perspective of what Eliade calls "modern nonreligious man"[17] is becoming dominant in Western Europe, and some of this is spreading to other modern democracies around the world. Do Eliade's (and Otto's) findings apply to modern man? Can modern man be considered *homo religiosus*?

Most religious people in the modern world (84 percent) still possess many, if not most, of the characteristics of *homo religiosus*.[18] They believe in an absolute transcendent reality that manifests itself in the

---

[17] Eliade, *Sacred and the Profane*, pp. 14, 17, 70, 89–90, 93–94, 146, 162, 203.

[18] As stated previously (in the Introduction and Chapter 1), a study by the Pew Research Center indicates that 84 percent of the world's population self-identify as believers who subscribe to religion; see Pew Research Center, "The Global Religious Landscape", December 18, 2012, http://www.pewforum.org/2012/12/18/global-religious-landscape-exec. The Pew study did not measure specifically for Eliade's characteristics of *homo religiosus*, but inasmuch as most world religions adhere to most of these general characteristics, and most individuals who self-identify as "subscribers to religion" are in general agreement with the basic tenets of religion, it seemed reasonable to infer that most of them subscribe to most of Eliade's characteristics of *homo religiosus*.

world, and in so doing, sanctifies the world and gives it significance (ultimate significance). They also believe that life has a sacred origin (and is therefore sacred) and that human potentiality can only be realized (both in this world and the next) through a vital connection with the sacred transcendent reality. Finally they make recourse to sacred stories, rituals, and symbols to commemorate and reenter sacred time and place in order to participate in holiness (the sacred) and to be strengthened in their capacity to follow the paradigmatic models provided by the sacred realities' entrance into the profane world. Inasmuch as they exemplify *homo religiosus*, they *satisfy* their desire for transcendent reality incited by the numinous experience and find a source of the ultimate meaning, fulfillment, and reality they yearn for. This ultimate meaning, fulfillment, and reality does not come from merely *intellectual* assent to the existence of a transcendent reality, but more from *connecting* with and *relating to* the sacred reality (through sacred ritual and sacred writings[19]) and following the goods, ends, and virtues elucidated by these sacred writings.

Evidently modern religious people experience the same problems arising out of natural causation, economic difficulties, political turmoil, and other worldly challenges as modern nonreligious people. However, religious people have a level of ultimate, transcendent, and sacred meaning, hope, happiness, dignity, and destiny that "modern *nonreligious* people" have implicitly or explicitly denied. Furthermore modern *homo religiosus* has an ultimate and transcendent sense of the good and virtue that "modern nonreligious people" do not recognize. For Eliade, this absence of the sacred in modern nonreligious people introduces a heightened anxiety about existence, meaning, and reality (what might be called "existential anxiety"[20]). It comes from "the absence of things yearned for", that is, the absence of the transcendent that we desire implicitly or explicitly (because of the numen's presence within us). For Eliade, the more modern nonreligious people reject the sacred and the transcendent, the more acute

---

[19] In modern cultures, sacred writings include more than the great myths. They also include theological histories (many of which accurately recount historical facts and events), wisdom sayings, prophetic utterances, prayers, and laws. Therefore when referring to "modern man", I will use "sacred writings" instead of "sacred myths".

[20] For a complete explanation of "existential anxiety", see Volume I, Chapter 5, Section I of this Quartet.

their alienation from self and reality becomes, which brings with it an increasing sense of existential anxiety.[21]

Does Eliade's contention here stand up to scrutiny? Interestingly, it is the hallmark of not only theistic existentialism but also *atheistic* existentialism (e.g., Sartre, Camus, Kafka, and so forth). In Volume I (Chapter 5, Section I) we discussed existential anxiety in both theistic and atheistic existentialist schools and described it in terms of "*cosmic* emptiness, alienation, loneliness, and guilt". These anxieties are frequently alleviated through religious faith. But is there more than philosophical and anecdotal evidence for the efficacy of religion in psychological health?

The 2004 study in the *American Journal of Psychiatry* correlated nonreligious affiliation with suicide rates and found that nonreligious affiliation was the strongest contributing factor to an increase in suicide (verifying the conjectures and predictions of Eliade and theistic existentialists). The study concluded:

> Religiously unaffiliated subjects had *significantly* more lifetime suicide attempts and more first-degree relatives who committed suicide than subjects who endorsed a religious affiliation. Unaffiliated subjects were younger, less often married, less often had children, and had less contact with family members. Furthermore, subjects with no religious affiliation perceived fewer reasons for living, particularly fewer moral objections to suicide. In terms of clinical characteristics, religiously unaffiliated subjects had more lifetime impulsivity, aggression, and past substance use disorder. No differences in the level of subjective and objective depression, hopelessness, or stressful life events were found.[22]

This statistical verification of the positive effects of religion on the human psyche supports Eliade's and existentialists' predictions about the alienation of many nonreligious people. If this trend continues, modern nonreligious culture may be headed for a crisis in which it no longer sees a call to higher principles, virtues, ideals, dignity, and destiny, progressively losing its sense of hope in a positive future,

---

[21] Eliade, *Sacred and the Profane*, p. 211.

[22] The statistical analysis for this conclusion may be found in Kanita Dervic et al., "Religious Affiliation and Suicide Attempt", *American Journal of Psychiatry* 161, no. 12 (December 2004): 2303–8, http://ajp.psychiatryonline.org/article.aspx?articleid=177228.

leaving its participants in a state of moral and metaphysical alienation, emptiness, and superficiality—reduced to little worlds of materialism, autonomy, and self-indulgence. Eliade believes that this crisis may be inevitable because modern nonreligious man's sense of self and freedom is based upon the rejection of the sacred:

> Modern nonreligious man assumes a new existential situation; he regards himself solely as the subject and agent of history, and he refuses all appeal to transcendence. In other words, he accepts no model for humanity outside the human condition as it can be seen in the various historical situations. Man *makes himself*, and he only makes himself completely in proportion as he desacralizes himself and the world. The sacred is the prime obstacle to his freedom. He will become himself only when he is totally demysticized. He will not be truly free until he has killed the last god.[23]

Is the viewpoint of modern nonreligious man justified? Is collective existential anxiety and crisis inevitable? Do freedom and self-identity have to come from the rejection of the sacred? Otto and Eliade think not. The remarkable cross-cultural and cross-historical coincidence of the human sense of the spiritual (the numinous experience) and expression of the sacred (hierophany) and the likelihood that these remarkable coincidences have an interior supernatural origin should give the modern person pause, for there may be good reason to suspect not only that individuals have a transcendental dimension (and are destined for transcendental fulfillment), but that they are created in a relationship with the transcendental reality that is at once mysterious, daunting, and wholly Other, as well as desirable, fascinating, good, and caring.

Some contemporary critics may object that the interior evidence of the numinous, and the cross-cultural evidence of religious expression, are not enough—no matter how omnipresent they are. This objection may be grounded in an inability to detect the numinous experience for themselves or to desire a connection with the sacred through ritual and sacred writings. No doubt these individuals see their inner world to be devoid of transcendent awareness and desire; however, this is not the only way of gaining access to the sacred.

---

[23] Eliade, *Sacred and the Profane*, p. 203 (emphasis mine).

Frequently, it is easier to detect its presence through the negative effects of rejecting it, that is, through the anxiety, alienation, and emptiness that arises out of ignoring or frustrating it. Is the reason that nonreligiously affiliated people have significantly higher suicide rates, less reasons for living, less contact with family, and greater anxiety merely a result of fear or unfulfilled wish—or rather, is it a result of radical incompleteness of being, purpose, and destiny? Nonreligious people must answer this question for themselves. However, if theistic existentialists are correct, the anxiety is not so much a matter of fear as emptiness and loneliness, not so much a matter of unfulfilled wishes as alienation from self and reality. If this is the truth, then Otto and Eliade hold out a solution to the existential anxiety of modern times, namely, an openness to the Transcendent Reality within us and to collective participation in religious community, ritual, and symbol.

There are other clues to our transcendental nature and our relationship to a transcendent reality beyond that of Otto and Eliade:

1. The origin of conscience (Section II)
2. Our awareness of a cosmic struggle between good and evil (Section III)
3. Four transcendental desires for perfect truth, love, goodness, and beauty (Chapters 3 and 4)
4. The evidence of survival of bodily death from medical studies of near-death experiences (Chapter 5)

These other clues corroborate the findings of Otto and Eliade, strengthening the plausibility and expanding the horizon of our transcendental nature and destiny.

II. Kant and Newman on the Divine Origin of Conscience

The Transcendent Reality has frequently been identified as the source of the *good*—the good in itself and the good in our consciousness. Otto's research indicates that the numinous is perceived to be good, while Eliade's research indicates that hierophanies concern not only the breakthrough of the sacred into the world, but also the revelation of paradigmatic models for personal behavior. The identification of the Transcendent Reality with the good is not only a part of religious intuition, but also of philosophical reflection since the time of the ancient Greeks.

Plato believed that the highest reality was the good itself,[24] and that the good itself was present to us, and that we could know it through questioning and dialectic. Saint Paul brought these considerations to a whole new level by showing that all individuals could know the good (as well as evil) through their *consciences*. In the Letter to the Romans, he reflects on the Gentile's ability to know God's law without having the benefit of Judeo-Christian revelation:

> When Gentiles who have not the law do by nature what the law requires, they are a law to themselves, even though they do not have the law. They show that what the law requires is written on their hearts, while their conscience [συνείδησις] also bears witness and their conflicting thoughts accuse or perhaps excuse them. (Rom 2:14–15)

For Saint Paul, "the law" is *God's law*, and he asserts that God writes this law on the hearts of all people so distinctly that it accuses and defends them.

Saint Thomas Aquinas concurred with Saint Paul, and formulated a general explanation of conscience that has become a cornerstone of philosophy up to the present time. Recall from Volume I (Chapter 1) that conscience has two components:

1. what Aquinas called "*synderesis*" (an attraction to and love of the good and a fear of and repulsion toward evil), and
2. awareness of certain *general* precepts of the good.

With respect to *synderesis*, our attraction to and love of the good leads to feelings of nobility and fulfillment when we do good (or contemplate doing it). Conversely, our fear of and repulsion toward

---

[24]Plato, *Republic*, trans. Paul Shorey, in *The Collected Dialogues of Plato*, edited by Edith Hamilton and Huntington Cairns (Princeton, N.J.: Princeton University Press, 1961), Book VII, pp. 747–51.

evil leads to feelings of guilt and alienation when we do evil (or contemplate doing it).[25]

Conscience not only has the above emotional and personal component; it also has an intellectual one. We have a sense of *what* is good or evil (in a general way). These precepts might include do good; avoid evil; do not kill an innocent person; do not unnecessarily injure another, steal from another, or otherwise unnecessarily harm another; give a person their just desserts; and be truthful to yourself and others.

Aquinas associated these precepts of conscience with the natural law, holding that the natural law is part of God's eternal law:

> Now among all others, the rational creature is subject to Divine providence in the most excellent way, in so far as it partakes of a share of providence, by being provident both for itself and for others. Wherefore it has a share of the Eternal Reason, whereby it has a natural inclination to its proper act and end: *and this participation of the eternal law in the rational creature is called the natural law.*[26]

A. Kant and the Divine Origin of Conscience

The above thinkers presume the existence of God and attempt to show that the good we know in our conscience comes from God. In the eighteenth century, Immanuel Kant looked at the reverse contention. Instead of assuming the existence of God and inferring His presence in our conscience, Kant begins with the moral obligation imposed by conscience and moves to the existence of God. He believed that the way in which the good was known through man's consciousness entailed its divine origin:

> Through the idea of the supreme good as object and final end of the pure practical reason the moral law leads to religion, that is, to the

---

[25] "It is fitting that we have bestowed on us *by nature* not only speculative principles but also practical principles.... The first practical principles bestowed on us by nature, do not belong to a special power but to a special *natural* habit, which we call *synderesis*. Thus *synderesis* is said to incite to good and to murmur at evil, inasmuch as we proceed from first principles to discover and judge of what we have discovered" (Thomas Aquinas, *The Summa Theologica of St. Thomas Aquinas*, vol. 1, trans. Fathers of the English Dominican Province [New York: Benziger Brothers, 1947], Part I, Question 79, Article 12, p. 407; emphasis mine).

[26] Aquinas, *Summa Theologica*, vol. 1, Part I–II, Question 91, Article 2, p. 997 (emphasis mine).

recognition of all duties as divine commands, not as sanctions, that is, as arbitrary commands of an alien will which are contingent in themselves, but as essential laws of every free will in itself, which, however, must be looked on as commands of the supreme Being, because it is only from a morally perfect (holy and good) and at the same time all-powerful will, and consequently only through harmony with this will, that we can hope to attain the highest good, which the moral law makes it our duty to take as the object of our endeavour.[27]

The essence of Kant's thought here may be summarized in two statements in his *Opus Postumum*: "In the moral-practical reason lies the categorical imperative to regard all human duties as divine commands";[28] this causes him to view God as follows: "The concept of God is the concept of an obligation-imposing subject outside myself."[29] Kant moves from an intrinsic awareness of an absolute moral duty (categorical imperative) to an awareness of a morally perfect will that is the source of that absolute duty, and then to an awareness of the supreme Being who is an "obligation-imposing Subject outside the person". Notice that this transition of awareness is not a formal set of inferences, but rather an unfolding of the meaning of the absolute duty, which is central to Kant's consciousness.

For Kant, the good (within our consciousness) is embedded within an absolute duty to do that good, which, in its turn, is embedded within a divine source of that absolute duty. He cannot conceive of the good without the duty to do it (for what makes the good recognizable is the duty or imperative to do it), and he cannot conceive of an *absolute* duty to do the good without an *absolute* obligation-imposing Subject outside himself. Goods cannot be recognized without the duty to do them, and the *absolute* duty to do them cannot be recognized without an *absolute* obligation-imposing Subject outside ourselves.

This line of thought may seem unsatisfying to a skeptic, but Kant is not trying to prove anything to a skeptic. He is trying to shed light on the implications of the good within our consciousness. For anyone who cares to probe the distinctive quality of the good within himself,

[27] Immanuel Kant, *Kant's Critique of Practical Reason and Other Works on the Theory of Ethics*, trans. T. K. Abbott (New York: Barnes and Noble, 2004), p. 233.

[28] Immanuel Kant, *Opus Postumum*, vol. 21, Berlin Critical Edition (Berlin: Georg Reimer, 1960), p. 12.

[29] Ibid.

God is an inescapable reality. Anyone who probes the qualities of that good will sense the presence of the obligation-imposing Subject within it. If we allow the good to reveal itself within us, we will not only know of its divine origin; we will know that the divine is present to us—at once outside of us and embedded in the absolute duty of the good within us. This presence of the divine within us makes us transcendental.

Notice that Kant has not constructed a *formal* proof *of* God here, but rather has given an *existential* inference *to* God. He makes no use of deduction or logic, but rather is interested in the existential (concretely experienced) content of his interior recognition of the good. The recognition of the good leads to the absolute duty that makes the good to be recognizable as good, and the absolute duty leads to the Supreme Subject who imposes that absolute duty.

B. Newman and the Divine Origin of Conscience

John Henry Newman brought the line of thought regarding the divine origin of conscience to a new level about eighty years later. Though he borrows the general structure of "existential inference" from Kant, he shifts the emphasis from an "obligation-imposing Subject outside ourselves" to an "interpersonal, caring, fatherly authority who is the source of goodness and law". Unlike Kant, who moves from the good to God through two existential inferences, Newman uses five inferences (detailed below)—being careful to distinguish his sense of conscience from other natural phenomena.

Unfortunately, Newman did not leave us with a formal rendition of his existential inference to God, but he did leave an unpublished manuscript with a set of organized passages from his sermons and additional notes. (Adrian J. Boekraad and Henry Tristram have published an edition of this unfinished work entitled "Proof of Theism".)[30] Since Newman presents his points quite systematically, I will

---

[30] Adrian Boekraad and Henry Tristram, eds., *The Argument from Conscience to the Existence of God according to J. H. Newman* [with an unpublished manuscript by Newman entitled "Proof of Theism"] (London: Mill Hill, 1961). I will cite the texts of Newman from this work, and then cite the page numbers from Newman's unpublished paper as given by Boekraad and Tristram.

here present only the main movements of the argument with a brief interpretation of his texts. His general argument proceeds as follows. He begins with an overview of his main contention:

> Ward thinks I hold that moral obligation is, because there is a God. But I hold just the reverse, viz. there is a God, because there is a moral obligation. I have a certain *feeling* on my mind, which I call conscience. When I analyse this, I *feel* it involves the idea of a Father and a Judge,—of one who sees my heart, etc.[31]

Newman then proceeds to an assessment of the unity of his consciousness and his existence, which shows that his consciousness is as undeniable as his existence (since one cannot be aware of the latter without being aware of the former). He further shows that he has an *immediate* awareness of his consciousness, and therefore he does not have to deduce it or believe in it. Belief occurs when one is not certain, but Newman is as aware of his consciousness as he is of his existence. He intends to show later that if conscience is intrinsic to his consciousness, then he can be just as immediately aware of his conscience as he is of his consciousness and existence. He then proceeds to a definition of conscience:

> Man has within his breast a certain commanding dictate, not a mere sentiment, not a mere opinion, or impression, or view of things, but a law, an authoritative voice, bidding him do certain things and avoid others. I do not say that its particular injunctions are always clear, or that they are always consistent with each other; but what I am insisting on here is this, that it commands, that it praises, it blames, it promises, it threatens, it implies a future, and it witnesses the unseen. It is more than a man's own self. The man himself has no power over it, or only with extreme difficulty; he did not make it, he cannot destroy it.[32]

For Newman, conscience "commands" (just as for Kant, the categorical imperative imposes duty). He is not so much concerned with whether the specific dictates of the command are always consistent

---

[31] Ibid., p. 103, citing Newman (unpublished), p. 1 (emphasis mine).

[32] John Henry Newman, *Sermons Preached on Various Occasions* (London: Longmans, Green, 1908), Sermon no. 64. See also Boekraad and Tristram, *Argument from Conscience*, p. 114, citing Newman (unpublished), pp. 11–12.

from person to person or from culture to culture, but is impressed by the seeming universality of what is ingredient to conscience's dictates, namely, "command", "praise", "blame", "promise", "a future", and "the unseen". These characteristics intrinsic to conscience's dictates imply something more than a mere standard or authority. They seem to have an origin outside the self, an origin that is not a matter of personal learning (controlled by an inquiring subject), but rather one that is *uncontrolled* by the self. The more we recognize, listen to, and obey this uncontrollable authority, the clearer it and its *dictates* become:

> Conscience implies a relation between the soul and something exterior, and moreover, superior to itself; a relation to an excellence which it does not possess, and to a tribunal over which it has no power. And since the more closely this inward monitor is respected and followed, the clearer, the more exalted, and the more varied its dictates become, and the standard of excellence is ever outstripping, while it guides, our obedience. A moral conviction is thus at length obtained of the unapproachable nature as well as the supreme authority of that, whatever it is, which is the object of the mind's contemplation.[33]

It seems that the dictates of conscience and the presence of its authority are somewhat dim in the unpracticed moral agent; but as one listens to and follows these dictates, the dictates themselves and the presence of their source become clearer and clearer to the point of being virtually undeniable. The presence of this authority is so strong that Newman is impelled to make his first inference:

> This is Conscience, and, from the nature of the case, its very existence carries on our minds to a Being exterior to ourselves; or else, whence did it come? And to a being superior to ourselves; else whence its strange, troublesome peremptoriness? ... Its very existence throws us out of ourselves and beyond ourselves, to go and seek for Him in the height and depth, whose voice it is.[34]

Newman is relating a dimension of his *experience* of conscience, namely, a presence that not only invites us out of ourselves, but draws

---

[33] Boekraad and Tristram, *Argument from Conscience*, p. 113, citing Newman (unpublished), pp. 10–11.

[34] Ibid., pp. 114–15, citing Newman (unpublished), p. 12.

us and even throws us out of ourselves. It is a presence that calls us to itself—sets us seeking "for Him in the height and depth, whose voice it is". If we respond to this invitation—if we follow the call of the "voice"—then its *personal* presence will become apparent. In an 1855 novel entitled *Callista*, Newman uses the voice of his protagonist to make this point:

> [God] says to me, Do this, don't do that. You may tell me that this dictate is a mere law of my nature, as is to joy or to grieve. I cannot understand this. No, it is the echo of a person speaking to me. Nothing shall persuade me that it does not ultimately proceed from a person external to us. It carries with it its proof of its divine origin. My nature feels towards it as towards a person. When I obey it, I feel a satisfaction; when I disobey a soreness,—just like that which I feel in pleasing or offending some revered friend.... The echo implies a voice; a voice a speaker. That speaker I love and I fear.[35]

In order to clarify and validate this experience, Newman contrasts the experience of conscience to the experience of what he calls "taste" (aesthetic experience), and he shows that aesthetic experiences do not call me out of myself in an interpersonal way as does the experience of conscience. If conscience were only intrapersonal (private), it would resemble aesthetic experience, but it is so much more:

> Now I can best explain what I mean by this peculiarity of feeling [intrinsic to conscience], by contrasting it with the rules of taste. As we have a notion of wrong and right, so we have of beautiful and ugly; but the latter set of notions is attended by no sanction. No hope or fear, no misgiving of the future, no feeling of being hurt, no tender sorrow, no sunny self-satisfaction, no lightness of heart attends on the acting with beauty or deformity. It is these feelings, which carry the mind out of itself and beyond itself, which imply a tribunal in future, and reward and punishment which are so special.[36]

He then focuses on these special feelings to distill the *interpersonal* nature of them, revealing that these feelings could not be experienced

---

[35] Ibid., p. 116, citing Newman (unpublished), p. 13.
[36] Ibid., pp. 117–18, citing Newman (unpublished), p. 14.

were it not through a relationship with another person—a person like a father:

> The feeling is one analogous or similar to that which we feel in human matters towards a *person* whom we have offended; there is a tenderness almost tearful on going wrong, and a grateful cheerfulness when we go right which is just what we feel in pleasing or displeasing a father or revered superior. So that contemplating and revolving on this feeling the mind will reasonably conclude that it is an unseen father who is the object of the feeling. And this father has necessarily some of those special attributes which belong to the notion of God. He is invisible—He is the searcher of hearts—He is omniscient as far as man is concerned—He is (to our notions) omnipotent.[37]

We may now summarize Newman's thought on this matter. First, he claims that he does not *believe* in conscience any more than he *believes* in his consciousness; he is *directly aware* of them, for consciousness is intrinsic to his awareness of everything, including his own existence, and conscience is intrinsic to his consciousness, presenting him with an awareness of interpersonal relationship and authority. He then describes in five steps how conscience is an *immediate* awareness or experience of a personal God:

1. He observes that conscience commands him, and that this command includes praise, blame, promise, a future, and the unseen (and is in *immediate* relationship with his consciousness when it does so).
2. He then observes that intrinsic to this praise, blame, promise, and so on is a concomitant awareness of an *external source* ("its very existence throws us out of ourselves and beyond ourselves, to go and seek for Him in the height and depth, whose voice it is").
3. He then shows that these feelings are not reducible to other kinds of feelings within our consciousness (such as aesthetic feelings): "[The feeling of beauty or ugliness] is attended by no sanction [and] no hope or fear, no misgiving of the future, no feeling of being hurt, no tender sorrow, no sunny self-satisfaction, no lightness of heart".

[37] Ibid., pp. 118–19, citing Newman (unpublished), pp. 14–15.

4. He then shows that there is a *personal* dimension intrinsic to these special qualities of the feelings of conscience: "The feeling is one analogous or similar to that which we feel in human matters towards a *person* whom we have offended; there is a tenderness almost tearful on going wrong, and a grateful cheerfulness when we go right which is just what we feel in pleasing or displeasing a father".

5. He then reveals that this personal dimension is not completely similar to those experienced with human beings, but has a divine dimension that is implicit in its supreme authority ("an authoritative voice, bidding him do certain things and avoid others.... The man himself has no power over it, or only with extreme difficulty; he did not make it, he cannot destroy it"). When this *supreme* authority is considered within the context of "the voice of a father", it manifests divine attributes ("so that contemplating and revolving on this feeling the mind will reasonably conclude that it is an unseen father who is the object of the feeling. And this father has necessarily the notion of God. He is invisible—He is the searcher of hearts—He is omniscient").

The more we recognize, listen to, and follow the urgings of conscience, the more clear and evident both the dictates of conscience and its personal, external, divine source become.

Newman has not formulated an *inferential* argument here; rather, he has rationally unfolded the fivefold dimension of his immediate experience of God in his conscience. He reveals, as it were, a dimension within a dimension within a dimension within the feelings and experience of conscience. What are these dimensions? A divine dimension (invisible, searcher of hearts, omniscient) *within* a personal dimension (a tenderness almost tearful on going wrong, and a grateful cheerfulness when we go right) *within* special qualities (sanction, hope, fear, misgiving of the future, feelings of being hurt, tender sorrow) *within* the feelings and experience of conscience (praise, blame, promise, etc.). This total experience of conscience ("the divine dimension within the personal dimension within the special qualities within the feelings and experience of conscience") is intrinsic to his consciousness, and, therefore, he is *immediately* aware of it.

Thus, Newman is not making an inferential argument; he is unfolding his own immediate experience of God through his conscience. Newman assures us that the more we listen to and follow our conscience, the more deeply and clearly we will experience the God who both guides and invites us to His life of transcendent and perfect goodness. Once again, we find God present to our consciousness—not only in the numinous experience and our religious intuition of the sacred, but also in the omniscient, invisible searcher of hearts who bids us to do good and avoid evil.

C. An Initial Conclusion about "the Soul"

Up to this point we have seen three ways in which the Transcendent Reality touches us:

1. The numinous experience—in which the numen presents itself as mysterious, daunting, uncontrollable, fascinating, good, and empathetic, and invites us into itself by inciting our interest and desire
2. The religious intuition—in which we sense that the sacred transcendent reality has broken into the world, which invites us to draw closer to the sacred reality through sacred place, ritual, and myth
3. Conscience—through which an omniscient, invisible searcher of hearts bids us to do good and avoid evil

These three dimensions of contact with transcendent reality invite us and bring us into the transcendent domain, and, in so doing, make us transcendent. Inasmuch as "soul" refers to a transcendental dimension of a person, we might call the three "points of contact with a transcendent reality" "three dimensions of the soul".

These three dimensions of the soul (connections with the sacred transcendent reality) are not static; they are interrelational and dialogical. Otto's numinous experience includes a dimension of empathy and invitation within the feeling-contents of fascination, desire, goodness, care, and comfort (see Chapter 1, Section VI); Eliade's religious intuition includes a dimension of sanctification by the transcendent reality within the desire for the sacred, and Newman's conscience includes an experience of an omniscient, invisible searcher of hearts within the feelings of guilt, hope or fear, misgiving of the future, being hurt, tender sorrow, sunny self-satisfaction, and lightness of heart. When the Transcendent Reality makes itself present to us, it manifests concern and care for us, calls us into a deeper relationship with itself, and offers us guidance and sanctification in our life's journey. Those who open themselves to the "transcendent presence within" will find not only the mysterious and sacred "wholly Other", but also a personal, empathetic, and loving being passionately interested in bringing us to the fullness of life through itself.

Each one of these three dimensions of the soul points to a personal transcendent reality independently of the others, and so each has its own probative value. The fact that they all point to the existence and presence of the same interpersonal transcendent reality makes them mutually corroborative, and so they form what Newman would call an informal inference with cumulative probative value. There are three other dimensions of the soul we will discuss throughout this book: our awareness of the cosmic struggle between good and evil, the four transcendental desires for perfect truth, love, goodness, and beauty, and the likelihood of a transphysical dimension of consciousness that can survive bodily death. When all of these dimensions are put together, they form a complementary and mutually corroborative network of evidence for the mysterious, fascinating, sacred, supremely good interpersonal transcendent presence within us.

III. Eliade, Tolkien, and Jung on the Myth of the Cosmic Struggle between Good and Evil

We might find it curious that J. K. Rowling's *Harry Potter* and J. R. R. Tolkien's *Lord of the Rings* are two of the most popular book series written for all time. They are also two of the most popular film series worldwide, along with George Lucas' *Star Wars*. Why is it that these three stories are so popular, not only in English-speaking countries, but everywhere in the world? Why do they resonate so deeply with so many different groups within international modern culture? Is there something about them that strikes us as not only significant and instructive, but expressive of ultimate truth, reality, and meaning?

The answers to the above questions are likely to be contained within the stories themselves—specifically the *common* elements among the stories. So what are these common elements? The first and foremost is that they concern a cosmic struggle between good and evil—the forces of goodness are pitted against the forces of darkness (evil). The outcome of the struggle will affect the entire world (or universe), not just the domain in which the battles take place. The "sides" of the cosmic struggle take the same general form. Cosmic goodness is portrayed as an unseen force of providence who interacts with high representatives and heroes through their *free* choices and actions. The high representatives of goodness have freely chosen to help the hero to defeat evil and restore universal goodness—the good wizard (Gandalf) in the Tolkien trilogy, the good wizard Dumbledore in *Harry Potter*, and the Jedi masters Obi-Wan Kenobi and Yoda in *Star Wars*.

Cosmic goodness is opposed by cosmic evil, which is manifest through a lord of darkness—Sauron in the Tolkien trilogy, Lord Voldemort in *Harry Potter*, and the Lord of the Sith in *Star Wars*. The dark lord has his high representatives who lead his armies or minions—Saruman in the Tolkien trilogy, Barty Crouch in *Harry Potter*, and Darth Vader in *Star Wars*.

The central protagonist is a *hero* who is unaware of his heroic role throughout his early life—Frodo Baggins in the Tolkien trilogy, Harry Potter in *Harry Potter*, and Luke Skywalker in *Star Wars*. The hero is given a mission by the representatives of cosmic goodness—Gandalf tells Frodo that he must throw the ring of power into Mount Doom; Harry Potter is told by Dumbledore that he must defeat Lord Voldemort; and Luke Skywalker is told by both Obi-Wan Kenobi and Yoda that he must defeat both Darth Vader and the Sith Lord. The hero is bewildered about being chosen for this immense task, but nonetheless accepts it as part of the central purpose of his life. He knows that his mission will entail sacrifice, but has no idea what it will really entail. At this point, the three modern myths resemble scores of other myths from various cultures and religions. Joseph Campbell describes the common features of virtually all hero myths as follows:

A hero ventures forth from the world of common day into a region
of supernatural wonder: fabulous forces are there encountered and a
decisive victory is won: the hero comes back from this mysterious
adventure with the power to bestow boons on his fellow man.[38]

The hero is given helpers either by the unseen hand of providence
or by the representatives of cosmic goodness—Samwise Gamgee,
Strider, Legolas (the elf), and Gimli (the dwarf) in the Tolkien
trilogy; Hermione Granger, Ron Weasley, and Ginny Weasley in
Harry Potter; and Princess Leah, Hans Solo, Chewbacca, R2-D2, and
C-3PO in *Star Wars*.

The hero and his assistants must summon the courage and virtue to
meet external struggles—confronting Orcs, the allies of Lord Voldemort, and the armies of Darth Vader. They also have to confront
internal struggles, because the forces of evil attempt to bring them
into their domain—the ring attempts to bring Frodo into its power,
Darth Vader is revealed to be the father of Luke Skywalker, and the
forces of evil try to "turn" Harry Potter. Ultimately, because of their
courage, fortitude, and belief in their mission, the hero and his com-
pany succeed in their mission by defeating the powers of darkness and
restoring the world to goodness and light.

What is so appealing about this common story that it rises—in its
many manifestations—to the top of best-seller lists? Why do people of all ages watch them multiple times? Some literary critics have
"panned" these works as shallow, juvenile fantasies—as merely escapist novels. Yet, if these "epic tales" are only an escape, why does every
other escapist book or series enjoy a mere fraction of the popularity as
these? Is it because English-speaking readers are drawn to Tolkien's
esoteric writing style? Probably not—contemporary readers don't
seem to be drawn to esoteric writing at all. Is it because J. K. Rowling wrote for an uncritical audience of children? This is not likely
either, because *Harry Potter* is at the top of the *adult* best-seller list. Is
it because of the visual effects in *Star Wars*? Very unlikely, given the
fact that there are many other action movies with even better visual
effects that haven't scratched the surface of *Star Wars'* popularity.

---

[38]Joseph Campbell, *The Hero with a Thousand Faces* (Princeton: Princeton University,
1949), p. 23.

What is it then about these three stories that catapults them ahead of other works of great literature, adventure stories, fantasy stories, and escapist novels? In a word, they all fit the technical description of *myths*. Though a myth is fictional, it is not fiction. Fiction concerns narratives that could be factual—"real in this world alone". Though fiction is purely imaginary, it portrays a narrative that *could* be real in the world around us. Myths, in contrast, are not concerned with "*worldly*" narratives, but rather with transworldly, transphysical, and spiritual narratives. The objective of myths is to express ultimate truth and meaning, and in order to do this they must reach beyond the contingent barriers of this world and universe and reveal the source of ultimate truth and meaning—that is, ultimate *reality*. Not only this, but myths must also reveal how and why ultimate reality connects with this world—and the people within it.

J.R.R. Tolkien knew well of the power, mystery, and truth of myths, and he wrote the *Lord of the Rings*, *The Silmarillion*, and *The Hobbit* to convey this most important dimension of man's existence and destiny. Before his conversion to Christianity, C.S. Lewis told Tolkien that "myths were nothing more than lies and therefore worthless, even though breathed through silver." Joseph Pearce reports Tolkien's response as follows:

No, they are not lies. Far from being lies they are the best way—sometimes the only way—of conveying truths that would otherwise remain inexpressible. We have come from God and inevitably the myths woven by us, though they contain error, reflect a splintered fragment of the true light, the eternal truth that is with God. Myths may be misguided, but they steer however shakily toward the true harbor, whereas materialistic "progress" leads only to the abyss and the power of evil.[39]

For Tolkien, myths presume that ultimate truth and meaning are not to be found in the natural world. They are based on the presumption that this world is too restricted, conditioned, and contingent to hold ultimate truth and meaning, and so they tell a story that expresses a "creed" about creation, a transcendent reality, gods, heroes, villains,

[39]Joseph Pearce, "J.R.R. Tolkien: Truth and Myth", *Lay Witness*, September 2001, p. 2, http://catholiceducation.org/articles/arts/alo107.html.

good and evil, virtues and vices—a story about adventure and challenge, darkness and light, wisdom, courage, fortitude, and temperance. Through this "high narrative", myths open upon an interior belief held by the vast majority of people, namely, that there is an ultimate reality beyond this world, and that this reality has come into this world to give us transcendent dignity, meaning, and destiny and to reveal *the way* to draw close to this ultimate meaning. If this is our common belief, then we should not be surprised that myths fascinate and captivate not only our imaginations but our very souls (the interior domain in which the transcendent makes contact with us).

Myths appeal not only to our intellect, but also to our emotions, intuition, and soul. When we read myths, we not only discover a truth about God, the transcendent, or the supernatural; we *feel* the ultimacy, mystery, and desirability of these transcendent realities. We not only think that transcendent reality has made contact with this world; we *feel* fascinated and enchanted with the place, the way, and the time of that connection. We not only learn how good and evil operate; we *feel* an attraction to the sublime goodness of the Transcendent Reality and *feel* the repulsion and horror toward evil. We not only learn about the edifying quality of virtue, and the disedifying qualities of vice; we *feel* ennobled by that virtue and disgusted by that vice. Thus, myths fuse together metaphysical and meta-ethical content with the feelings of the three dimensions of our transcendent soul (the numinous connection, the religious intuition, and conscience).

So how do myths work? How are they able to appeal to the numinous dimension, sacred dimension, and conscientious dimensions of our soul, as well as our intellect, emotions, and intuitions? They do so through the power of *symbols*, which do more than point beyond themselves; they use worldly images and concepts to make contact with the emotions and intuitions of the soul, with the numinous, the religious, and conscience. Eliade phrases it this way:

> The unconscious activity of modern man ceaselessly presents him with innumerable symbols, and each of them has a particular message to transmit, a particular mission to accomplish, in order to ensure or to re-establish the equilibrium of the psyche. As we have seen, the symbol not only makes the world "open" but also helps religious man to attain to the universal. For it is through symbols that man finds his way

out of his particular situation and "opens him-self to the general and the universal." Symbols awaken individual experience and transmute it into a spiritual act, into metaphysical comprehension of the world.[40]

Eliade goes on to describe every individual not only as *homo religiosus*, but *homo symbolicus*. Indeed, we could not be *homo religiosus* (in Eliade's sense) without being *homo symbolicus*. Were it not for the way that symbols connect with the numinous, religious, and conscientious dimensions of our soul, we would only be able to *understand* metaphysical *concepts*. We might be able to understand the proof of God's existence from physics or logic (see Appendixes 1 and 2, respectively, at the end of this volume), but we would not *feel* the mysterious, daunting, authoritative, good, powerful, glorious sublimity of the Transcendent Reality; we would not be able to praise, worship, adore, desire, and passionately pursue the Transcendent Reality. We could only think about it as the conclusion to a syllogism or a physical theorem.

The three dimensions of our soul enable symbol to point from the natural world to the transnatural one in intellection, emotion, and desire. They play a mediating role between our natural awareness and our supernatural awareness, natural feelings and supernatural feelings, and natural desires and supernatural desires. But how? How do symbols mediate the natural and supernatural domains?

For Eliade, the *unconscious* activities of our psyche contain and present us with certain images that are susceptible to both natural and supernatural meanings, each of which has its own message, mission, and mediative effect. Before asking where these "two-faced" images come from (pointing at once to the natural and supernatural domains), we will want to look at some examples of them.

Where would we find such "two-faced" images that can have the above mediative effects? Evidently, in religious rituals, events, and dreams. We can divide these symbolic images into two kinds:

1. those which are *learned* from a particular culture or religion, and
2. those which are transcultural—universal in virtually every culture and religion.

40 Eliade, *Sacred and the Profane*, p. 211.

Children learn various culturally and religiously conditioned symbols by hearing their culture's great myths, participating in their religion's rituals, and viewing religious art and architecture. These symbols are appropriated by the unconscious mind, and additional ones may be generated from the appropriated ones. Once appropriated or generated, these symbols can show up in dreams and can be used in religious worship and creative work.

Transcultural symbols are even more fascinating than those learned from a particular culture or religion. Such transcultural symbols are frequently called "archetypal" by Eliade, Carl Jung, and their followers. "Archetype" refers to the fact that these symbols are *originative* (from the Greek *archē*—"source" or "origin"). Eliade concentrates on the transcultural, cross-religious, and transmythical dimensions of these symbols, while Carl Jung explores an even more fundamental dimension of them, namely, that they appear to be *unlearned*, that is, already present in our unconscious from the moment our unconscious comes into being.

Carl Jung (1875–1961) was a Swiss psychiatrist and psychotherapist who started the school of analytical psychology. Though a student of Sigmund Freud, he disagreed with him, particularly in the area of empirical reductionistic method, believing that the psyche, particularly the unconscious, is beyond strict materialism. Jung believed that the unconscious dimension of the human psyche comes into the world with "archetypes", presumably from heredity. Since archetypes affect the dreams of children and adults in similar ways in virtually every culture, Jung believed that they came from a *common* heritage refined through thousands of generations. He calls this transgenerational common heritage "the collective unconscious". [41] Since many of the archetypes are found not only in dreams, but also in myths, a brief look at Jung's theory will prove helpful.

For Jung, archetypes are not images or symbols per se; they are the *potential* for symbols (that is, the potential that translates an image into a symbol when actualized in the conscious mind). Since they are "potentials" in the *unconscious*, they can only be *deduced* from dreams, rituals, myths, and art. These unconscious potentials have meanings

---

[41] See Carl Jung, *The Archetypes and the Collective Unconscious*, in *Collected Works of C. G. Jung*, vol. 9, pt. 1, trans. R. F. C. Hull (Princeton: Princeton University Press, 1981).

that are essential for knowing one's place in the world and the cosmos, one's meaning in this life and the next, and one's relationships with others and God. When these unconscious potentials surface within the conscious psyche, they attach themselves to images, enabling these images to convey the archetype's meaning.

Some prevalent archetypal figures are great mother, father, child, devil, god, wise old man, wise old woman, the trickster, and the hero.[42] We can see several of these archetypes within ancient and contemporary myths (such as those of Tolkien, Rowling, and Lucas).

The hero is the key archetype of contemporary myths, but the archetypes of God, the devil, the wise old man, and the trickster are also prevalent. Notice that there are no prescribed symbols for these archetypes; the hero can come from any culture, and the God archetype can be manifest as the unseen hand of providence or as "the good side of the force". The archetype of the devil or evil can be manifest in the various images of the lord of darkness and his minions, and the trickster can be manifest as Gollum or an imposter.

As noted above, Jung held that these archetypes are present in virtually every person in virtually every culture around the world from the moment our unconscious begins its activities. This suggests that the archetypes have not been learned, but are present to us, almost as a part of our "human nature". This is difficult to explain in any conventional way, and Jung ultimately decided that they were inherited, just as the content of animal instincts can be inherited from previous generations.

This may be a stretch for some readers, so we need to ask if there is a way to verify Jung's theory. The strongest verification comes from the presence of the archetypes in the dreams of young children. If the archetypes appeared only in the dreams of adults, we might be able to explain them as learned from religion or culture, but it is much more difficult to explain them in the dreams of young children who had little or no exposure to cultural and religious symbols. Children do not have to learn about the "boogeyman" (an image of the archetype of the devil or evil); they do not have to learn about the hero and his journey, or about a good "higher power" (a God archetype). If these archetypes are present to children at the time that their unconscious

---

[42] Ibid.

psyche begins its activities and they do not learn them from their culture, religion, or parents, then where did they come from, and why do children of virtually every culture and religion use the same archetypes?

Furthermore, young children not only use the same archetypes; they associate similar feelings with those archetypes from culture to culture. For example, the archetype of evil produces horror (as distinct from fear),[43] the archetype of God produces numinous feelings— mysteriousness and goodness, uncontrollableness and fascination— and the archetype of the hero produces feelings of nobility and dignity. But how can this occur in young children in virtually every culture? If there is not something akin to the collective unconscious, then the archetypes (and their associated feelings) would appear to be inexplicable.

Jung's explanation of the archetypes as coming from heredity is plausible, but it leaves open the question of where the archetypes of the first generation came from. Obviously the first generation did not inherit either the metaphysical and ethical content of the archetypes or the feelings associated with those contents. So the archetypes must have originated from another source. I would submit that one plausible source is the three dimensions of the soul (the numinous experience, religious intuition, and conscience). In my view, the first human being had a soul (as described above), which is precisely what made that person to be human. This first human being might have created the first archetypes from the metaphysical and ethical contents and feelings arising out of his soul. The numinous contents and feelings could have given rise to the God archetype; the religious intuition could have given rise to the hero archetype; the contents and feelings of conscience combined with the numinous feelings could have given rise to the *goodness* of the God archetype, and to the darkness and evil of the devil archetype. The combination of these archetypes could have given rise to the journey archetype, and so forth.

---

[43] Recall Otto's distinction between fear and horror. The former occurs when one's life is threatened by a danger—adrenaline is released, our heart rates increase, our faces become flush, and we move quickly. Alternatively, horror occurs in the presence of something spiritual, like a ghost, or an evil spirit. This produces precisely the opposite emotions of fear. We feel a sense of cold, our hearts slow down, the blood drains from our faces, and we freeze.

This gives rise to the question of whether the archetypes are inherited. Why would they need to be? If the first human being could connect the contents and feelings of the three dimensions of the soul with various archetypes, why wouldn't every subsequent generation of human beings be able to do the same? In my view, if one believes in a soul (and the above three dimensions of it), this explanation would be as plausible as Jung's hereditary explanation. Speaking personally, I had the contents and feelings of the numinous experience, religious intuition, and conscience from a very young age, and I have no difficulty believing that *I* associated these transcendent contents and feelings with archetypes and images. I don't think I had to inherit my images of God or the boogeyman from my parents (or from all previous generations of humanity); I think they could have arisen at the very moment the three transcendent dimensions of my soul began to manifest themselves.

It may be thought that this explanation does not explain the cross-*cultural* similarities among the archetypes as well as Jung's explanation. Jung's explanation is straightforward—we received the archetypes from a common ancestor and a common generational trajectory from that common ancestry, meaning that every person in every culture has a common source of the archetypes. However, I believe my explanation also provides a common source of the archetypes, namely, the same transcendent reality working through the same three dimensions of the soul in every person in every culture. My explanation simply shifts the common source of the archetypes from a common inherited memory to a common transcendent reality.

The above analysis provides yet another clue to our transcendent reality. For if we do not have a soul through which a transcendent reality has imparted numinous feelings, religious intuitions, and the contents and feelings of conscience, how can the appearance of the archetypes in the dreams and art of young children in virtually every culture be explained? If the above three dimensions of the soul were not present in the first human being, how could that first human being have transmitted the archetypes to subsequent generations (Jung's explanation)? Similarly, if we did not inherit the archetypes from a common ancestor, and the three dimensions of the soul are not present in all human beings, how could any of us use the archetypes in our dreams today (my explanation)?

It does not matter whether Jung's or my explanation is correct, the *absence* of a soul (and a transcendent reality connected with that soul) makes the cross-cultural presence of the archetypes in young children very difficult, if not impossible, to explain. This is yet another clue to the presence of a transcendental reality within us.

After that long digression, we must now return to the question we posed about the attractive and fascinating qualities of myths. So why are the above three contemporary "hero myths" so overwhelmingly popular? Why do they hold out an endless source of fascination for both young people and adults? The above analysis gives us a coherent explanation. The three dimensions of our soul provide the contents and feelings behind all the archetypes and symbols of the hero myth. The numinous connection provides not only an awareness of a transcendent, mysterious, daunting, fascinating, good "wholly Other", but also feelings of fear and fascination, mystery and desire, creatureliness and care.

Our awareness and attraction to this transcendent reality stands behind our archetype of the unseen sacred and providential Deity. Similarly, our religious intuition incites a belief that the sacred reality has broken into the world and has sanctified at least a part of it. These thoughts and feelings stand behind the division of the world into sacred and profane as well as the belief that the sacred is present in the world (often represented by the archetype of the wise old man). The content and feelings of conscience can be superimposed on the division of sacred and profane, turning it into a division between cosmic good and cosmic evil. The religious intuition can give rise to the archetype of the hero (who is connected to God by his own free will and has a mission of representing the Deity in the world). The feelings of conscience can give rise to the goodness of some people and the evil of others. When numinous feelings, religious feelings, and feelings and contents of conscience are combined, we can see not only the archetypes, but the rudimentary sketch of the hero myth, and we can associate this hero with ourselves, and the hero's journey with our lives (or some special mission or task within them).

Myths are attractive and fascinating, because they draw us into our numinous feelings and our religious intuition; they tell us about the truth of ourselves—that we are called to be heroes (or helpers of heroes) in a most noble mission: the defeat of cosmic evil and the restoration of cosmic good. Myths tell us that our lives are not purely mundane, but rather involved in matters of the highest consequence: eternal consequences. Though we may look at the hero as distinct from ourselves, we cannot help but think that the hero's challenges are in some way our challenges; his victories, our victories; his virtues, the virtues to which we aspire; his dangers, the dangers that confront us; and his internal struggles with vice, the ones that could befall us.

The hero is a pure form, an idealized symbol; and thank goodness for it, because we can admire him from afar and hope in his success without directly confronting his struggles and dangers—all the while seeing ourselves in his reflection, and knowing that there is something more to life than the merely mundane. The hero is immersed in a transcendent mystery in an obvious way—in a transcendent mission in an obvious way, and in the nobility of a cosmic struggle in an obvious way. Yet, enmeshed in his pure form is the subtle reminder that we too share in his experience of transcendent mystery, transcendent mission, and noble endeavor. Tolkien knew well what he wanted to convey in his hero myth *The Lord of the Rings*:

> [Myths are] the best way—sometimes the only way—of conveying truths that would otherwise remain inexpressible. We have come from God and inevitably the myths woven by us, though they contain error, reflect a splintered fragment of the true light, the eternal truth that is with God.[44]

Our attraction to and love of myths comes from within us—or better, from the presence of God within us—inviting us into His noble mission, into Himself, and into His destiny.

IV. Conclusion

Throughout the last two chapters we have uncovered several clues to the presence of a transcendent reality within us. We began with Otto's consideration of the numinous experience and noted that this

---

[44]Joseph Pearce, *Tolkien: Man and Myth* (London: Harper Collins, 1998), p. 58. This was copublished in the United States by Ignatius Press, San Francisco in 2001.

cross-cultural and cross-historical phenomenon can be either prominent or quite subtle. Even if it is quite subtle, it leaves us with a desire
for the mysterious, daunting, fascinating, good "wholly Other",
which incites both children's and adults' belief in a transcendent reality to which we can draw near and are ultimately called. If we were
unacquainted with the numinous experience, it would be quite difficult to explain why the vast majority of people (84 percent throughout the world) associate virtually the same characteristics and feelings
(e.g., mystery, fascination, dauntingness, and goodness in the wholly
Other) with transcendent reality.

We then considered a second clue: Eliade's analysis of religious
intuition in which he reveals the cross-cultural and cross-historical
phenomenon of *homo religiosus*—a common belief within virtually
every "traditional man", in an absolute transcendent reality, the
Transcendent Reality's breakthrough into the world, the sanctification of the world by this transcendent reality, and the possibility of
drawing near to that reality for our own sanctification and ultimate
meaning.

If we did not have a common religious intuition, it would be difficult to explain why so many people are not only drawn to religion,
but have a similar belief about the breakthrough of the transcendent
into the world, and the sanctification of the world through this event.
It would likewise be difficult to explain why people have a similar
attraction to myth, ritual, and holy places, and why so many people
feel fulfillment and dignity by participating in religious rituals and
recounting sacred myths.

We then considered a third clue implicit in Eliade's contention that
the abandonment of religion by some modern people should give rise
to existential anxiety. He predicts this because the abandonment of
religion is tantamount to a denial of our implicit intuition of an absolute reality, our transcendent identity and dignity, the potential to
encounter transcendent reality, the potential to obtain sanctification,
and the possibility of finding ultimate meaning and fulfillment. Eliade
surmised that if we really do have numinous feelings and religious
intuitions, then our denial of the Transcendent Reality would be a
denial of both ourselves and the substance of things yearned for. If
the transcendent is present to us, then our denial of it should lead to
anxiety—and so it does, as we have seen in the works of both theistic

and atheistic existentialists as well as the well-documented studies of the American Psychiatric Association (in the *American Journal of Psychiatry*).[45] Why would nonreligious people experience such higher levels of anxiety, aggression, meaninglessness, and distance from family, if they were not rejecting their perceived identity, dignity, and destiny? Why would they experience cosmic emptiness, alienation, loneliness, and guilt if the transcendent and religious were not at least implicitly significant and needed? Why would the nonreligious have such higher rates of suicide?

The fourth clue to the presence of transcendence within us came from conscience. We asked why such a large part of the world's population had certain feelings associated with good and evil—attraction and love of the good, and horror and revulsion to evil. Once again it seemed that our common moral contents and feelings would be inexplicable if they did not have a common source within us. We then examined the work of Immanuel Kant and John Henry Newman that showed how our moral conviction is grounded in a sense of responsibility or duty to a supreme interpersonal authority with whom we are personally familiar. Without this conviction, we would not have the specific thoughts and feelings that make the good obligatory and meaningful.

We then considered a fifth clue arising out of our attraction to and love of myth. We saw that the attraction to myth is linked to archetypes and symbols that convey certain central truths about a cosmic struggle between good and evil, and our place in it. We also saw that these archetypes are present in the dreams of very young children in virtually every culture and religion around the world. This provoked the question about how the archetypes could be present to them if they did not learn them from the outside world. We saw only two options: either they were inherited, or they are derived from the three dimensions of our transcendent soul (the numinous experience, the religious intuition, and conscience). Yet, if they were inherited, we have to ask the question of how the first human being possessed them so as to make them part of his genetic heritage. Since the first human being could not have inherited them, we were left with the implication that they had to come from the three dimensions of

---

[45] That is, in the well-documented studies in Dervic et al., "Religious Affiliation".

his soul. This provoked the following further question: Well, if he derived them from his soul, why wouldn't every person in every subsequent generation be able to derive them from their souls?

So it seems that transcendence is a virtually inescapable feature of every person. To deny this feature requires denying numinous feelings, religious intuition, and the supreme duty of conscience within ourselves. Moreover it leaves us without a suitable explanation for why nonreligious people suffer higher levels of existential anxiety than religious people, and how the archetypes universally present in the dreams of young children found their way into their unconscious activity. Whether we wish to acknowledge it or not, transcendent reality seems to play a part in all of our lives.

We now proceed to five additional clues to the presence of a transcendent reality within us: four transcendental desires for truth, love, goodness, and beauty (Chapters 3 and 4), and the evidence for a transphysical dimension of consciousness that can survive bodily death—from near-death experiences (Chapter 5).

Chapter Three

Mind and the Transcendent

Editor's Note

Readers who are not acquainted with philosophy and logical argument may find this chapter difficult, but profitable. You may want to begin with Sections III and IV—Lonergan's proof of God—and try to read it two or three times until you grasp the essence of the argument. You might then want to proceed to Sections I, II, V, and VI, which will take you through the basic steps of epistemology from perceptual ideas to conceptual ideas, heuristic notions, and the supreme heuristic notion.[1]

Introduction

We are now ready to explore yet another four clues to the presence of the Transcendent Reality to our consciousness. In the previous two chapters, we saw that the presence of the Transcendent Reality is interpersonal and dialogical. The numinous experience has a distinct element of both empathy and invitation, the religious intuition has a dimension of the sacred that breaks into the profane world to sanctify us, and conscience is embedded within the sense of an omniscient, invisible searcher of hearts. Finally, the unconscious archetypal myth calls us to be heroic companions of cosmic good in the struggle against cosmic evil.

---

[1] Personally speaking, during my sophomore year at college, I attempted to read Lonergan's *Insight* and was particularly interested in Chapters 14–19, Lonergan's approach to metaphysics and his proof of God. I recall being dazed after going through the material *slowly* for the first time, but on subsequent rereadings of the material, these chapters became foundational to my study and writing in philosophy. Sometimes "tougher texts", like "tougher teachers", are worth the most. See Bernard Lonergan, *Insight: A Study of Human Understanding*, in *Collected Works of Bernard Lonergan* 3, ed. Frederick E. Crowe and Robert M. Doran (Toronto: University of Toronto Press, 1992).

Our next set of clues is less interpersonal and more metaphysical. It points to the presence of something perfect, unconditional, and unrestricted within our consciousness that beckons us ahead of any imperfect and finite idea or ideal that causes us to seek greater love, goodness, justice, and beauty beyond anything previously learned or discovered. Some philosophers call this a "transcendent horizon" that can neither be described nor explained through any set of restricted, conditioned, or imperfect categories or realities.[2] If such a transcendent horizon is present to us, it implies that we too are transcendent—bestowed of a soul that supersedes the physical world and its finite structures.

In Chapter 2 of the previous volume, I briefly discussed the five transcendental desires that have impressed philosophers since the time of Plato: the desire for perfect truth, love, justice or goodness, beauty, and being. Neo-Platonists such as Plotinus, Boethius, and Saint Augustine thought they were the most important powers or capacities within us. Saint Thomas Aquinas and virtually all of his contemporary followers (such as Etienne Gilson, Jacques Maritain, Josef Pieper, Bernard Lonergan, and Karl Rahner) put these transcendental desires at the center of their philosophies. They believed that these desires not only point to our transcendental nature and transphysical soul, but also to our ultimate happiness, purpose in life, fulfillment, and destiny. If we do not acknowledge them, we cannot know who we truly are, and as a result, we cannot be truly free, for freedom requires knowing our true potential and how to orient our lives toward it.

Most transcendental philosophers believe that we cannot desire something without being at least tacitly aware of it. How can we desire something we are not aware of? So, we must have some awareness of perfect truth, love, goodness, beauty, and being (hereafter, the "five transcendentals"). This provokes an important question: Can we learn about perfect truth, love, goodness, beauty, and being from the world around us, sufficient to desire them? If the physical-empirical

---

[2] See ibid. and the following references: Emerich Coreth, *Metaphysics*, trans. Joseph Donceel (New York: Herder and Herder, 1968); Joseph Maréchal, *Le point de depart de la métaphysique: leçons sur le développement historique du problèm de la connaissance* (Bruges: Charles Beyaert, 1922); and Karl Rahner, *Spirit in the World* (New York: Herder and Herder, 1968). Rahner has written extensively about the "transcendent horizon".

world is conditioned by contingent and finite structures, then we cannot learn about the five transcendentals from it.

The above consideration leads to several additional questions: Could these five transcendentals be programmed in the physics, chemistry, and biology of our brains? Again, it seems highly unlikely, because quantum physics, macroscopic physics, chemistry, and biology are all conditioned by contingent and finite structures. Well then, where did our awareness and desire for the five transcendentals come from? They would need to come from something transphysical, something without the inherent limitations of the brain or physical reality around us. This is precisely what has led the transcendentalist school, since the time of Plato, to the belief that there must be something transphysical within every individual.

Is there any way of verifying the presence of these five transcendentals within us? Do the above-mentioned philosophers present any evidence or arguments for them? Is there any way to be sure that these desires are really for the unconditional and perfect? In a word, yes, which will be the subject of this and the next chapter. I will combine the consideration of truth and being in this chapter and will then consider the other three transcendentals—love, goodness, and beauty—in the next.

I. The Desire for Perfect Truth-Being: Lonergan's Proof of God and Human Transcedence

Though Plato, Aquinas, and other ancient medieval philosophers formulated arguments for our desire for and awareness of perfect truth, Bernard Lonergan provides the most contemporary cogent argument responding to the critical work of David Hume and Immanuel Kant, as well as relativity physics, quantum physics, and statistical heuristic structures. Lonergan's argument is presented through several chapters of his major opus, *Insight: A Study of Human Understanding*. Though it is complex, it has vast explanatory power—not only to answer some of the most vexing questions in cognitional theory, but also to prove the existence of God and human transcendence.

I will summarize Lonergan's argument for our desire for perfect truth (complete intelligibility) in four steps, using the titles of their respective sections below:

II. Clues to Our Transcendence from the Question *Why*

In *Insight: A Study of Human Understanding*, Lonergan examines the evidence for the transcendentality of consciousness intrinsic to our ability to ask questions about causation and our unrestricted desire to know. Though this capacity and desire may not seem to be an entry-way to the world of transcendence, Lonergan shows that they are deep and sweeping—manifesting not only our transcendentality, but also the presence of God to us. Before we can explain this extraordinary claim, we must begin with our everyday experience of asking the question, why is it so?

The following question is a highly complex mentative operation: Why is reality this particular way rather than some other? We sometimes fail to see how complex it is, because children do it so easily, almost as if they have been programmed to do it without recognizing its remarkable nature. So what is required for anyone to ask the foregoing question? First and foremost we must be aware that *particular* (finite and conditioned) manifestations of reality do not exhaust the whole of reality; the whole of reality is much greater. This provokes the following thought: If reality can be manifest in so many different ways, *why* is it manifest in this particular way—here and now? At this point, we are aware that the *particular manifestation* of reality could have been otherwise, and that the particular way that happens to be real is *not necessary*. It is only one possibility amid other possibilities, and the one possibility that happens to be real does not have to be real. This leads us to conclude that there must be something in reality that "caused" this one nonnecessary possibility to be real, but not the others. This "cause" is precisely what the question *why* is seeking.

Let's look at it the other way around. Would you have ever asked the question *why* if you were not seeking a cause for the particular way in which reality happens to be? And could you have known that reality needs a cause if you were not aware that reality could have been other than it is? And would you have been aware that reality could be other than it is unless you had some sense that reality is much greater than any of its particular manifestations? If so, then you might want to ask how you learned all of this information. How did you learn that reality had so much more potential than any particular way it happens to be at a particular place and time? Where did you learn that the particular ways "in which things are" are not necessary, and that they do not explain themselves? Where did you learn that if they cannot explain themselves, they must have some explanation beyond themselves—a cause. If all these things are necessary to ask the question, why is it so? coherently, could we have learned them from the outside world? Wouldn't we have to have used these concepts in order to learn them (a vicious circle)? Could they have been programmed into our organic brain with its physical parts and finite structures? Lonergan and a host of philosophers before him did not think so. They thought that it would have to come from something that is not limited by particular places, times, processes, and structures—something beyond the limitations of physics and finite structures. But we are getting ahead of ourselves here. In order to understand this question and its response, we will have to do far more preparation. For the moment, suffice it to say that the question, why is it so? seems to be beyond merely materialistic and mechanistic explanation.

Before delving into the conditions necessary for awareness of the need for causation, we will want to answer a commonsense objection, namely, "It does not seem that grasping the need for causation is so complex. After all, animals can memorize particular cause-effect sequences—like the squeak of the can opener means impending food or the master's return home means food, affection, and a walk. Isn't this the same as asking the question of why is it so?" Evidently, these are not the same mentative activities. The dog has only recognized a pattern of "before and after" (that can satisfy biological needs); it is truly not looking for a cause out of a belief that a particular reality cannot explain itself. It really is not concerned with why a particular state of affairs exists rather than some other. Children, however, do ask the foregoing question in a meaningful way, looking for a cause or explanation. Yet, how can they do this if they are not aware that a particular reality does not explain itself, and therefore needs an explanation?

Let us return to our original contention, namely, that if we are to ask the question, why is it so? meaningfully, we must have at least a tacit awareness[3] that reality ("the real" or "reality as a whole") allows for many more possibilities than the *particular* reality (state of affairs) that we happen to be experiencing. For example, would I ask for an explanation of why an electron is at a particular space-time point, if I did not have some awareness that *it could have been* at a myriad of *other* space-time points? This recognition that it could have been otherwise reveals our awareness that reality ("reality as a whole") allows for *other possibilities*. If we did not have such an awareness, we would see no need for a cause, and would therefore not ask the question of why is it so.

This gives rise to a further question: What is the condition necessary for us to be aware that "reality as a whole" allows for other possibilities besides the one we are experiencing? Evidently, we must have at least a tacit awareness of what might be called a "supercategory" of "the whole of reality", and this supercategory must include a tacit awareness of a wide range of possibilities beyond those that just happen to have occurred. Without this tacit awareness of the vast possibilities for the whole of reality, we would once again be unable to ask the question, why is it so? meaningfully.

A tacit awareness of "the vast possibilities for reality as a whole" would have to include a sense of both "everything that is real" and "the possibilities for reality that are *not* real", a sense of the universality of reality as well as its *unrealized* possibilities. Some people will balk at the idea that we have such a complex universal tacit awareness of the "vast possibilities for the whole of reality", because it seems as if it must originate within a highly mature reflective intellect. Yet, children apparently have it, enabling them to ask the question, why is it so? Where in the world could children have been exposed to such a complex universal concept?

As the reader might suspect, this complex universal awareness does not come from anywhere in the world. It will have to come from some other source that is truly *universal* and capable of imparting

---

[3] By "tacit awareness" here is meant an awareness of the meaning of an idea without a reflective understanding of it. This awareness is sufficient to *use* the idea in asking questions or contextualizing answers, but is not explicit enough to be reflectively grasped, defined, and understood.

a sense of both "what is realized" and "what is unrealized" in the whole of reality. If we admit that the question, why is it so? requires a tacit awareness that the whole of reality allows for possibilities other than the ones that have occurred, and that this tacit awareness in turn requires a tacit awareness of both the realized and unrealized possibilities of the whole of reality, then we will have to find an appropriate *universal* source of that tacit awareness. Before taking up this challenge, we must examine two other dimensions intrinsic to this question.

Is the tacit awareness of the "realized and unrealized possibilities for reality as a whole" enough to ask the foregoing question? Though it is the most fundamental condition for this question, it is not the *only* condition. We must also have a belief that an answer to our question can be found, that is, that an answer exists within "reality as a whole". Notice that questions (and even questioning) would be meaningless if we do not anticipate finding a correct answer. If we had no sense of a "correct answer to be discovered", we would have *nothing* to look for; our question would be bereft of an objective. Furthermore, we are not looking for just any answer; we are looking for a *correct* answer—a *true* answer, a *real* answer. If we were not looking for an answer corresponding to reality, the question, why is reality this way rather than some other? would once again be meaningless.

Let's take a closer look at this anticipation of a correct answer to our question. Clearly, it entails finding an answer from the whole of *reality.* This means that we have a tacit belief that an answer to our question exists within the whole of reality, awaiting our discovery of it. We not only have a tacit awareness of the "realized and unrealized possibilities of the whole of reality", but also an awareness that the whole of reality contains the correct answer to our question of why is it so. We have a sense of the *intelligibility* of the whole of reality, that is, that the whole of reality contains correct answers to our questions. Thus, we are decidedly "nonsubjectivists" in our questioning, for we will only be content with an answer that comes from "the whole of reality".

Once again, we are provoked to ask the question, what is the source of this belief in the intelligibility of the whole of reality, this belief that an answer to our question exists within the whole of reality, our anticipation of a correct answer to the question of why is it so? If the meaningful asking of this question requires a belief in (and anticipation of) a correct answer in the whole of reality, then there must be some appropriate source of that belief. Once again we must defer our response to that challenge until we have considered one final point.

Up to now we have elucidated two conditions required for asking the question of why is it so:

1. a tacit awareness of "realized and unrealized possibilities of the whole of reality", and
2. a tacit belief in the *intelligibility* of the whole of reality (a tacit belief that the whole of reality contains the answer to our question).

Without this tacit awareness and tacit belief, we simply could not ask the foregoing question meaningfully. Children would be much easier to put up with, but we would be reduced to the state of nonreflective animals.

Lonergan identifies one more dimension of our questioning process that is *not a condition required* for this question. Nevertheless, it is integral to our questioning process; we have a pure *unrestricted* desire to know, that is, a desire to know all that is to be known (everything about everything). When we examine this desire more closely, we see that it entails yet another belief, namely, that "everything about everything" is knowable—and is awaiting our discovery. We appear to believe that the *complete* set of correct answers to the *complete* set of questions exists within the whole of reality. For Lonergan, when we ask the question of why is it so, we are not simply looking for a partial or incomplete answer, but rather for a *complete and perfect answer*. With every asking of this question, we are anticipating a completely intelligible answer—we are seeking complete intelligibility. When we arrive at an answer that is only *partially* intelligible (that is, it is not "everything about everything"), our desire is only *partially* satisfied, and we naturally ask a subsequent question of why is it so in our quest to achieve the fulfillment of our desire, namely, complete intelligibility (the knowledge of everything about everything).

How can Lonergan be so sure that we desire to know *complete* intelligibility every time we ask this question? The answer lies in our reaction to the discovery that we have answered a question in only a *partially* intelligible way. As this answer emerges, we realize almost immediately that it is *not* what we are looking for (a completely intelligible answer), and that we must ask a further question to get to our goal. Yet, how do we know the *partial* intelligibility of our answers *every* time we have arrived at them? We must have a tacit awareness of what complete intelligibility is like. If we did not have this tacit awareness, we would not immediately recognize the *partial* intelligibility of *every* answer that is not completely intelligible. This tacit awareness is present not only in our recognition of *all* instances of *partial* intelligibility, but also in every question that we ask, for we are not simply seeking partial intelligibility, but complete and perfect intelligibility in our questioning; we are always seeking the complete satisfaction of our *unrestricted* desire to know. This tacit awareness within our questioning incites us to ask further questions *continuously* until we have reached the complete set of correct answers to the complete set of questions in the whole of reality.

As noted above, if we are to seek *complete* intelligibility every time we ask a question, and to have an awareness of the partial intelligibility of every answer that falls short of complete intelligibility, we must have a tacit awareness of what complete intelligibility is like—what qualifies for "the complete set of correct answers to the complete set of questions". Now we see that we not only have a tacit awareness of the intelligibility of reality as a whole, but a tacit awareness of the *complete* intelligibility of reality as a whole. We may now summarize the two dimensions of the tacit awareness intrinsic to our questions about causation:

1. an awareness of the realized and unrealized possibilities of the whole of reality, and
2. an awareness of the complete intelligibility of the whole of reality (that is, that the whole of reality contains the complete set of correct answers to the complete set of questions).

Once again we are provoked to ask the question, what is the source of this tacit awareness (with its two dimensions)? We will consider the answer in two steps:

1. whether our tacit awareness is innate (intrinsic to us, and *not* learned from the world around us), and
2. whether the source of this tacit awareness can be found in restricted or partially intelligible realities.

So, does our tacit awareness of the complete intelligibility of reality have to be *innate*? It seems that it must be innate because we would have to use this tacit awareness of completely intelligible reality in order to learn it from the outside world. Stated the other way around, we couldn't learn it from the outside world unless we already had it within our consciousness. Why so? Because the questioning process moves us from the domain of experience to that of understanding; so if we are to understand anything from experience, we will have to ask a question. The paradox now emerges: How could we learn the two dimensions of our tacit awareness for asking questions without already understanding them, so that we could use them to ask the question? A brief consideration of experience and understanding will prove helpful here.

Experience is awareness of the world around us, but this awareness occurs as *individual* perceptual ideas, like images or "picture thoughts". Individual picture thoughts represent very few of our concepts and words. The reader need only look at the previous two or three paragraphs and count the number of words that refer to individual perceptual ideas, to notice that they are few and far between. Most of our words refer to relational ideas that derive their meaning from *relationships* among perceptual ideas and even relationships among those relationships. We derive these relational ideas from various questions that set up a heuristic structure through which perceptual ideas and relational ideas can be organized. For example, the question *where* brings to mind a heuristic structure like a map in which various places can be set into *relationship* with one another. The question *when* brings to mind a heuristic structure like a clock or a calendar that allows us to set various times into *relationship* with one another. The question *what* brings to mind a heuristic structure of genre and species—similarities and differences—in which various perceptual ideas and relational ideas can be placed in *relationship* to one another. The question *why* brings to mind a heuristic structure of cause and effect, conditioned and conditions, that allows us to build explanatory relationships among perceptual and relational ideas, and so on. Each specific heuristic structure is organized around a "heuristic notion", which is a large domain of intelligibility through which various perceptual and relational ideas can be organized (e.g., location, time, similarity-difference, cause-effect, etc.). For Lonergan, the "*supreme* heuristic notion" is "the complete intelligibility of the whole of reality", because it underlies all other heuristic notions, and, therefore, all relational ideas.[4]

The moment we ask a question, it incites an organizing heuristic structure that allows us to set perceptual and relational ideas into relationship with one another, and these *relational* ideas can then be used as predicates or objects in a sentence. Perceptual ideas ("picture thoughts") cannot be used as predicates or objects, because they cannot represent more than the one individual object of experience from which they are derived. If we did not have relational ideas, we would only be able to speak in tautologies—"Socrates is Socrates", "Fido is Fido", and so on. However, relational ideas can stand for a multiplicity of perceptual objects and even a multiplicity of relationships among perceptual ideas—for example, "Socrates is a man" (in which man is a relational idea derived from similarities among many men and differentiated from women, nonrational animals, nonliving things, etc.). Furthermore, we can say "man is a noun" (in which noun is a second-degree abstraction, a relationship among relational ideas). We can even abstract relationships among "relationships of relational ideas" (e.g., "nouns are parts of speech in grammar"). These third-degree abstractions (e.g., "grammar", "mathematics", "metaphysics", "logic", etc.) enable us to organize relationships among "relationships of relational ideas". Without relational ideas, we would not be able to know or communicate anything *about* anything; we would not be able to grasp the significance of syntax,[5] let alone grasp complex thoughts in grammar, logic, mathematics, and so on.

---

[4] Lonergan, *Insight*, p. 380.

[5] As will be seen (Section VI below), Noam Chomsky provides a definitive test for the possibility of chimpanzees (or other higher animals) having understanding (the ability to know and say something *about* something) on the basis of syntax. If syntax is not significant for a particular animal species, then that species does not abstract or use relational ideas, and if it does not do this, then it has no understanding; it remains solely on the level of experience (perceptual ideas) as well as memories of perceptual ideas, including before-after sequences and here-now positioning of perceptual ideas.

We may now return to the question with which we began: Does our tacit awareness of the complete intelligibility of the whole of reality have to be *innate*? The above consideration shows that it *must be*, because if we were not aware of the heuristic structures and notions intrinsic to each question, we would not be able to ask those questions, and if we could not ask questions, we would be locked into the domain of experience and perceptual ideas—unable to abstract the simplest predicates and objects, and therefore unable to abstract the most complex ones (the heuristic notions underlying all of our questions).

Does this apply to the heuristic notion—the intelligibility of the whole of reality—that underlies the question of why is it so? It does, because this heuristic notion is a condition necessary for *all* questioning. Recall what was said above that if we are to meaningfully ask *any* question, we must be able to anticipate a correct answer in the whole of reality. Questioning that does not anticipate a correct answer is meaningless. Thus, if we do not have a tacit awareness of intelligibility (correct answers in the whole of reality), we will not ask *any* questions at all, and if we do not ask questions, we cannot move from the domain of experience to understanding, and if we do not do this, we cannot abstract even simple relational ideas from the perceptual world—let alone the heuristic notion of the intelligibility of the whole of reality. In sum, we need an awareness of the intelligibility of the whole of reality in order to ask the questions that allow us to learn this idea from the world around us. If we did not have it innately, we would never be able to learn it from the world around us.

In the previous paragraph we showed that our tacit awareness of the intelligibility of the whole of reality is innate, but we did not speak of *complete* intelligibility. So, is our tacit awareness of the *complete* intelligibility of the whole of reality also innate? It must be, because we could not have an awareness of the *complete* intelligibility of the whole of reality without simultaneously being aware of the intelligibility of the whole of reality. So, if the latter awareness must be innate, so also must the former, which is dependent on it.

We are now in a position to investigate the *source* of our tacit awareness of the complete intelligibility of the whole of reality.

Since this tacit awareness must be innate, we cannot learn it from the world around us. As we shall see, there is another reason for this—namely, that the world around us is restricted by individuation, space-time particularity, and other restrictions, but our tacit awareness of the complete intelligibility of the whole of reality must come from *a unique unrestricted act of thinking*. But we are here getting way ahead of ourselves. If we are to understand this contention, we will have to first establish that the whole of reality really is completely intelligible—as we anticipate. It just so happens that the proof of the complete intelligibility of the whole of reality entails the existence of at least one uncaused cause (a reality that exists through itself), which must be unrestricted in intelligibility and completely unique and an unrestricted act of thinking.

In order to establish this, we will have to leave our consideration of cognitional theory and epistemology for a moment and delve into the world of ontology and metaphysics, specifically Lonergan's proof of the complete intelligibility of the whole of reality (Section III.A below) and its consequence—the existence of a unique unrestricted act of thinking: God (Sections III.B–III.D below). When the latter investigation is complete, the source of our innate tacit awareness of the complete intelligibility of the whole of reality will become clear (Sections IV and V below).

III. Lonergan's Proof of God

Lonergan's proof may be stated as follows:

> If the totality of reality is completely intelligible, then God exists.
> But the totality of reality *is* completely intelligible.
> Therefore, God exists.[6]

We will begin with the minor premise—namely, that the totality of reality is completely intelligible—and then move to the major premise ("if the totality of reality is completely intelligible, then God exists").

[6] See Lonergan, *Insight*, p. 695.

A. Proof of the Minor Premise:
"The Totality of Reality Is Completely Intelligible"

The totality of reality must have at least one necessary reality, that is, a reality that exists *through itself* (and needs no cause outside of itself to exist). If there were not at least one necessary reality in the totality of reality, then the totality of reality would collectively require a cause in order to exist, implying that it would not exist without this cause. Look at it this way: if there is no "reality that exists through itself" in the totality of reality, then the totality of reality would be composed only of "realities that cannot exist without a cause". But if this were the case, then the totality of reality itself (collectively) could not exist without a cause. In the absence of such a cause the totality of reality would not exist—the totality of reality would be all hypothetical realities awaiting causation to exist, which means that there would be literally *nothing* in the totality of reality; it would be completely nonexistent. Therefore, there must be at least one necessary reality that can exist through itself in the totality of reality.

The existence of at least one "reality that exists through itself" enables not only the totality of reality to *exist*, but also to be *completely intelligible*, that is, that every question of why is it so and every other question that is premised upon it have a correct answer. This can be proven in two steps.

Step no. 1

Inasmuch as a necessary reality (that exists through itself) must exist, then it must be the *final* (ultimate) answer to every inquiry about causation (i.e., the question of why is it so). For example, if I ask, "Why is this electron at this space-time point?" and you respond, "Because of a cause that occurred at another space-time point", I then follow that up with the question, "Why was that cause at that particular space-time point?" and you identify yet another cause. Ultimately, we will reach an end to our questioning, because we will have to arrive at an uncaused cause (a necessary being existing through itself), without which the totality of reality would be nothing. Therefore, a necessary reality must be the final (ultimate) answer to every question of causation.

Step no. 2

If there must be a final answer to the question of why is it so, there must also be a final answer to every *other* question (e.g., *what, where, when,* as well as, how does it operate? etc.), because the latter is grounded in (dependent on) the former. Without a cause of existence, there would be literally *nothing* to be intelligible. There cannot be questions for *intelligibility* (e.g., what is it?) that go beyond the final (ultimate) cause of *existence*. If there were such questions, their answers would have to be nothing. Therefore, a final (ultimate) answer to the question of why is it so must ground the final (ultimate) answer to every other question. The answers to all possible questions must terminate in the final answer to this question. Since there must exist a final answer to this question: "Why is it so?" (a necessary being existing through itself), there must also be a final answer to every other question about reality. The complete set of correct answers to the complete set of questions really must exist—and reality, as Lonergan asserts, must be completely intelligible.[7]

B. Proof of the Major Premise:
"If the Totality of Reality Is Completely Intelligible, God Exists"

Why does Lonergan believe that if the totality of reality is completely intelligible, then God (i.e., a unique unrestricted reality that is an unrestricted act of thinking) exists?[8] As we saw in the proof of the minor premise, the totality of reality *must include* a "necessary reality which exists through itself". Without at least one necessary reality, there would be *nothing* in the totality of reality. This necessary reality brings finality to the answers to every question that can be asked about the totality of reality—and so makes the totality of reality (*completely*) intelligible. Lonergan recognizes that this necessary being must also be *unrestricted* in its intelligibility, and this requires that it be unique (one and only one) as well as an unrestricted act of thinking, and the Creator of the rest of reality. (The proof of these contentions is summarized below in this section and in Section IV.)

[7] See the extended treatment in ibid., pp. 674–79.
[8] This proof may be found in ibid., pp. 692–98.

We now turn to the proof of the first of these contentions, namely, that a "necessary reality existing through itself" must be unrestricted in its intelligibility. This may be shown in two steps.

Step no. 1

A necessary being must be unrestricted in its explicability (its capacity to explain *itself* from within itself). If it were restricted in its explicability, then within it there would be a restricted number of answers to the question of why is it so. This means that more questions could be asked about this reality than could be answered by the information intrinsic to it. If this were the case, then the necessary reality would not be able to explain *itself*. Recourse would have to be made to a reality outside of it to obtain the final answer to the above question. But this is an obvious contradiction, because a necessary being exists *through itself* and, therefore, must have all the information in it necessary to answer every question about its existence.

Step no. 2

If a reality is unrestricted in its explicability, it must also be unrestricted in its intelligibility. We were given a hint about the proof of this contention in the minor premise when it was shown that the final answer to the question of why is it so must also be the final answer to all other questions, that is, that the answers to *all* questions must terminate in a necessary reality existing through itself. Lonergan realizes that not only the *finality* of intelligibility follows from the *finality* of explicability (existence), but also that the *unrestrictedness* of intelligibility follows from the *unrestrictedness* of explicability (existence). If a reality were restricted in intelligibility (i.e., it did not answer some questions about itself), it would also imply a restriction of explicability. Because if there is not enough information in a reality to answer the questions *what* and *where*, as well as, how does it operate? there would not be enough information in that reality to answer every question about its existence. "What a thing *is*" is tied to the causes of its existence, so also where *it is*, when *it is*, and how *it is*, and so on.[9]

---

[9] See ibid., pp. 674–79.

This key insight came twenty-four hundred years before Lonergan in the *Physics* and *Metaphysics* of Aristotle, who delineated four causes of *both existence and intelligibility*:

1. *Material cause*—the underlying constituent parts that make a reality to exist. In the case of a cell, it would be the different molecules, atoms constituting those molecules, and protons and electrons constituting those atoms, and so on. Notice that the material cause not only answers the question about what makes the cell to *exist*, but also the following questions: *What* are its parts? *How* are its parts structured?
2. *Formal cause*—the internal activities (operations) that characterize a reality. For example, in a cell, the constituent parts—the material cause—are organized to perform activities that will keep the cell alive (ingestion, metabolism, replication, respiration, etc.). These activities require *information* to organize the cell's constituent parts to perform those activities. This information is part of the formal cause (along with the activities resulting from it). Notice again that the formal cause not only answers questions about what makes a cell *exist*, but also answers the following questions: *What* are its fundamental operations and activities? *How* do the parts produce those operations and activities?
3. *Efficient cause*—constituents and activities *outside* of a reality that cause it to exist. The efficient cause of a cell is the cell (or cells) from which it was generated, the conditions in the environment or in a host body that enable this generation to occur, and so on. Notice again that the efficient cause not only answers questions about what makes the cell *exist*, but also answers the following questions: *What* does it need from the environment to exist? *What* does it need from the environment to operate? *When* will it exist and operate? *Where* is it?
4. *Final cause*—the determinative information that brings a reality to its perfection, to "what it was meant to be". In a cell this would be genetic information that moves a cell from the initial stages of replication to its full functioning either by itself (e.g., protozoa) or in a complex organism (e.g., a muscle cell). Notice again that this cause explains what makes a cell to *exist* as well as *what* will it become and *how* will it develop.

We are now in a position to examine Lonergan's recognition that unrestrictedness of explicability implies unrestrictedness of intelligibility. As can be seen from the four causes of Aristotle, what makes a thing to exist also makes it to be intelligible; the two are inextricably intertwined. Thus, if a particular reality lacks information within itself to answer questions about what it is, where it is, and how it operates, and so on, it will also lack the corresponding information about what makes it exist (the explicability of its existence). This means that if a reality is restricted in its intelligibility, it will also be restricted in its explicability, and so it must follow that unrestricted explicability entails unrestricted intelligibility (*modus tollens*).

Conclusion

Since a "necessary being existing through itself" must be unrestricted in its explicability (Step no. 1), it must also be unrestricted in its intelligibility (Step no. 2). There is a further consequence of this, namely, that a reality which is unrestricted in its explicability will have no other logically possible alternatives to itself. It is in itself the totality of all possibilities for itself. Thus, the following is the answer to the question, why is this reality so? There is no other possibility than this reality because it exhausts all possibilities for reality within itself—and hence it also exhausts all possibilities for intelligibility within itself.

C. A Reality That Is Unrestricted in Intelligibility Must Be Completely Unique

The general argument is as follows. If there were more than one unrestrictedly intelligible reality, there would have to be a difference between the one and the other, and if there were such a difference, then one of the supposedly "unrestricted intelligibles" would have to be restricted in its intelligibility—an obvious contradiction. This proof can be set out in two steps.

Step no. 1

Suppose there are two unrestrictedly intelligible realities—UI_1 and UI_2. There would have to be some difference between UI_1 and UI_2.

If there were not some difference in intelligibility (difference as to activities, space-time point, qualities, and on on) between the one and the other, then the two would be the self-same, which means there would only be one of them (a priori). Therefore, if there are two or more unrestrictedly intelligible realities, there would have to be a difference between them.

Step no. 2

If there is a difference between UI_1 and UI_2, then one of them would have to be somewhere, be something, or have something that the other one did *not*. This would mean that one of them would *not* be intelligible in some way that the other one was (that is, one of them would not be able to answer a question from the information within itself that the other one was able to answer from within *itself*). The one that could not answer such a question from within itself would have to be *restricted* in its intelligibility. But this again is an obvious contradiction, because this hypothetical unrestrictedly intelligible reality would be restricted in its intelligibility.

Conclusion

Every hypothetical second, third, and so on, unrestrictedly intelligible reality is an intrinsic contradiction (i.e., a restricted unrestrictedly in-telligible reality). Therefore, there can be only one unrestrictedly intelligible reality in the totality of reality. Inasmuch as there must be at least one "necessary reality existing through itself" (proved in the minor premise), and such a reality must be unrestricted in its intelligi-bility (proved in the first part of the major premise in Section III.B), and there can only be one unrestrictedly intelligible reality (proved immediately above), there can be *only one* necessary reality that is unrestricted in its intelligibility.

D. The One Necessary Reality Is the Ultimate Cause of Everything Else in Reality

This contention follows from four conclusions of the proofs given above:

1. There must be at least one necessary being existing through itself, otherwise the totality of reality would be nothing (the minor premise; Section III.A).
2. Any "necessary being existing through itself" must be unrestrictedly intelligible (Section III.B).
3. There can only be one unrestrictedly intelligible reality (Section III.C).
4. The existence and intelligibility of all realities must ultimately be caused by (grounded in) a "necessary being existing through itself" (the minor premise; Section III.A).

Therefore, the existence and intelligibility of every reality must be caused by (grounded in) the one—and only one—"necessary reality existing through itself" that is unrestricted in its explicability and intelligibility. This one unrestrictedly intelligible necessary reality must therefore be the ultimate cause of the existence and intelligibility of everything in the totality of reality.

Conclusion

This "unrestrictedly intelligible necessary reality that is the cause of everything else in reality" may be viewed as a general metaphysical definition of "God". Therefore, God, as defined, exists.

IV. God Is an "Unrestricted Act of Thinking"

The reader may be wondering why we gave Lonergan's proof of God's existence in the context of discussing our desire for complete intelligibility. The brief answer is that our awareness of the complete intelligibility of reality requires a source, and as will be seen, this source must be the *idea* of complete intelligibility, and the idea of complete intelligibility must occur within an unrestricted act of thinking. In the above proof of God, we showed that the totality of reality must include a unique necessary reality that is unrestricted in its intelligibility. We will now show that unrestricted intelligibility can only occur through an unrestricted *idea*, which in turn can only occur through an unrestricted act of thinking. This means that the source of our awareness of complete intelligibility must be a unique unrestricted act of thinking that makes itself present to us—not as an idea, but as a notion or "horizon" impelling us not only to ask the question of why is it so, but also to make the creative leaps necessary to answer it. In this section we will present the evidence for the unique unrestricted act of thinking, and in the next section, we will present the way in which it presents itself to us.

As noted above, the one necessary reality that exists through itself is unrestricted in its intelligibility. This means that it can answer from within itself not only the question of why is it so, but also all other questions premised upon it. For Lonergan, this kind of intelligibility cannot be material (conditioned by space and time) or individuated (restricted to an instance and therefore unable to unify or relate distinct or opposed objects). It must therefore be transmaterial and transindividual—having the qualities of an *idea*. In order to explain what Lonergan means by "idea", it will be helpful to distinguish between two kinds of thinking: "picture thinking" and "conceptual thinking". Picture thinking results in what is called "perceptual ideas", ideas that correspond to an *individual* image (such as my dog Fido); and conceptual thinking corresponds to "conceptual ideas", which require more explanation.

Look at the words in the previous two paragraphs. How many of them correspond to an individual image (like my dog Fido)? As you can see, the vast majority of them do not correspond to any individual image. So what do these *abstract* words such as conjunctions, prepositions, logical terms, mathematical terms, verbs, adjectives, abstract nouns, and so on, refer to? In a word, *relationships* (or even relationships among relationships). Though some animals are capable of forming perceptual ideas, people alone are capable of forming conceptual ("relationship-based") ideas (see below, Section VI).

Recall what was said above about the heuristic structures and heuristic notions that stand behind every question. Notions are general inclusive concepts, and *heuristic* notions are among the highest of these inclusive concepts. They are capable of unifying (bringing together) all other less general concepts under their broad and inclusive intelligibility.

These high-level unifying concepts enable individuals to create superstructures through which to *interrelate* perceptual ideas among one another, perceptual ideas with conceptual ideas, and conceptual ideas among one another. These superstructures are like context for organization of particular ideas—like a map is a context for organizing specific places, or a clock or calendar for organizing specific times, or a table of genus and species for organizing similarities and differences among realities, and so on. Each superstructure has particular heuristic notions (high-level ideas) intrinsic to it that determine the way in which ideas are to be organized.

For example, the notions of "similarity and difference" are essential for organizing answers to the question *what*, "here and there" for the question *where*, "earlier-now-later" for the question *when*, and "causation-possibility-necessity-contingency-actuality" for the question *why*. Without heuristic notions to give intelligibility to organizational superstructures, we would have no way of relating ideas among one another, and if we could not do this, we would have no conceptual ideas. We would be reduced to about 4 percent of the words we use—limited only to those having direct pictorial referents.

As noted above (Section II), heuristic notions cannot be learned from the empirical world, because we would have to use them to transform perceptual ideas into the highest-level conceptual ideas. They must therefore be innate. Lonergan believes that all such heuristic notions are derived from the *supreme* heuristic notion—the notion of completely intelligible reality (what he terms "the notion of being";[10] see below, Section V).

We use heuristic notions ("categories") to create contexts (superstructures) for organizing relationships among ideas. In children, the ideas organized are mostly perceptual ideas, and so they "abstract" the first level of conceptual ideas (relationships among perceptual ideas). Simple though these are, they enable children to use the same word for many individuals (e.g., to use the word "man" to refer to many individual men) and to formulate predicates, adjectives, and direct objects. This enables young children to make syntactical distinctions that higher primates (even those trained for years) are not able to make. For example, a child can distinguish between "dog bites man" and "man bites dog" because they see the syntactical distinction between subject and object (which is a conceptual or relational

[10] See ibid., pp. 380–81.

idea), but higher primates cannot do this (because they are limited to perceptual ideas).[11]

The mind with its innate heuristic notions is not limited to relationships among *perceptual* ideas; it can also organize relationships among *conceptual* ideas. This gives rise to second-level abstractions (such as particular conjunctions, i.e., "and", "or", etc.) and particular prepositions (such as "here", "around", "below", etc.), and third-level abstractions (such as the concepts of "conjunction" and "preposition"). The mind can generate higher and higher levels of abstract ideas in language, logic, mathematics, and metaphysics. Currently the highest levels of logic are manifest in the ideas of heuristic notions mentioned above. In mathematics, the highest levels may be found in tensor geometry and the mathematics of higher dimensional space; and in metaphysics, the highest levels are found in the ideas of space, time, energy, being, and so on. Notice that these "mega-conceptual ideas" cannot be found in the physical world, which is limited by individuation and space-time particularity. They can only be found in the power of a mind that can host heuristic notions enabling it to transcend the limitations of the physical world.

Let us review. Humans move from the domain of individual things and individual images (perceptual ideas) to the domain of conceptual (relational) ideas through the use of heuristic notions (high-level ideas that act as superstructures to organize relationships among perceptual and conceptual ideas). These conceptual ideas go far beyond the domain of individual material objects and perceptual ideas, because they contain relational contents that underlie the whole of language, logic, mathematics, metaphysics, and every science and discipline that uses them. Conceptual ideas, then, are vehicles to convey not only meaning, but the intelligibility of reality. Such ideas cannot come from the world of material things; they must come from the domain of mind (thinking) in which heuristic notions organize relationships among individual perceptual ideas and the conceptual ideas derived from them. Inasmuch as notions are high-level ideas, they are not to be found in the physical world—but only in the domain of mind that is free from the limitations of individuation and space-time particularity and can therefore host these heuristic notions.

---

[11] See Section VI below for the studies from Chomsky and Terrace.

We may now proceed to the main point of this section, namely, that the source of our awareness of complete intelligibility must be a unique unrestricted act of thinking (God). Why so? Recall from Lonergan's proof of God that the ultimate source of complete intelligibility must be a necessary being that can exist through itself. This necessary being must be unique and unrestricted in its intelligibility. What kind of being has unrestricted intelligibility? As can be seen from the above analysis, it cannot be something physical or material that is limited by individuated and space-time particularity, and it cannot be something that is merely abstract (such as a conceptual idea), because an abstraction is restricted by the ideas from which it is derived. Furthermore, it cannot be a restricted act of thinking (which can still inquire), because it is not unrestrictedly intelligible. Well then, what is it? It must be mind (an act of thinking) that has the power not only to ground the complete intelligibility of reality but also to cause or create realities other than itself. Lonergan puts it this way (using "act of understanding" in the same way I have been using "act of thinking"):

> Intelligibility either is material or spiritual or abstract: it is material in the objects of physics, chemistry, biology, and sensitive psychology; it is spiritual when it is identical with understanding; and it is abstract in concepts of unities, laws.... But abstract intelligibility necessarily is in-complete, for it arises only in the self-expression of spiritual intel-ligibility. Again, spiritual intelligibility is incomplete as long as it can inquire. Finally, material intelligibility necessarily is incomplete, for it is contingent in its existence and in its occurrences, in its genera and species.... Moreover, it includes a merely empirical residue of indi-viduality, noncountable infinities, particular places and times.... It fol-lows that the only possibility of complete intelligibility lies in a spiritual intelligibility that cannot inquire because it understands everything about everything.[12]

So what is an unrestricted act of thinking like? Let's begin with what it is *not*. An unrestricted act of thinking cannot occur through a *material brain*, because a material brain cannot accommodate unre-stricted intelligibility, since it is restricted in both its intelligibility and its material functioning. The same can be said for artificial intelligence,

---

[12] Lonergan, *Insight*, pp. 696–97.

which also is restricted in its intelligibility and material (electromagnetic, electrochemical, or even biochemical) functioning. Indeed, we will have to eliminate any apparatus, power, or activity that is in any way material or restricted in its power to ground intelligibility.

This means that an unrestricted act of thinking must be a *power* that is capable of bringing together, in a single act, the interrelationship among unrestricted intelligibility and all restricted intelligibility. What kind of power could this be? It cannot be a material power. Rather, it must be a power that can be in relationship to itself and anything extrinsic to itself—a power that is not restricted by a spatial or temporal manifold; a power that has no intrinsic limitations or extrinsic restrictions that would prevent it from being unrestricted in its intelligibility; a power that can act as a fundamental unity for every restricted reality and idea as well as for itself; a power that can be completely self-reflective, self-appropriating, self-conscious, and self-transparent because it has no intrinsic restriction preventing it from being present to itself and everything distinct from itself (the whole domain of restricted reality and intelligibility).

This pure mentative power cannot be imagined (i.e., picture thinking), because that would subject it to individuation as well as space and time (which it completely transcends). We can only approach it through an appreciation of its unrestricted and self-transparent unitive and unifying power. Any attempt to further refine this generic notion will only serve to restrict and particularize it—which would render our conception false.

For Lonergan, then, the only possible source of complete intelligibility is an unrestricted act of understanding—what we have called an unrestricted act of thinking or mind. Insofar as an unrestricted act of thinking is the source of complete intelligibility itself, it must also be the source of our awareness of complete intelligibility that fills all heuristic notions with meaning and enables us to ask and answer the fundamental question of why is it so.

V. The Presence of God as Source of the Notion of Completely Intelligible Reality

We are now ready to answer the question about human transcendentality with which we started. Recall that our inquiry (in Section II) stemmed from our remarkable ability to ask and answer the question of why is it so. We noticed that this entailed recognizing *the need* for a cause, and this in turn is dependent on the following two conditions:

1. a tacit awareness of "realized and unrealized possibilities of the whole of reality", and
2. a tacit belief in the *intelligibility* of the whole of reality (a tacit belief that the whole of reality contains the answer to our question).

We then asked what could be the source of our tacit awareness of "the realized and unrealized possibilities for the whole of reality" and our tacit belief in its complete intelligibility. Recalling that we could never have derived this "superuniversal awareness" from the world around us (because we would need it in order to learn it), we asked, where did it come from? Suspecting that it would have to come from a source commensurate with its superuniversal content, we paused our epistemological investigation to delve into the world of ontology and metaphysics, because we needed to know whether the whole of reality is in fact completely intelligible. This led us to the minor premise of Lonergan's proof of God: "the totality of reality is completely intelligible", which led us to the major premise, that if the totality of reality is completely intelligible, then God (a unique unrestricted act of thinking that is the ultimate cause of everything else in reality) must exist.

We have now arrived at Lonergan's remarkable discovery, namely, that our superuniversal awareness of the complete intelligibility of the whole of reality must come from a source that is *unrestrictedly intelligible*, because if there were any restriction to the sources of intelligibility, then more questions could be asked of it than could be answered by the information (intelligibility) within it. If the source were *restricted* in its intelligibility, then it would leave many questions about existence and intelligibility of reality unanswered, in which case, it could not ground the complete intelligibility of the whole of reality—it could not be the final answer to all questions of existence and intelligibility. What Lonergan discovers is that the source of our tacit awareness of complete intelligibility of reality must be the *idea* of the complete intelligibility of reality, and the idea of the complete intelligibility of reality must be *unrestrictedly intelligible*. Since unrestricted intelligibility must be a unique unrestricted act of thinking (God), the unique unrestricted act of thinking must be the only possible source of our tacit awareness of the complete intelligibility of reality.

No other source would be capable of conveying the complete intelligibility of the whole of reality to our awareness (consciousness). It could not be a material source, because material realities, as we have noted, are restricted in space, time, and structure. It cannot be any number or combination of finite ideas, because their combination is still restricted in intelligibility. Similarly, it cannot be any number or combination of finite acts of thinking, because they too would be restricted in their combined intelligibility. Therefore, the one *unrestrictedly* intelligible reality—the unique unrestricted act of thinking—must be the source of our tacit awareness of the complete intelligibility of the whole of reality. For Lonergan, God alone must be the source of our ability to ask and answer the question of why is it so, because only God can be the source of our supreme heuristic notion of "the complete intelligibility of the whole of reality".

A. The Notion of the Complete Intelligibility of Reality

So how does "the complete intelligibility of reality" manifest itself within our consciousness? Lonergan calls it a "notion" and describes it as follows:

> The notion of being penetrates all cognitional contents. It is the supreme heuristic notion. Prior to every content, it is the notion of the to-be-known through that content. As each content emerges, the "to-be-known through that content" passes without residue into the "known through that content." Some blank in *universal anticipation* is filled in, not merely to end that element of anticipation, but also to make the filler a part of the anticipated. Hence, *prior* to all answers, the notion of being is the notion of the *totality* to be known through all answers.[13]

So what does Lonergan mean by "notion"? We saw above that "notion" has the general meaning of a high-level, general, inclusive

---

[13] Ibid., pp. 380–81.

idea. Lonergan certainly uses the term in this way, but he also uses it in a special way, that is, to distinguish it from an idea. For Lonergan, an idea occurs when we understand something, and understanding occurs when we put perceptual ideas or conceptual ideas into *relationship* with one another. We saw above that these relationships among perceptual and conceptual ideas occur through heuristic *notions* that are high-level ideas that function as superstructures through which we organize those relationships. We also saw that the heuristic notions had to be *innate* because we would have to use them in order to learn them from the world around us.

For Lonergan, we do not truly *understand* these heuristic notions. We only have an *awareness* of them sufficient to *use* them as organizational superstructures for our thinking process. This is particularly true for the supreme heuristic notion of "the complete intelligibility of reality". Why so? Consider the following. If we were to *understand* the *idea* of "the complete intelligibility of reality", we would also have to understand the one necessary reality that is *unrestricted* in its intelligibility (because the latter is an integral and necessary part of the former). As we saw above (Section IV), the only way of understanding something that is unrestricted in its intelligibility is through an unrestricted act of thinking. We know that we are not capable of such an unrestricted act of thinking by simply reflecting on our thinking process. Moreover, there can be only one unrestricted act of thinking, and it must ground the intelligibility of the whole of reality. If we had such an unrestricted act of thinking, we would not need to ask any questions, because we would already know everything about everything. However, I (and most of the people I know) still make inquiries in order to arrive at a partial understanding of reality.

For Lonergan, then, we do not *understand* the *idea* of completely intelligible reality. We can only be *aware* of it sufficient to use it in our thinking process. This limited awareness is not grasped or controlled by us; it is only made present to us by something else (the unrestricted act of thinking) that allows us to use it for every form of free inquiry and creativity. This is what Lonergan means by "notion", and why he says that the notion of completely intelligible reality ("the notion of being") is the supreme heuristic notion. This contention will be justified in the next section.

B. Universal and Unrestricted Heuristic Anticipation

Lonergan is by no means the first philosopher to have discovered something akin to the "notion of being". Since the time of Plato, philosophers have recognized that the ability to ask questions requires some preconsciousness of what is to be known. Plato saw clearly that if we did not have some sense of intelligibility beyond "the known", we would not desire to move beyond it—we would never ask a question. He attempts to demonstrate this in his early dialogue (see *Meno* 84b–85d) by showing that a slave boy (ignorant of geometry) has enough "innate knowledge of mathematical intelligibility" to respond to questions posed by Socrates. Whether or not one puts credence in Plato's demonstration of *particular* innate ideas of geometry, he shows that our logical and mathematical ideas require much more than can be learned from the empirical world. We must have something more than empirical data to move from the domain of particular individuals (in the material world) to the domain of conceptual ideas (which are free from individuation in space-time particularity).

Kant recognized the need for transcendental knowledge ("I call all knowledge transcendental if it is occupied, not with objects, but with the way that we can possibly know objects even *before* we experience them"[14]). The idea of preexperiential knowledge is not limited to Plato and Kant. Many other philosophers follow Plato in this contention until the present day—most notably the school of transcendental Thomism (Bernard Lonergan, Karl Rahner, Emerich Coreth, and Joseph Marechal), process philosophers (following Alfred North Whitehead), and nonreductionistic philosophers of science (following Michael Polanyi), as well as some physicists (such as Albert Einstein and Sir Arthur Eddington) and mathematicians (such as Kurt Gödel). We will first examine the views of the aforementioned physicists and the philosophers Whitehead and Polanyi, and then proceed to the transcendental Thomists—who move from the domain of "particular heuristic anticipation" to the domain of "*universal* heuristic anticipation".

Albert Einstein believed in an intuition or premonition of what Lonergan calls the "to be known", saying: "The intellect has little to

---

[14] Immanuel Kant, *Critique of Pure Reason*, trans. Norman Kemp Smith (New York: St. Martin's Press, 1965), A12.

do on the road to discovery. There comes a leap in consciousness, call it Intuition or what you will, the solution comes to you and you don't know how or why."[15] The idea of a "leap in consciousness" or a "solution comes to you" suggests a premonition of content beyond what we currently know or can obtain from the empirical world. Einstein only states *that* he has a premonition, but does not explain how it came to him.

Sir Arthur Eddington (Einstein's colleague) goes further than Einstein. He acknowledges not only a premonition of intelligibility beyond what he knows or what he can obtain from the empirical world, but also implies that it comes from God—"a light that beckons ahead": "Science can scarcely question [the] sanction [that there are regions of the human spirit untrammeled by the world of physics], for the pursuit of science springs from a striving which the mind is impelled to follow, a questioning that will not be suppressed.... The light beckons ahead and the purpose surging in our nature responds."[16]

The well-known American logician and philosopher of science Alfred North Whitehead took the path of Einstein, suggesting that he had an intuition or premonition of intelligibility beyond what could be learned from the empirical world, but he did not identify its source. He describes it as a "dim apprehension" or a "vague anticipation".[17]

The famous chemist (later turned philosopher and social scientist) Michael Polanyi dealt a devastating blow to positivism by showing that both biological and conscious activities could not be reduced to physical-chemical structures. They required additional higher-level information and systems to carry out their higher-level activities.[18] Polanyi went further and claimed that human knowledge required a tacit dimension that provides us with a *context* (like a heuristic

---

[15] William Hermanns, *Einstein and the Poet: In Search of the Cosmic Man* (Wellesley, Mass.: Branden Books, 1983), p. 115.

[16] Sir Arthur Eddington, *The Nature of the Physical World* (Cambridge: Cambridge University Press, 1928), pp. 327–28.

[17] See Thomas Hosinski, "Process, Insight, and Empirical Method: An Argument for the Compatibility of the Philosophies of Alfred North Whitehead and Bernard J. F. Lonergan and Its Implications for Foundational Theology" (Ph.D. dissertation, University of Chicago Divinity School, 1983), http://www.anthonyflood.com/hosinski12.htm.

[18] See Michael Polanyi, "Life's Irreducible Structure", *Science* 160, no. 3834 (June 21, 1968): 1308–12.

superstructure) through which our abstract language (conceptual ideas) can have meaning.[19] He notes also that this tacit dimension opens us to "a foreknowledge or heuristic anticipation of the solution that cannot be explicitly stated".[20] Though Polanyi realizes that there must be some principle of transcendence and self-transcendence enabling this "foreknowledge and heuristic anticipation" to occur, he does not specifically identify it.[21]

The history of science and philosophy, outside of the domain of naïvely reductionistic science, echoes a constant refrain that heuristic anticipation is a condition for personal knowledge. Insightful as these thinkers are in articulating this tacit domain, they do not reach the fundamental insight of transcendental Thomism (Lonergan, Rahner,[22] Coreth,[23] and Marechal)—namely, that heuristic anticipation is *universal*. What Lonergan realized is that we not only anticipate the solution to specific questions (in order to ask those questions); we anticipate the answer to *all* questions in order to ask a single question: Why is it so? This universal anticipation is what fuels our desire to know "everything about everything"—to know "the totality of all that is to be known".

How can we justify this move to *universal* anticipation? As noted above (Section II), the answer lies in the question for causation (why is it so?), and this, in turn, has two conditions:

1. a tacit awareness of "realized and unrealized possibilities of the whole of reality", and
2. a tacit belief in the *intelligibility* of the whole of reality (a tacit belief that the whole of reality contains the answer to our question).

As we saw above (Section II), we would not be able to ask the question of why is it so without a tacit awareness of the "realized and

---

[19] See Michael Polanyi, *The Tacit Dimension* (Chicago: University of Chicago Press, 2009), pp. 4–16; Michael Polanyi, *Personal Knowledge: Towards a Post-Critical Philosophy* (Chicago: University of Chicago Press, 1974), pp. 69–248.

[20] See Hosinski, "Process, Insight, and Empirical Method".

[21] See Michael Polanyi, "Transcendence and Self-Transcendence", *Soundings* 53, no. 1 (1970): 88–94.

[22] See Rahner, *Spirit in the World*, pp. 163–230, 387–406.

[23] Coreth, *Metaphysics*, pp. 103–97.

unrealized possibilities of reality as a whole", because we would have no sense that reality could be other than it is—that there would be other possibilities than "the way things are", that "the ways things are" is not necessary. Without these insights, the question *why* would not even occur to us.

Yet, we must have a tacit awareness of more than "the realized and unrealized possibilities of the whole of reality" to ask the question *why*. We must have some sense that a cause (an answer to our question) really exists in the whole of reality, otherwise we would have no objective to look for—our question would be meaningless.

C. Universal Heuristic Anticipation Is Unrestricted

Lonergan advances the discussion by showing that we have a tacit awareness of the *complete* intelligibility of the whole of reality, making his view of heuristic anticipation to be *universal*. As noted in Section II, we do not desire to know the answer to only *particular* questions; we desire to know everything about everything—the complete set of correct answers to the complete set of questions (universal knowledge). Whenever we ask the question of why is it so, we will never be satisfied with an *incompletely* intelligible answer. If our answer is partially (incompletely) intelligible, we will want to go further and ask another question—and another question, and another question—until we get to the complete intelligibility of reality. Our desire to know is not partial, and so it will be satisfied only when we reach complete intelligibility.

This provides a clue to the *universality* and *unrestrictedness* of our heuristic anticipation—our tacit awareness of *complete* intelligibility. We have a capacity to recognize *incomplete* intelligibility in seemingly *every* context in which it occurs. We seem to have an endless capacity to recognize every *incompletely* intelligible answer to the question of why is it so (and every other question dependent upon it). If we really do have such a capacity to recognize incomplete intelligibility whenever, wherever, and however it occurs, we must ask the following further question: How could we do so if we did not have some tacit awareness of what *complete* intelligibility would be like? Remarkable as this capacity to judge "incomplete intelligibility in seemingly every context" is, still more remarkable is our ability to *pre*judge the incompleteness of intelligibility in *every restricted* answer to every question. It is this capacity that reveals the *unrestrictedness* of our tacit awareness of *complete* intelligibility. To understand this, we will have to probe more deeply into the nature of our tacit awareness of complete intelligibility.

Consider the following. We must have awareness commensurate with our desire; so if we have a desire to know everything about everything—a desire for complete intelligibility—we must also be aware of this as the object of our desire, for we cannot desire what we are unaware of. Recall that we do not *understand* "everything about everything" (the complete intelligibility of reality), for this would entail having an unrestricted act of understanding and already knowing the answers to all coherent questions. Hence our awareness must be "tacit", or, as Lonergan calls it, "notional".

Karl Rahner provides a useful analogy for tacit or notional awareness—a *horizon*.[24] A horizon is beyond us, and we can't see everything within its scope, but it gives us the sense (the awareness) that there is something beyond, something to be reached. This sense of a "real beyondness which has not yet been reached, but which can be reached" is critical for asking questions. Think about it: in order to ask a question, we must see a *limit* to what we know, but we cannot recognize that limit unless we are aware of something *beyond* it. We will not see a wall as a limit unless we are aware that there is something beyond it. Without that awareness, it simply stands in front of us blocking our vision. As most epistemologists recognize, limits are imperceptible without horizons—without "beyondness".

The horizon that allows us to ask questions has no intrinsic limit; it provides us with a sense of "intelligibility beyond the known" sufficient to ask *every* question—it is *universal* heuristic anticipation. If we scrutinize our desire to know, we notice that we want to know *everything* that is to be known. We don't just want to get beyond one limit (get the answer to only one question); we want to get beyond *every* limit and get the answer to *every* question.

What is more interesting is our ability to know that an answer to a particular question will not be completely intelligible—*before* we

24See Rahner, *Spirit in the World*, pp. 163–230, 387–406.

answer the question. We can even anticipate that *all restricted* answers to questions will be inadequate to reaching our objective of complete intelligibility. How can we do this? We have a sense that *incompleteness* of intelligibility is connected with *restrictedness* of intelligibility.

What enables us to recognize incomplete intelligibility is awareness of a *restriction* to intelligibility, and what enables us to recognize a restriction to intelligibility is a horizon of intelligibility *beyond* that restriction. Recall that we cannot recognize restrictions or limits without having an awareness of something beyond them. But the remarkable character of human consciousness goes even further. We not only recognize restrictions to intelligibility in the answers to *particular* questions; we also recognize "restrictedness to intelligibility" in *general*—in a universal way. This awareness of "restrictedness to intelligibility" can be applied to *every* particular restriction we see, and can even be applied to every restricted intelligible we *fore*see. We are aware in general that *every* restrictedly intelligible answer will have a horizon of intelligibility beyond it and therefore will not qualify for complete intelligibility.

Here lies the crucial insight: if we really are tacitly aware that *every* restricted intelligible is incomplete, then the only way we could have done this is to have a tacit universal awareness of "restrictedness of intelligibility" and an awareness of its incompleteness—and the only way of recognizing this is to see it through an *unrestricted* horizon of complete intelligibility. We must have some sense, some *notional* sense of *unrestricted* intelligibility lying beyond *all* restricted answers to our questioning. Thus, we must be tacitly aware of an *unrestricted* horizon of intelligibility. If we are to prejudge the inadequacy of *all* restrictedly intelligible answers—to be aware that restrictedly intelligible answers will always lead to further questions whose answers lie beyond them (to be aware that restricted intelligibility is incomplete intelligibility)—then the horizon of our questioning must be completely *universal* and *unrestricted*.

This conclusion runs contrary to all materialistic assumptions about consciousness and intelligence, yet it is inescapable to anyone who affirms for himself that he has the capacity to prejudge the incomplete intelligibility of every restricted answer to every question before asking those questions—to anyone who has a sense that complete intelligibility must go beyond all restricted intelligibility. If we really affirm this capacity within ourselves, then we affirm that we have a tacit awareness that *complete* intelligibility includes *unrestricted* intelligibility and simultaneously affirm our tacit awareness of *unrestricted* intelligibility. As was noted in Section V.A above, the only possible source of this tacit awareness is the unique unrestrictedly intelligible reality itself, the unique unrestricted act of thinking—God. If we really affirm a tacit awareness of unrestricted intelligibility within ourselves, we simultaneously affirm that we are transmaterial, and that God is present to our consciousness as that unrestricted horizon of intelligibility.

Einstein, Whitehead, Polanyi, and others do not identify the source of their foreknowledge or premonition about "intelligibility beyond the known", because they did not recognize that heuristic anticipation extends to the *whole* domain of the knowable, which includes unrestricted intelligibility. However, Lonergan and Rahner *do* recognize this, because they probe the tacit awareness underlying our pure unrestricted desire to know. Here we discover our preawareness that complete intelligibility goes beyond all restricted intelligibility that requires a horizon of unrestricted intelligibility.

What is this horizon of unrestricted intelligibility like? According to the above thinkers, the horizon manifests itself as a premonition or a sense of anticipation imbuing our consciousness during all its acts of questioning, searching, conceiving, hypothesizing, and confirming. It fills these acts of intellection with the presence of "intelligibility to be discovered", including unrestricted intelligibility. This universal anticipation reveals not only that there is a correct answer to a *particular* question—but answers to questions beyond that answer, and even correct answers to every possible question about reality. It impels us to question unceasingly, seek answers unceasingly, create new systems of thought unceasingly, and confirm unceasingly. Our awareness of this horizon is not like taking a peak into the mind of God, but, rather, getting a *"feel"* for the vast and complete potentiality of "all that is to be known". We might say, therefore, that God shares His mind with us sufficient to engender a horizon of *complete* and *unrestricted* intelligibility,[25] giving rise to every form of free intellectual inquiry and creativity.

[25] See Lonergan, *Insight*, pp. 668 and 697.

The following list and diagram may help to synthesize the four levels of human intellection:

1. The horizon of complete and unrestricted intelligibility (the supreme heuristic notion)
2. Derivative heuristic notions providing the organization super-structure for all questions
3. Conceptual ideas that are the result of perceptual ideas related to one another through the heuristic notions
4. Perceptual ideas that come from experience and imagination

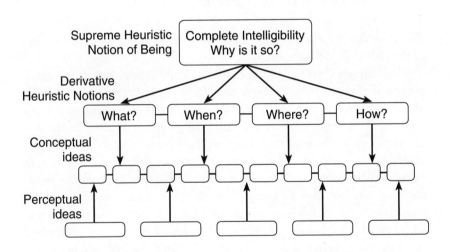

D. Human Intelligence versus Artificial Intelligence

Some readers may find it difficult to believe in a transmaterial ground of human consciousness and intellection, but this idea is not out of the mainstream of philosophical thought, as we have seen from Einstein's, Eddington's, Plato's, Kant's, Whitehead's, and Polanyi's belief in a preconsciousness or premonition of high-level concepts and solutions to particular problems. Lonergan does not separate himself from their central contention, but rather advances it to its logical conclusion. He proves that reality is completely intelligible and that

God (a unique unrestricted act of thinking grounding the intelligibility of all reality) must exist.

If God must ground the intelligibility of all reality, why is it so difficult to believe that He also grounds that notion in our consciousness? If we affirm that this conclusion is plausible and even probative, then we resolve three vexing problems:

1. the source of innate heuristic notions (particularly the supreme heuristic notion of the complete intelligibility of reality),
2. the capacity to seek the complete intelligibility of reality through universal heuristic anticipation, and
3. the challenge of Gödel's theorem.

We have already discussed the first two problems, so we will proceed to the third: Gödel's theorem.

The famous German mathematician Kurt Gödel first formulated the proof of the non-rule-based, nonalgorithmic, transcendent nature of human intelligence in 1931.[26] It was revised on several occasions by John R. Lucas[27] and by the eminent physicist Roger Penrose.[28] In brief, Gödel showed that there will always be unprovable propositions within any set of axiomatic statements in arithmetic. Human beings are able not only to show that consistent, unprovable statements exist, but also to prove that they are consistent by making recourse to axioms *beyond* those used to generate these statements. This reveals that human thinking is not based on a set of prescribed axioms, rules, or programs, and is, by nature, *beyond* any program. Stephen Barr, summing up the Lucas version of Gödel's argument, notes:

[26] See Kurt Gödel, "Über formal unentscheidbare Sätze der Principia Mathematica undverwandter Systeme I", *Monatshefte für Mathematik und Physik* 38 (1931): 173–98.

[27] See John R. Lucas, "Minds, Machines, and Gödel", *Philosophy* 36 (1961): 120; John R. Lucas, "Mechanism: A Rejoinder", *Philosophy* 45 (1970): 149–51; John R. Lucas, "Mind, Machines and Gödel: A Retrospect" (paper presented at the Turing Conference, Brighton, UK, April 6, 1990).

[28] See Roger Penrose, *The Emperor's New Mind* (Oxford: Oxford University Press, 1989); Roger Penrose, *Shadows of the Mind* (Oxford: Oxford University Press, 1994); Roger Penrose, "Beyond the Doubting of a Shadow", *Psyche* 2, no. 23 (1996): 23.

First, imagine that someone shows me a computer program, P, that has built into it the ability to do simple arithmetic and logic. And imagine that I know this program to be consistent in its operations, and that I know all the rules by which it operates. Then, as proven by Gödel, I can find a statement in arithmetic that the program P cannot prove (or disprove) but which I, following Gödel's reasoning, can show to be a true statement of arithmetic. Call this statement G(P). This means that I have done something that that computer program cannot do. I can show that G(P) is a true statement, whereas the program P cannot do so using the rules built into it.

Now, so far, this is no big deal. A programmer could easily add a few things to the program—more axioms or more rules of inference—so that in its modified form it can prove G(P). (The easiest thing to do would be simply to add G(P) itself to the program as a new axiom.) Let us call the new and improved program P′. Now P′ is able to prove the statement G(P), just as I can.

At this point, however, we are dealing with a new and different program, P′, and not the old P. Consequently, assuming I know that P′ is still a consistent program, I can find a Gödel proposition for *it*. That is, I can find a statement, which we may call G(P′), that the program P′ can neither prove nor disprove, but which I can show to be a true statement of arithmetic. So, I am again ahead of the game.... This race could be continued *forever*.[29]

Since people can *indefinitely* prove propositions that are not provable through the axioms from which they were derived, it would seem that human intelligence is *indefinitely beyond* any axiomatic or program-induced intellection.

Gödel's proof shows that human thinking is not only *always* beyond axioms, rules, and programs (to which artificial intelligence is limited), but also capable of *genuinely originative creativity* (that is, capable of thinking without deriving from or making recourse to any prior axioms, rules, or programs). How can this be explained? It must occur through the same vehicle that allows us to convert picture images and perceptual ideas into conceptual ideas (in language and logic), namely, *heuristic notions*. Recall that heuristic notions do not

[29] Stephen M. Barr, *Modern Physics and Ancient Faith* (Notre Dame: University of Notre Dame Press, 2003), p. 214 (emphasis mine).

operate from "below", so to speak (from other picture images and perceptual ideas), but rather from "above" (from the highest level of conceptual ideas that can be used as superstructures to *relate* ideas to one another).

Gödel's theorem shows that human creativity in mathematics cannot be explained from "below"—from previous sets of rules and algorithms (that are required for all computers). This means that human mathematical creativity will have to be explained from "above", suggesting that there must be heuristic notions in mathematics similar to those required for language and logic. It was implied above (in Section II) that the supreme heuristic notion of "the complete intelligibility of reality" is the source of all subordinate heuristic notions in language and logic; so we might suppose that it plays the same role in mathematics—and so it does.

Recall that the supreme heuristic notion of the complete intelligibility of reality enables us to see limits to our current understanding, and how to get beyond those limits. It does this for all areas of intelligibility, including mathematical intelligibility. So we might say that included within our horizon of complete intelligibility is a horizon of mathematical intelligibility, which includes everything from arithmetic to higher dimensional mathematics—and beyond.

This provides a solution to what might be called the "Gödel enigma" of how human intelligence can be beyond any set of prescribed rules and algorithms—and understand the higher mathematical intelligibility necessary to prove formerly unproven propositions. We seemingly have the capacity to see *any* mathematical theory in light of the horizon of "mathematical intelligibility", which reveals limits to our current knowledge and points to higher-level solutions within that horizon of intelligibility. This enables us to see the mathematical principles necessary to indefinitely prove new mathematical theories not derivable from previous ones.

When we situate an old theory into the horizon of complete intelligibility, it reveals the limits of that theory and gives clues about where to find new principles, rules, and justification. The horizon of mathematical intelligibility (within the horizon of complete intelligibility) enables us to generate higher rules and proofs *indefinitely* (just as Gödel suspected) until we reach complete mathematical intelligibility.

All forms of artificial intelligence are based on prescribed rules, algorithms, axioms, and programs.[30] If Lonergan's implied solution to Gödel's theorem is correct, then no artificial (machine) intelligence will ever be able to replicate human questioning and creativity—let alone our quest for complete and unrestricted intelligibility. Artificial intelligence has no consciousness of a horizon of greater intelligibility— let alone a horizon of complete and unrestricted intelligibility—and human beings will not be able to create such a horizon for it, because any such horizon is beyond the domain of individuation and space-time particularity, which means it is beyond the domain of macroscopic and quantum physics. Furthermore, human beings will never be capable of creating a horizon of *complete and unrestricted* intelligibility because such a horizon can only be created by "complete and unrestricted intelligibility itself". We will never be able to create artificial replicas of our own free and creative inquiry, because we are mere restricted beneficiaries of a capacity given to us by a truly unrestricted intelligence.

VI. Human Intelligence versus Animal Intelligence

There has been considerable speculation about higher primates having similar intellectual and linguistic capabilities to humans. Some

[30] Currently all forms of artificial intelligence can be replicated by a universal Turing Machine, which is bound by prescribed rules, axioms, algorithms, and propositions. "A Turing Machine" is a hypothetical device that models the basic mechanical, logical, and computational properties intrinsic to every computer. Alan Turing described this basic model which has helped computer scientists and philosophers to theorize about both the potential and limits to mechanical intelligence (logical and computational processing through scanning and binary circuitry). Turing's model has been sufficiently generalized to replicate any known form of mechanical intelligence, and it is called "a universal Turing Machine". It is theoretically possible to have non-Turing forms of machine intelligence, but these will not be able to escape the requirement for prescribed rules, axioms, algorithms, and propositions, because the only way to move beyond them is to be tacitly conscious of a horizon of higher intelligibility (and if Lonergan is correct, a horizon of *complete and unrestricted* intelligibility). Such a horizon is beyond all physical and mechanical processes, including quantum ones, for it cannot be limited by individuation and space-time particularity (see the explanation above in Sections IV and V.A). See Robert J. Spitzer, "Why Is Human Self-Consciousness Different from Artificial Intelligence and Animal Consciousness?" *Ultimate Reality and Meaning: Interdisciplinary Studies in the Philosophy of Understanding* 33, nos. 1–2 (2010): 5–27; see especially the response to Roger Penrose and S. R. Hameroff (pp. 19–23).

have conjectured that the difference between humans and higher primates is only a matter of *degree*, but the *essential* cognitional activity is the same. If these thinkers are correct, it would mean that higher primates have an awareness of the supreme heuristic notion and are, therefore, transcendent in the same way as humans. Is there any way of determining whether this is the case? As a matter of fact, there is.

The critical distinction between perceptual ideas (picture images) and conceptual ideas (relationships among ideas—justified in Section IV) dovetails felicitously with a behavioral test developed by the well-known philosopher of language Noam Chomsky, which can be applied to the socio-linguistic behavior of higher primates. A quick explanation of this reveals that human beings are categorically different from primates, not only in their linguistic capabilities, but also in their capacity to formulate conceptual ideas in language, logic, mathematics, natural science, social science, and philosophy. There is nothing in the socio-linguistic behavior of higher primates—even the best trained ones—that indicates the presence of conceptual ideas, heuristic notions, or a supreme heuristic notion. Primates appear to be limited to the domain of perceptual ideas, and linguistic signs that refer to those perceptual ideas. We shall now consider each of these points in more depth.

With respect to perceptual and conceptual ideas, let us first recall what we said about the vast majority of the words we use, namely, that they do not have any pictorial image as a referent, thus they are *not* perceptual ideas (picture images) but conceptual ones. We asked then how we give meaning to conceptual ideas (which are nonpictorial) and noticed that they were derived from *relationships* among ideas—first, relationships among perceptual ideas (that have pictorial referents, such as "cat" or "tree" or "man"), and then relationships among conceptual ideas (such as "noun", "verb", "too", and "add"). We saw that we could move to higher levels of abstraction—relationships among relationships among relationships, and so on. This was true in the domain of grammar, logic, mathematics, the natural sciences, and so on.

We then asked *how* we were able to create these relationships among ideas and noticed that there would have to be some *context* through which to organize them—something like a map or a clock or a table of genus and species, which could provide a background or superstructure through which ideas could be related in an organized way. It turned out that each of these superstructures have high-level ideas intrinsic to them that determine the way in which ideas are organized—for example, "similarity and difference" are essential for the question *what*; "here and there" for the question *where*; "earlier-now-later" for the question *when*; and "causation-possibility-necessity-contingency-actuality" for the question *why*. We then saw that all such heuristic notions are given meaning in the "real world" through the supreme heuristic notion of "the complete intelligibility of reality".

We are now in a position to make a judgment about animal intelligence (specifically the intelligence of higher primates). Do higher primates form conceptual ideas? Do they transform perceptual ideas into conceptual ideas through interrelationships within superstructures organized by heuristic notions? Noam Chomsky gave the first linguistic test to answer these questions and, on the basis of it, held fast to the belief that they do not. Chomsky realized that certain words in a sentence could have direct pictorial referents, but was certain that the *syntax* of a sentence could not be grasped pictorially. It can only be grasped by understanding relationships among ideas. A simple test of this would be to grasp the meaning of subject and object in the word order of a sentence, for example, "dog bites man" versus "man bites dog".[31] Even though one could grasp "dog", "bites", and "man" through perceptual ideas, one cannot grasp the difference between subject and object in a sentence's word order without some conceptual (relational) idea.[32] Do higher primates

---

[31] Chomsky was primarily concerned with the operation of *innate* structures for *syntax* capable of *creatively* combining and adapting intelligible phrases from words and signs. Control over syntax (e.g., understanding the difference between "dog bites man" and "man bites dog") is an essential test of this capability. See Noam Chomsky, interview by Matt Aames Cucchiaro, "On the Myth of Ape Language", 2007. Chomsky was highly critical of B. F. Skinner's functionalistic (behavioristic) explanation of language that implied commonality between animal linguistic functions and behaviors and human linguistic functions and behaviors, because it ignored this central test of creative combining, organizing, and adapting of words and signs manifest in syntactical control. See ibid.; Noam Chomsky, "The Case against B. F. Skinner", *The New York Review of Books*, December 30, 1971; and Noam Chomsky, "A Review of B. F. Skinner's *Verbal Behavior*", in *Readings in the Psychology of Language*, ed. Leon A. Jakobovits and Murray S. Miron (Englewood Cliffs, N.J.: Prentice Hall, 1967).

[32] Chomsky held that humans can both create and understand these syntactical differences (in the ordering of words within an expression) because they can apply transformation rules to universal core patterns and, therefore, do not need to be trained to understand and use every expression. It does not matter whether one accepts Chomsky's whole theory of human linguistic creativeness, because his syntactical control test for the presence of conceptual intelligence in animals is still valid whether or not one accepts his explanation of how syntactical control occurs.

grasp the syntactical difference between subject and object as small children do who laugh at the curious thought of a man biting a dog? Contemporary research indicates that they do not.

There is considerable evidence that vertebrates generate perceptual ideas, manifesting perceptual intelligence. For example, an animal can relate perceptual images, such as a rabbit and a tree, to one another spatially and temporally (as well as to itself). Notice that what the animal *perceives* is an individual object or image; it is a picture in the animal's consciousness. So does the animal go beyond relating perceptual ideas in space and time? Does it implicitly understand the most rudimentary implications of grammar communicated by word order? If it does not, then we can be sure that it does not grasp elementary conceptual (relational) ideas, and that it is restricted to the domain of perceptual ones.

Is *perceptual* intelligence sufficient for elementary language? Researchers have shown that it is. For example, primates have the ability to associate signs (such as those from American Sign Language) with their perceptual (picture) thoughts. However, these associations appear to have no other purpose than to name or identify specific things (such as Joe the trainer, or a banana, or a perceptual action like running or biting) to satisfy biological opportunities (such as obtaining food or shelter) or to communicate biological dangers (such as the approach of a predator). For example, a chimpanzee can be taught to use sign language to communicate a need for food or even a warning about danger, but cannot be trained to use language to say something *about* something (which would require syntactical control, the intelligible use of predicates and objects).

One of the more controlled experiments in this regard was carried out by Allen and Beatrix Gardner in 1967 (Project Washoe), in which a female chimpanzee named Washoe was raised in a very familial human environment with affection and other human-bonding qualities.[33] According to the Gardners, Washoe was able to learn 350 words of American Sign Language, which exceeds the capacity of virtually every other chimpanzee subjected to this kind of training (operative behavioral conditioning). The Gardners seemed to have

[33] See Allen Gardner, Beatrix Gardner, and Thomas Van Cantfort, *Teaching Sign Language to Chimpanzees* (New York: State University of New York Press, 1989).

achieved other successes: Washoe seemed to be able to adapt some of the learned signs for other uses and also taught other chimpanzees some of the signs she had learned.

The Gardners' results were challenged by Herbert Terrace, who indicated that the Gardners did not have a rigorous methodology to assess Washoe's use of language beyond codes or naming associated with biological opportunities and dangers. Furthermore, there was no real attempt to carry out Chomsky's syntactical control test in a rigorous way.[34]

Terrace decided to conduct a more controlled test of the Gardners' claims at Columbia University in 1974, because he believed that many of their claims were based on misinformation from the chimp. So Terrace designed experiments that would test specifically for syntactical control and understanding within a chimp's use of sign language.[35] Terrace used a famous chimpanzee named Nim Chimpsky (playing off the name of Noam Chomsky) in a much more controlled behavioral environment, which yielded more modest results than the Gardners'. Though Nim was able to master 125 signs (significantly less than the Gardners' claims about Washoe) and could be trained to use those signs precisely as his trainer indicated, there was no evidence that Nim had any syntactical awareness, understanding, or control over the use of his signs. Terrace summarized the results as follows:

> Unless alternative explanations of an ape's combinations of signs are eliminated, in particular the habit of partially imitating teachers' recent utterances, there is no reason to regard an ape's multisign utterance as a sentence.... For the moment, our detailed investigation suggests that an ape's language learning is severely restricted. Apes can learn many isolated symbols (as can dogs, horses, and other nonhuman species), but they show no unequivocal evidence of mastering the conversational, *semantic*, or *syntactic organization* of language.[36]

Though the Gardners claimed that Nim could have learned more signs had he been brought up in a more familial environment, no

---

[34]See Herbert S. Terrace et al., "Can an Ape Create a Sentence?" *Science* 206, no. 4421 (November 23, 1979): 891–902, http://www.sciencemag.org/content/206/4421/891.

[35]See ibid.

[36]Ibid., pp. 900–901.

subsequent experiment with higher primate language has been able to pass Chomsky's syntactical test. And so it seems that Chomsky's claims about exclusively human syntactical control over language remains unrefuted.

Inasmuch as syntactical understanding and control is foundational for all higher uses of language (such as using subjects, predicates, and objects to say something *about* something, as well as to formulate mathematical, scientific, or other theoretical expressions), it seems that human beings are the only species having the creative use of language (to create and understand expressions that they have not been trained specifically to use or understand). This further implies that human beings are the only species capable of higher-order conceptual ideas and language (going beyond perceptual ideas and language).

Several other philosophers have developed tests to assess intelligence in animals (particularly higher primates and dolphins). The most famous of these were formulated by Donald Davidson in the 1980s and 1990s—the intentionality test,[37] the argument from holism,[38] and what might be termed the "belief test".[39] Though these arguments are contested, including Davidson's final and main argument (the belief test), his analysis of the link between thought and language is quite instructive and can be used to provide a deeper insight into the differences between human and animal intelligence (beyond Chomsky's syntactical test).

There are other approaches to the absence of conceptual intelligence in animals, the most important of which are forwarded by Paul Moser,[40] Jonathan Bennett,[41] John Searle,[42] and José Bermúdez.[43]

---

[37] See Donald Davidson, "Thought and Talk", in *Inquiries into Truth and Interpretation* (Oxford: Clarendon Press, 1984), pp. 155–79.

[38] See Donald Davidson, "Rational Animals", in *Dialectica*, vol. 36, no. 4 (1982): 318–27.

[39] See Donald Davidson, "The Emergence of Thought", *Erkenntnis* 51 (1997): 7–17.

[40] See Paul Moser, "Rationality without Surprise: Davidson on Rational Belief", *Dialectica* 37 (1983): 221–26.

[41] See Jonathan Bennett, *Rationality: An Essay Towards an Analysis* (1964; repr., Indianapolis: Hackett, 1989).

[42] See John Searle, "Animal Minds", *Midwest Studies in Philosophy* 19 (1994): 206–19.

[43] See José L. Bermúdez, *Thinking without Words* (Oxford: Oxford University Press, 2003). There is an excellent summary of these philosophical arguments by Robert Lurz (a well-known researcher in the area of animal intelligence), which may be found in the *Internet Encyclopedia of Philosophy* (http://www.iep.utm.edu/ani-mind/#SH1c).

These confirm and extend the findings of Chomsky, Terrace, and Davidson, implying a categorical difference between human and animal intelligence. In view of this, humans seem to be the only species capable of generating conceptual ideas and therefore of having preexperiential awareness of heuristic notions and structures. This implies that humans are the only transcendental species tacitly aware of a horizon of complete and unrestricted intelligibility. As such, they are the only species capable of genuine creativity of new ideas, of surpassing the "Gödel limit to machine intelligence", and communication through complex syntax and semantics.

VII. Conclusion

Lonergan advances our exploration of human transcendentality not only by proving the existence of God (a unique unrestricted act of thinking that grounds the existence and intelligibility of the rest of reality), but also by showing that God is notionally present within our consciousness, making possible free inquiry and creativity. His analysis tells us that the source of the numinous, the sacred, conscience, and the mythical is not only transcendent and "wholly Other", but is also unique, unrestricted, and a Creator. In Chapters 1 and 2, we spoke about "the presence of transcendence" or "the presence of the numen" within our consciousness; now it seems probable that the source of these transcendent intuitions and feelings is a supreme Being (a unique, unrestricted Creator).

In Chapter 1 we discussed the presence of a mysterious, daunting, fascinating, good "wholly Other" who interacts with us empathetically, inviting us more deeply into its mystery. In Chapter 2, we discussed other clues to the presence of the transcendent within us—in our sense of the sacred, the authority of our conscience, and in the power of myth. We can now see, in light of Lonergan's analysis, that the transcendent source of the numinous, sacred, conscience, and mythical is also the source of reality, intelligibility, explicability, intelligence, and creativity. Some thinkers view these two sets of characteristics as opposed, but as can be seen, this cannot be the case, because they are all integral dimensions of the one, unrestricted act of thinking. No doubt these two sets of characteristics are distinct, but they can all emerge from the same transcendent reality. At the very least, this means that the one transcendent Being is not a computer (a kind of "Einsteinian God"), lacking empathy, morality, and emotion. Can we be sure that this conclusion is correct? Is there any other evidence to support the contention that the unrestricted act of thinking is also loving, good, ethical, beautiful, and passionate? In the next chapter, we will probe this evidence in our reflection on three other transcendental desires: the desire for perfect love, goodness, and beauty. This will provide additional clues to the personal qualities of the transcendent Being present to us.

Chapter Four

The Substance of Things Yearned For

Introduction

In the previous chapter, we examined our desire for perfect truth, arising out of our notional awareness of the complete intelligibility of reality. We now turn to the other three transcendental desires manifesting the interior presence of God: the desire for perfect love (Section I), perfect goodness (Section II), and perfect beauty (Section III). Like the desire for perfect truth, these other transcendental desires distinguish human transcendental consciousness from animal consciousness. It is not possible to give the same extensive treatment to these other transcendental desires as to the desire for perfect truth, because they do not show themselves as clearly and comprehensively as the desire for perfect truth. However, they are not completely hidden, for they manifest themselves through their distinct modalities within human consciousness—the empathetic mode (love), the ethical mode (goodness), and the aesthetic mode (beauty). Since the time of Plato, these modes of consciousness (like the rational mode, truth) have been seen to pursue perfect objectives, that is, perfect love, perfect goodness, and perfect beauty. A brief analysis of each will reveal striking similarities to the desire for perfect truth, providing essential clues to the diversity of human transcendental consciousness.

I. The Desire for Perfect Love

Human beings seem to have a "sense" of *perfect and unconditional love.* Not only do we have the power to love (i.e., the power to be naturally connected to another person in profound empathy, emotion, care, self-gift, concern, and acceptance); we have a "sense" of what this profound interpersonal connection would be like if it were perfect. This sense of perfect love has the positive effect of inciting us to pursue evermore perfect forms of love. However, it has the drawback of inciting us to *expect* evermore perfect love from others. This generally leads to frustrated expectations of others and consequently to a decline of relationships that can never grow fast enough to meet the expectation of perfection.

For example, as the first signs of imperfection and finitude begin to emerge in the beloved, the lover may show slight irritation, but have hopes that the ideal will soon be recaptured (as if it were ever captured to begin with). But as the fallibility of the beloved begins to be more acutely manifest (the other is not perfectly humble, gentle, kind, forgiving, self-giving, and concerned with the lover in all his interests), the irritation becomes frustration, which, in turn, becomes dashed expectation: "I can't believe I thought he was really the *one*." Of course, he wasn't the *one*, because he is not perfect and unconditioned. Nevertheless, the dashed expectation becomes either quiet hurt or overt demands, both aimed at extracting a higher level of performance from the beloved. When he does not comply, thoughts of terminating the relationship may arise.

The root problem was not with the authenticity of this couple's love for one another. It did not arise out of a lack of concern, care, and responsiveness, a desire to be self-giving, responsible, self-disciplined, and true. Rather, it arose out of a false expectation that they could reach *perfect* and *unconditional* love through one another.

Why do we fall prey to what seems to be such an obvious error? Because our *desire* for love and to love is unconditional, but our *actuality* is conditioned. Our desire is for the perfect, but our actuality is imperfect. We, as mere humans, therefore, cannot satisfy one another's desire for the unconditional and the perfect. If we do not have a *real* unconditional and perfect being to satisfy this desire, we start looking around to find a surrogate. Another person at first may seem like a very good one, because he may display qualities of self-transcendence. Hence, we confuse one another for the perfect and unconditioned, and undermine the very relationships that hold out opportunities for growth, depth, joy, common cause, and mutual bondedness.

The above reflection reveals a remarkable internal capacity—we can seemingly recognize *every* imperfect manifestation of love in others and ourselves. We can even recognize imperfection in the world's greatest saints and noblest heroes. We are masters of love's imperfections, yet this leads to an obvious question: How are we always able to recognize imperfection in love unless we have some sense of *what perfect love would be like*? This bears a resemblance to the previous analysis of perfect truth, in which we noticed our capacity to recognize *incompleteness* of intelligibility in *every restricted* manifestation of intelligibility. This revealed our notional awareness of an unrestricted horizon of intelligibility, capable of manifesting all restricted and incomplete instances of intelligibility.

Now let us return to love. If we really do have an awareness of what perfect love would be like, we must ask from where we learned or apprehended it. Clearly, we do not apprehend it from the people or the world around us, because every manifestation of love we encounter is *imperfect*. So where does our awareness of perfect love come from? It seems that it is intrinsic to us—prior to our experiences of love in the world around us.

Recall from the last chapter that the preexperiential presence of the heuristic notions (behind every question) within our consciousness is derived from the *supreme* heuristic notion—the notion of "the complete intelligibility of reality". Could our awareness of perfect love be yet another "universal heuristic notion" present to our consciousness? If so, then would it have come from the same source as the notion of the complete intelligibility of reality, namely, the unique unrestricted act of thinking? Though we cannot provide a *formal proof* to answer these questions about the source of perfect love in the same way we did for the source of perfect truth, we can adduce some probative evidence from the power of unification that points to the likelihood that both supreme notions come from the same source.

A. The Source of Perfect Unity Is the Source of Perfect Love, Goodness, and Beauty

The key clue to the source of our notion of perfect love comes once again from Plato and the Christian Neo-Platonists, who recognized that the power of unification is a kind of "perfection". For them, the more inclusive and unifying a reality is, the more perfect it is. Conversely, the less inclusive or unifying a reality is, the less perfect it is.

This view is premised on the idea that restrictedness leads to exclusion or opposition. For example, the restrictions (or boundaries) of a square *exclude* the boundaries of a triangle, circle, and trapezoid from itself in the same respect at the same place and time. Similarly, the restrictions of an electron's activities *exclude* the possibility of its acting like a proton or a positron in the same respect at the same place and time. Wherever there are restrictions and boundaries, there will also be *exclusion* of other restrictions and boundaries (in the same respect at the same place and time).[1]

Philosophers have long recognized that matter has more restrictions than mind. Matter is restricted by ways of acting (e.g., electron versus proton behaviors), individuation, and space-time particularity. As we saw (in Chapter 3, Section IV above), mind is not limited in these ways. It is capable of *unifying* every restricted reality and idea in order to relate these excluding ideas to one another. When it does this, it finds similarities and differences, causes and effects, and spatio-temporal relations among these excluding realities. This unifying power enables mind to transform perceptual ideas into conceptual ideas (which are free of individuation and space-time particularity). This allows conceptual ideas to be used as predicates and objects to say something *about* something.

Philosophers have also recognized that mind can unify at very high levels—not just relationships among perceptual (individuated) ideas, but relationships among relationships, and even relationships among complex relationships, achieving higher and higher levels of abstraction. These higher-level ideas in logic, grammar, mathematics, and metaphysics give us great powers of analysis and synthesis, enabling creative advancements in mathematics, science, and every other discipline. Thus, mind or consciousness is capable of greater unification than matter, and the more it unifies in a single conscious or mentative act, the more powerful and creative it is. We frequently identify genius with the capacity to apprehend and create enormously comprehensive unities among ideas, in mathematics, logic, natural sciences, and so on.

---

[1] See the extensive treatment of this in Robert J. Spitzer, *New Proofs for the Existence of God: Contributions of Contemporary Physics and Philosophy* (Grand Rapids, Mich.: Eerdmans, 2010), pp. 122–27.

Now we can get to our main point. The unique *unrestricted* act of thinking proved by Lonergan (in Chapter 3, Sections III and IV) must be the highest possible unifying power. Why so? Because the unique unrestricted act of thinking has no *restrictions* in its intelligibility, and as we saw, restrictions in intelligibility produce exclusions (contrary to unity and unification). Inasmuch as an unrestrictedly intelligible reality produces no exclusions, it is the highest (most inclusive) *perfect* unifying power.

What does all of this have to do with the source of our awareness of perfect love? If higher orders of unity indicate less exclusions, and less exclusions indicate less restrictions, then higher orders of unity also allow for greater *perfection* of reality. We have already seen that more inclusive mentation allows for greater unification of ideas and more perfect and comprehensive acts of thinking; but we cannot limit the power of inclusion and unity to the domain of mentation alone—for *wherever* there is greater unity (inclusion), there is less exclusion and less restriction to *reality*. Hence, we should suppose that wherever there are higher levels of unity in reality, there will also be higher levels of perfection in reality.

B. There Can Be Only One Perfect Unity

Judeo-Christian Neo-Platonists recognized at least three other areas of reality susceptible to greater and greater levels of unity: love, goodness, and beauty. These thinkers came to an important conclusion, namely, that the source of perfect unity in thinking must also be the source of perfect unity in love, goodness, and beauty. The following argument (proof) will make this clear:

1. Perfect unity can only occur through an *unrestrictedly* intelligible reality, because restrictions in intelligibility give rise to *exclusions* that are contrary to unity (see above, Section I.A).
2. There can only be one unrestrictedly intelligible reality (see the proof in Chapter 3, Section III.C).
3. Therefore, the one unrestrictedly intelligible reality must be the one source of *all* manifestations of perfect unity (unities of mind, love, goodness, and beauty).

4. And the one unrestricted act of thinking (proven in Chapter 3, Sections III and IV) must be the source of all manifestations of perfect unity.

I will discuss the perfect unity of love in Section I.C below, and then goodness in Section II, and beauty in Section III.

C. Perfect Love Is Perfect Unity

We now return to the question asked earlier in Section I, namely, what is the source of our awareness of perfect love (manifest in our ability to identify every imperfection in love both in others and ourselves)? We saw that this awareness was very likely innate, because we could not learn it from the imperfect manifestations of love in the outside world. Is the source of this innate awareness of perfect love the same as our notional awareness of "the complete intelligibility of reality"? If it can be shown that love, like mind, is a reality susceptible to greater and greater levels of unity, and there can only be one perfect unity, then it follows that the source of our awareness of perfect love is the same as the source of our awareness of perfect truth, namely, the unique unrestricted act of thinking. So, then, is love a reality susceptible of greater and greater unity or unification? Many philosophers, both ancient and contemporary, think that it is. We can see this unity in the power of empathy, care, and self-sacrifice.

Empathy (in-feeling; in Greek, *en-pathos*; in German, *ein-Fühlung*—coined by Rudolf Lotze in 1858) begins with a deep awareness of and connection to the other as both given and uniquely good. When we allow this awareness of and connection to the other to affect us, it produces an acceptance of the other and a consequent unity of feeling with the other, which opens upon an identification with the other tantamount to a sympathetic vibration. Though this unity with the feelings and being of another does not cause a loss of one's self or self-consciousness, it does cause a break with the autonomy we feel when we focus on the interior world of our self-consciousness. Were it not for the capacity to be open to the unique goodness of the other, we might be inexorably caught up in egocentricity and radical autonomy. However, empathy does not allow self-consciousness to become radically autonomous and absolute; it presents the possibility of relational personhood whenever we choose to accept our "unity of feeling with the other", and to identify with the being of the other.[2]

This acceptance and identification of the feelings and being of the other gives rise to concern for the other, which evolves into care for the other as the relationship grows. This care, in its turn, can completely reverse the human tendency toward autonomy (being over against the other) and can give rise to a self-giving that can become self-sacrificial (*agapē*). Through empathy, then, we go beyond ourselves to initiate a unity with the other, whereby doing the good for the other is just as easy, if not easier, than doing the good for ourselves.

Empathy is a natural power of unification, and love is its completion. When the unifying power of empathy takes hold in our free will and intentionality, we begin to care about the other and care for the other, intensifying our unity with the other. If this process continues, we can lose our sense of self-interest and open ourselves to self-sacrifice for the beloved. This self-sacrificial love (called *agapē*) is the highest form of interpersonal unity.

The unifying power of love does not seem to have any intrinsic or extrinsic limit. If love (empathy → concern → care → *agapē*) can unify the radical autonomy of *two* individuals, why would it not be able to overcome the autonomy of hundreds or thousands, or even millions, of people? Why would it not be able to unify all individual self-consciousnesses throughout all history? Indeed, why would it not be able to unify this totality of humanity with perfect self-consciousness (the perfect, self-transparent, mentating activity of the unrestricted act of thinking)?

If there is no intrinsic limit to the unifying power of love, then perfect love is capable of perfect unification. This implies that its source is the one unrestricted act of thinking (which has no restrictions that would produce exclusions contrary to unity; see the proof in I.B above).

We may now answer the question with which we started (concerning the source of our awareness of perfect love). It seems that this

---

[2]Edith Stein has written a powerful essay on this phenomenon in Edith Stein, *On the Problem of Empathy*, trans. Waltraut Stein (Washington, D.C.: Institute of Carmelite Studies Publications, 1989).

innate awareness must come from a source that is commensurate with the effect it produces within us, a source that is perfect love itself. If perfect love really is perfect unification, and there can only be one perfect power of unification (which has no restrictions to its intelligibility), then the one unrestricted act of thinking must be the source not only of our awareness of "the complete intelligibility of reality", but also our awareness of perfect love. The unique unrestricted act of thinking is perfect love, and it is the common source of the supreme notion of truth and love.

II. The Desire for Perfect and Unconditional Justice or Goodness

As with our awareness of perfect and unconditional truth and love, philosophers have long recognized man's desire for *perfect justice or goodness*. Not only do we have a sense of good and evil, a capacity for moral reflection, a profoundly negative felt awareness of cooperation with evil (guilt), and a profoundly positive felt awareness of cooperation with goodness (nobility); we also have a "sense" of what perfect, unconditioned justice or goodness would be like. We are constantly striving for ways to achieve the more noble, the greater good, the higher ideal. We even go so far as to pursue the perfectly good or just order.

An insight into this desire for perfect justice or goodness may be gleaned from children. An imperfect manifestation of justice from parents will get the immediate retort "That's not fair!" Adults do the same thing. We have a sense of what perfect justice ought to be, and we believe others ought to know this. When this sense of perfect justice has been violated, we are likely to respond with outrage. A violation of this sort always seems particularly acute. We seem to be in a state of shock. We really expect that perfect justice ought to happen, and when it doesn't, it so profoundly disappoints us that it can consume us. We can feel the same outrage toward groups, social structures, and even God.

As with our "sense" of perfect and unconditional love, our sense of perfect and unconditional justice or goodness has some associated risks. While it can fuel our strivings for an evermore perfect social order, a more just legal system, greater equity and equality, and even our Promethean idealism to bring the justice of God to earth, it can also incite our expectations for *perfect* justice in a *finite* and conditioned world, meaning that our Promethean ideals are likely to be frustrated. This causes disappointments with the culture, the legal system, our organizations, and even our families. We seem to always expect more justice and goodness than the finite world can deliver, and it causes impatience, judgment of others, and even cynicism when it does not come to pass.

Our discontent with imperfect justice and goodness seems to know no limits. Apparently we have the ability to recognize seemingly *every* imperfection in the justice or goodness of others, ourselves, groups, organizations, institutions, social structures, societies, governments, and international organizations. We are not only masters of love's imperfections, but also justice's and goodness' imperfections. Once again the following question arises: How can we recognize imperfections in every manifestation in justice and goodness if we do not have some awareness of what perfect justice and goodness would be like? If we had no sense of perfect justice or goodness, it seems unlikely that we would recognize imperfections everywhere around us; we would be as content with our "lot" as animals partaking of some good food.

Every person in our experience seems to manifest some injustice or unfairness, at least occasionally—so also do governments and legal systems, and so also socio-political and economic theories (e.g., capitalism, socialism, etc.). There does not appear to be any perfectly just or good person, institution, magistrate, body of law, government, or anything else of man's making. So it seems unlikely that the exterior or the outside world has provided us with the notion of perfect justice, making it likely that it is innate, that is, intrinsic to our consciousness from its very inception.

What is the source of this awareness of what perfect justice or goodness would be like? It is unlikely that the source of our perfect desire is in the world around us, because it is filled exclusively with imperfect manifestations of justice or goodness.

Is this awareness of "what perfect justice or goodness would be like" the same as the source of perfect truth and perfect love? If it can be shown that justice or goodness, like love and mind, is a reality susceptible to greater and greater levels of unity, and there can only be one perfect unity, then it follows that the source of our awareness of perfect justice or goodness is the same as the source of our awareness of perfect love and truth, namely, the unique unrestricted act of thinking. So, then, is justice or goodness a reality susceptible of greater and greater unity or unification? Many philosophers think that it is.

Let us begin with Plato's notion of justice, namely, giving every person his due (what belongs to him and is owed to him). In a broader sense, justice is the drive to keep a society cohesive and at peace—not by external coercion or force, but by our interior conviction to give people what they deserve (and not to deprive them of what rightfully belongs to them). So justice is at once a principle, an ideal, and an intrinsic drive. It is a principle because it is thought to be self-evident and the foundation for all other ethical precepts. It is an ideal because it is thought to be an end or goal (telos) of human conduct and life; and it is an intrinsic drive because this end of human conduct is not only *thought* but *felt* to be a foundational principle for good conduct and a good life. We not only know justice to be self-evidently good; we believe it is essential for a good life, and feel it as a driving force within us—so much so, that when we are unjust, we feel alienated and guilty (see the discussion about conscience in Chapter 2, Section II).

The effects of justice not only occur within the minds and hearts of individuals, but also in the collective conviction and *ethos* of *groups*, such as organizations, local communities, societies, and even states. This intrinsic drive within individuals and groups animates the desire for law and a legal system (even though laws and legal systems can impose obligations and burdens on individuals). We submit to the law, not only out of self-interest (for protection of our lives and property), but also because the law is noble and good—precisely because it is grounded in justice. Insofar as we *feel* that *justice* is good and noble, we also feel that the law and legal system (inasmuch as they are based upon it) are likewise good and noble.

Regrettably, human beings feel and practice an *opposing* tendency (counter to justice), namely, the desire to control, dominate, and use power to personal advantage. In certain personalities, this manifests itself as the socially destructive view of "might makes right". It is precisely this propensity that justice and the common good counteract.

Justice overcomes not only a barrier between individuals; it overcomes the *negative effects* of our pursuits of selfish self-interest.

Justice overcomes these invasive, negating propensities, not merely through a pragmatic urge, but through genuine *love* of the ideals embodied in it. The love of justice, law, and the common good strikes an uplifting Apollonian note within us. Instinctively, we seem to sense nobility, not only behind the power of the law, but behind the notion of justice that the law and its power seek to preserve— justice *inspires* us.

This natural power to love good and shun evil, to love justice and the common good and to shun injustice and the undermining of society, is essentially a *unifying* power. It transforms self-consciousness' propensity to be over against others and in conflict with others, into a sense of shared good, common cause, and esprit de corps. Henceforth I will refer to it as the "love of justice and the good".

The "love of justice and the good" is a natural unifier, for it overcomes the natural barriers and enmity arising out of competition for scarce resources, fear of strangers, natural animosity, survival of the fittest, and suspicion of others' potential injustices. It overcomes the natural barriers and enmity of irresponsibility (responsibility to myself alone, or the complete abdication of responsibility to others) by calling individuals to a higher duty to the just society. It can also lead to self-sacrifice (the sacrifice not only of one's advantage and aggrandizement, but also of one's very self) for the sake of the good of society and for goodness and justice within society. These unifying powers of the love of justice and the good appear to have no limit—the principle, ideal, and drive of justice can bring together individuals, individuals with groups, groups with one another, groups with communities, communities with one another, communities with society, societies with one another, societies with states, and states with one another. We might say, then, that justice has an unlimited power to overcome the depravity and misuse of power (arising out of greed, pride, and the resultant desire for control and domination), an unlimited power to inspire and unify an entire planet—and beyond.

We can now see the underlying rationale for the philosophical conviction that justice or goodness is a transcendental desire that has its origin in the presence of God (the one unrestricted act of thinking).

At the beginning of this section, it was noted that we have a desire for perfect justice, and that we are able to recognize *every* imperfection of justice in others and ourselves. This capacity to recognize universally "imperfections of justice" manifests our awareness of "what perfect justice would be like". If we did not have such an awareness, the universal recognition of imperfection would not be possible.

We then asked what the source of our awareness of what perfect justice would be like might be, noting that it very probably did not come from the world around us (since all concrete manifestations of justice in the world are imperfect). In view of this, we asked what the source of our *innate* awareness of perfect justice could be. We saw that justice is not only a unifier of individuals and groups (overcoming the misuse of strength, control, and power), but also a *universal* and *unlimited* unifier. As such, it is capable of being a *perfect unifier*—a *perfect unity*.

Recall that there can be only one perfect unity (see Section I.B above), and so it follows that the source of our awareness of perfect justice is the same as the source of our awareness of perfect love and perfect truth, namely, the one unrestricted act of thinking. Once again we see God's presence to us—not only in our capacity to seek perfection in love and truth, but also in our capacity to seek perfect justice and the common good. When God gives us the capacity to love justice and goodness—and to seek it until we have reached perfection—He also reveals Himself to be perfectly just and good.

III. The Desire for Perfect and Unconditional Beauty

Throughout history, great thinkers and artists have found themselves idolizing beauty. Our desire to be immersed in beauty and to possess and become beautiful is so powerful that it frequently becomes obsessive and all-consuming. Strangely, we can become intoxicated by something or someone beautiful and frustrated by the slightest imperfections in the next moment. We recognize imperfections in beauty not only in the world around us but also in our own appearance, and when we recognize these imperfections, we try to improve upon them. Once in a great while, we think we have arrived at consummate beauty. This might occur while looking at a scene of natural beauty—a sunset over the water, majestic green and brown mountains against a horizon of blue sky. But even there, despite our desire to elevate it to the quasi-divine, we get bored and strive for a different or an even more perfect manifestation of natural beauty—a *little* better sunset, another vantage point of the Alps that's a *little* more perfect.

As with the other three transcendental desires (for perfect truth, perfect love, and perfect justice or goodness), human beings seem to have an awareness of what is more beautiful. It incites man to a more perfect ideal, but also has associated risks. It fuels the continuous personal striving for artistic, architectural, musical, and literary perfection; we do not *passively* desire to create—we *passionately* desire to create, to express in evermore beautiful forms the perfection of beauty that we seem to carry within our consciousness. We do not simply want to *say* an idea; we want to express it beautifully—more beautifully, indeed, perfectly beautifully. We do not simply want to express a mood in music; we want to express it perfectly beautifully. This striving has left a legacy of architecture and art, music and drama, and every form of high culture.

The risk associated with this desire for perfect beauty is that it can produce boredom or frustration with any imperfect manifestation of beauty. This causes us to confuse what is imperfectly beautiful with our ideal of perfect beauty. It is true that a garden can achieve a certain perfection of beauty, but our continuous desire to improve it can make us grow terribly dissatisfied when we cannot perfect it indefinitely.

This is evidenced quite strongly in the artistic community. When one reads the biographies of great artists, musicians, and poets, one senses the tragedy with which art is frequently imbued. What causes these extraordinarily gifted men and women to abuse themselves, to judge themselves so harshly, to so totally pour themselves into their art? Perhaps it is when art becomes a "god", when one tries to extract perfect and unconditional beauty from imperfect and conditioned minds and forms.

We not only have a desire for perfect beauty; we also have a capacity to recognize *every* imperfection in beauty—in visual forms, auditory forms, tactile forms, and every combination of these forms. Even if we do not recognize these imperfections *reflectively*, we manifest our awareness of them by becoming disengaged by what formerly enthralled us, or by trying to improve our experience of what formerly captivated us (e.g., turning up the music, trying to find a better perspective, adding features to a home or garden, etc.). If we concentrate for a long period of time on "earthly beauties", we find ourselves becoming progressively less interested—and in the end, even bored with them. If something were perfectly beautiful, it would never fail to fascinate—but the beauty in the world around us does not have that power or perfection.

Once again, our capacity to recognize seemingly *every* imperfection in seemingly *every* manifestation of beauty we encounter (including the beauty of restricted ideas, restricted love, and restricted justice or goodness—the other three transcendentals) manifests our awareness of "what perfect beauty would be like". So what is the source of this transcendental awareness? The reader will by now know how transcendental philosophers are likely to answer this question—namely, by showing first that this transcendental awareness does not have a source in the restricted world around us (which is filled with only imperfect beauty), and then showing that perfect beauty is a perfect unity capable of perfect unification of distinct forms. Since there can be only one perfect unity—namely, the one unrestricted act of thinking—it must be the source of our awareness of perfect beauty as well as our awareness of perfect truth, love, and justice or goodness. So how does the argument about perfect beauty proceed?

I begin with the thoughts of the influential artist and art critic Roger Eliott Fry, who in the last paragraph of his essay "Retrospect" attempted to detach "the aesthetic quality" from all other practical and ethical concerns in order to appreciate it for itself:

> One can only say that those who experience [the purely aesthetic quality of significant form which is something other than agreeable arrangements of form, harmonious patterns, and the like] feel it to have a peculiar quality of *"reality"* which makes it a matter of infinite importance in their lives. Any attempt I might make to explain this would probably land me in the depths of mysticism. On the edge of that gulf I stop.[3]

[3] Roger Fry, "Retrospect", in *Vision and Design*, ed. J.B. Bullen (Mineola, N.Y.: Dover Publications, 1998), p. 211.

What does Fry mean by this pure aesthetic quality which will land him "in the depths of mysticism"? We may begin with a more basic question, namely, what is it about beautiful objects that evokes delight, repose, reveling, enjoyment, and even sublimity? Johannes Lotz, going back to Albert the Great, suggests that the following three characteristics give rise to the above aesthetic emotions: perfection of a particular form (essence), harmonious resonance, and "shining forth" (luster or splendor) pointing beyond itself.[4]

The first characteristic refers to what we enjoy in "natural objects coming to perfection". When something reaches its *to ti ēn einai* (what it was supposed to be—the perfection of its form), it is a delight to see. We not only revel in something coming to perfection in essence, but also in proportion and appearance. When things are disordered, dysfunctional, or flawed, they either evoke no emotion or cause a sense of disturbance or revulsion. In a sense, then, individual form brought to perfection is intrinsically beautiful.

The second quality of beauty, harmonious resonance, is perhaps the best recognized quality of beautiful objects. When different forms blend together, each form brings out hidden aspects of the other. In music, for example, the harmony of two notes brings out aspects of the individual notes that are unrecognized in their isolation. What note 1 does to note 2 is not recognized when note 1 stands by itself. The same holds true for the visual arts. When one form blends "harmoniously" with another, the two forms bring out aspects of each other that remain hidden when they are in isolation. The same holds true for architecture and poetry, and any other manifestation of beauty. Harmony (a complementary blending), then, is more than an absence of conflict or disorder. It is also a revealing of hidden beauty within individual forms.

Yet, there is more to harmony than the evoking of deeper delight, repose, reveling, and enjoyment. Certain harmonies reach to the deepest emotions—the *sublime* emotions within us. In the glory of a Brahms symphony (complex harmonies amid complex melodies), breathtaking architecture (having large scale amid minute proportionality), and Elliot's *Four Quartets* (filled with metaphysical ideas,

[4]Johannes B. Lotz, "Beauty", in *Philosophical Dictionary*, trans. and ed. Kenneth Baker (Spokane, Wash.: Gonzaga University Press, 1972), p. 30.

dense metaphors, and beautiful poetic form), beauty points beyond mere delight, repose, reveling, and enjoyment, to a kind of ecstasy, a sublime reveling, a *mysterium tremendum*, or a sense of being at home with the divine. The more complex, grand, and sustained the harmony, the more it evokes the sublime or exalted emotions, and the more it seems to connect us with the glorious, the beautiful, and the sublime itself. We are now beginning to approach Roger Fry's "matter of infinite importance" whose explanation lies in the "depths of mysticism".

The third quality of beauty—"shining forth", splendor, and luster—refers to "access to perfection of form or harmony". The less hidden the first two qualities of beauty are, the more we delight, repose, or revel in it. But "shining forth" is much more than this. As suggested above, complex, grand, and sustained beauty point beyond their complementary unified forms to unity, perfection, and sublimity itself. One might say that simple objects of beauty point to the perfection of the form through which it exists, but complex beauties tend to point beyond the perfection of a particular form to *perfection itself*. When one hears Mozart's *Requiem*, one recognizes and then reposes and revels in more than music brought to its perfection, more than the emotions evoked by the harmonies and melodies. One enjoys the more perfect manifestation of unity and then reposes and revels in it, feeling a deep and abiding sense of exaltation and glory. Now, when the *Requiem* is performed within a magnificent church with magnificent art, and the music, art, and architecture are unified as a whole, one feels drawn into a perfection bigger than all the forms combined. One is drawn into the perfection of complex unification to which one appends the name "glorious", or "magnificent".

Again, when one beholds not only a beautiful ocean, but a beautiful mountain and waterfall and sky forming a single contiguous whole, with the motion of the sea and the waterfall, and the flight of birds, and the movement of wind rustling through vegetation, the harmonious totality shines forth and points not only to a unity amid complexity, but offers a taste of unity itself, a taste of repose itself—perhaps stated best, a taste of ultimate home itself. Again, we find another manifestation of the blending of forms that not only demonstrates unity, but gives the felt perception of unity. It not only points to the perfection of a form, but points beyond any form to perfection itself.

This kind of unity seems to have no intrinsic limit. The susceptibility of form to intrinsic unification (as if the forms were created to be unified, created to complement one another, created as radically incomplete anticipating a home in their highest unifications—like mathematics), this kind of anticipatory completion, this perfect anticipatory unity of incomplete form, seems to have as its source "unity itself" or "beauty itself". As the notes are combined with other notes, as musical forms are combined with architectural, artistic, and natural forms, the origin of these partial manifestations of perfection is revealed, and so, at once, we resonate with (we say "we feel") unity itself, perfection itself, and beauty itself. When we resonate with perfection itself, we feel at once in ecstasy and at home, in a flurry of activity and at a still point.

It seems that *all* forms have an ideal complementarity with *all* other forms, revealing yet another kind of ideal or perfect unification within the phenomenon of beauty. This ideal or perfect complementarity among diverse forms suggests yet another manifestation of *perfect unity* (in addition to perfect truth, goodness, and love).

We may now return to the question with which we began, namely, what is the source of our awareness of what perfect beauty would be like? Recognizing that all worldly forms of beauty are imperfect, it seems unlikely that our awareness of perfect beauty comes from the outside world. So we ask once again what the source of our *innate* awareness of perfect beauty might be. As with our awareness of perfect truth, love, and justice or goodness, we see that perfect beauty is susceptible to perfect unity, capable of perfectly unifying every diverse form. There is no intrinsic limit to its "unifying power", and so it seems to be yet another manifestation of the one perfect unity, the one unrestricted act of thinking (see the proof above in Section I.B). This one unrestricted act of thinking is at once the unity of perfect mind, perfect love, perfect justice or goodness, and perfect beauty. We may now return to what Roger Fry intuited in his essay "Retrospect": "[Beauty has a] '*reality*' which makes it a matter of infinite importance.... Any attempt I might make to explain this would probably land me in the depths of mysticism." Without having a formal understanding of Platonic or transcendental philosophy, Fry recognized that his awareness of beauty, particularly sublime beauty, originated with the presence of God ("the infinite" "important One")[5] within his consciousness. Once again we see that God reveals Himself to us by allowing us to participate not only in the appreciation of and fulfillment through beauty, but also in our awareness of what His beauty would be like. At the very moment He imparts in us the power to appreciate, create, and critique beauty, He also calls us to Himself in our yearning for perfect beauty.

IV. The Unity, Meaning, and Depth of Our Transcendental Desires

At the end of Chapter 3 we asked whether the unrestricted act of thinking was more than "Einstein's God"—a perfect mentative act. We noted that Otto, Eliade, Newman, and Tolkien gave us good reason for thinking that God was also mysterious, good, sacred, daunting, fascinating, and empathetic. In light of our investigation of three other transcendental desires (the desire for perfect love, justice or goodness, and beauty), we now see an impressive reasonable validation of what was formerly a strong intrasubjective impression (a *feeling* and intuition of an empathetic transcendent "wholly Other").

Lonergan offers an initial entryway into the reasonable affirmation of this love, justice or goodness, and beauty by intimating that the power of mind occurs through higher-level unifications of ideas (including systems of ideas and even systems of systems of ideas). The higher the level of unity, the more ideas are related through it, and the more powerful the act of thinking. Thus, the unrestricted act of thinking would be one in which *every* idea, including an unrestricted idea, would be unified and interrelated.

The Platonists recognized that reality was more than intelligibility; it had dimensions of love, justice or goodness, and beauty with which the domain of intelligibility (explicability) is not directly concerned. These other dimensions of reality have their own distinctive qualities when they are manifest to restricted acts of consciousness in a restricted world. Yet, they all share one feature in common: they

---

[5] See ibid., p. 121.

are capable of unifying the whole of reality in their own distinctive ways—and hence, are all perfect unities. This led to a remarkable discovery that can be expressed in the following five-step argument:

1. Perfect unity can only occur through a purely inclusive reality, which excludes nothing from itself. (See above Section I.A.)
2. A purely inclusive reality cannot have any restrictions, because restrictions entail exclusions (e.g., the restrictions of square exclude the restrictions of circle in the same respect, at the same place and time). Therefore, a purely inclusive reality must be an unrestricted reality. (See above Section I.B.)
3. There can only be one unrestricted reality (i.e., the one unrestricted act of thinking). (See the proof in Chapter 3, Section III.C.)
4. Therefore, inasmuch as a perfect unity must be a purely inclusive reality, and a purely inclusive reality must be unrestricted, and an unrestricted reality must be absolutely unique (the one unrestricted act of thinking), the source of perfect unity must be *the one* unrestricted act of thinking.
5. The one unrestricted act of thinking must be the one source of every manifestation of perfect unity—the perfect unity of mind, love, justice or goodness, and beauty.

If Lonergan's proof of the unique unrestricted act of thinking (God) and the argument of the Neo-Platonists and Neo-Thomists for the perfect unity of love, justice or goodness, and beauty are correct, then there is rational access to God's love, goodness, and beauty—and even to God's *perfect* love, goodness, and beauty.

A. Reason and Revelation

The question has often been raised about whether the love and goodness of God could be known through reasonable and responsible proof, or whether such qualities were limited to the domain of revelation alone. The Neo-Platonists and Neo-Thomists have given us good *reason* to believe that these attributes belong to the one perfect unity (God). However, this rational approach to the love and goodness of God is limited; with respect to love, we can appreciate perfection in empathy and care, and with respect to goodness, the qualities of justice and equity—but beyond this, we can only hypothesize. We cannot be sure how such qualities manifest themselves, let alone how they affect our relationship with God, God's desires and hopes for us, God's involvement in suffering and redemption, and so on. To answer these more refined questions, we must turn to revelation.

This shows an important complementarity between reason and revelation. If we hold that the Neo-Platonists and Neo-Thomists are on the right track, then we will know by the light of reason what kind of revelation we are looking for, namely, one that is consistent with perfect empathy and care as well as perfect justice and goodness. Now if we find a source of revelation that is consistent with these two guiding principles from reason, that revelation should answer the questions that reason itself cannot answer, namely, our relationships with God, journey with God, inspiration by God, protection and guidance by God, the purpose of suffering, the reason for evil, the efficacy of prayer, the function of grace, and so on. The two criteria of reason can lead us to a true source of revelation, and the true source of revelation in turn can answer questions that are beyond the scope of reason. This will become quite important as we move into Volume III of this Quartet on the revelation of Jesus Christ.

B. Using One Transcendental Desire as an Interpretive Lens for the Others

We began our investigation of human transcendental nature (in Chapter 3) with the desire for perfect truth (the desire to know everything about everything) because this transcendental desire is open to considerable nuance and probative arguments—including a proof for the unique unrestricted act of thinking (God), and its presence in our consciousness as the universal anticipation of all that is to be known (the notion of being). This gave us a solid ground from which to probe more deeply into the nature of the unrestricted act of thinking. Inasmuch as there can only be one purely inclusive reality (which excludes nothing from itself), we recognize that the unrestricted act of thinking would have to be the source of all other purely inclusive realities (perfect unities)—namely, perfect love, perfect justice or goodness, and perfect beauty.

Though this procedure is clearly the best way to rationally understand and reasonably confirm the perfect love, goodness, and beauty of God, other thinkers such as Plato, Karl Rahner, and Hans Urs von Balthasar show that there is much to be gained by looking at our transcendental nature through the interpretive lens of perfect love, perfect justice or goodness, and perfect beauty, so that we do not limit ourselves to the interpretive power of perfect truth or intelligibility alone. Rahner advocates looking at truth, goodness, and beauty through the lens of love; Plato advocates looking at truth and beauty through the lens of goodness; and von Balthasar advocates looking at truth and goodness through the lens of beauty. Though these procedures do not lend clarity or probative force to the approach we have taken, they do add depth and comprehensiveness to it. This comprehensive approach is beyond the scope of our study, but a few quotations from the above thinkers may inspire readers to investigate them on their own.

Karl Rahner sees the unity and fulfillment of our transcendental nature in God's love, noting:

> God wishes to communicate himself, to pour forth the love which he himself is. This is the first and the last of his real plans and hence of his real world too. Everything else exists so that this one thing might be: the eternal miracle of infinite Love. And so God makes a creature whom he can love: he creates man. He creates him in such a way that he *can* receive this Love which is God himself, and that he can and must at the same time accept it for what it is: the ever astounding wonder, the unexpected, unexacted gift.[6]

Lonergan agrees with Rahner's view that love is our ultimate fulfillment, though he does not consider love to be the beginning point of inquiry. As we saw above, Lonergan proceeds from the desire to know perfect truth ("all that is to be known"); then, after proving the existence of God and grounding the horizon of our intellection within it, he shows that love is the fulfillment of all our transcendental

---

[6]Karl Rahner, *Foundations of Christian Faith* (New York: Crossroad Publishing, 1982), pp. 123–24.

notions: "I have conceived being in love with God as an ultimate fulfillment of man's capacity for self-transcendence; and this view of religion is sustained when God is conceived as the supreme fulfillment of the transcendental notions, as supreme intelligence, truth, reality, righteousness, goodness."[7] Though the desire for perfect truth is the beginning point of his inquiry, the desire for perfect love is the end, because he sees perfect love as the fulfillment of perfect truth and perfect goodness.

Plato advocates for the ultimate significance of the *good*. Though he admits that "the good" is not the first transcendental quality to be discovered, he believes it is the final and most important one, advocating that we look at truth, love, and beauty through its interpretive lens. In his famous "Allegory of the Cave" (in the *Republic*), he associates perfect goodness with the author of light that gives value to everything else in reality:

> But, at any rate, my dream [of the cave and the sun] as it appears to me is that in the region of the known the last thing to be seen and hardly seen is *the idea of good*, and that when seen it must point us to the conclusion that this is indeed the cause of all things of all that is right and beautiful, giving birth in the visible world to light, and the author of light and itself in the intelligible world being the authentic source of truth and reason,... and that anyone who is to act wisely in private or public must have caught sight of this, their souls ever feel the upward urge and the yearning for that sojourn above.[8]

For Plato, the "good" points us to the perfection of the other transcendentals: "all that is right and beautiful" and "all that is true and reasonable".[9] It is the perfection of being itself, and so it is the perfection of beauty itself and truth itself. When we attend to the good itself, we cannot help but notice its beauty and truth—and see beauty itself and truth itself within it.

Hans Urs von Balthasar offers yet another approach to man's transcendence—emphasizing the significance of beauty as an animator

---

[7] Bernard Lonergan, *Method in Theology* (New York: Herder and Herder, 1972), p. 111.

[8] Plato, *Republic*, trans. Paul Shorey, in *The Collected Dialogues of Plato*, ed. Edith Hamilton and Huntington Cairns (Princeton, N.J.: Princeton University Press, 1961), 517c–d, p. 750 (emphasis mine).

[9] Ibid.

of truth and goodness. He not only associates the notion of perfect beauty with God; he sees it as the unifying element between perfect truth and perfect goodness. This quality of perfect beauty is what makes the true and the good wholly attractive to us and reveals that beauty must be more than mere appearance. In Volume 1 of *The Glory of the Lord*, he establishes the basis for his theological aesthetics by noting:

> Beauty is the word that shall be our first. Beauty is the last thing which the thinking intellect dares to approach, since only *it* dances as an uncontained splendour around the double constellation of the true and the good and their inseparable relation to one another. Beauty is the disinterested one, without which the ancient world refused to understand itself, a world which both imperceptibly and yet unmistakably has bid farewell to our new world, a world of interests, leaving it to its own avarice and sadness. We no longer dare to believe in beauty and we make of it a mere appearance in order the more easily to dispose of it. Our situation today shows that beauty demands for itself at least as much courage and decision as do truth and goodness, and she will not allow herself to be separated and banned from her two sisters without taking them along with herself in an act of mysterious vengeance. We can be sure that whoever sneers at her name as if she were the ornament of a bourgeois past—whether he admits it or not—can no longer pray and soon will no longer be able to love.[10]

For von Balthasar, beauty is not merely a "good feeling", but a felt awareness of the perfect unity of God, which brings with it the perfect unity of truth and goodness. Though we might distance ourselves from beauty to gain the objectivity necessary to use the methods of the natural sciences, mathematics, logic, or the social sciences, we cannot help but be attracted to the beauty of truth itself, which we seek. Scientists and logicians are not looking for the most beautiful solution, but they are looking for the beauty *of* the truth awaiting their discovery—and not only this but the beauty *in* the truth they have discovered, in the symmetry and elegance of mathematical and physical equations, of physical and biological systems, of the motion

---

[10] Hans Urs von Balthasar, *The Glory of the Lord: A Theological Aesthetics*, trans. Erasmo Leiva-Merikakis, vol. 1, *Seeing the Form* (Edinburgh: T and T Clark, 1982), p. 18.

of planets, stars, and galaxies, and of the creativity of human beings in discovering them all.

Similarly, ethicists may try to detach themselves from aesthetics in their interpretation and application of the principles and theories of the good, but they should not detach themselves from the beauty *of* or *in* the good they are seeking—the beauty of self-sacrifice for justice, of increasing recognition and articulation of individual, political, and economic rights, in the creation of more just systems of governance within and among states and countries. If scientists, logicians, mathematicians, ethicists, and judges distance themselves from the beauty of goodness and truth altogether, they will lose their love of the object they seek and the transcendental quality within it. They will become the victims of von Balthasar's prophecy: "We can be sure that whoever sneers at [Beauty's] name as if she were the ornament of a bourgeois past—whether he admits it or not—can no longer pray and soon will no longer be able to love."

Plato was the first philosopher to articulate the unity of the transcendentals. In the previous citation from the *Republic*, he suggests that goodness is the unity of "all that is right and beautiful" and "true and reasonable". In the *Symposium*, Plato recognizes the power of beauty to unify truth, love, and goodness:

> He who would proceed aright in this matter should begin in youth to visit beautiful forms; and first ... to love one such form only.... Soon he will of himself perceive ... that the beauty in every form is one and the same ... and will become a lover of all beautiful forms; in the next stage he will consider that the beauty of the mind is more honorable than the beauty of the outward form ... until he is compelled to contemplate and see the beauty of institutions and laws, and to understand that the beauty of them is all of one family, and that personal beauty is a trifle; and after laws and institutions he will go on to the sciences, that he may see their beauty,... and at last the vision is revealed to him of a single science, which is the science of beauty everywhere.... He who has been instructed thus far in the things of love, and who has learned to see the beautiful in due order and succession, when he comes towards the end will suddenly perceive a nature of wondrous beauty ... a nature which in the first place is everlasting, not growing and decaying ... but beauty absolute, separate, simple, and everlasting, which without diminution and without increase, or

any change, is imparted to the ever-growing and perishing beauties of all other things.[11]

For Plato, beauty not only manifests itself in outward forms, but in the objects of the mind—in mathematics, science, and philosophy. This beauty awakens love of these objects ("*eros* of the mind"),[12] which finds its culmination in the love of the ground and unity of mind and truth itself. Beauty also manifests itself in the objects of justice and goodness (as well as the institutions of justice and goodness). Once again this beauty awakens our love for justice and goodness, which again finds its culmination in the ground and unity of justice and goodness itself. Finally, beauty is manifest in the unity of being itself, truth itself, and goodness itself. This awakens the highest kind of love that finds its culmination in the *one* ground of being, truth, and goodness, "a nature which in the first place is everlasting, not growing and decaying ... but beauty absolute, separate, simple, and everlasting, which without diminution and without increase, or any change, is imparted to the ever-growing and perishing beauties of all other things."

This passage makes clear how each transcendental reveals the depth of the others, as each note in the harmony or melody brings out beauty in the other notes. Beauty itself brings out the aesthetic dimension of truth itself, goodness itself, and love itself; truth itself brings out the intelligible dimension of goodness itself, love itself, and beauty itself; goodness itself brings out the perfection of truth itself, love itself, and beauty itself; and love itself brings out the fulfillment of truth itself, goodness itself, and beauty itself. In his vision of "perfect and wondrous beauty"[13] Plato sees the perfection, intelligibility, and fulfillment of truth itself, goodness itself, and love itself.

Von Balthasar adds to this by recognizing that this transcendent nature is also *spiritual*, attracting us and drawing us into a relationship

---

[11] Plato, *Symposium*, in *Symposium and Phaedrus*, trans. Benjamin Jowett (New York: Dover, 1993), 210a–211b, p. 33.

[12] This expression has its origins in Plato's blending of "eros" and "psych" in the *Symposium*—particularly the love (desire) of the soul, the love of wisdom, and the love of knowledge, which as objects of love are both good and immortal (see 210b–211b, ibid., pp. 32–33). The expression was later taken up by Plotinus and Augustine and others and ultimately becomes a central theme in Bernard Lonergan's *Insight*, pp. 97, 247, 355–56, 498.

[13] Jowett, *Symposium*, p. 33.

with the transcendent. For him, beauty is the underlying animating quality in love and prayer, which, in their turn, reveal the deepest dimensions of truth and goodness (see Volume I, Chapter 5, Section II.B, "Transcendent Beauty").

Though it is clearest and most probative to begin an investigation of the transcendental desires from the vantage point of the desire for perfect truth (the complete intelligibility of reality), we can gain considerable depth and comprehensiveness by looking at them through the lens of each—following the examples of Rahner and Lonergan with respect to love, Plato with respect to the good, and Plato and von Balthasar with respect to beauty. As we do so, we gain greater insight and access into not only the mind but the heart of God.

V. Our Transcendent Nature:
A Review of the Evidence

We now proceed to a synthetic account of the clues to our transcendent nature discovered in Chapters 1 through 4. We began with Rudolf Otto's articulation of a fundamental *interpersonal* experience of the numen (intrinsic to individuals in virtually every religion and culture) and found the numen to have two poles of "feeling-content": (1) a mysterious, daunting, spiritual, overpowering "wholly Other", and (2) a fascinating, energizing, good, and caring presence that draws us to itself. The numinous presence incites us (but does not force us) to worship, praise, and prayer.

In Chapter 2 we examined Mircea Eliade's study of the history of religion and found that the numinous experience not only incited us to worship, but to recognize sacred space and time in the world around us. People of virtually every culture and religion seem to have a *religious intuition*, an awareness that the transcendent has broken into the world and after doing so has left us with a means to reconnect with it, namely, in sacred places, myths, rituals, and communities. Thus the numinous experience has both interior and exterior effects; it works through individuals and groups, including communities, cultures, and societies. It causes us to be naturally religious, to seek and learn from the sacred domain, and to enter into our transcendent nature and destiny. When we ignore this part of our nature, we feel cosmic emptiness, alienation, and loneliness, which has a number of measureable negative clinical effects, such as increased suicide rates, increased distance from family members, fewer reasons for living, increased aggression, more lifetime impulsivity, and greater substance use disorder.[14] Whether we acknowledge our natural religious disposition or not, it will ultimately manifest itself by negative consequences if we ignore it, pointing to one of the most powerful dimensions of our consciousness and validating our nature as *homo religiosus*.

In the latter part of Chapter 2, we examined a third manifestation of the interior presence of transcendence to us: *conscience* (the felt awareness of and attraction to the good and revulsion at evil). Immanuel Kant and John Henry Newman pointed to the palpable quality of divine authority within the experience of conscience. This presence of divine authority is so integral to conscience that it cannot be experienced or conceived without it. For this reason, both Kant and Newman felt that it provided a pathway, a nonsyllogistic "proof", toward God. This experience of conscience is essential for social and civil conduct, for without it, we are sociopathic. If we ignore or repress it over the long term, we become progressively more egocentric, aggressive, unjust, and even criminal. However, if we acknowledge it, and attempt to follow it, we experience more acutely the presence of the Divine Authority within us.

We concluded Chapter 2 by combining the numinous experience, the religious intuition, and the experience of conscience, showing their combined effects in the origination of religious archetypal symbols (from Carl Jung's theory of the collective unconscious). We noticed that these archetypes are almost naturally woven into a powerful myth about the cosmic struggle between good and evil (articulated by J.R.R. Tolkien, J.K. Rowling, and George Lucas, among others). Intrinsic to this interior myth is a call to be a hero on the side of cosmic good—and to do our part to avert the prophecy of Edmund Burke that "all that is required for evil to triumph, is for a few good people to remain silent." The immense popularity of these so-called contemporary myths gives testimony to the likelihood of their presence within us.

[14] See Kanita Dervic et al., "Religious Affiliation and Suicide Attempt", *American Journal of Psychiatry* 161, no. 12 (December 2004): 2303–8, http://ajp.psychiatryonline.org/article .aspx?articleid=177228.

We concluded from this that we have a transcendent soul (a domain within our consciousness that dynamically encounters and relates to the transcendent, as mysterious, fascinating, sacred, and good). This encounter with the transcendent incites us to worship and prayer, to seek the sacred both individually and collectively, to pursue the good and avoid evil, and to enter bravely on the side of cosmic good in the struggle against cosmic evil.

Notice that each of the above characteristics is fundamentally *interpersonal*: the numen (the transcendent presence) attracts and invites us into itself, even as "wholly Other". Our awareness of the presence of the sacred in the *outer* world draws us to a collective (group) encounter with it through myth, ritual, and sacred places. The presence of the Divine Authority in conscience invites us to follow its lead (and not to avoid or ignore it). The following diagram reflects this threefold *interpersonal* dimension of our soul.

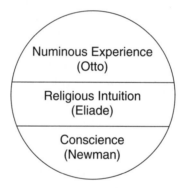

Numinous Experience
(Otto)

Religious Intuition
(Eliade)

Conscience
(Newman)

We then shifted our focus from our interior *experience* of the transcendent to a *rational* reflection on our transcendental awareness and desires. We followed the Platonic and Thomistic implications of four transcendental desires: the desires for perfect truth, love, justice or goodness, and beauty. We discovered that we do not have an interpersonal experience of these transcendental desires, but we can know them from their effects in our consciousness and the world around us. By using the tools of rational proof, we were able to demonstrate the existence of a unique, unrestricted act of thinking that is also perfect love, justice or goodness, and beauty—and then show that this unique being is the source of all four transcendental desires within us.

In Chapter 3 we examined the clearest and most probative of these transcendental notions, namely, the notion of being (the notion of the complete intelligibility of reality). We began by examining the preconditions for the question of causation (why is it so?) and discovered that it entailed preawareness of higher heuristic notions of "possibility", "necessity", "reality", and ultimately the supreme heuristic notion: the complete intelligibility of reality, "the notion of being" (Section II). This led to an examination of Lonergan's contention that reality is completely intelligible, which in its turn led to his proof for the existence of God. After showing the necessity of at least one reality that can exist through itself (otherwise there would be nothing in all reality), we demonstrated that this necessary reality would have to be unrestricted in intelligibility, and therefore absolutely unique and the ultimate cause (Creator) of everything else that exists (Section III). We then probed into the nature of completely intelligible reality and followed Lonergan's reasoning to the conclusion that it must be an unrestricted act of thinking (Section IV).

We were then in a position to determine the source of our tacit awareness (horizon) of complete and unrestricted intelligibility and determined that the only possible source would have to be unrestricted intelligibility itself: the unique unrestricted act of thinking. We concluded that God shares His mind with us sufficient to engender a horizon of the vast potential of *unrestricted* intelligibility, giving rise to every form of free intellectual inquiry and creativity (Section V).

This is an important realization, because it clarifies the nature of the source of our *interpersonal experience* of the transcendent (the numen, the sacred, and the Divine Authority), and reasonably confirms its unique, unrestricted, intelligent nature and existence. Though we do not directly experience the unique, unrestricted, intelligent, creative nature of the Transcendent Reality, we can prove its existence, and deduce its presence within us. This gives us the best of both worlds: the world of direct experience of the transcendent as interpersonal and emotional, and the world of logical proof (from effects to causes), which clarifies and confirms the unique, unrestricted, creative nature of the supreme act of thinking.

When we recognize that our two distinct methods (interior experience and rational proof) point to a similar transcendent reality, we are given additional confirmation of our conclusion through mutual corroboration. Furthermore, the convergence of the two methods allows the evidence from each to complement the other, revealing that the mysterious, sacred, and fascinating reality (of interior experience) is the same as the unique, unrestricted, intelligent, creative reality (of rational proof). We can now experience and understand that a reality of infinite and ultimate significance is not only present to us, but desires to be in relationship with us, and *nothing* could be more significant than that.

In Chapter 4, we completed our journey into the interior world of the transcendent by following the Neo-Platonic and Neo-Thomistic philosophers into the domain of love, justice or goodness, and beauty. Once again we found ourselves in a world of logical deduction rather than direct experience. We began with the insight that thinking (mind) is essentially a unifying activity and noticed that the higher the level of thinking, the more ideas would be unified through it, leading to the conclusion that the highest act of thinking would be a unity of all ideas. We were then provoked to ask the following question (posed by many philosophers): What is this perfect unity, this perfect unifying power? We began our answer with the fundamental insight that a perfect unity would have to be purely inclusive to every reality and idea. We then made recourse to the philosophical insight that restrictions of any kind cause exclusions (e.g., the restrictions of square exclude the restrictions of circle in the same respect at the same place and time). The more restrictions there are, the more exclusion there is, and the more exclusion there is, the less the unifying power. This led us to a double insight. First, a perfect unity (as perfectly inclusive) could not have any exclusions and therefore could not have any *restrictions*—it would have to be unrestricted. Second, an unrestricted reality must be unique (from the proof in Chapter 3, Section III.C). This means that every manifestation of perfect unity must have this *one* unrestricted source. Having already proven that the one unrestricted reality is an unrestricted act of thinking, we reasoned that this one unrestricted act of thinking would have to be the source of *every* manifestation of perfect unity.

We then returned to the Neo-Platonists and Neo-Thomists, who recognized not only the perfect unity within the unrestricted act of thinking (perfect truth), but also in perfect love, perfect justice or goodness, and perfect beauty (see the justification of this in

Sections I–III above). Given the insightfulness and apparent validity of their arguments, it seemed likely that the unrestricted act of thinking was the *source* of perfect love, goodness, and beauty. God is not just mind, but also love, goodness, and beauty—indeed, perfect love, perfect goodness, and perfect beauty.

This realization enabled us to complete our investigation of our transcendent soul, that is, the interior presence of God within our consciousness. Recognizing that we not only have the desire for perfect love, justice or goodness, and beauty, but also the capacity to recognize imperfection in *every* manifestation of them, we reasoned that we must have some awareness of what perfect love, justice or goodness, and beauty would be like. The source of these manifestations of transcendental awareness must be the one and only perfect unity: the unrestricted act of thinking who is perfectly loving, good, and beautiful.

We are now in a position to put together the evidence of our interior awareness of transcendence with the evidence of rational proof. The unique, unrestricted, creative act of thinking that is perfect love, goodness, and beauty (from rational proof) comes to our consciousness revealing His attractive, fascinating nature within His mysterious transcendent daunting presence. He inclines us (but does not force us) to search for Him, pray to Him, worship Him, and unite ourselves to Him. Through the manifestation of His divine authority, He reveals to us the path to the good—and helps us to feel the cold and dark of evil. Through archetypal symbols He gives us a sense of higher and heroic mission in life, suggesting that we not only avoid evil, but help others around us to avoid it—and even defeat it. His presence to us is not only an invitation to Himself, but also an invitation to virtue and heroic mission, and through these, to our highest purpose, dignity, and destiny.

The following diagram reflects the two dimensions of God's presence to us (our transcendent soul): the interpersonal dimension (the inner circle) and the unique, unrestricted, creative dimension (the outer circle).

Is there any other evidence of our transcendental nature and destiny besides the seven kinds mentioned above? There is—and it comes from a distinctive source: empirically testable data of transphysical survival of bodily death from near-death experiences. This evidence

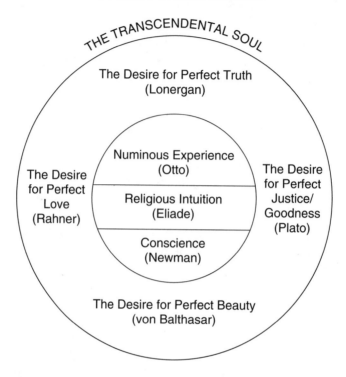

will further complement and corroborate the evidence from interior experience of the transcendent, Lonergan's proof of God, and the logical analysis of our transcendental desires. When these different kinds of evidence are set into corroborative relationship with one another, they show the high probability of our transcendental nature and destiny—a destiny toward perfect good and love.

Chapter Five

Clues to a Life Beyond

Introduction

I cite the evidence of near-death experiences (NDEs) with some trepidation, because there are many books written on this subject that are not scientific or based on any clinical, cross-cultural, long-term study, but rather on a few anecdotes taken to the extreme. Some of these nonscientific books have rather manipulative agendas, and some are quite cultic in character. These problematic accounts do not mitigate the excellent longitudinal studies that have been carried out by Sam Parnia at Southampton University[1] and by Pim van Lommel;[2] the two studies carried out by Kenneth Ring on near-death experiences,[3] and his later study of near-death experiences of the blind;[4] Dr. Janice Holden's analysis of veridical evidence in NDEs from thirty-nine independent studies;[5] and Raymond Moody's studies of them.[6] There are additional careful longitudinal studies cited throughout this

[1] See Sam Parnia et al., "AWARE—AWAreness during REsuscitation—A Prospective Study", *Resuscitation*, October 6, 2014, pp. 1799–1805, http://www.resuscitationjournal.com /article/S0300-9572%2814%2900739-4/fulltext.

[2] See Pim van Lommel et al., "Near-Death Experience in Survivors of Cardiac Arrest: A Prospective Study in the Netherlands", *The Lancet* 358, no. 9298 (2001): 2039–45.

[3] See Kenneth Ring, *Life at Death: A Scientific Investigation of the Near-Death Experience* (New York: Coward, McCann and Geoghegan, 1980).

[4] See Kenneth Ring, Sharon Cooper, and Charles Tart, *Mindsight: Near-Death and Out-of-Body Experiences in the Blind* (Palo Alto, Calif.: William James Center for Consciousness Studies at the Institute of Transpersonal Psychology, 1999).

[5] See Janice Holden, *Handbook of Near Death Experiences: Thirty Years of Investigation* (Westport, Conn.: Praeger Press, 2009).

[6] See Raymond A. Moody, *Life After Life* (New York: Harper Collins, 1975); *The Light Beyond* (New York: Bantam Books, 1988); *Reunions: Visionary Encounters with Departed Loved Ones* (New York: Random House, 1993).

chapter, as well as many studies reported in the *Journal of Near-Death Studies* published by the International Association for Near-Death Studies (peer-reviewed).[7]

Before responding to physicalists' objections, we will want to clarify some terms and circumstances surrounding this remarkable entry-way into the realm of survival of bodily death and the existence of transphysical consciousness.

I. Definitions and Descriptions

In 1982, a Gallup survey indicated that approximately eight million adults in the United States had had a near-death experience (a significantly large population from which to take accurate samples).[8] The people sampled reported having some of the following ten characteristics, eight of which appear to be unique to near-death experiences (in italics):

1. *Out-of-body experience*
2. *Accurate visual perception* (while out of body)
3. *Accurate auditory perception* (while out of body)
4. Feelings of peace and painlessness
5. *Light phenomena* (encounter with loving white light)
6. *Life review*
7. *Being in another world*
8. *Encountering other beings*
9. *Tunnel experience*
10. Precognition

According to the study by Parnia at Southampton University, approximately 9 percent of adults have a near-death experience after cardiac arrest[9] (van Lommel found that 18 percent had a NDE[10]), and according to the International Association of Near-Death Studies (that publishes the peer-reviewed *Journal of Near-Death Studies*),

[7]See the website of the International Association for Near-Death Studies at www.iands .org/publications/journal-of-near-death.html for a complete index of 135 topics concerned with research and longitudinal studies of NDEs.

[8]See George Gallup Jr. and William Proctor, *Adventures in Immortality* (New York: McGraw-Hill, 1982).

[9]Parnia et al., "AWAreness during REsuscitation", pp. 1799–805.

[10]Van Lommel et al., "Near-Death Experience", p. 2039.

approximately 85 percent of children have near-death experiences after cardiac arrest.[11]

The Transphysical Component of Near-Death Experience

The transphysical component of a person having a near-death experience may be described as follows: when a person undergoes clinical death (defined below), a transphysical component of that person leaves the physical body (frequently through a tunnel), emerging outside the physical body, and frequently looking down upon it. This transphysical component is completely intact without the physical body, and it is self-conscious and capable of seeing and hearing (without the biological organs associated with those functions). This transphysical component retains all its memories and appears to have acute recall and memory functions (without use of the brain). It is aware of its self-identity and its distinction from others, but it is more than self-consciousness. It has a remnant of its former embodiment, particularly the presence and sense of extendedness. Though it is *not* physical (constituted by and subject to the laws of physics), it is like an ethereal remnant of the physical body. It is not limited by physical laws (such as gravity), or the restrictions imposed by physical mass (such as walls or roofs). It can be called into a spiritual or heavenly domain in which it can encounter spiritual beings like itself (in human form) as well as wholly transcendent beings greater than itself (such as a loving white light). It can communicate with these beings without the use of voice and sounds. Though it has autonomy and self-identity, it does not have control over most dimensions of the out-of-body experience; for example, it is moved outside of its body, transported to a transphysical domain, and called back into its body by some higher transphysical power. In order to distinguish it from its former physical manifestation, I will refer to it as "a transphysical component".

Clinical Death

After a heart attack, drowning, or significant trauma, people frequently undergo severe oxygen deprivation leading to a gradual

[11] International Association of Near-Death Studies, iands.org/childrens-near-death-experiences.html.

reduction of electrical activity in the brain, resulting in a "shutdown" of higher cerebral functioning as well as most functions of the lower brain (after twenty to thirty seconds). This phenomenon is marked by a flat EEG (electroencephalogram), indicating an absence of electrical activity in the cerebral cortex (generating higher cerebral functioning), and the absence of gag reflex, as well as fixed and dilated pupils, indicating a significant reduction of lower brain functioning. In this state, sensory organs are nonfunctional, both in themselves and in the brain's capacity to process their signals. Furthermore, higher cerebral functions such as thinking, processing memories, and linguistic functions would either be completely absent or reduced to insignificance. Lower brain activity is also minimized, though there may be some sporadic and minimal "sputtering" of pockets of deep cortical neurons in those areas.

Dr. Eben Alexander, a neurosurgeon and professor at the University of Virginia Medical School who underwent a severe coma from encephalitis (and was monitored throughout his comatose state), described it as follows:

> My synapses—the spaces between the neurons of the brain that support the electrochemical activity that makes the brain function—were not simply compromised during my experience. They were stopped. Only isolated pockets of deep cortical neurons were still sputtering, but no broad networks capable of generating anything like what we call "consciousness". The E. coli bacteria that flooded my brain during my illness made sure of that. My doctors have told me that according to all the brain tests they were doing, there was no way that any of the functions including vision, hearing, emotion, memory, language, or logic could possibly have been intact.[12]

The Relationship between the Transphysical Component and the Brain

Given the above definition of "clinical death" and the description of the transphysical component, it appears that we will have to modify contemporary views of the origin of consciousness. Currently,

---

[12] Eben Alexander, "The Science of Heaven", *Newsweek*, November 18, 2012, www.newsweek.com/science-heven-63823.

consciousness is presumed to originate with brain functioning, but if the thousands of monitored cases of clinical death are accurate, and Alexander's and others' assessment of the absence or reduction of brain function are correct, and the verifiable reports of consciousness during clinical death are also accurate, then it seems highly unlikely that consciousness originates with the brain. Instead it seems that consciousness originates from a transphysical component, and that *it* interacts with the brain to channel the data of consciousness to our physical body. Thus, consciousness can exist apart from the body, but if its activities and effects are to be channeled through the body, it is done through the brain. (This is thoroughly discussed in Chapter 6.) There is a close parallelism between transphysical consciousness and the brain's interaction with it. It appears that there is some redundancy or overlapping in the subsidiary functions of consciousness produced by the transphysical component and the brain (such as memory, recall, visual and auditory imagination, and other similar functions). Alexander describes it as follows:

> Brain activity and consciousness are indeed profoundly tied up with one another. But that does not mean that those bonds can't be loosened, or even cut completely. The question of questions is whether the deep parallelism between brain function and human consciousness means that the brain actually produces consciousness. In the wake of my experiences during my week in a coma, my answer is a very confident "No."
>
> Many scientists who study consciousness would agree with me that, in fact, the hard problem of consciousness is probably the one question facing modern science that is arguably forever beyond our knowing, at least in terms of a physicalist model of how the brain might create consciousness. In fact, they would agree that the problem is so profound that we don't even know how to phrase a scientific question addressing it. But if we must decide which produces which, modern physics is pushing us in precisely the opposite direction, suggesting that it is consciousness that is primary and matter secondary.[13]

This view of the transphysical origin of man's consciousness arises primarily out of the studies of near-death experiences (see below),

[13] Ibid.

but is not accepted by some in the current scientific community. Some attempts have been made to explain near-death experiences from a purely physiological point of view to restore credibility to the prevailing view of a physical origin of man's consciousness.[14] (Several more contemporary physicalist explanations are assessed below in Section IV.) In general, these hypotheses do not account for the three kinds of verifiable evidence discussed in Sections II and III below: (1) verification of reports of empirical data occurring during clinical death by independent investigators, (2) visual perception by 80 percent of blind people during clinical death, and (3) verification of reports of previously unknown data given by deceased relatives and friends during clinical death. The inability of purely naturalistic explanations to account for this abundance of verified data seriously challenges their adequacy, allowing the possibility for transphysical explanations of consciousness (like the one given in Chapter 6).

Near-death experiences give strong evidence for a transphysical ground of consciousness, though studies in physics, medicine, and philosophy are also beginning to lean in this direction. The Nobel Prize-winning neurophysiologist Sir John Eccles has set out a serious theory of *tri*alist interactionsim.[15] Dualist theories hold that there is a separate transphysical ground of consciousness (termed "mind" or "soul" or "self") that works through the brain to produce activities within physical embodiment.[16] In order to avoid the perennial problem of dualism—an immaterial substance (such as a conceptual

---

[14]For example, see the following: R. S. Blacher, "To Sleep, Perchance to Dream ...", *Journal of the American Medical Association* 242, no. 21 (November 23, 1979): 2291; Susan Blackmore, *Dying to Live: Science and the Near-Death Experience* (London: Grafton, 1993); S. B. Nuland, *How We Die: Reflections on Life's Final Chapter* (Norwalk, Conn.: Hastings House, 1994); E. Rodin, "The Reality of Death Experiences: A Personal Perspective", *Journal of Nervous and Mental Disease* 168 (1980): 259–63.

[15]In his early work, Eccles declared himself to be an "interactionist *dualist*", but when he realized the need for a "field of mediation" between the immaterial "soul" and the material body, and saw quantum field theory as a viable candidate for this mediation, he along with his "co-theorist", Sir Karl Popper, moved to a theory of "trialistic" interactionism. See Chapter 6 (Section IV.A) for a detailed explanation. See also Sir John Eccles, *Evolution of the Brain: Creation of the Self* (London, UK: Routledge, 1989); Sir John Eccles, "A Unitary Hypothesis of Mind—Brain Interaction in the Cerebral Cortex", *Proceedings of the Royal Society—Biological Sciences* B 240 (1990): 433–51; Karl Popper and John Eccles, *The Self and Its Brain: An Argument for Interactionism* (New York: Routledge, 1984).

[16]Eccles has provided a book of essays by scientists and philosophers about the cogency of strong interactionist dualism in Sir John Eccles, ed., *Mind and Brain: The Many-Faceted Problems* (St. Paul, Minn: Paragon Books, 1983).

idea) affecting and being affected by a material substance (e.g., the biophysical constituents of the brain)—Eccles proposes a "trialist" interactionism in which quantum fields mediate the interaction of the immaterial soul and the material brain.[17] As will be seen, this proposal has considerable explanatory power not only to account for the data of near-death experiences, but also heuristic notions, Lonergan's horizon of complete intelligibility, the implications of Gödel's enigma, and the hard problem of consciousness (see Chapter 6, Section IV.A).

Several other philosophers agree with Eccles' viewpoint, and J. N. Watson has argued convincingly that current brain physiology cannot explain many of the activities of man's consciousness.[18] The well-known philosopher of mind David Chalmers[19] has formulated what is called "the hard problem of consciousness", showing that the inner world of subjective experience is not explicable by physical-biological processes (found in the brain). This implies that some transphysical component is necessary to explain conscious activity fully. Other philosophers such as Thomas Nagel[20] concur with this assessment and develop additional arguments to substantiate the need for a nonreductionistic metaphysical solution to the hard problem of consciousness. "Nonreductionistic" refers to models of consciousness that advocate the improbability or impossibility of explaining conscious activities through physical processes alone.

Physicists such as Henry Stapp[21] and Friedrich Beck[22] substantiate Eccles' trialist interactionism by using John von Neumann's orthodox interpretation of quantum field theory to show the possibility

---

[17] See Eccles, *Evolution of the Brain*, and Eccles, "Unitary Hypothesis of Mind".

[18] See J. N. Watson, "Mind and Brain", in *Mind and Brain: The Many-Faceted Problems*, ed. Sir John Eccles (St. Paul Minn.: Paragon, 1983), pp. 315–25.

[19] See David Chalmers, *The Character of Consciousness (Philosophy of Mind)* (London: Oxford University Press, 2010). See also David Chalmers, *The Conscious Mind: In Search of a Fundamental Theory* (London: Oxford University Press, 1997).

[20] See Thomas Nagel, "What Is It Like to Be a Bat?" *Philosophical Review* 83 (1974): 435–50. See also Thomas Nagel, *Mind and Cosmos* (London: Oxford University Press, 2012).

[21] See Henry Stapp, *Mindful Universe: Quantum Mechanics and the Participating Observer* (New York: Springing Publications, 2007).

[22] See Friedrich Beck, "Synaptic Quantum Tunneling in Brain Activity", *NeuroQuantology* 6, no. 2 (2008): 140–51. See also Friedrich Beck and John C. Eccles, "Quantum Aspects of Brain Activity and the Role of Consciousness", *Proceedings of the National Academy of Sciences—USA* 89 (1992): 11357–61, and Friedrich Beck and John C. Eccles, "Quantum Processes in the Brain: A Scientific Basis of Consciousness", in *Neural Basis of Consciousness*, ed. Naoyuki Osaka (Philadelphia: John Benjamins, 2003), pp. 141–65.

of immaterial-material interaction through the mediation of quantum fields. Inasmuch as observation (immaterial input) can collapse a quantum wave function to an eigenstate (a state that can affect classical physical systems, such as biological systems in the brain), quantum fields may in fact mediate immaterial and material components of consciousness (see Chapter 6).[23]

The eminent physicist Roger Penrose and his medical colleague Stuart Hameroff [24] distinguish themselves from Stapp, Beck, and Eccles by using quantum theory to construct a *physicalist* model of consciousness. Unlike Stapp, Beck, and Eccles, Penrose and Hameroff do not seem to be aware of the fuller problem of human consciousness (e.g., Chalmers' hard problem of consciousness and the problem of conceptual ideas). They are, however, acutely aware of Gödel's enigma, and how this enigma suggests that human intelligence is beyond *any* set of deterministic rules or algorithms. They believe they have a solution for how the human brain (considered to be a *physical* entity alone) can transcend rules and algorithms through quantum activity (producing quantum computation) in brain microtubules. They theorize that quantum vibrations in the microtubules in brain neurons may account for the possibility of nondeterministic quantum computation in the brain. However, problems and gaps in their theory may compel them to look for a mindlike or conscious component in addition to physical systems.[25] (See Chapter 6.)

Neuroscientists (such as Mario Beauregard and Denyse O'Leary) have tried to make a case for "a spiritual brain" (i.e., a transphysical

---

[23] See Stapp, *Mindful Universe*.

[24] See Stuart Hameroff, "Quantum Computation in Brain Microtubules? The Penrose-Hameroff 'Orch OR' Model of Consciousness", *Philosophical Transactions Royal Society London* (A) 356 (1998): 1869–96, www.old.quantumconsciousness.org/penrose-hameroff /quantumcomputation.html. See also Roger Penrose and S.R. Hameroff, "What 'Gaps'? Reply to Grush and Churchland", *Journal of Consciousness Studies* 2, no. 2 (1995): 99–112; and Stuart Hameroff and Roger Penrose, "Orchestrated Reduction of Quantum Coherence in Brain Microtubules: A Model for Consciousness", in *Toward a Science of Consciousness—The First Tucson Discussions and Debates*, edited by S.R. Hameroff, A. Kaszniak, and A.C. Scott (Cambridge, Mass.: MIT Press, 1996), pp. 507–40; also published in *Mathematics and Computers in Simulation* 40 (1996): 453–80.

[25] Penrose and Hameroff have been criticized for making unexplained (and seemingly unjustified) leaps from quantum activity in brain microtubules (which is hypothetical) to quantum computation in the brain and then to man's self-consciousness. The difficulties with this theory are assessed in Chapter 6, Section I.

soul interacting with a physical brain) on the basis of near-death experiences applied to neuroscientific research[26] (see below, Section IV).

It would not be surprising to see the evidence of a transphysical
ground of consciousness from near-death experiences find a theoretical confluence with trialist interactionist theories (Eccles, Popper,
and Beck), nonreductionistic philosophies (Chalmers and Nagel),
orthodox interpretations of quantum theory (Stapp and Beck), and
quasi-dualistic neuroscientific theories (Beauregard and O'Leary). (I
have attempted to formulate a case and model for such a confluence
in Chapter 6.) It combines the trialist interactionist model of Eccles
with a hylomorphic model based on the physical and ontological theories of Michael Polanyi[27] and Bernard Lonergan.[28] This combined
model, which I term "hylomorphic trialist interactionism", is capable
of addressing five major areas of transphysical self-consciousness:

1. The survival of self-consciousness after bodily death implied by
   near-death experiences (see below in this chapter)
2. The transphysical nature of heuristic notions and conceptual
   ideas (see Chapter 3, Sections V.A. and V.B)
3. The transphysical nature of the horizon of complete intelligibility (see Chapter 3, Sections V.A and V.B)
4. The transphysical implications of Gödel's enigma (see Chapter 3,
   Section V.C)
5. The transphysical nature of the inwardness and self-apprehension
   of self-consciousness (Chalmers' hard problem of consciousness;
   see Chapter 6, Section III)

We may now proceed to the evidence of transphysical consciousness
from near-death experiences.

[26] See Mario Beauregard and Denyse O'Leary, *The Spiritual Brain: A Neuroscientist's Case for
the Existence of the Soul* (New York: HarperOne, 2008), and Mario Beauregard, *Brain Wars:
The Scientific Battle over the Existence of the Mind and the Proof That Will Change the Way We Live*
(New York: HarperOne, 2012).

[27] Michael Polanyi, "Life's Irreducible Structure", *Science* 160, no. 3834 (June 21, 1968):
1308–12; Michael Polanyi, *Being and Knowing* (London: Routledge and Kegan Paul, 1969);
Michael Polanyi, "Transcendence and Self-Transcendence", *Soundings* 53, no. 1 (1970): 88–94;
1970.

[28] Bernard Lonergan, *Insight: A Study of Human Understanding*, in *Collected Works of Bernard
Lonergan* 3, ed. Frederick E. Crowe and Robert M. Doran (Toronto: University of Toronto
Press, 1992), pp. 270–78.

II. Important Studies

The studies of Dr. Sam Parnia[29], Pim van Lommel,[30] Dr. Kenneth Ring and Evelyn Valarino,[31] Dr. Raymond Moody,[32] and Dr. Janice Holden[33] provide significant verifiable evidence of survival of man's consciousness after clinical death.[34] Dr. Bruce Greyson and Dr. Emily Kelly have made longitudinal studies of near-death phenomena (with control groups) at the University of Virginia's Division of Perceptual Studies (in the Department of Psychiatry in the School of Medicine), which is partially dedicated to the scientific study of near-death experiences.[35]

A. The Parnia-Southampton University Study

In 2014, scientists under the direction of Dr. Sam Parnia at Southampton University completed the largest study of near-death experiences. It was a four-year study of 2060 patients who had suffered cardiac arrest in hospitals in the United States, United Kingdom, and Austria. The researchers found that *9 percent* of the survivors (185 patients) had a *near-death experience* (NDE), though many more—an

[29] See Parnia et al., "AWAreness during REsuscitation".

[30] See van Lommel et al., "Near-Death Experience".

[31] See Kenneth Ring and Evelyn Elsaesser Valarino, *Lessons from the Light: What We Can Learn from the Near-Death Experience* (New York: Insight Books, 2006).

[32] Moody, *Life After Life*.

[33] See Janice Holden, "More Things in Heaven and Earth: A Response to Near-Death Experiences with Hallucinatory Features", *Journal of Near-Death Studies* 26, no. 1 (Fall 2007): 33–42.

[34] There are many other careful studies, which corroborate and extend their finding that are not explicitly discussed here but are important for readers interested in more extensive research. For example, see the following: T.K. Basford, *Near-Death Experiences: An Annotated Bibliography* (New York: Garland, 1990); P. Fenwick and E. Fenwick, *The Truth in the Light: An Investigation of Over 300 Near-Death Experiences* (New York: Berkley Books, 1995); B. Greyson and C.P. Flynn, eds., *The Near-Death Experience: Problems, Prospects, Perspectives* (Springfield, Ill.: Charles C. Thomas, 1984); G. Roberts and J. Owen, "The Near-Death Experience", *British Journal of Psychiatry* 153 (1988): 607–17; M.B. Sabom, *Recollections of Death: A Medical Investigation* (New York: Harper and Row, 1982); C. Zaleski, *Otherworld Journeys: Accounts of Near-Death Experience in Medieval and Modern Times* (Oxford: Oxford University Press, 1987).

[35] See the Department of Psychiatry and Neurobehavioral Sciences website at http:// www.medicine.virginia.edu/clinical/departments/psychiatry/sections/cspp/dops/case _types-pages#NDE.

additional 30 percent (618 patients)—had some sense of postmortem consciousness and feelings that did not meet the full description of an NDE (see above, Section I). Some of the patients (who had an NDE) maintained visual awareness for up to three minutes after cardiac arrest—long after the brain shuts down (which occurs twenty to thirty seconds after cardiac arrest).

This study advanced those of van Lommel, Ring, and Holden by taking account of experiential markers showing how long patients maintain awareness after clinical death (after electrical activity in the brain is almost completely absent). For example, a patient reported hearing two "bleeps" from a machine that sounds in three-minute intervals, revealing that he maintained awareness for more than three minutes after cardiac arrest. This patient was not only aware of sounds in the room but was also able to accurately report with heightened visual acuity what was going on in the operating room. The events reported were verified by researchers after resuscitation.[36]

B. The Van Lommel Study

The longitudinal study of near-death experiences by van Lommel and four researchers in Holland surveyed 344 cardiac patients who were successfully resuscitated after cardiac arrest in ten Dutch hospitals. It compared demographic, medical, pharmacological, and psychological data between patients who reported near-death experiences and patients who did not (controls) after resuscitation. It studied life changes after NDE and compared the groups two and eight years later.[37]

This study found that sixty-two adult patients (18 percent, roughly one out of every five) resuscitated from cardiac arrest experienced an NDE with some of the characteristics described above. No patients reported distressing or frightening NDEs. The 18 percent positive response does not necessarily mean that the others did not have an NDE. In fact, the researchers in the Parnia study believe that many of those who could not remember having an NDE may have been

[36] See Parnia et al., "AWAreness during REsuscitation".
[37] See van Lommel et al., "Near-Death Experience".

adversely affected by morphine or other medications administered during the resuscitation procedure.[38] There may be other mitigating factors such as age or prolonged CPR, and some may have been unwilling to recount it (for fear of being thought to be unbalanced). This percentage enabled the van Lommel researchers to conclude that the experiences associated with NDEs were *not* likely to have been caused by physiology alone: "With a purely physiological explanation such as cerebral anoxia for the experience, most patients who have been clinically dead should report one."[39] The researchers concluded from this that

> our most striking finding was that Near-Death Experiences do not have a physical or medical root. After all, 100 percent of the patients suffered a shortage of oxygen, 100 percent were given morphine-like medications, 100 percent were victims of severe stress, so those are plainly not the reasons why 18 per cent had Near-Death Experiences and 82 percent didn't. If they had been triggered by any one of those things, everyone would have had Near-Death Experiences.[40]

Van Lommel's rationale does not conclusively rule out a physiological explanation of near-death experiences, because there might be other physical factors beyond those mentioned in his study. However, when van Lommel's rationale is combined with the three kinds of verifiable evidence (discussed in Section III below), it virtually rules out the possibility of a purely physiological explanation of near-death experiences, indicating the survival of one's consciousness after clinical death.

Of the sixty-two patients reporting an NDE, all of them experienced some of the following ten characteristics, according to the following distribution:

1. Awareness of being dead (50 percent)
2. Positive emotions (56 percent)
3. Out-of-body experience (24 percent)
4. Moving through a tunnel (31 percent)

[38] See Parnia et al., "AWAreness during REsuscitation".
[39] Van Lommel et al., "Near-Death Experience", p. 2039.
[40] Ibid., p. 2044.

5. Communication with light (23 percent)
6. Observation of colors (23 percent)
7. Observation of a celestial landscape (29 percent)
8. Meeting with deceased persons (32 percent)
9. Life review (13 percent)
10. Presence of border (8 percent)[41]

This study also reported corroborative veridical out-of-body experiences. These experiences enabled patients to have sensorial knowledge, which they were not able to have through their physical bodies. In other words, if these patients had not been in an "out-of-body" state, they would never have been able to experience the data they accurately reported.

The corroborated veridical sensorial knowledge by both sighted and blind patients is very significant because there does not appear to be any physical explanation for these corroborated phenomena, leading to the conclusion that there must be some form of nonphysical conscious existence (including self-consciousness, memory, intelligence, and self-identity). Van Lommel and his team conclude as follows:

> How could a clear consciousness outside one's body be experienced at the moment that the brain no longer functions during a period of clinical death with flat EEG? ... Furthermore, blind people have described veridical perception during out-of-body experiences at the time of this experience. NDE pushes at the limits of medical ideas about the range of human consciousness and the mind-brain relation. In our prospective study of patients that were clinically dead (flat EEG, showing no electrical activity in the cortex and loss of brain stem function evidenced by fixed dilated pupils and absence of the gag reflex) the patients report a clear consciousness, in which cognitive functioning, emotion, sense of identity, or memory from early childhood occurred, as well as perceptions from a position out and above their "dead" body.[42]

Notice that van Lommel's study indicates that blind people see during clinical death. This finding is corroborated in greater detail by Dr. Kenneth Ring and his team (see below, Section II.C).

[41] Ibid., p. 2041.
[42] Ibid., p. 2045.

C. Dr. Kenneth Ring's Studies of the Blind

Ring, Cooper, and Tart,[43] also reported in Ring and Valarino,[44] focused their research on near-death experiences of the blind. Ring, Cooper, and Tart studied thirty-one blind patients (twenty-one of whom had a near-death experience, and ten of whom had out-of-body experiences only). Of these thirty-one, fourteen were blind from birth and evidently had no experience of seeing, and seventeen had some experience of seeing *in the past* (though they were blind at the time of their near-death experience or out-of-body experience). Ring summarizes his findings as follows:

> Among those narrating NDEs, not only did their experiences conform to the classic NDE pattern, but they did not even vary according to the specific sight status of our respondents; that is, whether an NDEr was born blind or had lost his or her sight in later life, or even (as in a few of our cases) had some minimal light perception only, the NDEs described were much the same. Furthermore, **80 percent** of our thirty-one blind respondents claimed to be able to see during their NDEs or OBEs, and, like Vicki and Brad, often told us that they could see objects and persons in the physical world, as well as features of otherworldly settings.[45]

Ring, Cooper, and Tart also found that the quality of perception was quite high among the majority of blind patients who reported seeing during their near-death experience:

> How well do our respondents find they can see during these episodes? We have, of course, already noted that the visual perceptions of Vicki and Brad were extremely clear and detailed, especially when they found themselves in the otherworldly portion of their near-death journey. While not all of our blind NDErs had clear, articulated visual impressions, nevertheless enough of them did, so that we can conclude that cases like Vicki's and Brad's are quite representative in this regard.[46]

[43] See Ring, Cooper, and Tart, *Mindsight*.
[44] See Ring and Valarino, *Lessons from the Light*.
[45] Ibid., p. 81.
[46] Ibid.

What about the 20 percent who reported that they could not remember themselves seeing? There are two explanations: (1) they did not, in fact see anything during their near-death experience, or (2) even though they seem to have had some kind of perception, they did not recognize it as "seeing". Ring comments about the latter phenomenon with respect to one of his patients as follows: "As one man, whom we classified as a nonvisualizer, confessed, because 'I don't know what you mean by seeing,' he was at a loss to explain how he had the perceptions he was aware of during his NDE."[47] This study is particularly important because there is no physical explanation for the phenomenon described by it. The sight of these patients was completely impaired or almost completely impaired—*in their physical bodies*. Thus the only explanation for their sight would seem to be the capacity for visual perception in their *transphysical* state. This requires their continued existence after bodily death.

D. The Moody Study and Its Consistency of Data with Ring and Van Lommel

In 1975, Dr. Raymond Moody wrote his first study of near-death experiences entitled *Life After Life*.[48] It was based on more than one hundred case studies, but left several questions unanswered while revealing the need for a more sophisticated longitudinal study. Between 1975 and 1988, he completed that study after interviewing more than one thousand patients who had had a near-death experience. He noticed that patients having near-death experiences reported having one or more of the following nine characteristics:

1. A sense of being dead
2. Peace and painlessness
3. The tunnel experience
4. People of light
5. The Being of Light
6. The life review

[47] Ibid.
[48] Raymond A. Moody, *Life After Life*.

7. Rising rapidly into the heavens
8. Reluctance to return
9. Out-of-body experiences or different time and place[49]

Moody's findings closely correlate with Ring's and van Lommel's. Ring divides his study into five *stages* of near-death experiences, while van Lommel divides his findings into ten *features* of near-death experiences. Ring's stages are as follows:[50]

1. Peace	60 percent
2. Bodily separation	37 percent
3. Darkness or tunnel	23 percent
4. Light or beings of light	16 percent
5. Inner setting or paradise	10 percent

Notice the correlation with van Lommel's features:[51]

1. Awareness of being dead	50 percent	(not reported by Ring)
2. Positive emotions	56 percent	(compared to Ring's 60 percent for what he describes as "peace")
3. Out-of-body experience	24 percent	(compared with 37 percent in Ring's study)
4. Moving through a tunnel	31 percent	(compared with 23 percent in Ring's study)
5. Communication with light	23 percent	(compared with 16 percent in Ring's study)
6. Observation of colors	23 percent	(not reported by Ring)
7. Observation of a celestial landscape	29 percent	(compared with 10 percent in Ring's study)

[49]Raymond A. Moody, *Light Beyond*, pp. 7–20.

[50]Kenneth Ring, *Life at Death: A Scientific Investigation of Near-Death Experience* (New York: William Morrow, 1980), p. 145.

[51]Van Lommel et al., "Near-Death Experience", p. 2041.

8. Meeting with deceased persons	32 percent	(not reported by Ring, but reported by Moody[52])
9. Life review	13 percent	(not reported by Ring)
10. Presence of border	8 percent	(not reported by Ring)

Evidently, the larger, more longitudinal study of Dutch patients experienced the tunnel, being or beings of light, and celestial land-scapes more often than the smaller, less longitudinal, American group, while the American group experienced out-of-body survival more often. The differences in the data may be explained by the fact that most patients only experienced *some* of the above-mentioned features of near-death experiences.

E. Dr. Janice Holden's Assessment of Thirty-Nine NDE Studies

Dr. Janice Holden made a compendium of 107 cases in thirty-nine studies by thirty-seven authors in 2007[53] in which veridical (verifiable) experiences were reported. Christopher Carter writes about her conclusions as follows:

> Using the most stringent criterion—that a case would be classified as inaccurate if even one detail was found to not correspond to reality— Holden found that only 8 percent involved some inaccuracy. In contrast, 37 percent of the cases—almost five times as many—were determined to be accurate by an independent objective source, such as the investigation of researchers reporting the cases.[54]

The other 55 percent did not involve inaccuracies, but could not be completely independently verified by other sources. Therefore, of the 48 cases (45 percent of Holden's sample) qualifying as veridical (an unusual or unique report corroborated by an independent source),

---

[52] Moody's study is significant because it indicates how patients were transformed by these encounters with departed loved ones. See Moody, *Reunions*.

[53] Holden, "Response to Near-Death Experiences", pp. 33–42.

[54] Christopher Carter, *Science and the Near-Death Experience: How Consciousness Survives Death* (Rochester, Vt.: Inner Traditions, 2010), p. 217.

8 cases (17 percent) had some inaccuracy while 40 cases (83 percent) were reported completely accurately (using the strictest criteria).

It is difficult to believe that this degree of verifiably accurate reporting which occurred at a time when there was no electrical activity in the cortex can be attributed to a physical or physiological cause.

In view of this fact, as well as the fact that many of the reported incidents reached beyond bodily capabilities of the patient, it is not unreasonable to conclude that these perceptions (as well as the self-consciousness that accompanied them) existed independently of bodily function and could therefore persist after bodily death.

III. Three Kinds of Verifiable Evidence

There are three ways of verifying the transphysical nature of near-death experience reports:

1. Veridical reported data (all major longitudinal studies)[55]
2. Visual perception of the blind (primarily Ring and van Lommel)
3. Personal information about deceased individuals[56]

As will be seen since each of these kinds of evidence can be verified by independent researchers after the fact, and all of them are

---

[55] Explored in all fourteen studies mentioned in this chapter: Parnia et al., "AWAreness during REsuscitation"; van Lommel et al., "Near-Death Experience"; Ring and Valarino, *Lessons from the Light*; Holden, "Response to Near-Death Experiences"; Basford, *Near-Death Experiences*; Fenwick and Fenwick, *Truth in the Light*; Greyson and Flynn, *Near-Death Experience*; Roberts and Owen, "Near-Death Experience"; Sabom, *Recollections of Death*; Zaleski, *Otherworld Journeys*; Moody, *Light Beyond*; Bruce Greyson, "Seeing Dead People Not Known to Have Died: 'Peak in Darien' Experiences", American Anthropological Association, November 21, 2010, http://onlinelibrary.wiley.com/doi/10.1111/j.1548-1409.2010.01064.x /abstract; E. W. Cook, B. Greyson, and I. Stevenson, "Do Any Near-Death Experiences Provide Evidence for the Survival of Human Personality After Death? Relevant Features and Illustrative Case Reports", *Journal of Scientific Exploration* 12 (1998): 377–406; E. W. Kelly, B. Greyson, and I. Stevenson, "Can Experiences Near Death Furnish Evidence of Life After Death?" *Omega: Journal of Death and Dying* 40 (2000): 39–45.

[56] Primarily the following: Greyson, "Seeing Dead People"; Pim van Lommel, *Consciousness beyond Life* (New York: HarperOne, 2010); Moody, *Reunions*; Cook, Greyson, Stevenson, "Do Any Near-Death Experiences Provide Evidence?"; Kelly, Greyson, and Stevenson, "Can Experiences Near Death Furnish Evidence?"

exceedingly difficult (if not impossible) to explain by merely physical or physiological theories (such as hallucinations, anoxia, narcotics, etc.), it is highly likely that they have a transphysical cause (see Section IV). We will examine each kind of evidence and then assess the combined data.

A. Reported Veridical Data

Frequently during near-death experiences, the transphysical component leaves the body but does not go immediately to an otherworldly domain. Instead, it remains in the resuscitation room or in close or remote proximity to the body. As noted above, this transphysical component is self-conscious, and can see, hear, and remember. Its memories can be recalled after patients return to their bodies. Some of these reports have highly unusual or unique characteristics that are not part of ordinary resuscitation or hospital procedures. Many of these reports can be verified by independent researchers after patients return to their bodies. When all of these conditions have been met, and the unusual accounts have been verified to be 100 percent accurate, they are termed "veridical". Virtually every peer-reviewed study reports multiple instances of such veridical data. The following cases typify a much larger array of reports, many of which have been assessed by Dr. Janice Holden (see above Section II.E).

In the Pim van Lommel study discussed above (see Section II.B), one man who had been in a deep coma later told a nurse that he recognized her and saw where she had placed his dentures during resuscitation efforts, and he even described the cart into which she placed them.[57] They were there, precisely as he described it.

Melvin Morse and Kim Clark report that a woman had knowledge of a shoe on a window ledge outside the hospital (not near the room where the patient was resuscitated, but next to a third-floor office where she was being interviewed). The psychologist who did the interview (Kim Clark) had to crawl along the ledge outside her window to verify the claim. The shoe was indeed there, precisely as

[57]Van Lommel et al., "Near-Death Experience", p. 2042.

the patient had described it.[58] Though the shoe could have been seen from a window, the detail with which the NDE patient described it could not have been detected from that window (a worn little toe, a shoelace beneath the heel). Clark concluded that "the only way she [the patient] could have had such a perspective was if she had been floating right outside and at very close range to the tennis shoe. I retrieved the shoe and brought it back to Maria; it was very concrete evidence for me."[59]

Raymond Moody also reports similar veridical out-of-body experiences,[60] the most frequent of which are people who leave the operating room (after seeing the resuscitation efforts going on) and visit their relatives and friends in hospital waiting rooms (literally moving through walls). One patient reported seeing her young daughter wearing mismatched plaids (which was highly unusual and only knowable if she had actually been in the waiting room). Another woman overheard her brother-in-law talking to a business associate in the hospital waiting room in a very derogatory manner and was able to report this back to him later.

These veridical experiences are evidenced in every major study and help to corroborate the authenticity of the patients' claims to have been in an out-of-body state (with sensorial capabilities). These findings have been corroborated by many other studies, and the results have been correlated by Dr. Janice Holden (see Section II.E above), using the strictest criteria to determine the accuracy of those cases. She found that only 8 percent of patients reporting veridical data (who experienced unusual or unique occurrences during clinical death and corroborated by an independent source) had some degree of inaccuracy. Thirty-seven percent were reported perfectly accurately, while 55 percent did not qualify as veridical.

These findings lend considerable probative force to the survival of human consciousness after bodily death, because they cannot be explained by physical causation. They apparently require a capacity to see and hear independently of the physical body, which cannot be explained by a physical model alone (such as hallucination arising

---

[58] Melvin Morse, *Closer to the Light: Learning from the Near-Death Experiences of Children* (New York: Random House, 1990), p. 20.

[59] Kim Clark, "Clinical Interventions with Near-Death Experiencers", in *Near-Death Experience*, ed. Greyson and Flynn, p. 243.

[60] Moody, *Light Beyond*, pp. 17–20.

out of narcotics, oxygen deprivation, revival of brain cells and neural functions). Such hallucinatory activity would be random and sporadic while the reports of patients correspond precisely to empirical data verified after the fact.

B. Visual Perception of the Blind during Clinical Death

As noted above, van Lommel (Section II.B) and Ring, Cooper, and Tart (Section II.C) did focused studies on the near-death experiences of the blind. These patients (most whom were blind from birth) were able to see (most for the first time) during their near-death experience. These accounts show that patients who do not have the physical capacity to see report visual data accurately about their experiences during clinical death. Some of this data is veridical (highly unusual and therefore difficult to guess).[61]

As noted above, Ring found that 80 percent of blind people had visual perception during clinical death, and that these perceptions were clear and accurate. Even though 20 percent of those in the study could not remember or understand themselves seeing, the 80 percent who *were* able to report sensorial knowledge were accurately reporting what they could not have seen with their physical bodies. Given the insurmountable difficulties of explaining this phenomenon physically (hallucinations, narcotics, oxygen deprivation, and so on; see below, Section IV), it corroborates the likelihood of transphysical existence after clinical death. Furthermore, it shows the possibility of *transphysical* causes, not only of consciousness, but also of vision, hearing, and memory. No adequate physical explanation has been offered for the visual perception of the blind during clinical death (see below, Section IV).

C. Meeting Deceased Persons in a Transphysical Domain

Many patients undergoing clinical death are moved from the physical world to an otherworldly or heavenly domain. Some of them see themselves crossing a border into a beautiful paradise in which many are greeted by deceased relatives or friends, Jesus, or a loving

---

[61] See Ring, Cooper, and Tart, *Mindsight*, and Ring and Valarino, *Lessons from the Light*, pp. 80–82.

white light. Some patients may experience two or more of these phenomena. Some patients who are greeted by deceased relatives do not recognize them because they died before the patient was born. They often introduce themselves and reveal facts about themselves that the patients' relatives or friends are subsequently able to verify. Though this kind of evidence is not veridical (because it can't be corroborated as occurring during a patient's clinical death by an independent source), it has probative circumstantial value, particularly because it occurs in so many different cases of near-death experiences.

As cited previously, Raymond Moody has written a book on these experiences entitled *Reunions: Visionary Encounters with Departed Loved Ones*. It has also been studied by Dr. Jeffery Long[62] and van Lommel,[63] all of whom show patients' knowledge of facts about or from deceased relatives and friends not formerly known. Dr. Bruce Greyson has made a detailed study of these cases in his work entitled "Seeing Dead People Not Known to Have Died: 'Peak in Darien' Experiences". His colleague Dr. Emily Kelly at the Division of Perceptual Studies (University of Virginia) gives a careful report of their research in her article entitled "Near-Death Experiences with Reports of Meeting Deceased People".[64] This article arose out of two previous studies (the Cook, Greyson, and Stevenson study,[65] and the study by Kelly, Greyson, and Stevenson[66]). These researchers found that out of 553 cases of people reporting near-death experiences, 13 percent experienced a deceased relative or friend (a lower statistic than the 37 percent reported by Fenwick and Fenwick[67]). Most of these individuals reported seeing deceased *relatives* (and only 5 percent reported seeing deceased friends). Most of them were from a previous generation (parents or grandparents). Several individuals reported seeing a

---

[62] See Jeffery Long, *Evidence of the Afterlife* (New York: HarperOne, 2010), Chapter 8.

[63] See van Lommel, *Consciousness beyond Life*, pp. 310–19.

[64] Emily Kelly, "Near-Death Experiences with Reports of Meeting Deceased People", *Death Studies* 25 (2001): 229–49, http://www.medicine.virginia.edu/clinical/departments/psychiatry/sections/cspp/dops/emily-kelly-pdfs/KEL13%20NDEwithReports%20of%20Meeting%20Deceased%20People.pdf/view.

[65] Cook, Greyson, and Stevenson, "Do Any Near-Death Experiences Provide Evidence?", pp. 377–406.

[66] Kelly, Greyson, and Stevenson, "Can Experiences Near Death Furnish Evidence?", pp. 39–45.

[67] Fenwick and Fenwick, *Truth in the Light*, p. 163.

religious figure, usually Jesus, and several also reported seeing unrecognized figures along with relatives.[68]

One of the more important findings among these studies was the large number of patients who reported seeing people who were not close or even known. This finding militates against the hallucinatory expectation hypothesis—that dying individuals project an image of deceased loved ones whom they would want to see in the afterlife. Kelly notes in this regard:

> Although most people identified were emotionally close relatives, there were nonetheless a substantial number (32%) of people seen who were emotionally neutral or distant or whom the participant had never met. Many participants commented that seeing these people was unexpected and a "surprise." The expectation hypothesis seems a bit strained when we try to account for these numerous instances in which the deceased person was not someone the participant would particularly care about seeing.... Furthermore, even among those participants who did see a loved one, the person seen was not always one whom the participant would presumably most expect or want to see.[69]

When this is combined with the disclosure of information not previously known from deceased people,[70] it suggests that clinically dead individuals encounter deceased people who are not a projection of wishful expectations. Though this kind of evidence is not as strong as veridical evidence (see Section III.A), and the visual perception of blind people during clinical death (see Section III.B), it provides another clue to a transphysical ground of consciousness and human existence.

IV. Response to Physicalist Explanations

Before responding to physicalists' explanations, it may be helpful to briefly summarize the four kinds of evidence for transphysical consciousness after clinical (bodily) death:

[68] Kelly, "Near-Death Experiences", pp. 238–39.
[69] Ibid., p. 244.
[70] In Greyson, "Seeing Dead People"; van Lommel, *Consciousness beyond Life*; and Moody, *Reunions*.

1. Remarkable consistency surrounding ten features of the experience, seven of which are *unique* to near-death experiences, two of which are shared with physical embodiment (positive emotions, and visual or auditory perception), and one of which is shared with out-of-body experiences (seeing one's body from above)—in all 14 studies cited in Sections II and III above[71]

2. Corroborated, veridical, sensorial knowledge by patients who were unconscious (more than thirty seconds after cardiac arrest)—in all 14 studies cited in Sections II and III above

3. Corroborated, veridical, sensorial knowledge by *blind* patients who were unconscious (primarily Ring, Cooper, and Tart, *Mindsight*; Ring and Valarino, *Lessons from the Light*; and van Lommel, "Near-Death Experience")

4. Reports of encounters with deceased people who were unexpected or unknown, and reports of unknown information disclosed by deceased people (primarily Greyson, "Seeing Dead People"; van Lommel, *Consciousness beyond Life*; Moody, *Reunions*; Cook, Greyson, and Stevenson, "Do Any Near-Death Experiences Provide Evidence?"; and Kelly, Greyson, and Stevenson, "Can Experiences Near Death Furnish Evidence?")

As we shall see, physicalist explanations of near-death experiences do not (and probably cannot) explain these combined phenomena. Though they can explain how a hallucination might be possible during clinical death, they do not explain how people can accurately report empirical data, how the blind can see, and how people can acquire previously unknown information about deceased individuals during the time of clinical death. A brief examination of the six major physicalist explanations will make this clear.

As noted above, several physicians and neuroscientists have tried to explain near-death experiences by making recourse to hallucinations and other possible physical triggers. Dr. Mario Beauregard, neuroscientist at the University of Arizona, has responded to these

---

[71] See Parnia, "AWAreness during Resuscitation"; van Lommel et al., "Near-Death Experience"; Ring et al., *Lessons from the Light*; Moody, *Life After Life*; Holden, "More Things in Heaven and Earth".

physicalist explanations in his recent book, *Brain Wars*.[72] His findings and responses have been verified by the Parnia study that concludes that known physical explanations do not account for visual awareness, clarity of thought, and positive emotions associated with NDEs.[73] The following is a brief summary of some of Beauregard's responses excerpted from that book.[74]

Perhaps the most famous physicalist explanation of OBEs (out-of-body experiences) was proposed by Olaf Blanke in 2002,[75] which received an accolade from the journal *Nature* claiming that Blanke's research discovered the part of the brain in which OBEs are induced. Blanke and his team placed electrodes in the angular gyrus of the parietal lobe, which triggered an "OBE-like" experience in a forty-three-year-old patient with epilepsy. She claimed that she had left her body, but could only see the lower half—her legs and lower trunk. As the experience progressed, she perceived her legs to be getting shorter and shorter.[76] In 2004 Blanke and his team reported that they had induced an atypical and partial OBE in three patients and autoscopy in four patients, in which the patient perceives a double from the vantage point of her physical body.[77]

Beauregard responds to this with van Lommel's critique—first, Blanke's stimulations of the parietal lobe produce *abnormal* bodily experiences; second, these abnormal experiences give rise to a *false* sense of reality[78] (e.g., legs growing shorter and seeing body doubles). These experiences are *illusory* whereas typical OBEs are not illusory. Patients leave their bodies and see (and accurately remember and report) what is going on inside the operating room and how their physical bodies are situated relative to the people, events, and instruments in that room. Greyson adds to van Lommel's criticism by noting that if we accept Blanke's stimulations as typifying an OBE,

---

[72] Mario Beauregard, *Brain Wars: The Scientific Battle over the Existence of the Mind and the Proof That Will Change the Way We Live* (New York: HarperOne, 2012).

[73] See Parnia et al., "AWAreness during REsuscitation", pp. 40–47.

[74] See Mario Beauregard, "Near Death, Explained", *Salon*, April 21, 2012, http://www.salon.com/2012/04/21/near_death_explained.

[75] Helen Pearson, "Electrodes Trigger Out of Body Experience", *Nature*, September 19, 2002, www.nature.com/news/2002/020916/full/news020916-8.html.

[76] See ibid.

[77] See ibid.

[78] See ibid.

we would be constrained to think that OBEs are illusions; but as we have seen throughout this chapter, there is nothing illusory about them—they give accurate descriptions of verifiable data almost all the time (only 8 percent minor inaccuracies, according to Holden; see Section III.A).

Beauregard then turns to Susan Blackmore's hypothesis that anoxia (oxygen deprivation in the dying brain) could lead to the firing of neurons responsible for visual perception, possibly leading to an experience of a white light at the end of a tunnel.[79] Beauregard responds first with van Lommel's criticism—that 100 percent of dying people suffer from anoxia; so if anoxia is the cause of near-death experiences, 100 percent of patients should have them (but in fact only 18 percent of adults do).[80] Furthermore, the studies of Sam Parnia show that several people have had near-death experiences while feeling well—and therefore not suffering from anoxia.[81]

Beauregard also looks into James Whinnery's hypothesis that "dreamlets" are a possible explanation of NDEs.[82] "Dreamlets" occur in the stressed brain (e.g., of a fighter pilot) immediately prior to unconsciousness. This does not seem to be a plausible explanation of NDEs because Whinnery's research indicates that these individuals wake up confused and anxious—instead of having lucid recollections and positive life-transforming experiences.[83]

Beauregard then turns to the hypothesis of narcotically induced hallucination as a possible explanation of NDEs. Researcher Karl Jansen conjectured that he could produce an NDE by inhibiting NMDA receptors (by ingesting small quantities of ketamine, a veterinary anesthetic).[84] Though this did induce a sense of being out of body, the images in the hallucination were "weird" and perspectives were exaggerated.[85] In contrast to this, patients having a near-death

---

[79] See Blackmore, *Dying to Live*, pp. 49–62.

[80] See van Lommel et al., "Near-Death Experience", p. 2044.

[81] Sam Parnia, *Erasing Death: The Science That Is Rewriting the Boundaries between Life and Death* (New York: Harper Collins, 2014), pp. 159–60.

[82] See Beauregard, "Near Death, Explained", p. 3. See also Edward Kelly, Adam Crabtree, and E. W. Kelly, *Irreducible Mind: Toward a Psychology for the 21st Century* (Lanham, Md.: Rowman & Littlefield, 2007), pp. 379–80.

[83] See ibid.

[84] Karl Jansen, "Response to Commentaries on 'The Ketamine Model of Near-Death Experience'", in *Journal of Near-Death Studies* 16 (1997): 79–95.

[85] See Beauregard, "Near Death, Explained", p. 3.

experience perceive their surroundings in precisely the way they exist, for example, inside the operating room (many of these perceptions have been verified by independent researchers after the fact; see above Section III.A).

Another recent explanation has been offered by neuroscientist Michael Persinger, who proposes that he, too, can stimulate an NDE by using weak transcranial magnetic stimulation (TMS) of the temporal lobes.[86] Beauregard, citing Greyson and the literature of epilepsy, shows that NDEs do not resemble the psychic states experienced by epileptic patients, and that transcranial stimulation of the temporal lobes does not result in experiences similar to NDEs, but rather in the psychic states associated with epilepsy.[87]

In 2013 (after Beauregard's book), Jimo Borjigin proposed another possible physicalist explanation for NDEs. During his experiments with rats, he discovered that a surge of electrical activity occurred in the brain (which he hypothesized *might* produce consciousness and an image) when rats experienced cardiac arrest.[88] This hypothesis is not on the same level as the ones mentioned above for three reasons: (1) it was restricted to rats (not humans), (2) there is no evidence that the electrical surge in the brain produced either consciousness or an image, and (3) even if there were evidence that it produced consciousness and an image, there is no evidence that this consciousness-image resembles near-death or out-of-body experiences. In short, this hypothesis does not give researchers *anything* to compare to NDEs or OBEs—it is a pure speculation without an identifiable frame of comparison, meaning that it does not yet qualify as a scientific hypothesis.

At the present time, neuroscience is not able to generate a credible physical explanation for the verified out-of-body phenomena in near-death experiences. There is reason to believe that such explanations will never be able to do this. First, there is a radical discontinuity between those experiencing NDEs and those experiencing physically induced illusory states (e.g., in the studies of Blanke,[89] Whinnery,[90]

[86] See ibid. See also Kelly, Crabtree, and Kelly, *Irreducible Mind*, p. 383.

[87] Ibid., pp. 3–4.

[88] Jimo Borjigin, "Surge of Neurophysiological Coherence and Connectivity in the Dying Brain", *Journal Proceedings of the National Academy of Sciences*, August 2013.

[89] See Pearson, "Electrodes Trigger Out of Body Experience"; and Beauregard, "Near Death, Explained".

[90] See Kelly, Crabtree, and Kelly, *Irreducible Mind*, pp. 379–80; and Beauregard, "Near Death, Explained".

Jansen,[91] and Persinger[92]). The former group (NDEs) has no electrical activity in the cerebral cortex (marked by a flat EEG) and
virtually no electrical activity in the lower brain (fixed and dilated
pupils and absence of gag reflex). However, the latter group (physically stimulated illusions) has both a functioning cortex and lower
brain. Susan Blackmore presents the only case of a "dying brain",
in which electrical activity is being diminished because of anoxia.
Though this hypothesis resembles the diminished electrical activity
in the brain during clinical death, it falls prey to both van Lommel's
criticism (since 100 percent of dying people experience anoxia, 100
percent should have a near-death experience if anoxia is the cause
of NDEs), and Parnia's criticism (there are patients who have NDEs
without anoxia).

The second major difference between NDEs and physically stimulated illusion (PSI) is that the latter do not resemble the former. Blanke's
PSI gives rise to abnormal bodily experiences and a false sense of
reality (instead of a clear and accurate perception of reality and one's
place in it);[93] Whinnery's PSI gives rise to a state of confusion and
anxiousness in its aftermath (instead of clarity and lifelong positive
transformation). Jensen's narcotically induced hallucination gives
rise to false and weird images and exaggerated perspectives (unlike
NDEs), and Persinger's PSI gives rise to psychic states associated with
epilepsy (which are quite distinct from those associated with NDEs).

The third major difference between NDEs and physicalist explanations concerns the accurate veridical experience of both sighted
and blind people during clinical death. There is no evidence of this
occurring during anoxia or any of the above PSI phenomena. Even
if PSIs could produce these effects, it would *not* prove that those
effects had their origin in physical reality *alone* (i.e., that there is no
transphysical dimension of consciousness). Indeed, there *must be* such
a transphysical dimension of consciousness so that clinically dead
individuals can accurately see and hear apart from and above their

[91] See Jansen, "The Ketamine Model of Near-Death Experience", pp. 79–95; and Beauregard, "Near Death, Explained".

[92] See Kelly, Crabtree, and Kelly, *Irreducible Mind*, p. 383; and Beauregard, "Near Death,
Explained".

[93] See Beauregard, "Near Death, Explained"; and Pearson, "Electrodes Trigger Out of
Body Experience".

physical bodies. PSIs have certainly not given a *physical* explanation of how clinically dead individuals can see and hear apart from their physical bodies. Thus, even if PSIs could produce the effects of NDEs (which they are currently unable to do), it would only show that they had caused a *trans*physical state of consciousness to occur—a state of consciousness that can accurately see and hear apart from and above a clinically dead physical body. If PSIs could produce the same effect as NDEs, it would only serve to show that stimulation of the brain caused a *separation* of a *trans*physical dimension of consciousness from the physical body—it would not disprove the existence of that transphysical dimension.

In sum, it is highly unlikely that physicalist explanations will ever be able to account for this last line of reasoning because it would require them to prove that merely physical phenomena can have unmistakably transphysical effects—which is at best a contradiction. Physicalist explanations per se are limited to showing how physical causes produce *physical* effects—nothing more. Therefore, the physicalists will have to either open the door to transphysical explanation or leave the explanation of near-death experiences to those who are open to the transphysical domain.

V. Near-Death Experiences, Love, and Resurrection

As we have seen, there is considerable evidence of survival of human consciousness after clinical death, implying a transphysical dimension of human nature and a transphysical origin of consciousness. However, it does not show that this transphysical dimension of consciousness is *eternal*. Nevertheless, there are some *clues* that this transphysical condition is eternal—for example, the love and benevolence of the white light as well as the love of Jesus and deceased relatives and friends, which seem to betoken the intention of a loving Deity to fulfill our greatest desire, namely, unconditional love and joy with that Deity throughout eternity. This last point deserves special consideration because in every instance of an encounter with the "being of light" in all of the above studies, patients reported the experience to be one of intense love. The following case resembles hundreds of others reported by the above researchers:

I became very weak, and I fell down. I began to feel a sort of drifting, a movement of my real being in and out of my body, and to hear beautiful music. I floated on down the hall and out the door onto the screened-in porch. There, it almost seemed that clouds, a pink mist really, began to gather around me, and then I floated right straight on through the screen, just as though it weren't there, and up into this pure crystal clear light, an illuminating white light. It was beautiful and so bright, so radiant, but it didn't hurt my eyes. It's not any kind of light you can describe on earth. I didn't actually see a person in this light, and yet it has a special identity, it definitely does. It is a light of perfect understanding and perfect love.... And all during this time, I felt as though I was surrounded by an overwhelming love and compassion.[94]

This experience of overwhelming love by those who encountered the "being of light" may legitimately provoke the intuition that this being's intention is not only *transitory* benevolence, but to give unconditional and *eternal* love—which corresponds to the fulfillment of our greatest desire.

Furthermore, the reports about the loving being of light, the presence of Jesus, the love and joy of the deceased, and the presence of a paradise closely parallel the revelation and Resurrection of Jesus Christ, and this revelation does indicate the intention of an unconditionally loving God to bestow an *eternal* life of love upon all who are willing to accept and abide by that love.

Moving from the domain of empirically verifiable data to the domain of Christian revelation might seem to be stretching too far, but the close parallels between both approaches to life after death may reveal a justifiable complementarity worth investigating. The empirical investigation of transphysical survival (from near-death experiences) corroborates and complements the historical investigation of Jesus' Resurrection and revelation,[95] and vice versa. Each approach has its own distinct methodology and source of evidence, but they find a confluence in three areas.

[94] Moody, *Life After Life*, pp. 53–54.

[95] See the following studies that use the latest historical-critical method for approaching the validity of accounts of Jesus' Resurrection: N.T. Wright, *The Resurrection of the Son of God* (Minneapolis, Minn.: Fortress Press, 2003); Robert B. Stewart, ed., *The Resurrection of Jesus: John Dominic Crossan and N.T. Wright in Dialogue* (Minneapolis, Minn.: Fortress Press, 2006), particularly Gary R. Habermas, "Mapping the Recent Trend Toward the Bodily Resurrection Appearances of Jesus in Light of Other Prominent Positions", pp. 78–92. See also Volume III, Chapter 4 of this Quartet.

First, we will continue to possess some elements of our embodiment after physical death (e.g., vision, hearing, extendedness, and a recognizable bodily form). The transphysical features enable the deceased to transcend physical laws and structures (e.g., to pass through walls, to go upward, to move to a transphysical domain, etc.). Though there are some similarities between the descriptions of postmortem embodiment (reported in near-death experiences) and Jesus' glorified body (reported by Saint Paul and the Gospels),[96] Jesus' glorified body goes far beyond human postmortem embodiment; it is transformed and glorious—Godlike (see Volume III, Chapter 4). The ethereal embodiment in near-death experiences is more "ghostlike" and not really glorious or divine. According to Christian revelation, our bodies will be like that of Jesus (transformed in glory) when we reach the fullness of our salvation in the heavenly kingdom (see 1 Cor 15:49).

Second, the essence of eternal life is love (both the capacity to love and to receive the love of others). This is the central part of Jesus' revelation and is manifest in near-death experiences by the loving white light (associated with God), the love of Jesus, and the love and joy of deceased relatives.

Third, there is a dimension of beauty, joy, and paradise in many accounts of near-death experiences as well as Christian revelation (see Volume III, Chapter 4 of this Quartet). When we put the two sources of evidence together, they complement each other. Near-death experiences give *directly corroborateable evidence* of a transphysical life that the Resurrection appearances cannot give (since they are historically remote). Alternatively, the Resurrection and revelation of Jesus show that this transphysical life is *eternal, glorious,* and destined for *unconditional* love and joy. When this is combined with the seven dimensions of our transcendent nature (discussed in Chapters 1–4), they converge upon a single conclusion: that we are created by an unconditionally loving Deity who calls us to an eternal life of unconditional love through an invitation embedded in our psyches. In view of this convergence, we will want to look more closely at the revelation of Jesus—not only about the unconditional love of God, but about our eternal destiny and the path to reach it. We will take this up in Volume III of this Quartet.

[96] See, for example: Lk 24:37, Mt 28:17, Jn 20:19–20, 1 Cor 15:42–50. See also Volume III, Chapter 4 for a complete explanation of these passages and their historicity.

Chapter Six

The Soul and Its Brain: Toward a Theory of Transphysical Self-Consciousness

Introduction

This chapter may be difficult for those unacquainted with epistemology and the problem of consciousness. It is not necessary to understand this material in order to grasp the general conclusions about human transcendence in Chapters 1 through 5. Hence, some readers may elect to skip this chapter and proceed to the conclusion of this volume. However, readers may want to venture onto this new ground because it is the field upon which the academic and cultural battle between materialism, panpsychism, and transcendentalism is being waged—termed "brain wars" by Dr. Beauregard. Are we merely molecules, atoms, and quantum systems, or are we dimensions within a cosmic consciousness embedded in physical processes—or do we possess a unique transcendent soul? As explained in Chapters 1–5, the evidence for our unique transcendent soul is considerable *and* indispensable for defining our life's purpose and destiny—*if* we believe it and resist the pull of the current prevailing materialism. Hopefully, this chapter will help readers to do this and believe in the high dignity and destiny for which they have been created.

Given the inadequacy of physicalist hypotheses[1] to explain near-death experiences—particularly the verified accounts of vision, hearing, memory, and recall of self-consciousness away from and above an almost completely incapacitated brain-body (including perceptions of

---

[1] "Physicalist" refers to the school of thought holding that *all* reality is physical and can be completely explained by physical processes and systems. It does not refer to the scientific method or the physical sciences. It stands in contrast to schools of thought that are open to transphysical reality (i.e., realities that transcend the limits of space-time individuation, and physical laws).

people blind from birth)—we may want to follow the lead of some of the thinkers mentioned in Chapter 5 (i.e., Mario Beauregard, John Eccles, Friedrich Beck, and Denyse O'Leary) in advocating for what Beauregard has called "a spiritual brain" or what Eccles calls a "trialist interactionist theory".

The evidence of near-death experiences (as explained above) strongly suggests that consciousness has a transphysical ground not requiring a physical brain. This view runs against the prevailing physicalist view of consciousness, namely, that consciousness originates in the physical brain alone. If we are to follow the implications of transphysical consciousness manifest in near-death experiences, we will want to respond to two questions:

1. Is there any other reason for believing in a transphysical ground of consciousness besides near-death experiences?
2. Is there a ground of interaction between transphysical self-consciousness and the brain—between the transphysical and physical domains?

We will take up the first question in Sections I and II, and the second question in Sections III and IV.

As the reader may by now know, the evidence of near-death experiences is not the only reason to believe in a transphysical ground of consciousness. In Chapters 1 and 2, we talked about "the soul" as a mediator between our consciousness and the transcendent—through which we experience the numen, the sacred, and the authority behind conscience. In Chapter 3 (Section V), we addressed the need for heuristic notions (the organizing ideas behind the questions of what, where, when, why, and how) and the supreme heuristic notion (the horizon of complete and unrestricted intelligibility) required to pursue knowledge of "*all* that is to be known". We also saw in Chapter 3 (Section V.C) that Gödel's theorem presents a significant problem for physicalist models because it implies a horizon of higher mathematical intelligibility beyond *any* set of rules or algorithms that is accessible to man's consciousness. As will be seen, these three enigmas (heuristic notions, the horizon of complete intelligibility, and Gödel's theorem) point (along with near-death experiences) to a transphysical ground of consciousness.

There is a fifth indication of a transphysical ground of consciousness: what might be called "human subjectivity" or "self-consciousness". This phenomenon is difficult to explain in physicalist terms, and has become what David Chalmers calls "the hard problem of consciousness".[2] We will briefly examine each of these five indications of transphysical consciousness in turn.

Before examining the five indications of transphysical consciousness, we will want to consider a common error in physicalists' justification of their restrictive assumptions. Typically, physicalists make the following general argument: stimulation of the brain causes bodily movements; therefore, all bodily movements are caused by *only* physical processes in the brain.

As will be explained below, such arguments commit the common fallacy of "arguing from a particular to a universal". A rather stark example of this fallacy may be found in Stephen Hawking's and Leonard Mlodinow's work *The Grand Design*:

> For example, a study of patients undergoing awake brain surgery found that by electrically stimulating the appropriate regions of the brain, one could create in the patient the desire to move the hand, arm, or foot, or to move the lips and talk. It is hard to imagine how free will can operate if our behavior is determined by physical law, so it seems that we are no more than biological machines and that free will is just an illusion.[3]

As the reader may have already surmised, Hawking and Mlodinow have not proven physical determinism and reductionism, because they have not shown that the *only* cause of *all* bodily movement is physical processes in the brain. They have only shown that brain stimulation causes movements of the hand, arm, foot, and lips, but they have not *eliminated other* possible causes. For example, an idea or intention arising within *transphysical* consciousness could cause the brain to cause the body to move (i.e., a cause of a cause

---

[2] See David Chalmers, *The Conscious Mind: In Search of a Fundamental Theory* (London: Oxford University Press, 1997); and David Chalmers, *The Character of Consciousness (Philosophy of Mind)* (London: Oxford University, 2010).

[3] Stephen Hawking and Leonard Mlodinow, *The Grand Design* (New York: Random House, 2010), p. 32.

of an effect). This is envisioned by many thinkers such as Eccles, Popper, Beck, and Beauregard, who believe that conceptual ideas must originate within transphysical consciousness that affect the brain (through the mediation of quantum fields), which then affects the body (see below Section III.A). Evidently, Hawking and Mlodinow have not disproved this contention of Eccles, Popper, Beck, and Beauregard, because they have *only* shown that stimulation of the brain can move the body—a fact that Eccles and others assumed to be true. Thus, Hawking and Mlodinow have *not* disproved the Eccles contention that transphysical consciousness can cause the brain to cause bodily movement. Thus they have not proven either physicalism or determinism.

As noted above, this fallacy is called "arguing from a particular to a universal". It tries to demonstrate that because a *particular* cause produces an effect, it is the *only* cause of that effect (a universal claim). Such arguments are frequently wrong, because they overlook, ignore, or intentionally screen out a multiplicity of causes in order to unjustifiably restrict reality to a single cause. Recall the most fundamental rule of informal logic: "There are far more errors of omission than commission." Arguing from a particular to a universal almost invariably causes significant errors of omission, because reality is bigger than any one cause-effect model we generate at any particular point in time.

We may now proceed to an investigation of the five indications of transphysical activity in human consciousness.

I. Clues to Transphysical Consciousness

The reader may recall several indications of transphysical self-consciousness besides those implied by near-death experiences—Otto's numinous experience (Chapter 1), Eliade's religious intuition (Chapter 2, Section I), Newman's conscience (Chapter 2, Section II), the need for innate heuristic notions to convert perceptual ideas to conceptual ideas (Chapter 3, Section V.A), the need for a horizon of complete and unrestricted intelligibility to explain our capacity to pursue the complete set of correct answers to the complete set of questions (Chapter 3, Section V.B), the need for a horizon for higher mathematical intelligibility independent of *any* particular set of rules or algorithms required by Gödel's proof (Chapter 3, Section V.C), and the transcendental awareness of and desire for perfect and unconditional love, goodness, and beauty (Chapter 4). All these indications of transphysical self-consciousness have probative force, but only two are emphasized by the current discussion within the philosophy of mind and consciousness:

1. *Heuristic notions,* which come up in the discussion of conceptual ideas, abstract language, and understanding of syntax (Eccles, Popper, Chomsky, and Davidson)
2. *Gödel's theorem* (Lucas, Barr, Penrose, and Hameroff)

A new indication of transphysical consciousness has emerged in recent years championed by David Chalmers called the "hard problem of consciousness", implying an ontological distinction between the inwardness of human subjectivity and the mere outwardness of physical processes (see below Section III.B).

As noted above, another indication of transphysical consciousness is surfacing with greater intensity: near-death experiences that are discussed more by physicians and neuroscientists (e.g., Beauregard, O'Leary, Parnia, Alexander, and van Lommel) than philosophers.

Though Lonergan's horizon of complete and unrestricted intelligibility is not included in contemporary discussions of philosophy of mind and the implications of near-death experiences, I include it here because it has considerable explanatory power within those discussions. In this chapter, I will restrict myself to the above five indications of transphysical consciousness pertinent to the contemporary discussion and debate by philosophers, neuroscientists, and physicians. By doing this, I do not mean to imply that the other indications (the numinous experience, the transcendental desire for love, goodness, and beauty, etc.) are less probative or important. I restrict myself to the above five indications only to help readers integrate this account of transphysical consciousness with the contemporary discussion. In the conclusion (Section VI below), I will reconsider the other indications that are more pertinent to philosophy of religious experience, philosophy of religion, philosophical theology, and spiritual theology.

A. Heuristic Notions, Gödel's Theorem, and Transphysical Consciousness

Let us begin with heuristic notions. Recall from Chapter 3 (Section V) that perceptual ideas (pictorial images) do not yield understanding, but only pictures of images within our perceptual or imaginative field. Understanding is the ability to grasp or say something *about* something, which entails the capacity to use *syntax* and to set ideas in *relationship* to one another (conceptual ideas). These relationships among ideas, in turn, require some higher ideas (called "heuristic notions") to be an "organizing superstructure" through which ideas can be related—such as a map to organize data answering the question of where, or a clock or a calendar to organize data responding to the question of when; "similarities and differences" to respond to the question of what; or "causes and effects, possibilities and actualities" to respond to the question, why is it so? We showed that these heuristic notions could not have been derived from the world of experience because we would have to have used them *before* we derived them in order to derive them. This gives us a clue that we have what Kant called "transcendental knowledge" ("I call all knowledge transcendental if it is occupied, not with objects, but with the way that we can possibly know objects even *before* we experience them"[4]).

We then saw that the capacity for all questioning—and the heuristic notions necessary for it—is derived from the supreme heuristic notion: the horizon of complete intelligibility, because we would not be able to continually recognize limits to our knowledge (incomplete intelligibility) without a tacit awareness of what complete intelligibility is like. We then saw that a tacit awareness of complete intelligibility includes *unrestricted* intelligibility. This enables us to recognize restrictedness of intelligibility whenever it occurs, revealing the need for continued questioning until we have reached unrestricted intelligibility (complete intelligibility)—the ultimate objective of our pure unrestricted desire to know.

Even if one does not accept Lonergan's and Rahner's view that we have a tacit awareness (a horizon) of complete and unrestricted

---

[4] Immanuel Kant, *Critique of Pure Reason*, trans. Norman Kemp Smith (New York: St. Martin's Press, 1965), A12.

intelligibility, it is difficult to see how we can avoid Kant's idea of transcendental knowledge—innate heuristic notions necessary for the organization of relationships among ideas. Recall that heuristic notions are already high-level *conceptual* ideas (which do not and cannot exist in the physical world conditioned and determined by space-time particularity and individuation). If man's consciousness is merely physical—conditioned by space-time particularity and individuation—how can it have an awareness of a reality that is *not* so determined or conditioned? If we restrict consciousness (the cause) to the merely physical, do we not also restrict its contents (its effects) to physical conditions and limits? Can we really produce a transphysical effect from merely physical causes, create a higher-order reality out of a lower-order one? Can we free reality from the determinations and conditions of space-time particularity and individuation without making recourse to something that is already free from those conditions and restrictions? If not, then it would seem that we have some transphysical dimension to our consciousness.

Heuristic notions are not the only reason for believing that man's intellection entails transphysical consciousness. Recall what was said in Chapter 3 (Section V.C) about Gödel's theorem. We saw there that people do not have to rely upon predetermined prescribed rules, algorithms, and programs to create solutions to arithmetical and mathematical problems. We have the capacity to create new solutions to mathematical problems (beyond any previously known set of rules or algorithms) *indefinitely*, suggesting that we have a tacit awareness of mathematical intelligibility at a higher level than can be expressed by any set of rules or algorithms. But if this awareness is *beyond* any set of prescribed rules or algorithms, it must be nondeterministic or trans-deterministic, which puts it beyond the domain of classical physics (based on deterministic rules and structures).

The above three enigmas (heuristic notions, the horizon of complete intelligibility, and Gödel's theorem) along with near-death experiences and Chalmers' hard problem of consciousness (see below Section II) show that classical physicalist explanations have run their course and are no longer capable of explaining the full range of data from contemporary epistemology, linguistics, mathematics, and philosophy of mind. This has caused philosophers and physicists to formulate three distinct responses to this challenge:

1. *Quantum physicalism.* A physicalist model that tries to respond to Gödel's theorem and the hard problem of consciousness by appealing to the nonlocality and randomness of quantum field theory (Penrose and Hameroff).

2. *Protomentalism (panpsychism).* A nonphysicalist system that attempts to infuse consciousness within physical processes and systems (usually through quantum field theory) so that consciousness on higher levels (e.g., in human beings) can be derived from consciousness in physical processes (David Chalmers, David Ray Griffin, Christian de Quincey, and Peter Russell). Imagine a universe in which some form of elementary consciousness or soul is the fundamental building block of all reality. Thus, quantum fields, protons, complex molecules—everything—has some form of consciousness. As reality becomes more complex, so also does the capacity of the consciousness which results from the aggregation and interaction among the "ensouled" parts.

3. *Trialist interactionism and hylomorphism.* A transphysical system that proposes the existence of a distinct transphysical soul (self-consciousness) capable of existing apart from the body that is mediated to the physical processes of the body through quantum fields (Eccles, Popper, Beck, Polanyi, and Lonergan).

We will begin with quantum physicalist models because they do not separate consciousness from the physical processes of the brain (see below in Section B). We will then proceed to protomentalism, because it *does* distinguish consciousness from physical processes—however, it infuses this distinctive conscious principle into physical processes (see below Section II.A). We will conclude with trialist interactionism and hylomorphism because these two systems separate consciousness from physical processes and advocate that consciousness can exist apart from the physical brain. These models must overcome the problem of dualism, and if they do, hold out the best explanation for all the indications of transphysical self-consciousness—heuristic notions, the horizon of complete intelligibility, Gödel's theorem, the hard problem of consciousness, and near-death experiences (see Sections IV.A and IV.B).

B. A Quantum Physicalist Explanation—Penrose and Hameroff

Responding to the challenge of Gödel's proof, Roger Penrose and Stuart Hameroff propose an explanation of how nondeterministic mathematics can originate from *brain*.[5] Their proposal attempts to find a domain of *physics* that can, as it were, have the best of both worlds: the nondeterministic and nonalgorithmic dimensions of random quantum systems and the coherent ordered characteristics of deterministic classical systems. Quantum computing could provide a possible means for the physical brain to move beyond deterministic mathematics. How would such quantum computation occur within the brain that is in a great part described by the classical physics of biological systems?

The Penrose and Hameroff proposal suggests that quantum computation may be possible in brain microtubules. They suggest that protein assemblies called microtubules within the brain's neurons be viewed as self-organizing quantum computers.[6] In order for this proposal to work, they would have to show the following:

1. Quantum activity can affect classical physical structures of the brain.
2. The quantum activities in brain microtubules really constitute quantum computers.
3. Quantum computation can actually resolve the Gödel enigma.
4. We will examine each of these requirements in turn.

[5] There is an excellent summary of the basic elements of the transcomputational problem in brain activity and an excellent list of references in Stuart Hameroff, "The New Frontier in Brain Mind Science", *Philosophical Transactions Royal Society London (A)* 356 (1998).

[6] See Roger Penrose and Stuart Hameroff, "What 'Gaps'? Reply to Grush and Churchland", *Journal of Consciousness Studies* 2, no. 2 (1995): 99–112; and Stuart Hameroff and Roger Penrose, "Orchestrated Reduction of Quantum Coherence in Brain Microtubules: A Model for Consciousness", in *Toward a Science of Consciousness—The First Tucson Discussions and Debates*, ed. S. R. Hameroff, A. Kaszniak, and A. C. Scott (Cambridge, Mass.: MIT Press, 1996), pp. 507–40 (also published in *Mathematics and Computers in Simulation* 40 [1996]: 453–80).

The first requirement (that quantum activity can affect the classical physical structures of the brain) is theoretically possible. The orthodox interpretation of quantum theory allows intention and observation to collapse the quantum wave function (a state of potentiality) to an eigenstate (an actual state) that can affect classical physical systems (in the brain). These proposals have been seriously considered by the Nobel Prize-winning neurophysiologist Sir John Eccles, and physicists Friedrich Beck and Henry Stapp (among others), and may well hold the key to resolving the problem of mind-body interaction (see below Section IV.A).

The Penrose-Hameroff proposal goes further than the Eccles-Beck-Stapp proposal because it advocates for quantum computation within brain microtubules, which is far more granular than the collapse of the whole system to an eigenstate. It requires that *specific* inputs and outputs of quantum systems affect classical physical systems, which faces two significant (though not theoretically insurmountable) challenges: interfacing input-output to the system and protecting the system from environmental decoherence.[7]

"Input-output interface with the system" refers to the challenge of integrating quantum inputs and outputs with classical ones. In order to achieve a successful interface between quantum systems and classical systems, it will be necessary to convert quantum inputs and outputs to classical ones, and classical inputs and outputs to quantum ones, in a way that maintains the essential character of both sets of inputs and outputs. Such conversions are exceedingly intricate and delicate and may not be possible at the level needed by Penrose and Hameroff.

"Environmental decoherence" refers to the problem that occurs when a very weak quantum input or output is made incoherent by the environmental noise of much larger and stronger classical systems with which the quantum system is interacting. Hameroff describes the problems as follows:

At first glance the possibility of macroscopic quantum states in biological systems seems unlikely, appearing to require either extreme cold (to avoid thermal noise) or laser-like energetic pumping to achieve coherent states. And as in technological proposals, perfect isolation of

---

[7]See Hameroff, "New Frontier in Brain Mind Science", p. 1871.

the quantum state from the environment (and quantum error correction codes) would be required while the system must also somehow communicate with the external world.[8]

Again, this challenge may not be able to be met at the fine level required by Penrose and Hameroff.

Penrose and Hameroff must meet a second critical challenge to their proposal; they must show that quantum computation can actually take place in brain microtubules. Quantum computation offers the possibility of moving beyond the strictly deterministic and algorithmic characteristic of classical computation, but it is complex and layered. It entails superposed states using multiple computations simultaneously, in parallel.[9]

It is one thing to show that quantum activity can affect classical physical structures in the brain (and that quantum inputs and outputs can interact with classical ones), but quite another to say that the quantum activity is actually quantum *computing*—in superposed states using multiple computations simultaneously, in parallel. Penrose and Hameroff have not established how quantum activity in brain microtubules can and does self-organize into this complex, computational system. How can the leap from quantum interaction to quantum computing be explained? Penrose and Hameroff have not yet shown *how* such complex activities originate within microtubules (or anywhere else in the brain). If they cannot show this, their proposal would lack explanatory power.

The Penrose-Hameroff proposal must meet yet a third and far more challenging requirement: they must show how quantum computation can resolve the Gödel enigma. Though quantum computation can break free of deterministic mathematics by introducing randomness into deterministic systems, it does not show how such randomness within deterministic systems can generate higher-order mathematical intelligibility. Moving from one set of rules and algorithms to a *higher* set of rules and algorithms (along the lines of Gödel) is *ordered* toward a higher mathematical objective, and there is no guarantee that the randomness of quantum computation can do anything like

---

[8] Ibid., p. 1872.
[9] Ibid., pp. 1869–96.

this. Indeed it seems unbelievably improbable. It will take more than randomness within deterministic systems to generate the calculus or the Riemannian Curvature Tensor[10] from lower-order algebras and geometries. Patricia Smith Churchland sums up the challenge succinctly: "Pixie dust in the synapses is about as explanatorily powerful as quantum coherence in the microtubules."[11]

When we combine the above three challenges with the fact that quantum computation is not able to explain heuristic notions, the horizon of complete and unrestricted intelligibility, and the transphysical ground of consciousness implied by near-death experiences, it seems unlikely that this kind of physicalist explanation—albeit quantum physicalist—will be able to explain transphysical activity in man's consciousness. We will have to look elsewhere—beyond physicalist explanations—to find a solution to the above *trans*physical phenomena in human consciousness and thought. Such a solution will need to acknowledge a nonphysical or transphysical dimension of human consciousness and distinguish itself from physicalist models that try to derive transphysical activities from physical ones. Physicalist models are unlikely to be successful because they contain a flawed assumption that physical systems can extricate themselves from their intrinsic limitations (individuation, space-time particularity, and physical laws) by aggregation and complexification. However, aggregating and complexifying individuated, spatio-temporal physical systems only leads to more complex individuated, spatio-temporal physical systems—not to transphysical ones. It seems, then, that a solution to the challenges of transphysical activities in human consciousness (Gödel's theorem, heuristic notions, the horizon of complete intelligibility, and the transphysicality of near-death experiences) will have to consider a nonphysical or transphysical source of consciousness. This leads us to three alternative models of consciousness: protomentalism or panpsychism (Section II.C), trialist interactionism (Section IV.A), and hylomorphism (Section IV.B). Before proceeding to an

[10] This is a highly creative and complex way of mathematically defining the intrinsic curvature of complex surfaces and objects in n-dimensional space. The idea that this system could be generated from random combinations or integrations of lower-order algebra or geometry is exceedingly improbable.

[11] Patricia Smith Churchland, *Brain-Wise: Studies in Neurophilosophy* (Cambridge, Mass.: MIT Press, 2002), p. 197.

investigation of these models, we will want to explore David Chalmers' hard problem of consciousness.

II. The Hard Problem of Self-Consciousness

In addition to the evidence of near-death experiences, heuristic notions, and Gödel's theorem, another indication of transphysical consciousness has emerged in contemporary philosophy championed by David Chalmers and Thomas Nagel,[12]—what has been variously called "the problem of personal experience", "subjective presence", "self-possession", and "self-consciousness". These are all variations of a common problem: Can the subjective component of personal experience be explained by an aggregation of physical (neuro-biological, chemical-mechanical) processes in the brain? Or is there something about subjective experience that will always elude (be above) physical processes? David Chalmers phrased it this way:

> Why is it that when our cognitive systems engage in visual and auditory information-processing, we have visual or auditory *experience*: the quality of deep blue, the sensation of middle C? How can we explain

[12] See David Chalmers, "Facing Up to the Problem of Consciousness", *Journal of Consciousness Studies* 2, no. 3 (1995): 200–19; Chalmers, *Conscious Mind*; Chalmers, *Character of Consciousness*; Thomas Nagel, "What Is It Like to Be a Bat?" *Philosophical Review* 83 (1974): 435–50; and Thomas Nagel, *Mind and Cosmos* (London: Oxford University Press, 2012).

Though both thinkers advocate for a strong distinction between consciousness and physical processes, they interpret this distinction in different ways. Chalmers is the least physicalist (advocating for panpsychism or panprotopsychism to explain man's consciousness). Nagle does not go this far but maintains a hard distinction between the inwardness and self-possession of consciousness versus the outwardness and non-self-possession of physical processes.

John Searle is sometimes associated with the hard problem of consciousness, but he does not draw any *ontological* conclusions from his *phenomenal* distinction between "human first person subjective experience" and "objective particles in fields and force". He simply (and inexplicably) combines them, indicating that consciousness is a real *subjective* experience caused by the *physical* processes of the brain. Though he makes a phenomenal distinction between subjectivity and objectivity, he is an ontological physicalist. As will be explained below, Chalmers' conclusion about the *ontological* distinction between consciousness and physical processes is more explanatory (and realistic) than Searle's simple aggregation of them. See John Searle, *Intentionality* (New York: Cambridge University Press, 1983); John Searle, *The Rediscovery of the Mind* (Cambridge, Mass.: Bradford/MIT, 1991); John Searle, "Animal Minds", *Midwest Studies in Philosophy* 19 (1994): 206–19; and John Searle, *Rationality in Action* (Cambridge, Mass.: MIT Press, 2001).

why there is something it is like to *entertain* a mental image, or to experience an *emotion*? It is widely agreed that experience arises from a physical basis, but we have no good explanation of why and how it so arises. Why should physical processing give rise to a rich *inner life* at all? It seems objectively unreasonable that it should, and yet it does.[13]

Each of the italicized words in the above passage points to a quality that physical processes cannot seem to produce: a subjective quality of "appreciation" or "enjoyment" or "amazement" or "awe". These "experiences" do not happen only in the aesthetic domain (e.g., the appreciation of color, visual form, and music), but also in the domain of cognition itself (e.g., solving a puzzle, wanting to know, enjoying mathematical symmetry, fascination with scientific discovery, etc.).

Chalmers works backwards from what he calls "the easy problems of consciousness"[14] (i.e., any phenomenon that can be explained by an aggregation of physical processes) to the "hard problem of consciousness" (i.e., any phenomenon such as the previously mentioned experiences that do not seem to be able to be explained by an aggregation of physical processes).

The problem with describing *inner* experiences by means of physical processes is that physical processes have no "inner sense", that is, no "presence to self", no "awareness of self". Physical realities have no "inwardness" (no "interior depth"), but only "outwardness", which can interact or be aggregated with other physical ("outward") realities.

Thomas Nagel looks at it the other way around: from the vantage point of physical processes. He notes that physical processes are "objective"—they can be *shared* in a consistent way with anyone who has the means to observe them—but subjective "experiences" ("inner appreciation and enjoyment") cannot be shared with anyone. They are unshareable because the "inwardness" of subjective experience cannot be objectified ("made outward").[15]

Some readers might be thinking that the above analysis applies only to classical physics (deterministic mechanical physics), but not to quantum physics (in which information can be shared with an entire system, even incredibly large ones, simultaneously). (This question

[13] Chalmers, "Facing Up to the Problem of Consciousness", p. 200 (emphasis mine).
[14] See ibid., pp. 3–91.
[15] See Nagel, "What Is It Like to Be a Bat?", pp. 435–50.

will be taken up below in Section IV.B.) For the moment, suffice it
to say that this remarkable characteristic of quantum systems does not
explain "the *inwardness* of subjective experience", but only simultaneous system-wide transfer of information. The inwardness of subjective experience is far more than this.

Before describing this inwardness of subjective experience, we will
first examine the limits of what Chalmers calls "physical processes",[16]
processes that can be described by either classical or quantum physics.
As will be seen, the inwardness of subjective experience is not the
only domain that classical and quantum physics cannot by themselves
explain. There are two more fundamental domains: living systems
(Section II.A) and animal consciousness (Section III.A).

Human self-consciousness is far richer than the previous two
domains and includes apprehension, inwardness, independence, and
privilege over the "outside world". (We will examine this closely in
Section III.B.)

A. Living Systems

We might begin by making a fundamental distinction between
"being-for-itself" and "being-in-itself".[17] "Being-for-itself" refers
to any being that acts for itself—for its survival, sustenance, and replication, pursuing what will enhance it and avoiding what threatens
it. Every living system, even a single-celled bacterium, acts for itself.

In contrast, "being-in-itself" does not act for itself and is insensitive to its existence. Systems describable by classical and quantum
physics are "beings-in-themselves". Though living systems are constituted by physical systems, they are more than this. They have a
higher self-organizing principle and laws that direct physical processes
to higher ends, such as metabolizing, seeking sustenance, avoiding
threats, and replication. Without these higher self-organizing principles and laws, these physical systems would not direct their activities

---

[16]See Chalmers, "Facing Up to the Problem of Consciousness", pp. 3–91.

[17]These terms do not carry the philosopher Jean-Paul Sartre's (1905–1980) existential
interpretation with them. They are used only in an ontological sense to describe two different
modes of being.

toward metabolism, sustenance, and survival. They would act only in the ways described by classical and quantum physics.

In the important essay "Life's Irreducible Structure", the eminent chemist-philosopher Michael Polanyi made this point clear and showed that the compounding of physical systems alone will not give rise to the biological activities mentioned above—they would only result in more complex *physical* systems (beings-*in*-themselves). The compounding of merely physical systems does not enable the resulting complex to act *for* itself, but only to be a complex being-*in*-itself.

Systems that act *for* themselves (living systems) depend on systems that exist *in* themselves (physical systems), but they are more than this—they have a higher level of self-organization than physical systems. The higher level of self-organization constitutes a higher-level system (a *living* system) toward which all subordinate physical processes are oriented. Viewed the other way around, all physical processes within a being-for-itself are oriented toward the preservation and replication of the *higher*-order system.

We might say that, in living systems, physical processes are oriented toward objectives that lie beyond them—toward preserving the higher-order system with its higher level of self-organization.[18]

Physical systems by themselves (that are not part of a living system) do not perform higher-order activities (such as metabolism) to maintain, support, and preserve a higher level of self-organization such as a living system. They simply act in prescribed ways without regard to the benefit of a higher-ordered system. Protons attract electrons and repel other protons, but they are indifferent to their own good or the good of anything else. If protons acted for themselves, they would act like single-celled organisms—but the fact is, they do not. Therefore, we must join with Polanyi in asserting that living systems are not reducible to physical systems (classical or quantum) alone. Living systems must have two *additional* components along with the physical systems that comprise them:

1. A higher level of self-organization giving rise to a higher-order system (a living system)

[18]See Michael Polanyi, "Life's Irreducible Structure", *Science* 160, no. 3834 (June 21, 1968): 1308–12.

2. Higher-order information that orients physical systems toward the end of maintaining, preserving, and replicating the higher-order system

As we shall see (Section IV.B), Polanyi calls these additional components of living systems "a higher order principle of design orienting physical and chemical processes toward ends not intrinsic to them".[19]

If Polanyi is correct, then the hard problem of consciousness really begins with the hard problem of living systems. If a living system cannot be reduced to physical processes, then how much more irreducible will be consciousness in animals and self-consciousness in humans, which have even higher-order self-organization directed toward even higher-order ends.

Materialists have difficulty accepting the existence of higher-order self-organization directed toward higher-order ends because they cannot *identify* it through standard scientific instruments or tests. There are several problems with this materialistic objection. First, not all physical realities (let alone biological ones) can be identified by standard scientific tests or instruments. For example, the laws of physics described by standard equations (e.g., $E = Mc^2$) cannot be identified by direct observation or standard scientific instruments or tests. Where is the law behind $E = Mc^2$ to be found? In what process or physical reality can it be located? Yet, no one will deny its existence and effects within the universe as a whole. How can we be so sure about the existence of physical laws? We know about them not because of direct observation or location, but by their *effects*, which tell us of their existence and operation.

The same procedure can be used to infer the existence of higher-order self-organization directed toward higher-order ends in living systems. The effects of this are evident in living systems, but conspicuously absent in merely physical ones. They will be apparent in the *new* activities that physical processes perform when they are immersed in living systems (e.g., bacteria), but do not perform outside living systems. Such activities include metabolism, self-preservation, and replication.

What kind of existence could higher-level self-organization directed toward higher-order ends have? They could exist in the

---

[19] Michael Polanyi, *Being and Knowing* (London: Routledge and Kegan Paul, 1969), p. 225.

same way as physical laws and constants—as determinative *information* in the universe as a whole. This determinative information is *not* a physical "thing", but rather a controlling influence on things and the relationships among things in the universe. Lonergan's distinction between "conjugates" and "things" will help to clarify this distinction.

B. Lonergan's Levels of Reality—"Conjugates" and "Things"

We will want to pause here and consider Lonergan's distinction between "conjugates" (what we have called "a determinative influence in the universe as a whole") and a "thing".[20] Physicists will probably understand the reality of conjugates. As noted previously, the universe, from the moment of the Big Bang, was filled with information that determines the whole range of physical cause-effect relationships among all differentiated forces and fields within space-time. As the universe unfolds, this information continues to influence not only the emergence of distinct forces and fields, but also their interrelationships and unification within a system. We refer to this "determinative or influential information" as "physical laws". As noted above, these physical laws are real—the most fundamental constituents of physical reality. If there were no physical laws (no determinative influence to govern the emergence and interrelationship among forces and fields), there would be pure chaos.

In contrast to conjugates, a thing, for Lonergan, is a unity-identity-whole—an individuated unity of specific forces and fields (governed by conjugates, physical laws):

> ["Thing"] denotes a unity, identity, whole; initially it is grasped in data as individual; inasmuch as it unifies spatially and temporally distinct data, it is extended and permanent; inasmuch as the data it unifies also are understood through laws, conjugates become its properties, and probabilities govern its changes.[21]

[20] See Bernard Lonergan, *Insight: A Study of Human Understanding*, in *Collected Works of Bernard Lonergan* 3, ed. Frederick E. Crowe and Robert M. Doran (Toronto: University of Toronto Press, 1992), pp. 271–78.

[21] Ibid., p. 276.

For Lonergan, a "thing" is distinct from a "body". The latter is a *descriptive* term (which relates data to an *observer*), while the former is *explanatory* (relating data to *data*). Lonergan is careful not to confuse things with bodies, because the latter are merely ways in which unity-identity-wholes *appear* to observers. As Lonergan notes, they appear as "already out there nows".[22] In contrast, the idea of "thing" *explains* how conjugates can be unified and individuated in space and time (it relates data to data, i.e., individuation, conjugates, and space-time).

How can we use Lonergan's ideas of things and conjugates to understand living systems? We must first extricate ourselves from the naïve worldview that reduces realities to *bodies* (already-out-there-nows). As noted above, bodies are not explanatory, and therefore they do not give us an insight into physical reality independently of commonsense observation. An *explanation* of physical reality requires discovering the most fundamental principles underlying the inter-relationships among data (conjugates) and the unification and individuation of data (things). Everything else, for Lonergan, is naïve realism—a confusion of description for explanation.

So what are these "most fundamental principles"? There are three kinds:

1. Principles governing the emergence, metric, and geometry of space-time
2. Principles governing the emergence and interrelationship of forces and fields ("conjugates" or "physical laws")
3. Principles governing unification and individuation of conjugates, forces, and fields that give rise to "things"

Strange as it may seem, things are not the most fundamental manifestation of reality. They are derived from three more fundamental principles that are "lawlike" or "informationlike", rather than "thing-like". Notice that these three kinds of lawlike governing principles allow for the complex, organic, and serendipitous universe of contemporary cosmology. They can explain not only classical physics but quantum physics, the relativity of space-time, the possibility of

[22] Ibid., p. 277.

quantum cosmology, the variation of time within quantum and GTR (General Theory of Relativity) contexts, and so on. In other words, they are capable of explaining all known interrelationships among data in the physical universe. Once we have transcended "naïve realism" and moved to an explanatory view of the universe, we see that determinative information (the above three principles) are the most fundamental manifestation of physical reality—not things (which arise out of a *synthesis* of the three fundamental principles), and certainly not bodies (which are merely descriptions about how things appear to us as observers).

We may now return to the question with which we started, namely, how can we explain the higher-order self-organization and higher-order laws and ends governing living systems? By now it may be apparent that higher-order *self-organization* (of biological systems) arise out of a higher-order principle of *unity and individuation* that is present in the universe as a whole from its inception. It may also be apparent that higher-order *laws and ends* (of biological systems) arise out of higher-order *conjugates* (principles governing the interrelationships among forces and fields) present in the universe from its inception. Just as there are principles of unity and individuation on the level of *physics*, so also there are principles of unity and individuation on the higher level of *biology* (living systems). The same is true for biological *laws and ends*—just as there are conjugates (principles governing the interrelationship among forces and fields) giving rise to the laws of physics, so also there are conjugates giving rise to the higher-order laws of living systems (biology).

For Lonergan, the principles governing unity and individuation, and the principles governing interrelationships among forces and fields, can have multiple levels—physics, chemistry, biology, sensitive psychology (sensate consciousness), and rational psychology (human self-consciousness). The above three fundamental principles are intrinsic to the universe as a whole from its inception, and all of them influence unification and interrelationships within the universe when the conditions of their activation and operation are met. So, for example, when the physical and chemical processes needed for a living system are present and appropriately interrelated, the higher-order principles of unification and individuation and the principles of interrelationship among forces and fields (for living systems) can be activated and begin governing those physical and chemical processes toward biological ends.

Higher-order principles of unity and individuation and higher-order conjugates (principles of interrelationship) are not more mysterious or inexplicable than lower-order ones. We will never see them with microscopes or telescopes, but we will know them by their effects, and if we do not slip into the fallacies of physicalism and naïve realism, we will recognize these principles to be the most fundamental manifestation of reality.

Lonergan's explanation of physical reality (the above three fundamental principles) provides Michael Polanyi with an explanation for his key insight about living systems and will be indispensable for explaining the sensate consciousness of animals as well as human self-consciousness. As we shall see, human self-consciousness requires more than the above three fundamental principles of physical reality, because each instance of self-consciousness is unique and transphysical (as revealed by the above five indications; see Section I). Before exploring this distinctive dimension of human self-consciousness, we will want to consider the protomentalist explanation of the hard problem of consciousness (favored by many contemporary philosophers and physicists, such as Chalmers himself).

C. Protomentalist Solutions to the Hard Problem of Consciousness

Protomentalism or panpsychism has reemerged today in response to the hard problem of consciousness (e.g., by David Chalmers, David Ray Griffin, David Skrbina, Christian de Quincey, and Peter Russell). It holds that the most fundamental physical systems are conscious in some elementary "proto" way. This position resolves the hard problem of consciousness without advocating a discontinuous hierarchy of reality—between physical systems and living systems, between living systems and sensate animal consciousness, and between sensate consciousness and rational human self-consciousness. This distinguishes protomentalists from Lonergan and Polanyi, who do advocate for distinct (hierarchical) levels of reality. By postulating that consciousness exists within *physical* processes, panpsychists can *reduce* rational self-consciousness, sensate consciousness, and living systems to *physical* processes and systems. This allows the physical brain to be the sole source of human self-consciousness. By postulating the presence of protomental properties in physical realities to support quasi-materialistic reductionism, it argues for a new kind of materialism—only this time, matter has been given "consciousness".

Though protomentalism and panpsychism respond to Chalmers' hard problem of consciousness by proposing a blending of consciousness with physical processes and systems at the most fundamental physical levels, it does not respond to Lonergan's and Polanyi's arguments for nonreductionistic hierarchical levels of reality. These arguments show that higher-order self-organization and higher-order laws and ends cannot be explained by the aggregation of lower-order ones. Recall that living systems require additional laws (conjugates) to direct physical processes and systems toward *biological* ends that are *not* intrinsic to those physical processes and systems. Without these additional laws organized at a higher level than that of physical systems, physical systems would only be able to perform more complex physical activities—but not biological ones (e.g., metabolism, self-preservation, and replication). The lack of a cogent protomentalist response to the ontological levels proposed by Lonergan and Polanyi weakens the protomentalists' reductionistic contention—that human consciousness can be reduced to physical processes and systems fused with an elementary form of consciousness. Without such a response, it seems more likely that reality has what Polanyi calls "truly irreducible levels of self-organization and activity".[23]

Furthermore, protomentalism and panpsychism are significantly challenged by three other issues related to *self*-consciousness and its transphysicality. First, as we saw in Chapter 5, near-death experiences strongly suggest that self-consciousness has a *transphysical* ground that can survive the death of the physical body (and brain). If self-consciousness is truly transphysical (if it really can survive bodily death), then protomentalist solutions will be unsatisfactory because rational self-consciousness cannot be explained by the physical brain alone. If self-consciousness lives on after the death of the physical brain, it must have a distinct ontological ground apart from the physical brain—it must be transphysical.

---

[23] See Polanyi, "Life's Irreducible Structure".

There is yet another reason to be skeptical about protomentalist solutions to the hard problem of consciousness. Recall from Chapter 3 (Section V) that human consciousness appears to have three transphysical dimensions: heuristic notions operative in the formation of conceptual ideas, a horizon of complete and unrestricted intelligibility entailed by our unrestricted desire to know everything, and a horizon of higher mathematical intelligibility implied by Gödel's theorem. This means that human self-consciousness cannot be intrinsically restricted by the limitations of physical properties in the brain. There must be some dimension of consciousness going beyond, not just the brain, but all physical systems. Recall that protomentalist solutions embed elementary consciousness within physical processes and systems. If this is really the case, then self-consciousness—which is supposedly reducible to these "conscious physical processes"—would participate in the restrictions of those physical processes. However, this cannot be the case if self-consciousness can perform transphysical processes, such as being aware of heuristic notions, a horizon of complete and unrestricted intelligibility, and a horizon of nonalgorithmic mathematical intelligibility.

There is still another reason to be skeptical about protomentalist solutions to the hard problem of consciousness. If self-consciousness is intrinsic to physical processes and systems, then it would begin to manifest itself at the moment that physical conditions are minimally met for its emergence. It seems that this could occur at the level of chimpanzees, which have enough development of the cerebral cortex to manifest and process self-conscious prehensions and apprehensions.[24] If *self*-consciousness emerged in chimpanzees, we would further expect them to have the same apprehension of "inwardness" and "inner world" as human infants, who, according to Piaget, are capable of *absolutizing* their "ego"—their inner

---

[24] Recent studies indicate that chimpanzees are born with significant capacity in the cerebral cortex, including the prefrontal cortex, which is responsible for social functions. Though a child's cortex develops much more than a chimpanzee's, a chimpanzee seems to have enough fine brain tissue to accommodate self-consciousness and its primary effects. See Dan McLerran, "Chimps, Humans Share a Key Evolutionary Development, Study Says", *Popular Archaeology* 3 (August 11, 2011), http://popular-archaeology.com/issue/june-2011/article /chimps-humans-share-a-key-evolutionary-development-study-says.

world and their ownership of experience (see Section III.B). If this were the case, chimpanzees would act very differently, emphasizing autonomy, independence, centrality of self, and they would have early egocentric, domineering, and narcissistic impulses. If they had such impulses, we could clearly expect them to exemplify conduct betokening the film *Planet of the Apes*. Evidently, they do not. If self-consciousness really does exist in physical processes, then we might expect not only self-consciousness in chimpanzees, but also in lower biological species, having even minimal development of the cerebral cortex. This would present us with a very different world than the one we live in.

Where do we go from here? We saw from near-death experiences, heuristic notions, and the horizon of mathematical intelligibility (implied by Gödel's proof) that physicalist explanations (including quantum physicalist explanations) are inadequate to explain these transphysical dimensions of consciousness. We also saw that proto-mentalist solutions do not respond to Lonergan's and Polanyi's arguments for irreducible levels of reality, the transphysicality of near-death experiences, heuristic notions, and Gödel's proof. Furthermore, they do not correspond to what we might expect to find in the animal kingdom, if physical processes and systems really did have consciousness (e.g., chimpanzees absolutizing their egos).

So can the hard problem of consciousness be resolved without making recourse to the two extremes of physicalism and proto-mentalism? There is considerable potential in the trialist interactionist model of Sir John Eccles, Sir Karl Popper, Friedrich Beck, and Henry Stapp (see Section IV.A) in combination with the hylomorphic model of Bernard Lonergan[25] and Michael Polanyi[26] (see

---

[25] Bernard Lonergan's notion of "thing" has remarkable explanatory power. He speaks of it as a concrete unity of diverse data extended in space and having a concrete duration. This unity-identity-whole not only unifies diverse data within it, but also has laws and operators that orient these diverse data to an end of the whole. This idea can be applied, not only to quantum systems, but living systems (such as cells), sensate systems (such as vertebrates), and even self-conscious "systems" in humans. As such, it holds out the possibility of obtaining a hylomorphic solution to the hard problem of consciousness (see below Section IV). See Lonergan, *Insight*, pp. 271–75.

[26] Polanyi proposes the idea of a "principle of design that harnesses diverse physical and chemical processes" to explain what I have called "higher levels of self-organization and ends" (Polanyi, *Being and Knowing*, p. 225). See Section IV.B for additional quotations from this work.

Section IV.B). These models acknowledge a transphysical and irreducible ground of human self-consciousness, which can act as the higher-order self-organization and ends of physical processes and systems. Just as higher-order self-organization and ends of living systems can orient the activities of physical systems toward metabolism, sustenance, survival, and replication, so also the higher-order self-organization and ends of transphysical self-consciousness can orient physical systems toward self-reflectivity, unrestricted rational inquiry, conceptual thinking, and mathematical creativity.

Before explaining this solution in greater detail (Section IV), it will be helpful to clarify what philosophers mean by the following:

- Sensate consciousness—"prehensive" (feeling) of self within a field of perception (Section III.A)
- Rational self-consciousness—an inward *ap*prehension of self over and above the field of perceptions (Section III.B)

To do this, we will first turn to the exploration and descriptions of phenomenology.

III. Sensate Consciousness and Self-Consciousness

Phenomenologists have made the most comprehensive contribution to the study of "self-presence", "inwardness", and "interior experience" underlying the hard problem of consciousness. Phenomenological method was initially proposed by Edmund Husserl, who was interested in describing phenomena as they presented themselves to us. For Husserl, perceptions never just exhibit themselves (as they are); they are always embedded in conscious experience, and so, in lived experience, they are always exhibitions of a synthesis of multiple dimensions of both perceptions and the experiencing subject.[27]

The phenomenological investigation of self-consciousness has focused on four characteristics, or perhaps better, layers, constituting our sense of self:

[27] Edmund Husserl, *The Crisis of European Sciences and Transcendental Philosophy*, trans. D. Carr (Evanston, Ill.: Northwestern University Press, 1970), Sec. 45, pp. 157–58.

1. Prethematic sense of self within experience
2. Sense of ownership or possession of experience
3. An inner sense of time
4. Reflective awareness of our inner self

We need only discuss the first two characteristics of consciousness for the purposes of our investigation because they will justify and explain Chalmers' and Nagel's contention that consciousness (through which subjective experience occurs) cannot be reduced to or replicated by physical processes.

A. Animals, Sensate Consciousness, and the "Feeling" of Self

"Pre-reflective sense of self" refers to a sense or prehension of self-presence embedded in experience. It is prereflective because it does not result from reflection (thinking about ourselves to gain explicit self-understanding), but rather is a given (a fundamental or elementary given) embedded in the way our experience presents itself. Edmund Husserl[28] and Maurice Merleau-Ponty[29] give detailed accounts of this phenomenon.

So what is this elementary sense of self? It is perhaps best described as a "feeling" of self. This feeling is more elementary than awareness—the feeling is called "prehension", while awareness (attending to the prehension of self) is called "apprehension". Philosophers have long reflected on the difference between these two states. The former is like a feeling (an intrusion into one's perceptual field), while the latter refers to some basic form of awareness (attending) that foregrounds the felt intrusion as an object of desire or interest. We might generalize by saying that prehensions are "feelings of self" without awareness (attending to the feeling of self), but apprehensions are "feelings of self" that include some elementary form of awareness or attending to that feeling.

---

[28] See Edmund Husserl, Erste Philosophie II, Husserliana VIII (Den Haag: Martinus Nijhoff, 1959), pp. 189, 412.

[29] Maurice Merleau-Ponty, Phénoménologie de la perception (Paris: Éditions Gallimard, 1945), translated by C. Smith as Phenomenology of Perception (London: Routledge and Kegan Paul, 1962), p. 488.

Both man and higher-level vertebrates (e.g., cats, dogs, dolphins, and primates) prehend themselves in their field of perception. They also "feel" the presence of themselves within the imaginary stream of dreams. This enables them to feel or sense themselves *in relation* to everything else in the perceptual or imaginary field. So, for example, a dog can feel itself in relation to a rabbit or a lion (both in its perceptions and dreams). This is sufficient to situate and pursue biological opportunities and to avoid biological threats.

This feeling or sense of self occurs *within* the perceptual or imaginary field. It is not sufficient to stand *outside* of or *apart from* the perceptual stream. It seems that even the highest species of animals (e.g., primates) are locked *into* their perceptual stream. They feel themselves to be distinctive *within* that perceptual stream, but they do not apprehend themselves *apart from* or above it (as human beings do).

Gordon Gallup has developed a "mirror test" of self-awareness in which he attempts to discover whether various animal species can recognize themselves in a mirror. Some species are interested in the object in the mirror, but don't recognize it to be a proxy for themselves. However, great apes do seem to recognize that the mirror image is such a proxy. When they are marked on the forehead, they touch the mark after they look in the mirror, indicating that they recognize the mark to be on *their* heads. No other species engages in consistent "mark touching" behavior and therefore does not pass the mirror test. This means that they do not have even a minimal sense of self-awareness.[30]

Does this mean that great apes have self-awareness in a similar way to human beings? Peter Carruthers denies this on the basis of his "higher order thought" theory. He asserts that self-consciousness is present only when a mental state is "available to be thought about directly by that subject". If a species' mental state is not available to be used or thought about by it, it cannot be self-conscious in the same way as human beings.[31]

[30] See Gordon Gallup Jr., J.R. Anderson, and D.J. Shillito, "The Mirror Test", in *The Cognitive Animal*, ed. M. Bekoff, C. Allen, and G. Burghardt (Cambridge, Mass.: MIT Press, 2002), pp. 325–34.

[31] Peter Carruthers, "Meta-Cognition in Animals: A Skeptical Look", *Mind and Language* 23 (2009): 58–59. See Peter Carruthers, *Phenomenal Consciousness: A Naturalistic Theory* (Cambridge: Cambridge University Press, 2000).

William Lycan (and earlier David Armstrong) has a modified view of the Carruthers proposal that corresponds well with the phenomenological account of self-consciousness given below. Instead of requiring the availability of a *mental* state to be thought about by a subject (as in Carruthers), he proposes only the availability of a state of *experience* to be thought about.[32] It seems that great apes and chimpanzees cannot meet either Carruthers' criterion or Lycan's and Armstrong's criterion. Lycan's and Armstrong's criterion has the advantage of allowing children under four to be phenomenally self-conscious, whereas Carruthers' criterion does not.

Herbert Terrace (of "Nim Chimpsky" fame) has proposed an additional criterion for self-consciousness, namely, autonoetic episodic memory, which enables a subject to project himself into the past or future. In order to do this, a species would have to be aware of itself sufficiently to extricate the thought of itself from its present perceptual field and to move that thought of itself within its memory of the past and anticipation of the future. If a species cannot do this, it would not have sufficient self-awareness to extricate itself from its *present* perceptual field—in which case it would be, as we have said, at the level of *prehension* alone, a feeling of self *within* a perceptual field. Terrace believes that only human beings have this capacity: "I argue that only human beings possess 'autonoetic' episodic memory and the ability to mentally travel into the past and into the future, and that in that sense they are unique."[33]

If Gallup is correct in observing that no animal species except great apes can pass a "mirror test" of self-recognition (a minimal behavioral standard of self-consciousness), and if Carruthers, Armstrong, Lycan, and Terrace are correct that great apes and chimpanzees do not meet their criteria for phenomenal self-consciousness, it is unlikely that any animal species exemplifies self-apprehension—an awareness of being aware, or experiencing oneself experiencing. As will be seen in the next subsection, this uniquely human dimension of self-consciousness

---

[32]See William Lycan, *Consciousness and Experience* (Cambridge, Mass.: MIT Press, 1996), and David Armstrong, *The Nature of Mind and Other Essays* (Ithaca, N.Y.: Cornell University Press, 1980).

[33]Herbert Terrace, "Episodic Memory and Autonoesis: Uniquely Human?", in *The Missing Link in Cognition: Origins of Self-Reflective Consciousness*, ed. Herbert Terrace and Janet Metcalfe (New York: Oxford University Press, 2005), p. 4.

is precisely what makes it transphysical. We may now proceed to our phenomenological exploration of human self-consciousness.

B. Human Self-Apprehension and Self-Consciousness

Humans prehend not only themselves *within* perceptions, but also outside the perceptual field. This enables us to *apprehend* ourselves as the owners or possessors of our experiences and to apprehend our *independence* from the *whole* perceptual world.

Phenomenologists as well as other philosophers (e.g., Nagel) recognize that we not only have a sense of ourselves *apart* from our perceptual stream; we can use that autonomous sense of self to *unify* a *variety* of diverse experiences. It is the *same self* that possesses, not only our perceptual experiences, but also dream experiences, memories of perceptual experiences, and beliefs about perceptual experiences, and so on. Thus our apprehension of self provides a single substrate within the many diverse elements of our experience—all of them are "mine". Without this apprehension of self, the unity of our experiential stream would be inexplicable.[34]

In sum, if we did not sense ourselves as distinct from and independent of our perceptual stream, we would not be able to sense ourselves as owning our experiences, and if we did not sense ourselves owning our experiences, we would not have a sense of the unity of our experiential stream. We would be reduced to punctuated diverse experiences, without any sense of unity whatsoever.

Incidentally, this experience of "same self" having or possessing diverse experiences is the condition necessary for "narrative consciousness" (the ability to embed oneself in a story, and even to interpret the meaning of oneself within a story). This seems to be a universal and natural human ability from childhood, not explicitly manifest in the rest of the animal kingdom.[35]

---

[34] See Nagel, "What Is It Like to Be a Bat?", pp. 435–50.

[35] Higher primates do not have a sense of being in a story—a higher-level integration of the experiences of their *whole* lives. The work of Hebert Terrace ("Episodic Memory and Autonoesis") confirms that nonhuman species lack autonoetic episodic memory enabling them to project the thought of self into the past and future. The reason that primates do not have this ability is that they do not have a sense of having or possessing these experiences.

Now we must ask what the source of this "subjective sense of having or possessing our *whole* experience" is. Is it similar to the prehensive feeling of self that animals and man have *within* their perceptual and imaginative streams? The prehension of ourselves having or possessing our experiences is much more than this. In order to have a sense of self as a possessor, we would also have to have a prethematic sense of the following:

1. Interiority—we are not merely something *within* perceptions; we are something *in which* perceptions can be. This requires some kind of interiority or inwardness ("an inner world") that remains the same throughout our diverse experiences, memories of experiences, and so on.

2. Independence from the perceptual world—the above sense of interiority gives rise to a distinction between the inner world and the outer world manifest in my perceptual stream. It seems that the awareness of "in me" and "outside of me" begins at this fundamental, prethematic level and enables us to sense ourselves as *independent* of the *whole* outer world. Through this prethematic awareness of the "self being independent of the outside world", we can stand outside of the whole stream of perceptions and make them our own.

3. The inner self as above the outside world—this "inner world" (which is distinct from the outer world) is viewed in a privileged position; it is the possessor of the whole perceptual stream, and so it senses itself as above or "over" the outer world. This is probably the source of the human capacity to absolutize the ego (the inner world) as well as the tendency to be not only self-centered, but also self-obsessed and narcissistic.

Higher primates not only lack autonoetic episodic memory, they also lack what Husserl called "inner-time consciousness" (*inneren Zeitbewusstseins*)—a sense of the flow of time per se. (See Edward Husserl, *The Phenomenology of Internal Time Consciousness*, trans. James S. Churchill [Bloomington, Ind.: Indiana University Press, 1964]). Finally, primates lack the ability to form conceptual ideas about the past experiences they remember. As noted in Chapter 3, Section VI, they fail Chomsky's syntactical test (See Noam Chomsky, "The Case against B. F. Skinner", *The New York Review of Books*, December 30, 1971; interview by Matt Aames Cucchiaro, "On the Myth of Ape Language", 2007); and "A Review of B.F. Skinner's Verbal Behavior", in *Readings in the Psychology of Language*, eds. Leon A. Jakobovits and Murray S. Miron (Englewood Cliffs, N.J.: Prentice Hall, 1967).

Jean Piaget noticed that little children naturally "absolutize" their egos (inner worlds). They have such a strong sense of ego that they put themselves in the center of reality and relegate the rest of experience to the periphery (the outside). Thus, it is not unusual for children to think that the sun is following *them* instead of moving around the earth for *everybody*. Indeed, children's perceptions of self-possession or "mineness" can be so strong that they believe their own perspective to be central and infallible, and it takes continuous correction from parents to convince them that there are other perspectives that need to be reconciled with theirs. This leads to the disconcerting insight (which has to be learned) that they are not always right, and indeed, frequently wrong.[36]

Can we get to an even deeper explanation of how this "prethematic sense of interiority that we feel to be outside and above our whole perceptual stream" is produced? Several observations can be offered. First, this particular sense of self must go beyond the mere "prehension of self" embedded *within* a perceptual experience. It is one thing to feel a sense of self (within a perception) and quite another to *ap*prehend that the self has interiority. This *ap*prehension of self goes beyond a mere feeling of the *fact* of self, to an awareness of *what* the self is. This sense of self is laden with meaning—interiority, independence, privilege (being above the perceptual world), and possession or ownership. This meaning moves our sense of self from *pre*hension (a *feeling* of self) to *ap*prehension (an awareness of meaning within the self).

What could be the origin of this *ap*prehension of our interior-privileged-possessor self? Our sense of inwardness brings out the "otherness" of the outside world as well as the possession of our experiences. This, in turn, brings out a sense of being above our whole stream of experiences. Thus, our sense of inwardness in contrast to the rest of our experiential field brings out various meanings, moving us from mere feeling to the foregrounding of ourselves as interior, independent, and privileged.

How can this be done? We must have a reflective act of prehending that can prehend *itself* prehending (feel *itself* feeling; experience

[36] See Jean Piaget, *The Essential Piaget*, ed. Howard E. Gruber and J. Jacques Voneche (London: Routledge and Kegan Paul, 1977), p. 137; and Jean Piaget, *The Child's Conception of Physical Causality* (New York: Harcourt Brace, 1930).

itself experiencing) at the very same moment that it is prehending data outside itself. We not only experience images in our perceptual field; we also experience *ourselves* experiencing those images. This causes us to *contrast* our experience with the images in our perceptual field. At the very moment we experience ourselves experiencing, we are aware that we are the experienc*ers* and that the sensory images are not us. Thus, our prethematic, reflective experience of experiencing enables us to apprehend at once our interiority and our independence from and superiority to *"what is not us"* in the experience.

This multidimensional experience of experiencing does not happen in stages over time, that is, in the first moment, we experience the perceptual field, in the second moment, we experience ourselves experiencing, and in the third moment, we experience our inwardness—and then our independence and then our superiority and then our ownership. Conversely, all these dimensions occur at the same time. Intrinsic to our experience of the perceptual field is our experience of experiencing, which provides the contrast for all the other meanings in our self-apprehension.

This experience of ourselves experiencing makes humans *categorically different* from that of chimpanzees and other higher vertebrates. As noted above, there is no indication that chimpanzees experience themselves as independent of and superior to the images in their perceptual field—no indication that they separate the inner world from the outer world, and no indication that they are unifying the whole of their experiences. If chimpanzees were capable of such self-apprehension, they would be able to meet the criterion of Armstrong and Lycan—they would have experiential states available to be thought about by them. This does not appear to be the case. Furthermore, they would meet Terrace's criterion of being able to extricate themselves from their perceptual field to project a thought of themselves into the past and future (autonoetic episodic memory). However, chimpanzees do not display behaviors that would be naturally associated with this criterion either.

Additionally, if chimpanzees had man's self-consciousness, they would absolutize their ego in the same way that very young children do. According to Piaget,[37] at around eighteen months, children begin

---

[37] See Piaget, *Essential Piaget*, p. 137, and Piaget, *Child's Conception.*

the absolutizing of the ego. Though their language skills are not fully developed, they manifest a belief that they are autonomous, central, and infallible. They try to protect their autonomy and independence by resisting and disobeying commands, and they will try to impose their will on those who allow them to do so. Though chimpanzees can display behaviors that appear self-seeking and domineering, most of these activities originate with pursuing *biological* opportunities (e.g., food, shelter, and procreation) and avoiding biological threats. Selfishness, excessive rage, and imposition of will for its own sake are not clearly manifest in chimpanzees as they are in children.

The uniqueness of human self-awareness (experiencing ourselves experiencing, with all of its attendant contrasts to our perceptual field) reveals a problem with protomentalist solutions to the hard problem of consciousness. Recall that protomentalists hypothesize that consciousness is embedded in the physical world. If this is truly the case, then chimpanzees (who have sufficient cerebral capacity) should be self-conscious because all of the physical components necessary for self-consciousness to emerge through the chimpanzee brain are in place.[38] This is not the case if Carruthers, Armstrong, Lycan, Terrace, and Piaget are correct. This casts doubt on the presence of consciousness in physical processes and systems. This leads to the obvious question: If self-consciousness is uniquely present in humans, and not present in the biophysical constituents of humans, what is its source? I would propose that it is the same as the source of the transphysical ground of consciousness manifest in near-death experiences, heuristic notions, the horizon of complete and unrestricted intelligibility, and the horizon of mathematical intelligibility indicated by Gödel's theorem. This will be shown in the following subsection.

C. *The Transphysical Nature of Human Self-Consciousness*

Why consider human self-consciousness to be transphysical? Is there something about it that suggests transphysicality, like survival of bodily death, heuristic notions, and horizons of intelligibility? There seems to be good reason for thinking this. In order for us to experience our experiencing (in a single act), our experiencing cannot be

[38]See McLerran, "Chimps, Humans".

bound by the parameters of a space-time manifold, for space-time prohibits a single reality or action from occurring at more than one relative position at the same time—that is, the position of experienc*er* and experienc*ed* in the very same act.

How can the very same act of experiencing be in two relative positions with respect to itself simultaneously as experienc*er* and experienc*ed*? For the purposes of illustration, we might analogize the *mental* phenomenon of self-consciousness with the *physical* phenomenon of, say, trying to put a briefcase inside of itself (making it be in two relative positions with respect to itself simultaneously). There are only two ways in which this could be done: ·

1. By travelling at an infinite velocity so that it could be at two relative positions simultaneously, inside and outside of itself
2. By not being conditioned by space-time; if the briefcase were unaffected by space-time, it could be in multiple relative positions with respect to itself simultaneously

Both ways of enabling a single reality to be in two relative positions with respect to itself simultaneously require transcending the conditions of space *and* time.

Some readers may be thinking that quantum systems (*physical* systems) also avoid the conditions of *both* space *and* time, as manifest in quantum entanglement. If this were true, then quantum systems would be transphysical, and the protomentalist solution to the hard problem of consciousness would seem to have merit. Before explaining why this is not the case, we will want to briefly summarize what quantum entanglement is.

Quantum entanglement occurs when pairs of particles closely interact with one another over arbitrarily large distances such that the quantum state of each particle cannot be described independently of the other. It suggests that measurement of quantum systems can occur only within the system *as a whole*. For example, measurement of the momentum, position, or spin of one entangled particle will affect momentum position or spin of the other particle (no matter how far the other particle is from the first). If one entangled particle (in a pair whose total spin is zero) is measured to have a clockwise spin, the other will be measured to have a counterclockwise spin—even over arbitrarily large distances. Thus, the measurement of one particle in an entangled pair affects the measurement of the other regardless of the distance between them. This phenomenon has caused many to think that quantum systems are not conditioned by space and time.

This contention is not correct, because quantum systems as a *whole* are conditioned by space and time, but they are free from the conditions of locality and local realism. The principle of locality states that a physical object is influenced only by its *immediate* surroundings. Quantum entanglement clearly violates this because one particle has effects on another at great distances. The principle of local realism states that an objectively measurable aspect of an object must preexist the measurement. Quantum entanglement also violates this principle because the measure of a particle can occur at the time of measurement.

How can this be explained? One possible explanation is that information introduced into a quantum system by, for example, a measurement affects the disposition of the *whole* system. Information introduced at one point affects potential measurements at all points within the system.

Does this mean that a quantum system is free from the conditions of both space *and* time? It does not. Certain spatial conditions (locality and local realism) are negated *within* a quantum system. However, quantum systems (as a *whole*) exist within and are conditioned by space and time. Whole systems are extended in *space* and subject to *temporal* constraints; for example, the *whole* system cannot collapse into two distinct eigenstates simultaneously or give rise to two distinct outcomes simultaneously.[39]

[39] Some readers might be thinking that the prohibition of two distinct eigenstates occurring simultaneously from the collapse of a single quantum system can be avoided by appealing to Hugh Everett's "many universes" interpretation of quantum mechanics (see Hugh Everett, "Relative State Formulation of Quantum Mechanics", *Reviews of Modern Physics* 29 [1957]: 454–62). In this view, there is no "collapse" of the wave function, because all possible outcomes exist in their *own* distinct universes. Thus, two contradictory outcomes—such as Schrödinger's cat alive in our universe and dead in another hypothetical universe—can seemingly occur simultaneously. Aside from the fact that there is no evidence for these other universes, and the "many universes" interpretation has physical and ontological problems, this hypothesis does not imply that quantum systems are transtemporal, that they can give rise to two distinct outcomes *simultaneously*, that is, without temporal separation, for example, the cat alive at one moment and then dead at a *later* moment. The very fact that we would have to postulate another universe (with a *distinct temporal continuum*) shows that a single quantum system cannot produce two distinct outcomes at the *same* time in the *same* temporal continuum (in the same universe). Thus, hypothesizing other universes does not show that quantum systems can avoid the conditions of space and time; it only serves to *affirm* it. See Joseph Gerver, "The Past as Backward Movies of the Future", *Physics Today* 24, no. 4 (1971): 46–47;

If quantum systems cannot give rise to two distinct outcomes simultaneously (in the same universe),[40] then it seems that a single quantum system cannot be in two distinct relative positions with respect to itself simultaneously. Human self-consciousness appears to do precisely this. When we experience our experiencing, the same act of experiencing has two relative positions with respect to itself simultaneously. This characteristic of human consciousness strongly suggests that it is transphysical. Though transfer of information *within* a quantum system is free from the conditions of locality and local realism, the *whole* quantum system is not free from the conditions of space and time (and is not able to be in two relative positions with respect to itself simultaneously).

We have already seen the likelihood of transphysical consciousness in the capacity to survive bodily death, the innate presence of heuristic notions, and the presence of a horizon of complete intelligibility—and now we see yet another indication of it in *self*-consciousness' capacity to be in two relative positions with respect to itself simultaneously. If the above analysis is correct, the inwardness of *human* experiencing requires that the same act of experiencing be both experiencer and experienced simultaneously. This quality transcends the conditions of space *and* time, implying transphysicality. As such, it seems that human self-consciousness comes from the *same transphysical* ground as our capacity to survive bodily death, and to be aware of heuristic notions and the horizon of complete intelligibility. The origin of our self-consciousness is not the brain or its physical processes or constituents, but rather this transphysical ground.

IV. Dualism, Trialism, and Hylomorphism

If we take seriously the implications of the transphysical nature of self-consciousness, then we will have to explain how it can interact with the physical brain. This brings up the age-old problem of dualism,

---

Henry Stapp, "The Basis Problem in Many-World Theories", *Canadian Journal of Physics* 80 (2002): 1043–52; and David Baker, "Measurement Outcomes and Probability in Everettian Quantum Mechanics", *Studies in History and Philosophy of Science Part B: Studies In History and Philosophy of Modern Physics* 38, no. 1 (2007): 153–69.

[40] See the above footnote.

which has its origins in Plato, and in the Modern Period in René Descartes. Dualism respects the distinctive transphysical nature of the human mind (and self-consciousness) as well as the physical constituents of the brain. However, since it treats the transphysical and physical components as completely distinct substances, it is beset by a vexing problem: How can the two separate substances interact? If we maintain the distinct character of transphysical consciousness and the physical processes of the brain, there is only one way of resolving this problem: there must be what we might term a "third substance" that can mediate the transphysical and physical domain, a substance that is both constrained and unconstrained by space and time. As we saw above, the most likely candidate for this third substance is a quantum system that as a *whole* is constrained by space and time, but *within* is free from certain conditions of spatiality (locality and local realism). Furthermore, in the orthodox interpretation of quantum theory (von Neumann, Margenau,[41] Beck, and Stapp; see below Section IV.A), a whole quantum system (which does not have mass-energy when it is in its pure potential state) can be affected by a purely mental phenomenon (e.g., a conceptual idea, an intention, or an observation), which can convert it from its potential state (expressed by a wave function) to a precise actual state (an "eigenstate") capable of interacting with the classical physical systems of the brain. This is the model proposed by Sir John Eccles and his colleagues, which he terms trialist interactionism.

A. Trialist Interactionism—Eccles, Popper, Beck, and Stapp

Sir John Eccles, the Australian neurophysiologist who won the Nobel Prize for his research on brain synapses, has proposed one of the most

[41] Henry Margenau was a German physicist (1901–1997) who worked with Sir John Eccles to create a trialistic interactionism (see below Section IV.A). He believed that quantum fields could mediate the relationship between the classical physics of the body and consciousness, but insisted that quantum fields could not replace mind or consciousness. He noted in this regard, "Our thesis is that quantum mechanics leaves our body, our brain, at any moment in a state with numerous (because of its complexity we might say innumerable) possible futures, each with a predetermined probability. Freedom involves two components: chance (existence of a genuine set of alternatives) and choice. Quantum mechanics provides the chance, and we shall argue that only the mind can make the choice by selecting (not energetically enforcing) among the possible future courses" (Laurence Le Shan and Henry Margenau, *Einstein's Space and Van Gogh's Sky* [New York: Macmillan, 1982], p. 240).

enlightened theories of "consciousness and brain" in recent history. In his early work (pre-1989), he called himself a "*dualist* interactionist", but in his later work (post-1989), a "*trialist* interactionist" because he believed that quantum field theory had the potential to mediate the transphysical self ("soul") and the material brain. Few scientists have understood brain functioning more profoundly than Eccles, and still fewer have studied philosophy sufficiently to understand the "inner self", "subjective experience", and "pure ego". Eccles understood the hard problem of consciousness long before its contemporary articulation by David Chalmers and Thomas Nagel. Through his extensive knowledge of physical processes in the brain, he was able to articulate the incapacity of the brain's (physical) processes to describe and explain mental phenomena, particularly conceptual ideas, creativity, experience of self, and pure ego.

His theory of trialist interactionism (developed in conjunction with Sir Karl Popper[42]) holds out the possibility for explaining not only the phenomenon of near-death experiences, but also heuristic notions, the horizon of complete intelligibility, the phenomenon of "experiencing ourselves experiencing", and the uniqueness of each manifestation of self-consciousness. Though his theory of consciousness and brain has broader explanatory potential than any other I have encountered, it can be supplemented and assisted by some insights from hylomorphism (particularly in Michael Polanyi and Bernard Lonergan; see below Section IV.B).

Eccles complemented his medical studies at the University of Melbourne with philosophical studies at Oxford University, specifically focusing on the "mind-brain" problem. He was undoubtedly familiar with the problem of heuristic notions and conceptual ideas (described above in Section I.A. and Chapter 3, Section V). Recall that heuristic notions and conceptual ideas cannot occur through the space-time particularity and individuation of physical processes—not even quantum ones. Yet, their existence in our cognitional activity cannot be denied; for without them, we would not be able to pass Chomsky's syntactical test (see Chapter 3, Section VI). This led him to conclude:

---

[42] See Karl Popper and John Eccles, *The Self and Its Brain: An Argument for Interactionism* (New York: Routledge, 1984).

The materialistic view of mind is simply an illusion—a monism borne out of ignorance of either the philosophical problem of mind or the physical dynamics of brain physiology.... The more we discover scientifically about the brain, the more clearly do we distinguish between the brain events and the mental phenomena, and the more wonderful do the mental phenomena become.[43]

Eccles' philosophical studies also led him to the analytical and phenomenological study of the self. He was aware of the problem of inner subjectivity, "experiencing ourselves experiencing", and absolute ego, and he concluded that, like conceptual ideas and heuristic notions, these phenomena were also incapable of being explained by physical processes in the brain—a remarkably lucid statement of the hard problem of consciousness twenty years before Chalmers. This led him to the consequence that each "inner world" is unique and unduplicatable, requiring a unique transphysical origin, a "creation of an individual soul":

> Since the materialistic conception is incapable of explaining and accounting for the experience of our unrepeatability, I am forced to accept the supernatural creation of the unique, spiritual, and personal "I"—that is, the soul. Or, to put it in theological terms, every Soul is a new Divine creation infused into the human embryo.[44]

Though Eccles' view of a unique transphysical soul is derived mostly from conceptual ideas and the inwardness and unrepeatability of our experience of self, it can also explain the phenomenon of near-death experiences. The major longitudinal scientific studies of NDEs[45] were completed after Eccles' death (1997), but he had a

---

[43] Sir John Eccles, "A Unitary Hypothesis of Mind—Brain Interaction in the Cerebral Cortex", *Proceedings of the Royal Society—Biological Sciences* B 240 (1990): 434.

[44] Sir John Eccles, *Evolution of the Brain: Creation of the Self* (London, UK: Routledge, 1989), p. 237.

[45] For example, Sam Parnia et al., "AWARE—AWAreness during REsuscitation—A Prospective Study", *Resuscitation*, October 6, 2014, pp. 1799–805, http://www.resuscitation journal.com/article/S0300-9572%2814%2900739-4/fulltext; Pim van Lommel et al., "Near-Death Experience in Survivors of Cardiac Arrest: A Prospective Study in the Netherlands", *The Lancet* 358, no. 9298 (2001): 2039–45; Janice Holden, "More Things in Heaven and Earth: A Response to Near-Death Experiences with Hallucinatory Features", *Journal of Near-Death Studies* 26, no.1 (Fall 2007): 33–42; Kenneth Ring, Sharon Cooper, and Charles Tart, *Mindsight: Near-Death and Out-of-Body Experiences in the Blind* (Palo Alto, Calif.: William James Center for Consciousness Studies at the Institute of Transpersonal Psychology, 1999).

strong intuition that the "unique transphysical soul" did not have to cease after the death of the physical brain; it could—indeed it should—be able to persist:

> I believe that there is a fundamental mystery in my existence, transcending any biological account of the development of my body (including my brain) with its genetic inheritance and its evolutionary origin.... I cannot believe that this wonderful gift of a conscious existence has no further future, no possibility of another existence under some other unimaginable conditions.[46]

As might be expected, Eccles' view of transphysical self-consciousness ("soul") almost inevitably encounters the problem of dualism. If the ground of self-consciousness is truly transphysical, and the brain is truly physical, how can they interact? He proposes a third mediating reality: quantum fields, which exist in the physical world, but have a transphysical property, that is, they can be affected by purely mental phenomena (such as a conceptual idea). This third mediating component moves him from "dualism" to "*trialism*". Responding to his materialistic critics, he notes:

> The materialist critics argue that insuperable difficulties are encountered by the hypothesis that immaterial mental events can act in any way on material structures such as neurons. Such a presumed action is alleged to be incompatible with the conservation laws of physics, in particular of the first law of thermodynamics. This objection would certainly be sustained by nineteenth century physicists, and by neuroscientists and philosophers who are still ideologically in the physics of the nineteenth century, not recognizing the revolution wrought by quantum physicists in the twentieth century.[47]

Eccles uses Margenau's interpretation of orthodox quantum theory, postulated by John von Neumann,[48] to show the real possibility of immaterial realities (such as conceptual ideas) affecting classical physical processes (such as the biophysical constituents of the brain)

---

[46] Sir John Eccles, *Facing Reality: Philosophical Adventures by a Brain Scientist* (Heidelberg: Heidelberg Science Library, 1970), p. 83.

[47] Eccles, "Unitary Hypothesis of Mind", p. 433.

[48] John von Neumann, *Mathematical Foundations of Quantum Mechanics*, trans. Robert Beyer (Princeton: Princeton University Press, 1996).

through the mediation of quantum fields. According to that theory, observation (*immaterial* input) can collapse a quantum wave function (a state of probabilistic potentials) to an eigenstate (an actual physical state that can affect and be affected by classical physical systems, such as the biophysical systems of the brain). Accordingly, intentions, self-consciousness, conceptual ideas, and other immaterial contents of consciousness can have an effect on the classical physical systems of the brain. Eccles notes in this regard:

> Following Margenau, the hypothesis is that mind-brain interaction is *analogous* to a probability field of quantum mechanics, which has neither mass nor energy yet can cause effective action at microsites. More specifically it is proposed that the mental concentration involved in intentions or planned thinking can cause neural events by a process analogous to the probability fields of quantum mechanics.[49]

Eccles continued to develop this theory in conjunction with the German physicist Friedrich Beck. Their research has made important contributions to the field of neuroquantology.[50]

Though some contemporary quantum theorists view von Neumann's orthodox interpretation of quantum theory as controversial, there is good reason to believe that it is "realistic" and applicable to the mind-body problem. The particle physicist Henry Stapp uses the quantum "Zeno effect" to show the possibility of a *whole* system collapse to an eigenstate (a classical physical state that can affect and be affected by the biophysical constituents of the brain). The quantum Zeno effect refers to the effects of a person's observation on a quantum system; if one observes or measures the system frequently enough, one can suspend the decay of that system (a classical physical effect brought about by observation). For example, if one observes an unstable particle continuously, it will not evolve from its first known state. Inasmuch as the Zeno effect exemplifies the effects

[49] Eccles, *Evolution of the Brain*, p. 189.
[50] See Friedrich Beck and John C. Eccles, "Quantum Aspects of Brain Activity and the Role of Consciousness", *Proceedings of the National Academy of Sciences—USA* 89 (1992): 11357–61; and Friedrich Beck and John C. Eccles, "Quantum Processes in the Brain: A Scientific Basis of Consciousness", in Naoyuki Osaka, *Neural Basis of Consciousness* (Philadelphia: John Benjamins, 2003), pp. 141–65.

of observational intention on physical systems, it can ground Eccles' trialist interactionism.

Notice that Eccles and Stapp are concerned only with the *global* effect of one's intention and observation on the collapse of the *whole* system to a classical physical state within synapses of the brain. They are not concerned with a much finer and granular problem of producing quantum computation within brain microtubules (Penrose and Hameroff). This makes two of the problems faced by Penrose and Hameroff—the input or output problem and the environmental decoherence problem (see above Section I)—much less difficult for Eccles and Stapp.[51]

In sum, the trialist interactionism of Eccles (along with Popper, Stapp, and Beck) has considerable potential to explain how five seemingly transphysical dimensions of consciousness interact with the biophysical systems of the brain:

1. Capacity of consciousness to survive bodily death (implied by near-death experiences)
2. The need for heuristic notions to transform perceptual ideas (material images) into conceptual ideas (free from space-time particularity and individuation)
3. The need for a horizon of complete and unrestricted intelligibility to explain our awareness of the incompleteness of *all* restricted intelligibility
4. The need for a horizon of mathematical intelligibility to explain how human consciousness can continuously transcend rules and algorithms in the development of higher mathematics (implied by Gödel's theorem), and
5. The need for consciousness to be in two relative positions with respect to itself simultaneously (implied in the inwardness and self-apprehension of man's experience—the hard problem of consciousness)

If human intentionality, ideas, and observation truly do collapse the potential of the whole quantum system to a determinate classical state

---

[51] For example, see Henry Stapp, "Reply to a Critic: Mind Efforts, Quantum Zeno Effect and Environmental Decoherence", *NeuroQuantology* 10, no. 4 (2012): 601–5.

(that can interact with biophysical processes in brain synapses), then human *transphysical* self-consciousness can interact with the physical processes of the brain. It would not be surprising to see additional advances in quantum theory continue to corroborate this conclusion.[52] Indeed a whole new area of biophysics is developing around it: "neuroquantology".[53]

Does the Eccles-Popper-Stapp-Beck trialist theory solve the whole problem of the interconnection between "transphysical consciousness" and *its* brain? Though it provides a cogent solution to the most fundamental problem of transphysical-physical interaction, it does not explain why physical and chemical processes are so perfectly oriented toward transphysical objectives (such as transforming perceptual ideas into conceptual ideas, the pursuit of mathematics beyond rules and algorithms, and the integration of subjective inwardness with the mere outwardness of perception). This transphysical orientation of merely physical processes can be explained by what Polanyi terms "a higher principle of design orienting diverse physical and chemical processes toward ends not intrinsic to them"—the central insight of hylomorphism.

B. Contemporary Hylomorphism—Polanyi and Lonergan

In Sections II.A and II.B, we briefly mentioned two contemporary philosophers who provide, not only a conceptual, but an ontological basis for a hylomorphic solution to mind-brain interaction: Michael Polanyi and Bernard Lonergan. The idea of "hylomorphism" goes back to Aristotle, who had a teleological view of reality in his work *On the Soul*.[54] A telos (end) represents what Aristotle termed "the what it was meant to be" (*to ti ēn einai*). So, for example, the telos of a living thing orients the parts (the material cause) and their activities

---

[52] For example, see Beck and Eccles, "Quantum Aspects of Brain Activity", pp. 11357–61; and Friedrich Beck, "Synaptic Quantum Tunneling in Brain Activity", *NeuroQuantology* 6, no. 2 (2008): 140–51.

[53] See the developments reported in the journal *NeuroQuantology* at http://neuroquantology .com.

[54] See Aristotle, *Aristotle's On the Soul*, trans. and ed. Hippocrates Apostle (Grinnell, Iowa: Peripatetic Press, 1981), 413a20–21; 414a3–9; 412a20; 414a15–18.

(the formal cause) to their final *end* or objective (i.e., life). For Aristotle, a "soul" is not necessarily transphysical in the ways mentioned above—capacity to survive bodily death and to accommodate heuristic notions and a horizon of unrestricted intelligibility, and simultaneous reflectivity (experiencing our experiencing). He had a more general view of the soul as the principle of organization and determinative ends (*teloi*). Thus, plants have "souls" oriented toward nourishment and growth, animals have "souls" oriented toward sensate consciousness and motion, and human beings have souls oriented toward rationality.

We might interpret Aristotle's idea of the soul in the contemporary context by saying that the soul is a principle that organizes physical processes and systems toward ends and activities that are beyond those intrinsic to physical processes themselves. So, for example, a vegetative (plant) soul would be a principle that organizes the nonliving physical processes toward a higher end (living) than is intrinsic to those physical processes. Thus, a "plant soul" is a principle of organization with the "information" necessary to orient nonliving physical processes toward the end or objective of life (nourishment and growth). An "animal soul" is a principle of organization with the information necessary to orient physical processes toward sensation and self-movement. Finally, a human soul is a principle of organization with the information necessary to orient physical processes toward rationality.

Notice that Aristotle does not hold to a compounding of souls—so, for example, an animal does not have both a plant soul and an animal soul, and a human being does not have a plant soul, an animal soul, and a human soul. For Aristotle, the animal soul alone contains all the information necessary to bring about the activities of nourishment, growth, sensation, and self-movement. Likewise, the human soul alone has all the information necessary to bring about the activities of nourishment, growth, sensation, self-movement, and rationality. The higher the soul, the more sophisticated the information—the "program" organizing and orienting physical processes toward higher ends. An adaptation of Aristotle's essential idea to contemporary physics has the potential to explain the "leap" from nonliving to living beings, nonsensate to sensate beings, and nonrational to rational beings.

Michael Polanyi has done this in his work *Being and Knowing*, using the analogy of a machine to illustrate "a higher order principle of design orienting physical and chemical processes toward ends not intrinsic to them: So the machine as a whole works under the control of two distinct principles. The higher one is the principle of the machine's design, and this harnesses the lower one, which consists in the physical chemical processes on which the machine relies."[55] Though Polanyi does not use the term "soul" here, he has come very close to describing in contemporary terms what Aristotle meant by that term. Like Aristotle's "soul", Polanyi's "higher order principle of design orienting physical processes" provides a solution to the problem of how lower-order physical processes can be oriented toward objectives that are not intrinsic to them. Polanyi views this principle as a sort of "information field" which provides the "instructions" or "program" (the design) to orient or guide physical processes toward the end or objective of life.

An analogy can be made to computer languages. The most fundamental language (machine language or assembly language) is based on simple binary commands (on-off, 0-1, yes-no). In order to make more sophisticated programs (higher-level programs), programmers develop compilers to convert binary commands to more complex commands (which are easier to use) such as "do" or "go" or "if-then" (compiler commands). Now imagine that you had never heard about a compiler, and you only knew that computers operated on machine code (binary commands). You then went to a computer lab and saw a programmer putting in commands such as "do" or "go", and so on, and the computer interpreted these commands and carried out the implied function perfectly—time after time. You probably would not have thought to yourself, "Wow, what a remarkable coincidence that the machine language of this computer is consistently carrying out programing functions with commands like 'do' or 'go' all by itself." More likely, you would conclude, "There must be some program that translates low-level binary commands to higher-level, user-friendly commands." If you did this, you would have inferred the existence of the compiler from its *effects*, without actually seeing it or having heard about it. This is precisely what Polanyi does when

[55] Polanyi, *Being and Knowing*, p. 225. See also Polanyi, "Life's Irreducible Structure".

he infers the existence of a "higher order principle of design orienting physical and chemical processes toward ends not intrinsic to them". Recognizing that metabolism, respiration, replication, and so on are activities beyond the parameters of physical and chemical processes and systems, he infers the existence of a higher principle of design guiding those processes to higher ends.

We should not be disturbed that the information in "higher order principles of design orienting physical and chemical processes toward higher order ends not intrinsic to them" has not yet been located. Locating such information in specific places (space-time points) may well be futile. It is far more likely that this information exists within a *system* (like a quantum system) in which information is equally available throughout the *whole* system, even if it should span great distances like the whole universe. The idea that determinative or organizing information must exist in a particular place or take the form of a particle or molecule has long since been abandoned— not only because of quantum theory, but also because of plasma theory, field theory, and the universality of physical laws, such as $F = G\ (m_1 m_2)/r^2$ or $E = mc^2$. Recall that the equations of physics describe *real effective* laws of physical processes and systems everywhere in the universe. We do not doubt their existence because of a failure to locate a *particular* source of origin. We not only infer the existence of these efficacious laws of nature; we believe that they are somehow really present throughout the whole universe ("system-wide"). Why would we not infer the very same thing with respect to "higher order principles of design orienting physical and chemical processes toward higher order ends not intrinsic to them"?

Notice that Polanyi's "higher order principle of design toward higher order ends" resembles Lonergan's notion of "conjugates", principles (physical laws) in the universe as a whole that guide forces and fields toward particular ends. Lonergan proposes an additional principle of unity and individuation that governs the ways in which "things" (unity-identity-whole) are formed. When the principles (physical laws) governing the interrelationship among forces and fields (for physical, chemical, biological, sensate, and rational ends) interface with the principles governing unity and individuation, they govern the emergence and activity of *multiple levels* of reality—the physical, chemical, biological, sensate, and rational levels.

Lonergan provides the explanatory apparatus for Polanyi's "higher order principle of design toward higher order ends". Polanyi does not provide such an explanation, but only an inference that there *must* be such higher principles in the universe; otherwise, we would be forced to explain higher-order activities (e.g., biological processes) by means of lower-order activities (physical processes) *alone*. As he notes, this is virtually impossible without additional determinative information ("design") to direct physical processes toward objectives that are not intrinsic to them. Lonergan's idea of "conjugates" shows *how* these "higher-order principles" can exist in the universe as a whole (like physical laws) and further shows how they can form multiple levels of reality and multiple levels of "things". When we combine Polanyi's inference with Lonergan's explanation, we have a coherent hylomorphic theory that can complement Eccles' trialist interactionist theory to give a comprehensive explanation of the unity of transphysical self-consciousness (soul) with physical embodiment.

What about the question with which we started about transphysical *self-consciousness*? Can the combination of trialism and hylomorphism avoid the pitfalls of physicalism, dualism, and protomentalism? I believe it can. As we saw above, there are several indications that our self-consciousness is transphysical (not conditioned by space, time, or any other physical law or parameter). We might organize these indications as follows:

1. Near-death experiences show that our self-consciousness can survive bodily death, indicating that the ground of self-consciousness cannot be in the brain alone.
2. The presence of heuristic notions and a horizon of complete and unrestricted intelligibility in our consciousness as well as the implications of Gödel's theorem all indicate transphysical information and operations within self-consciousness.
3. Human self-consciousness appears to be transphysical inasmuch as "experiencing our experiencing" implies that the same act of experiencing be at two relative positions with respect to itself simultaneously.

This implies that our self-consciousness and its heuristic notions and horizons of intelligibility have the same transphysical ground as that implied by near-death experiences. If this is the case, then self-consciousness does not originate in the physical brain, but rather in a distinctive transphysical ground.

This does not imply dualism between the transphysical ground of self-consciousness and the physical brain, because, as we have seen, Eccles shows the plausibility of mediation between the two realms through quantum field theory. Lonergan and Polanyi go beyond the issue of mediation to explain a more profound connection between transphysical self-consciousness and the brain. The transphysical ground of consciousness can act like a "higher order principle of design orienting physical and chemical processes to higher ends not intrinsic to them". As such, it can orient physical processes toward transphysical ends. The transphysical ground of consciousness exerts an influence on the physical and chemical processes of the brain much like Lonergan's universal conjugates and principles and Polanyi's "higher principle of design". Lonergan's and Polanyi's universal principles exert an influence on physical and chemical processes to achieve the ends of *living* systems and *sensate consciousness*, while transphysical self-consciousness exerts an influence on physical and chemical processes to orient them toward *transphysical* activities (e.g., continuous questioning, formation of conceptual ideas, abstract reasoning, development of mathematical theory, etc.). There is one other important difference: Lonergan's and Polanyi's conjugates and principles are *universal* (system-wide—like physical laws), while the transphysical soul is and can only be *individual* (see below in this section for an explanation). In what specific ways does our individual transphysical soul influence and direct physical processes? There are dozens of ways, but some of the major ones are as follows:

- To connect the biophysical processing of perceptual ideas with transphysical heuristic notions so that transphysical conceptual ideas can be derived from perceptual ideas (images processed by the physical brain)
- To connect the biophysical field of perception with transphysical self-consciousness, resulting in "experiencing our experiencing of the perceptual field"
- To connect the biophysical perceptions of lengths, shapes, and individuals with the transphysical horizon of mathematical

intelligibility, resulting not only in mathematics but in continuously developing higher levels of theory and applications
- To connect the biophysical field of perception with the transphysical horizon of complete and unrestricted intelligibility, giving rise to unrestricted questioning of experience and ideas

Transphysical self-consciousness positions the brain's physical processes and contents (perceptions, images, perceptual ideas, and perceptual memories) within its transphysical horizon of higher intelligibility (including heuristic notions, the horizon of mathematical intelligibility, and the horizon of complete intelligibility) as well as the inner world of self-consciousness. This positioning of lower-order contents within higher-order contents results in what we might call a "fusion of higher- and lower-order activities"—such as curiosity, continuous questioning, the formation of conceptual ideas, the ongoing development of mathematics, narrative consciousness, self-analysis, and other creative pursuits. The contents of these "fused activities" can be used, remembered, and communicated through the physical brain. Indeed, the physical brain is necessary to mediate these activities and contents to the rest of the body—from the nervous system to the musculoskeletal system.

This last point is important, because it responds to physicalists' major challenge to the transphysicalists. Recall Steven Hawking's and Leonard Mlodinow's contention that because brain stimulation produces movements of the mouth and arms, it shows that the brain *alone* is responsible for the body's activities. The Eccles-Lonergan-Polanyi model acknowledges that the brain stimulates and causes electrical activity in the central and peripheral (autonomic and enteric) nervous system. However, it does not restrict conscious causal activity to the brain *alone*, because this would require that the brain perform by itself activities of which it is not capable—that is, "fused activities" such as the desire to know everything, formation of conceptual ideas, development of mathematics, and so on. If such contents cannot be explained by the physical processes of the brain alone (a thesis upon which many philosophers agree), then the physicalist hypothesis is insufficiently explanatory, and another system that does explain these "fused contents and activities" (such as Eccles-Lonergan-Polanyi) should be considered.

The brain's activity—not only in its participation in "fused activities and contents" but also in the mediation of those activities and contents to the rest of the body—can give rise to physical problems if it is hindered or injured. For example, if some malfunction should occur in the brain, it could prevent the production of "fused contents and activities" and the mediation of those contents and activities to the rest of the body. This might cause some theorists—particularly physicalists—to conclude that consciousness is not present in such individuals. In the Eccles-Lonergan-Polanyi model this conclusion is erroneous because transphysical consciousness may well be present, but its connection with and mediation through the brain is hampered. If this were true, then, one might conclude that an Alzheimer's patient—with severely limited physical memory and verbal capacity—has minimal or no self-consciousness. However, this does not correspond with current research on Alzheimer's patients that shows that many aspects of self-consciousness that are less associated with the physical brain are not severely affected by Alzheimer's disease, but *only* those aspects associated with "cortical areas and information sent to the associative frontal cortex from memory, language and visuospatial areas".[56] According to the study of Roger Gil,

> The least disturbed aspects [of self-consciousness] were awareness of identity and of mental representation of the body. Items relating to anosognosia and moral judgements were significantly correlated with the Mini Mental State score, whereas affective state, body representation disorders, prospective memory, and capacities for introspection were *not* related to the severity of the dementia. *Consciousness of identity was sound, regardless of Mini Mental State score.*[57]

This research supports the Eccles-Lonergan-Polanyi model that self-consciousness exists apart from the physical brain because features of self-consciousness that require less input from the brain seem to function well irrespective of the severity of dementia. In other words, the less that self-consciousness is dependent on *inputs* from

[56]Roger Gil et al., "Self-Consciousness and Alzheimer's Disease", *Acta Neurologica Scandinavica* 104, no. 5 (2001): 296.
[57]Ibid. (emphasis mine).

the physical brain, the better it *functions* independently of the physical brain—suggesting that it *exists independently* of the physical brain.

Now let us return to the interrelated activity of transphysical consciousness and the physical brain. When transphysical self-consciousness positions the brain's *contents* within the transphysical horizons of heuristic notions and higher intelligibility as well as the inner world of self-consciousness, it elevates the brain's contents in several respects:

- It positions the brain's *restricted* contents within the horizon of *unrestricted* intelligibility, giving rise to questioning and creativity.
- It positions the physical brain's perceptual ideas within the transphysical horizon of heuristic notions, giving rise to conceptual ideas that enable abstract thinking, abstract communication, and meaningful syntax.
- It positions the physical brain's field of perception within the transphysical horizon of inwardness and self-apprehension ("experiencing our experiencing"), giving rise to the absolutizing of ego, projection of ego into the past and future, narrative consciousness, self-interpretation, and self-analysis.
- It positions the physical brain's perceptions of lengths, shapes, and individuals within the transphysical horizon of mathematical intelligibility, giving rise to the continuous development of new mathematical theories.

Thus, transphysical self-consciousness not only orients the physical and chemical *processes* of the brain toward higher *objectives*; it also positions the *content* of the physical brain (perceptions, images, perceptual ideas, and perceptual memories) within a transphysical horizon of higher intelligibility and self-apprehension to yield the *fused* contents and activities of advanced thought, abstraction, syntactical language, unrestricted questioning, and every creative endeavor.

Earlier in this section we noted that transphysical self-consciousness orients the brain's physical processes toward higher-order objectives in a similar way to Lonergan's conjugates and principles, but with one notable exception—Lonergan's conjugates and principles are *universal* (system-wide throughout the universe, like physical laws), while self-consciousness is *individual*. There is good reason to infer this from the evidence we have already seen.

It should not be thought that the transphysical ground of consciousness is like a "world soul" orienting *every* person's physical brain toward the transphysical domain. There are two major reasons for this: first, self-consciousness is *by its very nature* uniquely individualistic; its experience of its experiencing is, as it were, within itself. This is precisely what the phenomenologists term "the experience of inwardness that leads us to possess our *own* experiences" ("They are all *mine*"). A "world soul" is completely the opposite; it would not yield an experience of our own inwardness and ownership of experience, but absorb us and our individuality into its totality. Eccles recognized the necessity of each soul's individuality as clearly as the phenomenologists—"Since the materialistic conception is incapable of explaining and accounting for the experience of our unrepeatability, I am forced to accept the supernatural creation of the unique, spiritual, and personal 'I'."[58] Notice that Eccles—prior to Chalmers' articulation of the hard problem of consciousness—recognized that the experience of the inwardness of self is not shareable or repeatable. In this respect, it is precisely the opposite of a physical process that is by nature objective—"outward", shareable, and, therefore, repeatable.[59] From this Eccles concludes that each transphysical self-consciousness ("soul") *must* be a unique individual.

Second, near-death experiences are decidedly individual. When we leave our physical bodies, we experience ourselves as *self*-conscious, individual, and autonomous. When we move to "the other side", we see ourselves in *relationship* to the consciousness of the white light— but not *absorbed* by it. Furthermore, we see ourselves in relation to our relatives and friends in the same way we do in this world: personally and interpersonally.

Inasmuch as there cannot be two identical self-consciousnesses, we do not share a single ground of self-consciousness. Rather, the ground of self-consciousness *must be our own*. This is why Eccles concludes that each of us has our own *individual* transphysical "soul" initiating and grounding all transphysical capacities and activities.[60] He conjectures from this that a transcendent power creates each of these unique souls individually.[61]

[58] Eccles, *Evolution of the Brain*, p. 237.
[59] See Nagel, "What Is It Like to Be a Bat?", pp. 235–50.
[60] See Eccles, *Evolution of the Brain*, p. 237.
[61] See ibid.

We are now in a position to combine the "trialist interactionist" theory of transphysical-physical interaction (Eccles, Popper, Stapp, and Beck) with the hylomorphic theory of a "higher order principle of design orienting physical and chemical processes toward ends which are not intrinsic to them" (Polanyi) and self-consciousness positioning the contents of the physical brain within a transphysical horizon of higher intelligibility and self-apprehension (Lonergan). At the end of Section III we noted that neuroquantology (as articulated by Eccles) resolves the first problem of transphysical self-consciousness' interaction with the physical brain. However, it does not explain why the brain's physical and chemical processes are so perfectly oriented toward ends that are transphysical, or why the contents of the physical brain generate transphysical activities and contents, such as conceptual ideas, higher mathematical systems, abstract reasoning, self-apprehension, and the desire to know everything about everything.

The above hylomorphic analysis (of Polanyi and Lonergan) gives us the answers to the many lingering questions about how the restricted processes and contents of the physical brain can generate unrestricted and transphysical activities and contents. The most prominent questions might be the following:

- How do the brain's perceptual ideas—which are restricted by individuation, space-time particularity, and physical conditions— generate conceptual ideas that are not so restricted?
- How do the brain's perceptual ideas—which are limited by the perceptual images from which they are derived—generate an awareness of complete and unrestricted intelligibility sufficient to incite *unrestricted* curiosity, questioning, and creativity?
- How do the brain's physical processes—which cannot generate the inwardness of "experiencing ourselves experiencing"—be immersed within the interior world of self-apprehension?
- How do the brain's physical processes—which require rules and algorithms—generate higher-level mathematics *beyond* any set of rules and algorithms?

If *transphysical* self-consciousness did not orient the brain's physical processes and contents toward transphysical activities and contents, then the above activities and contents would be completely

inexplicable—much like a computer performing sophisticated operations without an operating system or a program, or like a chimpanzee (incapable of syntactical language) solving complex problems
in calculus or writing a book on the General Theory of Relativity.
Synthesizing physical processes and contents will not produce transphysical effects without the intervention or mediation of a transphysical cause, because physical processes and contents cannot extricate
themselves from their inherent individuated, space-time, and physical
restrictions. Without a transphysical cause we are left only with the
aggregation (even the complex aggregation) of inherently restricted
physical processes—nothing more.

Trialist interactionism is compatible with hylomorphism because
these two systems are not giving opposed answers to the same question. Trialist interactionism answers the question of how transphysical self-consciousness can *interact* with the physical brain,
while hylomorphism responds to the question of how the physical
processes of the brain can be *oriented* toward transphysical activities
and contents. The answer to the first question concerns the mediating
capacity of *quantum fields*, while the answer to the second question
concerns the capacity of transphysical self-consciousness to orient
physical processes toward transphysical objectives. Thus, we might
say hylomorphic trialist interactionism provides a comprehensive
solution to the question posed by the interaction between transphysical self-consciousness and its physical brain.

V. Comparisons and Contrasts

Throughout this chapter (and in Chapters 3 and 5), we have considered five indications of transphysical consciousness that challenge
classical physicalist models:

1. The evidence of transphysical consciousness from near-death
   experiences
2. The need for innate heuristic notions to convert perceptual
   ideas into conceptual ideas
3. The need for a horizon of complete and unrestricted intelligibility to explain our *unrestricted* capacity to recognize incomplete
   and restricted intelligibility

4. The need for a horizon of mathematical intelligibility beyond all rules and algorithms to explain the Gödel enigma
5. The need for a transphysical ground of self-consciousness to explain how our "experience of experiencing" can have two relative positions with respect to itself simultaneously

As explained above, classical physicalist explanations do not explain any of these indications of transphysical consciousness, and so we explored four other approaches to consciousness that hold out the potential to do so:

1. Quantum physicalist explanations (e.g., Penrose and Hameroff)
2. Protomentalist explanations (e.g., Chalmers, Griffin, de Quincey, and Russell)
3. Trialist interactionist explanations (e.g., Eccles, Popper, Stapp, and Beck)
4. Contemporary hylomorphic explanations (e.g., Polanyi and Lonergan)

We examined each model and determined that the first two were incapable of explaining the above five indications of transphysical consciousness (for the reasons mentioned below). We then determined that a combination of the third and fourth models could best explain them. The following is a summary of the difficulties with the first two models (quantum physicalism and protomentalism) and the apparent sufficiency of the combined third and fourth models (trialist interactionism and hylomorphism).

A. Difficulties with Quantum Physicalist Explanations

Recall that quantum physicalist explanations are *reductionistic*; they try to explain consciousness in terms of quantum systems intrinsic to the brain. This is a more sophisticated physicalist explanation than the classical physicalist one. The latter does not account for the quantum properties of randomness and nonconstraint by locality and local realism.

Inasmuch as quantum physical models are limited to the physical domain, they cannot explain the transphysical ground of consciousness implied by near-death experiences. According to these models, when the brain dies, consciousness should also die with it. However, as noted in Chapter 5, there is considerable evidence from near-death experiences showing consciousness' capacity to survive bodily death.

Furthermore, quantum physical models cannot explain heuristic notions or the horizon of complete and unrestricted intelligibility. The transspatial qualities of nonlocality and nonlocal realism are not sufficient to explain the absence of physical conditions (individuation, space-time particularity, and physical laws) in heuristic notions and are likewise incapable of explaining the unrestrictedness of our horizon of intelligibility.

As noted in Section I, Penrose and Hameroff take Gödel's enigma very seriously. They believe it shows the human ability to transcend deterministic mathematics. In order to give this transcendental capacity a physicalist explanation, they propose the possibility of quantum computation in brain microtubules. Ingenious as this hypothesis is, it does not explain the full extent of Gödel's proof—that human intellection can transcend *any* rule or algorithm. It is one thing to say that human intellection can transcend deterministic mathematics (by quantum computation in brain microtubules), and quite another to say that human intellection can continuously (and seemingly indefinitely) create new mathematical systems without making recourse to any known rule or algorithm. The creation of new mathematical systems entails a grasp of mathematical intelligibility *beyond any* rules or algorithms. Generating such highly ordered viewpoints by randomness applied to previous algorithms is *exceedingly improbable*. For this reason, quantum physicalist solutions fall short of the requirements needed to explain the Gödel enigma.

B. Protomentalist Explanations

Many protomentalists recognize the intractable problems of purely physicalist explanations (both classical physicalist and quantum physicalist explanations) to resolve the hard problem of consciousness. Most protomentalists are less concerned with explaining Gödel's enigma than explaining Chalmers' "hard problem of consciousness" (i.e., the irreducibility of human inward self-apprehension to physical processes alone). To resolve this "hard problem", they propose that consciousness inheres in physical realities and processes. Quantum theory seems to provide justification for this because quantum systems are not constrained by locality and local realism. However, as explained above, this explanation of "consciousness in physical processes" does not resolve the hard problem.

Recall that Chalmers' problem concerns *human* consciousness—particularly the inwardness and subjectivity intrinsic to human experience. As explained above (Section III.B), this inward dimension of human consciousness requires that our act of experience be both experienc*er* and experienc*ed* simultaneously—that it be in two relative positions with respect to itself simultaneously. This quality of self-consciousness is not and cannot be found in quantum systems (see Section III.C). Furthermore this transphysical quality of inwardness and self-apprehension is qualitatively different from anything in living systems (e.g., a bacterium, plant, or insect) and also from anything in sensate consciousness (e.g., higher vertebrates). Thus, in order for the protomentalists' solution to work, they will have to hypothesize that *human self*-consciousness is intrinsic to *physical* processes. If they do not, they will not be able to resolve the hard problem of consciousness. The following reflection will clarify this.

If physical processes have only a "low form" of consciousness (such as quantum systems), then human self-consciousness will have to be explicable through an aggregation of quantum systems. But as we have seen, a quantum system cannot be in two relative positions with respect to itself simultaneously. If one quantum system cannot produce this effect, then any combination of them will not be able to do so. Why? Because compounding quantum systems will not remove their intrinsic restrictions or enable them to transcend those restrictions. The only way of doing this is through the intervention of a transcendent causal principle or agent not affected by those restrictions.

Furthermore, in Sections II.A and II.B we explained why Polanyi and Lonergan hold not only to the irreducibility *of self-consciousness* to physical processes but also to the irreducibility of *sensate consciousness* and *living systems* to those processes. For them, compounding classical and quantum physical systems will not be able to produce a living system (let alone a conscious system or a self-conscious one) without a "higher order principle of design orienting physical and chemical processes toward ends *not* intrinsic to them". Without such a higher-order principle or a higher-order cause, compounding physical and chemical processes will yield only more of the same. Inanimate molecules plus inanimate molecules (without a higher principle or cause of design for a living system) will only yield more (and possibly more complex) *inanimate* molecules. The same holds true for sensate consciousness and rational self-consciousness. Without a higher-order principle or cause of design to orient lower-order processes and systems to higher-order ones (thereby transcending their inherent limitations), lower-order systems and processes are doomed to remain mere aggregations of themselves.

If Polanyi and Lonergan are correct, then the protomentalist position will not work to solve the hard problem of consciousness unless the higher-order principle for human self-consciousness is intrinsic to physical processes and systems. Why? If self-consciousness cannot be produced by any aggregation or complexification of lower-order consciousness or systems (e.g., sensate consciousness, living systems, or quantum systems), then the only way physical processes will be able to generate human self-consciousness is if they have *higher-order* self-consciousness in them.

However, this presents two significant challenges to the protomentalist position. First, if the "higher order principle of design for self-consciousness" is present in physical processes and systems, then when the appropriate physical processes underlying self-consciousness are in place, some form of self-consciousness should be actualized. As noted above (Section III.B) the brain of a chimpanzee more than adequately meets this minimum requirement for physical processes. Why aren't chimpanzees self-reflective? Why aren't dolphins and rhesus monkeys self-conscious? Yet, none of these species meets current criteria for human self-consciousness—for example, Carruthers' criterion (having a mental state available to be thought about by a subject), or the criterion of Lycan and Armstrong (having an experiential state available to be thought about by a subject), or even Herbert Terrace's criterion of autonoetic episodic memory (ability to project self into memories of the past and anticipation of the future).

The second challenge to the protomentalist position concerns the *individuality* of human self-consciousness. Recall from Section IV.B that there cannot be a *universal* "higher principle of design for self-consciousness" (like there can be for living systems or sensate consciousness), because the inwardness of self-apprehension is unshareable and unrepeatable—and hence it must be individual and unique. As such, the proposition "universal self-consciousness" is tantamount to the proposition "universal unique individual"—which is an obvious contradiction. Thus, self-consciousness will only be realized when a *uniquely individual* principle of design orients physical and biological processes toward its higher end.

This puts protomentalists in a curious position: in order for them to resolve the hard problem of consciousness, they will have to postulate that unique acts of self-consciousness are intrinsic to physical processes. Aside from the rather humorous scenario this implies—uniquely self-conscious quantum systems, atoms, and molecules—there is the further problem of restricting self-consciousness to the limits of classical and quantum physics, which is yet another contradiction. Recall from above that self-consciousness cannot be subject to physical limits (individuation, space-time particularity, and physical laws) if it is to be in two relative positions with respect to itself simultaneously.

In addition to the above two challenges, the protomentalist explanation faces the same challenge as the quantum physicalist explanation, namely, that if the evidence of near-death experiences is correct, then human self-consciousness can survive bodily death. This means that self-consciousness can exist apart from the brain, and therefore apart from the physical systems constituting the brain. But this runs contrary to the protomentalist position that hypothesizes that consciousness is intrinsic to those physical processes and systems.

Though the protomentalist explanation of consciousness avoids some of the problems of the quantum physicalist explanation, it does not appear able to face successfully the challenges of survival of consciousness after bodily death, and the nonoccurrence of self-consciousness in primates. Moreover it is constrained to hypothesize *higher-order* self-consciousness in physical systems, which is both fanciful and contradictory. In view of this, we were obliged to seek another solution to the hard problem of consciousness. We considered two other potential candidates (trialist interactionism and hylomorphism) and discovered that a combination of both models could provide an explanation of the five indications of transphysical consciousness and a solution to the mind-body (transphysical-physical) problem.

Trialist interactionism (Eccles, Popper, Beck and Stapp) provides a plausible explanation for how quantum fields can mediate the transphysical content of consciousness (such as conceptual ideas) and the classical biophysical processes of the brain. However, it does not explain how the brain's physical processes and perceptual contents can orient themselves toward transphysical activities and contents (such as the formation of conceptual ideas, the unrestricted desire to know, the development of higher mathematical principles, and the experience of our experiencing).

We turned to Michael Polanyi's "higher order principle of design orienting physical and chemical processes toward ends not intrinsic to them" and Bernard Lonergan's "conjugates", "things", and "horizon of higher intelligibility" to explain this phenomenon. Polanyi reveals the need for higher-order principles of design to orient inanimate physical and chemical systems (which do not act *for* themselves) toward objectives appropriate to animate systems (which do act *for* themselves). The same higher principle can be used to explain how inanimate physical processes can be oriented toward sensate consciousness and human self-consciousness. We discovered one very important difference between self-consciousness and the other two systems (living systems and sensate consciousness): there can be no *universal* system of self-consciousness (as there can be for living systems and sensate consciousness), because every instance of self-consciousness must be unduplicatable and unique.

We used Lonergan's idea of "horizon of higher intelligibility"[62] to show how the brain's perceptual *contents* could be oriented toward transphysical contents and activities. When the brain's individuated contents (e.g., perceptions, images, perceptual ideas, and perceptual memories) are positioned within the transphysical horizon of higher intelligibility, they can contribute to conceptual ideas, syntactical language, abstract thought, higher mathematical theories, continuous and unrestricted curiosity, and every other creative endeavor.

---

[62] The term "horizon" is derived from Karl Rahner, but applied here to Lonergan's "notion of being" or "notion of complete intelligibility". Since Rahner's "horizon" and Lonergan's "notion" are compatible and similar (see Chapter 3, Sections V.A and V.B), I combined them and credited it to Lonergan.

Without this transphysical horizon of higher intelligibility, we would be reduced to perceptual ideas and nonsyntactical language—to the domain of the great apes.

Thus, trialist interactionism provides the explanation for how transphysical self-consciousness can interact with the physical brain. Hylomorphism as articulated by Polanyi and Lonergan provides the explanation for how the brain's physical *processes* (e.g., perception) can contribute to transphysical *activities* (e.g., continuous and unrestricted questioning), and also how the brain's individuated *contents* (e.g., perceptual ideas) can contribute to transphysical content (e.g., conceptual ideas and mathematical theories). Currently, hylomorphic trialist interactionism is the most comprehensive way of explaining the five indications of transphysical self-consciousness and its interaction with its physical brain.

VI. Conclusion: The Impact of Transphysical Self-Consciousness

When trialist interactionism and hylomorphism are combined, the resultant model of human consciousness is as follows:

1. There exists a unique instantiation of transphysical consciousness in every person that is the source and ground of heuristic notions, the unrestricted desire to know, the awareness of higher mathematical intelligibility, and the inwardness and self-apprehension of "experiencing our experiencing".
2. This transphysical ground of self-consciousness is independent of the brain (and all physical systems), meaning that it can perform all cognitional functions without the brain and survive bodily death.
3. If Eccles, Beck, and Stapp are correct, then each unique instantiation of self-consciousness can interact with a physical brain through the mediation of quantum fields in brain synapses. These quantum fields can be affected by transphysical activity and content (such as conceptual ideas, intentions, and observations) that can collapse the whole field to an eigenstate capable of interacting with the classical physical systems of the brain.

4. If Polanyi and Lonergan are correct, each unique instantiation of self-consciousness can act as a "higher order principle of design to orient the physical processes of the brain toward transphysical activities", such as unrestricted inquiry, conceptual thought, higher mathematics, and self-reflectivity.

5. Each unique instantiation of self-consciousness can act as a horizon of higher-order intelligibility in which the brain's perceptual contents (perceptions, images, perceptual ideas, and perceptual memories) can be positioned to yield transphysical contents (e.g., conceptual ideas, abstract theories, and mathematical theories).

The above transphysical activities and contents are the mediating ground through which man's self-consciousness interacts with *divine* self-consciousness, particularly in the experience of the numen and the sacred, the awareness of moral authority through conscience, and the awareness of a cosmic struggle between good and evil. They are also the vehicle for appropriating and interpreting love (empathy) and beauty (aesthetics) on both the temporal and transcendent level. The following diagram lists the central role of each unique instantiation of transphysical self-consciousness, showing the extent of our transcendent nature and activities.

We began this chapter by noting the limitations of physicalist models of consciousness. We can now see that those limitations have consequences beyond the problems of explaining heuristic notions, the unrestricted desire to know, Gödel's theorem, self-consciousness, and near-death experiences. These transphysical activities affect the way we view ourselves, the meaning of life, our sense of dignity, and our ultimate destiny. If we detach ourselves from these transphysical activities and consider ourselves mere classical and quantum physical systems, we eclipse the true mystery of our being, negating the significance of virtually everything on the above diagram. We no longer see our nature and dignity as unrestrictedly inquisitive and creative, seeking perfection in truth, love, goodness, and beauty; we ignore or screen out the experience of the numen, which calls us interiorly into relationship with itself; we become insensitive to the guidance of conscience and the cosmic struggle surrounding us; we circumscribe the unrestricted potential of our goodness and love; and we reduce

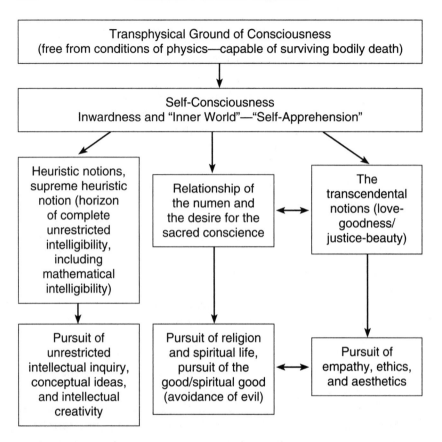

ourselves to the temporal and material—becoming disconnected from our eternal and transcendent purpose and destiny.

Why would we do this when the evidence for our transphysical activities is significant, based on careful studies of near-death experiences, Gödel's proof, the necessity of heuristic notions (recognized from the time of Plato), the hard problem of consciousness (the inwardness of self-apprehension), and our awareness of complete unrestricted intelligibility (intrinsic to our unrestricted desire and pursuit of universal knowledge)?

This evidence is not, strictly speaking, empirical and therefore cannot be considered "scientific". However, knowledge is *not* limited to observation and science. There is also a priori knowledge (based on the principle of noncontradiction from which we derive logic, mathematics, and methodological principles); the knowledge of interior experience (through which we apprehend inwardness, self-awareness, the numen, and conscience); and the evidence of corroborateable eyewitness testimony (from which we learn about history and the data of near-death experiences). Though these kinds of evidence are not strictly speaking empirical and scientific, they are nevertheless valid—and we would not want to preclude the data derived from them from the domain of reality by unjustifiably and arbitrarily limiting reality to the empirical domain alone. If we did so, we would have no logic, mathematics, psychology, philosophy, history, ethics, law, and so on. Indeed, this arbitrary restriction of evidence would present tremendous problems to the pursuit of science itself that is dependent on mathematics, logic, and methodological principles *not* derived from empirical observation or scientific methodology.

We have frequently noted that there are far more errors of omission than commission—and that reality is bigger and richer than the explanatory power of any particular method or causal model. If there is any legitimacy to the above kinds of nonscientific knowledge (and the clues to the transcendent they reveal), then it would seem more prudent to open ourselves to their breadth of data, rather than imposing an a priori limitation to legitimate evidence (restricting it to the domain of observation and science alone). Evidently, such an aprioristic limitation of evidence cannot be justified by either observation or science—and so it is a self-refuting enterprise.

We began this chapter by noting that our view of consciousness is the new field upon which the academic and cultural battle between materialism, panpsychism, and transcendentalism is being waged. We now see that the outcome of this battle will not only affect our personal view of life's purpose, the world, human dignity, and human value, but also the culture's outlook on these important ideas and ideals. Jesus' proclamation that "the truth will make you free" (Jn 8:32) is particularly important here—for if we and the culture falsely underestimate our purpose, dignity, value, and destiny, we will also unnecessarily restrict our freedom and potential to reach beyond the material world into the domain of perfect truth, love, goodness, and beauty. This would be one of the greatest avoidable travesties we could collectively impose upon ourselves. To avoid this, we need to consider seriously our transcendental nature, dignity, value, and destiny—and upon finding it, act on it.

CONCLUSION

In Chapters 1–4, we endeavored to describe the evidence for our transcendental nature and destiny from two kinds of sources:

1. Interior evidence of an interpersonal transcendent reality, which manifests itself within our consciousness in three distinctive ways:
   a. As the mysterious, daunting, fascinating, good, accessible "wholly Other" (Otto's numinous experience)
   b. As the Sacred Reality who breaks into the world, allowing us to reconnect with it both individually and collectively through sacred places, myths, rituals, and community (Eliade's religious intuition)
   c. As the Divine Authority who draws us more deeply into His goodness while revealing the coldness and darkness of evil (Newman's conscience)
2. Logical-empirical evidence of a unique, uncaused, unrestricted act of thinking that is the Creator of all else that exists. This was demonstrated by Lonergan's proof of God in Chapter 3 (Sections III and IV). We also showed that this unique, unrestricted act of thinking manifests itself in four distinctive ways:
   a. As the source of our innate tacit awareness of the complete intelligibility of reality (perfect truth)
   b. As the source of our innate tacit awareness of perfect love
   c. As the source of our innate tacit awareness of perfect justice or goodness
   d. As the source of our innate tacit awareness of perfect beauty

We diagramed these seven dimensions of our transcendental consciousness as follows:

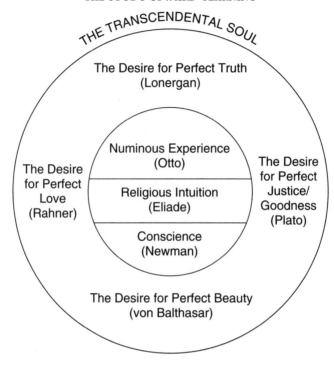

The complementarity between the two sources of evidence is important, because each does something the other cannot do. The first source tells us of the personal and interpersonal dimension of an experienced transcendent reality, but does not reveal its attributes (unique, uncaused, unrestricted, creative act of thinking). In contrast, the second source (including Lonergan's proof of God) proves the existence of a unique, unrestricted act of thinking that is the Creator of all else that is—and implies that this Being is perfect love, goodness, and beauty. However, the second source does not provide experiential access to the transcendent Being's personal consciousness. When we combine the two kinds of evidence, we arrive at a unique, uncaused, unrestricted, creative, intelligent, personal, empathetic, moral, and passionate *God*.

The above evidence of God and our transcendental nature is further complemented by the evidence of near-death experiences—which reveals our transphysical self-consciousness ("soul") capable of surviving bodily death (Chapter 5). It also reveals a domain independent of the physical universe, which is intensely beautiful and loving (where a loving white light, Jesus, and deceased relatives and friends may be encountered).

The above three kinds of evidence (interior evidence, logical-empirical evidence, and corroborated accounts of postmortem consciousness) come from three distinct sources and three distinct methods; this evidence is not only complementary but *mutually corroborative*. In view of this, it is reasonable and responsible to affirm the likelihood of a transcendental and transphysical soul capable of surviving bodily death and called by a unique divine consciousness into a destiny of perfect truth, love, justice or goodness, and beauty.

The existence of God and our transcendental soul does not exhaust the scope of transcendence accessible to reason and experience. Through interior experience, the numinous and sacred reality—God—incites us to discover and create greater truth, love, justice or goodness, and beauty and calls us to pursue good and avoid evil, and to be His companions in a cosmic struggle between good and evil.

If we are open to the full range of God's *interior* manifestation, we will see that He is not a disinterested God (e.g., the god of Aristotle or Einstein), nor a dispassionate God (the god of the rationalists), but rather a God who is calling us to develop our virtuous character, and to share it with the world, a world that is in need of everything we could offer—teetering on the brink of darkness.

If this sounds curiously like the contemporary myth of J.R.R. Tolkien, we might recall what he had to say about the power of myth:

> [Myths] are not lies. Far from being lies they are the best way—sometimes the only way—of conveying truths that would otherwise remain inexpressible. We have come from God and inevitably the myths woven by us, though they contain error, reflect a splintered fragment of the true light, the eternal truth that is with God.[1]

Where does this leave us? As the reader might suspect: with more questions than answers. The moment we see the breadth and depth of the universal revelation we have been given through interior experience and logical deduction, we want to know how to relate to this transcendent Being. What is His love and goodness like? How

[1] Joseph Pearce, *Tolkien: Man and Myth* (San Francisco: Ignatius Press, 2001), p. 58.

does He manifest it without undermining our freedom? Why would a perfectly loving God allow suffering? Why would a perfectly good God allow evil? What is God's purpose in suffering? How do we enter into the cosmic struggle between good and evil? How should we pray? Does God answer prayers? How does God inspire us, and how can He guide us without undermining our freedom? What is our eternal destiny like? Is there any possibility of being separated from God—even eternally?

These questions reveal the need for revelation *from God*, provoking yet another question: Does God reveal Himself in some *special* way besides the universal way of interior experience and logical reasoning (discussed in the last five chapters)? Does God give special revelations of Himself through prophets and holy people? If so, can He use the ideas and categories of these people to answer the above questions? If God does not reveal Himself in special ways to answer the above questions, then He would leave us radically incomplete—at the brink of a chasm—without sufficient knowledge of how to get across it.

If, as we have seen, God is perfectly good and loving—if He is really the God of our conscience, and the God of the sacred who has broken into the profane world—it seems unlikely that He would leave us in such a state. Why bother to give us an interior revelation of Himself without giving us the special revelation to complete it? Why would He create us in a condition in which we are not only incomplete, but incapable of reaching the transcendental destiny to which He seems to be calling us? In view of this, it seems likely that the God who reveals Himself to us interiorly (what ancient Christian philosophers called "the inner word") would also be the God of a special exterior revelation ("the outer word").

How would God reveal Himself in this special way? If He is to reveal Himself in a restricted and conditioned world, He will have to limit Himself to *particular* places, times, cultures, worldviews, and so on. God will have to accommodate Himself to these particularities and therefore answer the above questions in many different times, places, and cultures. This will entail differences among the doctrines of various religions—and we do not have to look far to see this. Nevertheless, as we saw in Chapter 1, there are certain similarities among the vast majority of the world's religions. Friedrich Heiler's seven similarities merit a review:

1. There is a reality of the transcendent, the holy, the divine, the Other.
2. The transcendent reality is immanent in human awareness.
3. This transcendent reality is the highest truth, highest good, and highest beauty.
4. This transcendent reality is loving and compassionate and seeks to reveal its love to human beings.
5. The way to God requires prayer, ethical self-discipline, purgation of self-centeredness, asceticism, and redressing of offenses.
6. The way to God also includes service and responsibility to others.
7. The highest way to eternal bliss in the Transcendent Reality is through love.

Two clarifications are in order. First, Heiler does not indicate the degree of importance of each of these common doctrines in world religions. So, for example, in the fourth and seventh doctrines, he indicates that love is a high path to a loving God, but he does not indicate whether this is found in one or two passages of a religion's mystical literature or whether it is central to the religion itself (and all its doctrines). There are significant differences in degree about "love being the highest path to God" among the world's religions. For example, in the teaching of Jesus, love is established as the highest commandment to which all other virtues and commandments are subordinated. Love (*agapē*) is defined very carefully—in parables, beatitudes, prescriptions, and most importantly in the actions of Jesus Himself. This cannot be said of other religions—many of which do not place this doctrine at their center, do not define it with great precision, and see it as qualified by other virtues and doctrines. This point will be important in our consideration of the *ultimate* source of revelation in Volume III of this Quartet.

With respect to our second clarification, it will come as no surprise that the first two common characteristics of religion (elucidated by Heiler) can be directly traced to the universal interpersonal revelation of the transcendent (the numinous experience, the religious intuition, and conscience). The third characteristic can also be traced to the universal interior revelation of the Transcendent Reality—the four transcendental desires for perfect truth, love, justice or goodness, and beauty. What is most interesting about Heiler's study is the fifth and sixth characteristics, which are considered quite important in *virtually all* religions, but are not specifically manifest in the universal interior revelation, namely, that the way to God requires prayer, ethical self-discipline, purgation of self-centeredness, asceticism, redressing of offenses, service, and responsibility to others. Though there are different emphases on the way these disciplines are to be carried out, their remarkably similar occurrence in world religions gives us pause. If God is not truly the *common source* of special *exterior* revelations to different cultures at different times, could these universal characteristics have manifested themselves so similarly within those different times and cultures? It seems highly unlikely, and so it seems that God's revealing hand is everywhere to be found in world religions.

This leaves us with a few major questions: Would God want to make a *personal* revelation to us? Would He want to reveal Himself to us face-to-face and peer-to-peer—or would God be content to use only *human* intermediaries (such as prophets and holy people) to reveal Himself? Would He come to us personally and be part of our existence? Would He want to be with us in a state of perfect empathy and self-gift? If so, how would God go about making such a personal revelation? Recall that if He does so, *He Himself* will be subject to the limitations of place, time, and culture. If He is to make a *personal* appearance, it would have to be at a *particular* place, time, and culture. What time and culture would He choose?

It is here that we encounter the peculiar and radical claim of Christianity that God has sent His only Son into the world, not only to reveal Himself in word, but also in unconditional self-sacrificial action—that He is unconditional, compassionate, and humble love, and that He prepared the Jewish people and the surrounding Gentile cultures with both the revelation and philosophy necessary to interpret and understand the arrival of His Son.

If there is any candidate for a personal and *ultimate* revelation, this is it. It is ultimate in the One chosen to give the personal revelation: God's only Son; ultimate in the content of revelation, that God is *unconditional*, compassionate, humble love; ultimate in the manifestation of that unconditional love, not only in word, but in complete self-sacrificial action (suffering and death). If it can be shown that this *ultimate* revelation is truly connected to God—and is not simply the ultimate revelation of an unconditionally loving *man*—then it should be taken with utmost seriousness, not as an invalidation of other religions, but as the ultimate revelation that fulfills and completes them. As we shall see in Volume III, there is an abundance of clues to Jesus' divinity: His Resurrection, gift of the Holy Spirit, miracles, claims about Himself, and the unconditional quality of His love.

Appendix One

Evidence for an Intelligent Creator from Contemporary Science

Introduction

In Volume 1 (Chapter 2), I indicated that there was not only evidence for the transcendent from experience and philosophical reasoning, but also from the domain of science, particularly contemporary astrophysics. The following is a summary of recent findings on creation and supernatural intelligence from contemporary Big Bang cosmology. I have written about this evidence extensively in *New Proofs for the Existence of God: Contributions of Contemporary Physics and Philosophy.*[1]

The evidence will be discussed in six sections:

1. Can Science Indicate Creation?
2. Fr. Georges Lemaître, the Big Bang Theory, and the Modern Universe
3. Space-Time Geometry Proofs and the Beginning of Physical Reality
4. Entropy and the Beginning of Our Universe

[1] See Robert J. Spitzer, *New Proofs for the Existence of God: Contributions of Contemporary Physics and Philosophy* (Grand Rapids, Mich.: Eerdmans, 2010), pp. 1–103. This appendix has new material (beyond the book) in four areas:

   1. A response to claims from physicists who say that the universe does not need a Creator (Section I)
   2. A brief consideration of the contributions of Fr. Georges Le Lemaître, who discovered the Big Bang theory (Section II)
   3. An extensive logical explanation of the Borde-Vilenkin-Guth proof for a beginning of all expansive universes and multiverses (Section III)
   4. An extensive explanation of recent physicists' foray into the metaphysics of nothing and purely intelligible realities (Section V)

278THE SOUL'S UPWARD YEARNING

5. From Physics to Metaphysics
6. Fine-Tuning "for Life" at the Big Bang—Implications of Supernatural Intelligence

I. Can Science Indicate Creation?

We should begin by clarifying what science can tell us about a beginning of the universe and supernatural causation. First, unlike philosophy and metaphysics, science cannot *deductively* prove a creation or God. Natural science is concerned with the physical universe and with the regularities we call "laws of nature", obeyed by the phenomena within that universe. But God is not an object or phenomenon or regularity within the physical universe; so science cannot say anything about God.

Moreover, science is an empirical and inductive discipline. As such, science cannot be certain that it has considered all possible data relevant to a complete explanation of particular physical phenomena or the universe itself. It must always remain open to new data and discoveries that could alter its explanation of particular phenomena and the universe. This can be seen quite clearly in the movement from the Newtonian view of the universe to the Einsteinian one or from the Ptolemaic view of the solar system (geocentric) to the Copernican one (heliocentric).

So what *can* science tell us? It can identify, aggregate, and synthesize evidence indicating the finitude of past time in the universe (as we currently know it and conceive it could be). Science can also identify the exceedingly high improbability of the random occurrence of conditions necessary to sustain life in the universe (as we currently know it and conceive it could be).

Though scientific conclusions are subject to change in the light of new data, we should not let this possibility cause us unnecessarily to discount the validity of long-standing, persistent, rigorously established theories. If we did this, we might discount the majority of all scientific theories. Thus, it is reasonable and responsible to attribute qualified truth value to such theories until such time as new data requires them to be modified.

The arguments that suggest the finitude of past time, that is, that time had a beginning, are basically of two types:

1. Arguments about the possible geometries of space-time
2. Arguments based on the second law of thermodynamics (entropy)

Though the arguments we shall give may conceivably have loopholes, in the sense that cosmological models or scenarios may be found in the future to which these arguments don't apply, their persistence and applicability to a large number of existing cosmological models gives them respectable probative force. Until such time as they are shown to be invalid or inapplicable to empirically verifiable characteristics of our universe, they should be considered as justifying the conclusion that it is probable that the universe had a beginning.

When we speak of a beginning (a point prior to which there is no physical reality), we stand at the threshold of metaphysics (beyond physics). Even though science cannot be validly used to prove a metaphysical claim (such as "a Creator or God exists"), it can be used (with the qualifications mentioned above) to show the high probability of a limit to past time *in* our universe, and even *in* physical reality itself. This *scientific* evidence for a beginning can be combined with a *metaphysical* premise (such as "from nothing, only nothing comes") to render a *metaphysical* conclusion that there must be *something* beyond physical reality that caused physical reality to exist (i.e., a transcendent cause).

There are other indications of supernatural causation arising out of contemporary cosmology besides the implications of a beginning—namely, the occurrence of several highly improbable cosmological conditions essential for the development and sustenance of *any* life form. These seemingly highly improbable conditions (which are sometimes called "cosmic coincidences" or "anthropic coincidences") imply an element of supernatural fine-tuning if no satisfactory naturalistic explanation can be found.

The existence of a Creator need not rest on scientific evidence alone. There are sufficient rational grounds to affirm the existence of a Creator without modern science (see Chapter 3, Section III, and Appendix 2).[2] The findings of modern science complement and corroborate these philosophical arguments. This complementarity and corroboration constitute a network of evidence. John Henry

[2] See the three proofs in Spitzer, *New Proofs for the Existence of God*, Chapters 3–5.

Newman termed such a network of evidence an "informal inference",[3] that is, reaching a conclusion by considering the accumulation of converging independently probable data sets. This allows for
possible modification of one or more of the sets without significantly
changing the general conclusion.

Using the foregoing methodological considerations as a foundation, we may now respond to three naturalistic claims that have
become widely accepted in popular culture:

1. Science can and has disproved the existence of a Creator.
2. Science currently knows everything about the universe sufficient to conclude that the universe does not need a Creator.
3. Science can give no evidence for a transcendent Creator.

Let us begin with the first naturalistic claim (science can disprove
a Creator). This claim is completely beyond the domain of science,
because scientific evidence must be observational (whether it be
directly observed, measured, or inferred from an experiment, etc.).
This observational evidence is limited to our universe (and even
to our event horizon within the universe). However, a *transcendent*
Creator would have to be beyond the confines of our observational
data (because it would be *beyond* our universe), and so science cannot
disprove the existence of a transcendent Creator. An elaboration of the
problem will make this clear.

It is much more difficult to disprove something by means of observation than to prove it. For example, if I want to prove the existence
of an alien, I need to see only one; however, if I wish to *disprove* the
existence of aliens by observational method, I would have to observe
everything that there was to observe in the universe, know with certainty that all realities within the universe come within my experiential
purview and observational powers, and then notice that it is not there.
Thus, *disproving* by means of observation requires a comprehensive
search and infallible certitude that all realities can be observed by the
observer (which itself cannot be known through observation!).

The problem becomes much more challenging when we are speaking about a reality *outside* of the observable universe (such as a transcendent Creator, or God). This would entail observing everything

---

[3] See John Henry Newman, *An Essay in Aid of a Grammar of Assent* (Notre Dame, Ind.:
University of Notre Dame Press, 1992), pp. 259–342 (Chapter 8).

there was to observe *outside* the universe, knowing that all realities outside the universe are in fact observable, and noticing that it is not there. This is evidently an impossible task—enough said. The claim that science can disprove God can never be sustained, because God necessarily lies beyond the methodological parameters of science.

Let us turn to the second naturalistic claim—namely, that science now knows enough about the universe to know with certainty that the universe does not need a Creator.[4] This contention cannot be the case today or at any other time in the future, because science is an *inductive* discipline. This means that science proceeds from specific observational data to theories that coherently unify this data. Sometimes scientists are able to formulate "rigorously established" theories that are corroborated by several different data sets and a convergence of the mathematics intrinsic to those data sets (such as the Big Bang theory). Though rigorously established theories have probative value, they can never be known with infallible certitude, because scientists can *never* know what they do not know until they have discovered it. Theories are not theorems (proofs). They are only coherent unifications of *currently available* data (observations). Thus, scientists can never know whether their theories are *completely* explanatory (i.e., that they explain all relevant data in the universe). Inasmuch as the completeness of a theory cannot be known by observational evidence, it cannot be known by science, and for this reason science must remain open to further discoveries—always.[5] Therefore, science can never know with certainty that the universe does not need a

---

[4] This is the contention of Stephen Hawking and Leonard Mlodinow. See their book *The Grand Design* (New York: Random House, 2010). See also the interview by Larry King regarding *The Grand Design* from *Larry King Live*, CNN, September 10, 2010, when Larry King first interviewed Stephen Hawking, then interviewed Leonard Mlodinow, Deepak Chopra, and me. The interview is available on YouTube in three parts: Part 1 can be found at http://www.youtube.com/watch?v=9AdKEHzmqxA; Part 2, https://www.youtube.com/watch?v=BCoTGTRfDyo; and Part 3, https://www.youtube.com/watch?v=tIttENo2eOM.

[5] The idea that M-theory (see explanatory note on p. 288) is perfectly explanatory is doubly fallacious. Though M-theory *can* show how an eleven-dimensional vibrating string configuration can explain much of quantum theory and general relativity theory, no scientist can know that M-theory exhausts the whole of physical reality (for the reasons mentioned above). There is a second problem with this contention—namely, that we currently do not have any evidence for string theory (or M-theory) (see explanatory note on p. 288), and it looks as if these theories may be inapplicable to some aspects of the observable universe. See Michael Dine, "Is There a String Theory Landscape: Some Cautionary Remarks", February 17, 2004, http://arxiv.org/pdf/hep-th/0402101v2.pdf; and see Bruce Gordon, "Inflationary Cosmology and the String Multiverse", in Spitzer, *New Proofs for the Existence of God*, pp. 75–103.

Creator, because it cannot know with certainty that it has accounted for all data in the universe affecting the answer to this question. Furthermore, this claim conflicts directly with the evidence for a creation of the universe discussed below (and in Chapter 3 and Appendix 2).

We proceed finally to the third naturalistic claim—namely, that science can give no evidence *for* a transcendent reality (such as a Creator or God). At first it might seem that if science *cannot* give evidence *against* a Creator, then it should not be able to give evidence *for* a Creator. However, recall from above that it is much easier to prove something with observational evidence than to disprove it, because disproving requires observing everything that is real, and noticing that a hypothetical entity is not there. Accomplishing this task for an entity outside the universe (outside of our observational horizon) is impossible. However, if one could show that the universe (and even physical reality itself) cannot explain its own existence, then it would be possible to give evidence for a reality beyond the universe. So is there any evidence *within* the universe that shows that the universe cannot explain its existence? As a matter of fact, there is—a finite limit to past time or what is commonly called "a beginning". As noted above, if science could show through observational evidence that the universe (and even physical reality itself) must have a beginning, then this datum could be combined with a metaphysical premise (showing that physical reality was absolutely nothing before the beginning) leading to the conclusion that the universe could not have moved itself from nothing to something before the beginning. This conclusion requires that physical reality have a transcendent Creator to move it from nothing to something when it was nothing (prior to the beginning).

Well then, can science give evidence for a beginning of the universe, the beginning of a hypothetical multiverse, and even the beginning of physical reality itself? We now proceed to Sections II through IV for that answer.

II. Fr. Georges Lemaître, the Big Bang Theory, and the Modern Universe

Monsignor Georges Lemaître, a Catholic priest, noted cosmologist, and colleague of Einstein's, proposed the premise for the Big Bang theory in 1927.[6] As will be explained below (in the first step in Section III), Lemaître ingeniously solved the problem of how the recessional velocities of distant galaxies could be greater than those of nearer galaxies. The idea was really quite radical—so much so that Einstein, though impressed with Lemaître's mathematics, rejected it at first. Lemaître theorized that galaxies were not moving in fixed space, but rather that the space between the galaxies was stretching and growing. This might be analogized by an inflating balloon. Think for a moment about a balloon with many dots on it, and liken the elastic of the balloon to the spatial manifold (spatial field) and the dots on the balloon to galaxies. Now circle one of the dots on the balloon and call it the Milky Way (our galaxy), and begin blowing up the balloon. Notice that every time you exhale into the balloon and stretch the elastic more, the farther dots from you expand more than the nearer dots. Why did the farther dots move farther away from you than the nearer dots? Because there was more space (more balloon) between them and you (than between the nearer galaxies and us). So, Lemaître reasoned that the more space there was to stretch and grow, the more stretching and growing would occur per unit time, and the more stretching and growing that occurs per unit time, the greater the recessional velocity would be (distance a galaxy moves away from us per unit time).

Lemaître knew that Einstein's General Theory of Relativity allowed not only for the spatial field to have a variable geometry (such as a curved geometrical configuration surrounding dense fields of mass-energy), but also for space to stretch and grow like the expansion of a balloon. He showed with great mathematical precision that the expansion of the universe as a whole was the best explanation of the recessional velocities of distant galaxies, but his conclusion was so radical that Einstein and others found it difficult to accept. Furthermore, it had the consequence that the universe may have had a beginning (a creation), which was a true departure from previous

---

[6] Recently, there was debate about who was the first person to propose that the universe is expanding. Originally, American astronomer Edwin Hubble was given the credit, due in part to censorship of a very important paper by Fr. Georges Lemaître. See Mario Livio, "Mystery of the Missing Text Solved", Comment, *Nature* 479 (November 10, 2011): 171–73, http://www.fisica.ufmg.br/~dsoares/cosmos/11/mario-livio.pdf.

Also worthy of note is that Fr. Georges Lemaître did not use the term "Big Bang", but, rather, "the Theory of the Primeval Atom". Sir Fred Hoyle (when he was in his atheistic phase) sneeringly dubbed Lemaître's theory "the Big Bang" to trivialize and insult it.

scientific assumptions. Why does Lemaître's theory have such a consequence? If the universe truly is expanding as a whole (irrespective of whether it expands uniformly like a balloon or in some other way), it must have been less expanded in the past, and even less expanded still as we go even further back into the past. Today there is only a finite distance between galaxies, and so we know that the universe could not have been expanding forever in the past. All of the points must have been arbitrarily close to one another at some time *in the finite past*. If the Big Bang marks the initial expansion of the universe, then it could be the *beginning* of the universe. We have very good evidence today that this event occurred about 13.8 billion years ago (plus or minus 100 million years).

Nothing like this had ever been considered in the natural sciences before Fr. Lemaître's theory. Aristotle[7] and Saint Thomas Aquinas[8] believed that the evidence of reason could not establish a beginning of time, and so natural philosophy would have to assume the *eternity* of the universe. Saint Thomas thought that the finitude of time in the universe could only be known through the revelation of God (requiring faith). Sir Isaac Newton made the same assumption, and so did his followers, right up to the time of Fr. Lemaître. Though Lemaître did not prove that the Big Bang was the beginning of the universe, his theory implied that it *could* be, and this radically changed the intellectual landscape (and horizon) of the natural sciences. Lemaître put it this way:

> We can compare space-time to an open, conic cup. The bottom of the cup is the origin of atomic disintegration: it is the first instant at the bottom of space-time, the now which has no yesterday because, yesterday, there was no space.[9]

Lemaître's theory was first confirmed two years later by Edwin Hubble's survey of the heavens (at Mt. Wilson Observatory), in which he

---

[7] See Aristotle, *Physics*, Book I, Chap. 7.

[8] Aquinas believed that the world had a beginning, as an article of faith, but held that a beginning of time could not be proven through the *philosophical* arguments of his day. He wrote a short work on this called "De Aeternitate Mundi". He also brings up these arguments in other works. See, for example, *Summa Theologica*, Part I, Question 46—"The Beginning of the Duration of Creatures".

[9] Georges Lemaître, *The Primeval Atom* (New York: University Press, 1943), p. 133.

showed through a well-known technique called redshifting that more distant galaxies are indeed moving away from our galaxy faster than those nearer to us. Hubble invited Einstein to Mt. Wilson to check the results, which apparently caused Einstein to change his mind. When Einstein and Lemaître co-presented at a conference at Mt. Wilson in 1933, Einstein was reported to have said, "This is the most beautiful and satisfactory explanation of creation to which I have ever listened."[10] Since that time, Lemaître's theory has been confirmed in a variety of different ways, making it one of the most comprehensive and rigorously established theories in contemporary cosmology.

After Hubble's confirmation of Lemaître's theory (through the redshifts detected in his survey of the heavens), Arno Penzias and Robert Wilson made another remarkable confirmation in 1965 through a very different approach. They inadvertently discovered cosmic microwave background radiation (a 2.7 degree Kelvin uniformly distributed radiation) throughout the universe, which could have occurred only at a very early, cosmic-wide event (the Big Bang and its immediate aftermath).[11] They received the Nobel Prize for this discovery in 1978.

The Big Bang was subsequently confirmed by data from NASA's cosmic background explorer satellite (COBE),[12] the Wilkinson Microwave Anisotropy Probe (WMAP),[13] and very recently by the Planck satellite.[14] These confirmations verify Fr. Lemaître's general concept of the Big Bang and add considerably more data to it—such as quantum gravity, inflationary theory, dark matter, and dark energy (described briefly below).

[10] David Topper, *How Einstein Created Relativity Out of Physics and Astronomy* (New York: Springer, 2013), p. 175. See Simon Singh, "Even Einstein Had His Off Days", Opinion, *New York Times*, January 2, 2005, http://www.nytimes.com/2005/01/02/opinion/02singh .html?_r=0.

[11] See Arno A. Penzias and Robert W. Wilson, "A Measurement of Excess Antenna Temperature at 408^0 Mc/s", *Astrophysical Journal* 142 (1965): 419–21.

[12] See NASA, "COBE: Cosmic Background Explorer", accessed February 23, 2015, http://lambda.gsfc.nasa.gov/product/cobe/.

[13] NASA, APPEL [Academy of Program/Project and Engineering Leadership] News Staff, "This Month in NASA History: WMAP Began to Transform Cosmology", June 25, 2014, http://appel.nasa.gov/2014/06/25/this-month-in-nasa-history-wmap-began-to-transform -cosmology/.

[14] NASA, "Planck Mission Brings Universe into Sharp Focus", March 21, 2013, www .nasa.gov/mission_pages/planck/news/planck20130321.html. See also the latest news about the Planck space mission at www.nasa.gov/planck.

So what do physicists think happened 13.8 billion years ago? It seems that our universe took a quantum cosmological form in which all four forces (the electromagnetic force, the strong nuclear force, the weak force, and the gravitational force—in a quantized form) were completely unified and then exploded. At that moment the space-time manifold came into existence, and energy emerged in it (in a fashion explicable by Einstein's General Theory of Relativity). The strong nuclear force separated from the electroweak force, and then the weak force separated from the electromagnetic force, which then moved through a Higgs field,[15] slowing it down to produce the "rest mass" of particles (such as protons and neutrons), making up the visible constituents of the universe. A plasma era ensued, followed by stellar nucleosynthesis and galactic formation, eventually giving rise to planets—and even some very special planets similar to the Earth.[16]

The observable universe appears to have approximately 10^{55} kilograms of visible matter, about five times more dark matter (25 percent of the universe), and considerably more dark energy (about 70 percent of the universe).

Dark matter is somewhat theoretical but probable (for both observational and theoretical reasons). It does not emit or absorb light or heat, so it is not detectable by traditional methods. It is currently thought to take the form of very fine particles that interact with the space-time manifold in the same way as visible matter (causing an increased curvature of the manifold in proportion to its density). It is what keeps the galaxies of the observable universe from flying apart (in the accelerated fashion of the space between the galaxies).

---

[15]The Higgs field was initially proposed in 1964 by the British theoretical physicist Peter Higgs. The discovery of the Higgs boson in 2012 confirmed the Higgs field which was the final piece in elementary particle theory. This Higgs boson is sometimes called the "god particle", but has nothing to do with God, creation, or a beginning. Rather, it is an explanation of how the electromagnetic force acquired rest mass after the Big Bang.

[16]The current estimate of such special planets in the Milky Way is approximately forty billion, according to researchers Erik Petigura and Geoffrey Marcy of the University of California, Berkeley, along with Andrew Howard of the University of Hawaii, using data from the Kepler satellite (a space telescope designed to detect planets in our galaxy and beyond). See Nell Greenfield-Boyce, "Galaxy Quest: Just How Many Earth-Like Planets Are Out There?" NPR, November 5, 2013, www.npr.org/2013/11/05/242991030/galaxy -quest-just-how-many-earth-like-planets-are-out-there.

Does life exist on any of these planets? Nobody knows. There is a possibility that some of these planets may be able to sustain life and, therefore, may have life, but current investigations have not found any data to support this (such as the Mars Curiosity Rover).

Dark energy is the opposite of dark matter and visible matter. Instead of interacting with the space-time manifold in a way that causes contraction, it causes repulsion. It seems to have a fieldlike quality that causes the space-time manifold to stretch and grow at an accelerated rate, causing the phenomenon known as inflation. There is some convincing evidence of inflation from the Planck satellite and other observations, and the best current explanation for this inflation is dark energy.

The visible and dark matter is distributed within 10^{11} galaxies (containing approximately 10^{22} stars). The galaxies maintain their volume (do not fly apart) because of visible matter, dark matter, and a giant black hole in their centers. The space *between* the galaxies is stretching at an accelerated rate (inflating) because of dark energy. It is highly unlikely that the universe will collapse in the future (in a big crunch followed by a bounce), because its probable flat geometry and dark energy will cause it to expand indefinitely. Therefore, the universe will reach a point of either a "big freeze" (in which the gases necessary for star formation will be exhausted, and all formed stars will use up their supply of gases) or "heat death" (in which the universe reaches maximum entropy) at a finite time in the future (somewhere between one trillion and one hundred trillion years from now).

This brings us to three central questions: Was the Big Bang the beginning of our universe? Does our universe exhaust the whole of physical reality (or is there some dimension of physical reality beyond our universe)? If physical reality does extend beyond our universe, must it too have a beginning?

Quantum gravity[17] and inflation theory[18] allow for the formation of four major speculative theories that might expand our view of physical reality far beyond our observable universe:

---

[17] Quantum gravity is a hypothetical field of physics that tries to describe the quantum behavior of the force of gravity. The classical description of gravity is explained in Einstein's General Theory of Relativity (through a malleable space-time manifold). Some theories of quantum gravity are used to explain a pre–Big Bang condition (prior to the advent of the space-time manifold described by the General Theory of Relativity). The two most popular theories are string theory and loop quantum gravity. This field of physics may remain quite hypothetical into the future, because its effects can only be observed near the Planck scale, which is far too small to be currently detected.

[18] Inflation theory (first described by Dr. Alan Guth to resolve various problems in the standard Big Bang model) describes the extremely rapid exponential expansion of the early universe by a factor of at least 10^{78} in volume. The inflation epoch seems to have taken place

1. The *multiverse hypothesis*—inflationary theory allows for the possibility of a giant inflating universe that can produce a multiplicity of bubble universes indefinitely into the future. One such bubble universe would be our own.

2. The *bouncing universe hypothesis*—since the time of Albert Einstein, the conventional bouncing universe hypothesis took the general form of a cyclic universe that expanded and then contracted in a "big crunch" and then bounced and reexpanded repeatedly. The expansion from the Big Bang until today is theorized to be one such cycle—the last one amid many others.

3. The *pre–Big Bang eternally static hypothesis*—quantum gravity allows for the possibility of a pre–Big Bang era in which the universe was perfectly stable for a long period of time prior to the Big Bang.

4. The *higher-dimensional space universe hypothesis*—string theory[19] (particularly M-theory[20]) allows for the possibility of universes to exist in higher-dimensional space (consisting of, say, eleven dimensions), permitting unusual complex expanding and bouncing universes.

---

in the first part of the electroweak era (when the universe was only 10^{-36} seconds to 10^{-33} seconds old). Inflation arises out of vacuum energy (dark energy), which has the opposite effect of mass-energy on the space-time manifold. In the General Theory of Relativity, the density of mass-energy causes an increased curvature of the space-time manifold (giving rise to a force of attraction). However, the density of vacuum energy causes the space-time manifold to expand and stretch at an accelerated rate, causing a repulsive effect.

[19] *String theory* is one way of describing quantum gravity, in which gravity is not the result of the curved geometry of the space-time continuum (as it is in the General Theory of Relativity), but rather is in a quantized state which strongly interacts with the other three forces in the universe—the electromagnetic force, the strong nuclear force, and the weak force. In order to accomplish the unification of all four forces (through the quantizing of gravity), particles are reduced to one-dimensional vibrating "strings" within extra-dimensional space. Some of these extra dimensions are compactified (reduced to extremely small scales). The first attempt at string theory was only able to account for one out of two major particle groups—bosons. Later, in "super string theory" the other group—fermions—was integrated into the theory through super symmetry.

[20] *M-theory* is an extension of string theory. In the 1990s, five consistent versions of string theory were developed which formed the basis of one eleven-dimensional theory which is thought by some, such as Stephen Hawking, to be a "theory of everything". Though this theory is tremendously powerful as an explanatory tool for integrating virtually all facets of quantum theory and general relativity theory, there is no evidence for it—so many well-known physicists (such as Richard Feynman, Roger Penrose, and Sheldon Glashow) are reticent to call it "real", let alone the "explanation of everything".

All of these hypotheses extend our view of physical reality beyond our observable universe, which may allow physical reality to exist prior to our 13.8 billion-year-old history (since the Big Bang)—and even eternally into the past. As noted above, they are all completely hypothetical and lie beyond our current capacity to observe. They may, in principle, be unobservable. As will be seen (below in Sections III–V), every one of these scenarios very probably requires a *beginning in the finite past* and, for this reason, brings physics to the threshold of metaphysics.

III. Space-Time Geometry Proofs and the Beginning of Physical Reality

Lemaître's discovery of the expansion of space-time in the universe (as a whole) enabled physicists to formulate theorems (proofs) about the necessity of a beginning. All such proofs are based on conditions (which can be confirmed by observation). If all the conditions are true, the conclusion must also be true. They take the following general form: If condition A, condition B, and condition C are true, then there must be a *beginning* of the universe (or the *beginning* of a multiverse or the *beginning* of physical reality itself).

The first space-time geometry proof (called a singularity theorem) was proposed by Stephen Hawking and Roger Penrose between 1968 and 1970,[21] which was based on five conditions. In 1980 Hawking declared "a curvature singularity that will intersect every world line ... [makes] general relativity predict a beginning of time."[22] Twenty years after they formulated the proof, Alan Guth proposed inflationary theory that appeared to violate the third condition of the Hawking-Penrose proof ("the mass density and pressure of matter never become negative"). Inflation (presumably caused by dark energy) produces negative pressure (accelerating expansion), which violates the third condition of the proof.

[21] See Stephen Hawking and Roger Penrose, "The Singularities of Gravitational Collapse and Cosmology", *Proc. Roy. Soc. Lond. A* 314 (1970): 529–48.

[22] Stephen Hawking, "Theoretical Advances in General Relativity", in *Some Strangeness in the Proportion*, ed. H. Woolf (Reading, Mass.: Addison-Wesley, 1980), p. 149.

This was only a temporary setback for space-time geometry proofs for a beginning of the universe. In 1994, Arvind Borde and Alexander Vilenkin devised a proof for a singularity (and beginning of the universe) accounting for *inflationary* cosmology.[23] However, they found an exception to their proof in 1997 with regard to the weak energy condition. Even though this exception was highly unlikely in our universe, it reopened the possibility of an eternal universe (in the past).[24] During the same period, Alan Guth showed that all known mathematical configurations of inflationary model cosmologies required a beginning:

> In my own opinion, it looks like eternally inflating models *necessarily* have a beginning. We believe this for two reasons. The first is the fact that, as hard as physicists have worked to try to construct an alternative, so far all the models that we construct have a beginning; they are eternal into the future, but not into the past. The second reason is that the technical assumption questioned in the 1997 Borde-Vilenkin paper does not seem important enough to me to change the *conclusion*.[25]

Though Guth's study was comprehensive, it did not constitute a proof of a singularity in all inflationary cosmologies.

In 2003, all three joined together to formulate an elegant proof of a boundary to past time in all cosmologies where the average Hubble expansion is greater than zero. This proof is not dependent on the weak energy condition (which allowed for possible exceptions to the 1994 Borde-Vilenkin proof). They formulated their findings as follows:

> Our argument shows that null and time-like geodesics are, in general, past-incomplete [requiring a boundary to past time] in inflationary models, whether or not energy conditions hold, provided only

[23] See Arvind Borde and Alexander Vilenkin, "Eternal Inflation and Initial Singularity", *Physical Review Letters* 72, no. 21 (1994): 3305–8.

[24] Arvind Borde and Alexander Vilenkin, "Violation of the Weak Energy Condition in Inflating Spacetimes", *Physical Review D* 56 (1997): 720.

[25] Alan H. Guth, "Eternal Inflation", paper presented at *Cosmic Questions*, National Museum of Natural History, Washington, D.C., April 14–16, 1999, p. 13.

that the averaged expansion condition $H_{av} > 0$ hold along these past-directed geodesics. This is a stronger conclusion than the one arrived at in previous work in that we have shown under reasonable assumptions that almost all causal geodesics, when extended to the past of an arbitrary point, reach the boundary of the inflating region of spacetime in a *finite* proper time.[26]

This proof (which is explained in detail below in this section) has extensive general applicability—that is, to *any universe* with an average Hubble expansion greater than zero. In particular, it applies to the eternal inflation scenario. Vilenkin states it as follows:

> We made no assumptions about the material content of the universe. We did not even assume that gravity is described by Einstein's equations. So, if Einstein's gravity requires some modification, our conclusion will still hold. The only assumption that we made was that the expansion rate of the universe never gets below some nonzero value, no matter how small. This assumption should certainly be satisfied in the inflating false vacuum. The conclusion is that past-eternal inflation without a beginning is impossible.[27]

The implications of Vilenkin's statement should not be underestimated, for he is claiming that the proof is valid almost *independently of the physics* of any universe (except for the one physical condition that the average expansion rate of the universe or multiverse be greater than zero). He is further claiming that such a universe without a beginning is *impossible*.

This proof is virtually universally applicable (not only to our universe, but also to multiverses and universes in the higher-dimensional space of string theory). It will be difficult to disprove because it has only one condition. Its importance merits further explanation (which can be done through logical steps with very little mathematical analysis). The following five steps indicate the logical and empirical validity of the proof.

[26] Arvind Borde, Alan Guth, and Alexander Vilenkin, "Inflationary Spacetimes Are Not Past-Complete", *Physical Review Letters* 90, no.15 (2003): 151301-3.

[27] Alexander Vilenkin, *Many Worlds in One: The Search for Other Universes* (New York: Hill and Wang, 2006), p. 175.

The First Step

The first step comes from Fr. Georges Lemaître's discovery in 1927—the farther a galaxy is from our galaxy, the greater will be its recessional velocity (its speed going away from the observer). Recall what was said about the universe expanding like a balloon—if space is stretching (growing like the elastic of our balloon), then the farther a galaxy is from us (the observer), the greater its recessional velocity will be. Why? Because galaxies are not simply moving away from each other in fixed space; the space between the galaxies is actually stretching and growing (like the balloon). Thus, the more space there is between our galaxy and another, the more space there is to stretch and grow, and so we would expect that there would be more growing of space between our galaxy and a far-distant galaxy than between our galaxy and a nearer one. This should increase the recessional velocity in proportion to a galaxy's distance from our galaxy.

Hubble had a precise equation to calculate this: $v = H_0 D$ (where "v" is the recessional velocity of a galaxy, "D" is the proper distance of that galaxy from our galaxy, and "H_0" is the Hubble constant, which transforms proper distance into recessional velocity). Today the Hubble constant is thought to be 69.32 ± 0.80 (km/s)/Mpc—(kilometers per second) per megaparsec. A parsec is a unit of length used in astronomy to measure the large distances to objects beyond our solar system.

We can illustrate this very simply with a rubber band. Take out a rubber band and put it on top of a ruler. Now draw a dot on the rubber band at point zero, another dot at one inch, and yet another dot at two inches. Now, take the rubber band and hold it with your left hand at point zero. With your right hand stretch the rubber band so that the dot that was at two inches is now at four inches. Evidently the dot that was at two inches from origin has expanded another two inches (to the four-inch mark). But notice that the dot that was at the one-inch mark has moved only to the *two-inch* mark (an expansion of *only* one inch). Thus, if space as a whole is growing like a balloon (or like our rubber band), the farther away a galaxy is from our galaxy (at point zero on the ruler), the more it expands per unit time. Since recessional velocity is "expansion per unit time", Lemaître proved his point—the farther away the galaxy is, the greater its recessional velocity will be, if space between the galaxies is expanding (instead of galaxies moving away from each other in fixed space).

The Second Step

We must now learn yet another concept—namely, relative velocity. This term refers to the velocity of a projectile (say, a rocket) approaching a galaxy that is moving away from it. Alexander Vilenkin gives the following example:

> Suppose, for example, that [a] space traveler has just zoomed by the earth at the speed of 100,000 kilometers per second and is now headed toward a distant galaxy, about a billion light years away. That galaxy is moving away from us at a speed of 20,000 kilometers per second [kps], so when the space traveler catches up with it, the observers there will see him moving at 80,000 kilometers per second [100,000 kps minus 20,000 kps].[28]

Now let's extend Vilenkin's example. Suppose that there are observers on a more distant galaxy—twice as far away as the first galaxy (two billion light years from here). Its recessional velocity should be approximately twice as much as the first galaxy's recessional velocity (approximately 40,000 kps away from us). The observers on that more distant galaxy would see the rocket coming at 60,000 kps (100,000 kps minus 40,000 kps).

As can be seen, relative velocity is inversely proportional to recessional velocity. So the greater the distance a galaxy is from us, the *greater* will be its recessional velocity; however, the *relative* velocity of a projectile approaching that more distant galaxy will be *smaller* than its relative velocity approaching a *nearer* galaxy. We can generalize by saying that the greater the distance of an object (such as a galaxy) is from a projectile (like a spaceship) moving toward it, the *greater* will be the *recessional* velocity of that object; however, the *relative* velocity of a projectile approaching it will be *smaller* (in inverse proportion to the recessional velocity).

---

[28] Ibid., p. 176.

The Third Step

There are two ways of having greater distance between our galaxy and other distant galaxies. The first way is the one described above (where galaxy no. 2 happens to be farther away than galaxy no. 1). The second way is by going into the *future*. If the universe's average rate of expansion is greater than zero, then as we move into the future, the space between galaxies will grow from past expansion. Thus, between moment number one and moment number two there is more space between the galaxies, and if there is more space between the galaxies, there will be more space to stretch and grow per unit time, which means that the recessional velocities will *increase* as we move into the future. Every moment our universe moves into the future, the recessional velocity of distant objects will get greater and greater.

The Fourth Step

Now let's apply the above insight (about *recessional* velocities) to *relative* velocities. Recall that recessional velocity and relative velocity are inversely proportional; so if *recessional* velocities are *increasing* into the future, *relative* velocities of approaching projectiles must be *decreasing* into the future. Since all galaxies are moving away from each other (because the universe's spatial manifold is expanding as a whole), all relative velocities of objects will have to get slower and slower into the future.

The Fifth Step

What is the consequence of Step 4? If the relative velocities of all objects must be getting slower and slower into the future, they must have been *faster* in the *past*. Vilenkin puts it this way:

> If the velocity of the space traveler relative to the spectators gets smaller and smaller into the future, then it follows that his velocity should get larger and larger as we follow his history into the past. In the limit, his velocity should get arbitrarily close to the speed of light.[29]

[29] Ibid.

So what is the point? It is not possible to have a relative velocity greater than the speed of light in our universe. Thus, when all relative velocities were arbitrarily close to the speed of light (in the distant past), then the past time of our universe could not have gone back any further. It represents a *beginning* of the universe.

Could this consequence of a beginning of the universe (in the Borde-Vilenkin-Guth proof) be avoided if scientists discover a velocity higher than the speed of light in the future? No, because it does not matter what the upper limit to velocity is; it will always be reached in a *finite* proper time in the past. The only thing that matters is that there *is* an upper limit to velocity in the universe (no matter what it is). This upper limit would have to be reached in a finite proper time in the past. Thus, in *any* scenario in which a universe (or multiverse) has an average rate of expansion greater than zero, it will have to have a beginning in the finite past. This beginning must occur irrespective of the value of the upper limit to velocity in that scenario.

Let's suppose scientists discover a tachyon (a particle which can travel faster than the speed of light) next year. Suppose further that this tachyon can travel at twice the speed of light (600,000 kps). Would this affect the Borde-Vilenkin-Guth (BVG) proof? No, because the relative velocities of all projectiles would have been decreasing into the future (in the same fashion mentioned above) throughout the universe's history; so at an earlier point in the universe's past, all relative velocities would have been 600,000 kps— which would again constitute a beginning (because the past time of the universe could not have existed before that point). We can postulate any finite velocity we want as the upper limit to velocity in our universe (or a multiverse), and we can know with certainty that every projectile in that universe or multiverse would have been travelling at that relative velocity sometime in that universe's or multiverse's *finite* past. Accordingly, *every* scenario in which a universe's (or multiverse's) average rate of expansion is greater than zero will have to have a *beginning*.

Does *every* universe or multiverse have to have a *finite* maximum velocity? Yes, because if that finite upper limit did not exist, then physical energy could travel at an *infinite* velocity, in which case physical energy could be everywhere in the universe or multiverse simultaneously. This gives rise to two irresolvable problems. First, the same physical energy would exist at every space-time point in the universe. This leads to a second problem—namely, that every space-time point would be simultaneously occupied by different incompatible forms of energy (such as protons and electrons or matter and antimatter). The whole universe or multiverse would be filled with contradictions—an obviously impossible state of affairs. The avoidance of these problems requires a finite maximum velocity in every universe *or* multiverse (because every multiverse must be inflationary and must therefore have an average expansion rate greater than zero). If all universes and multiverses must have a finite maximum velocity, and inflating universes and multiverses must have an expansion rate greater than zero (the single condition of the BVG proof), then they would all have to have a *beginning*.

There is one important nuance that should be clarified. The BVG proof establishes a boundary. To the extent that classical gravity is operative near that boundary, the boundary is a singularity and therefore a beginning of time. However, if quantum gravity effects are important near that boundary (which would be the case in some scenarios), the boundary could merely be a gateway to another earlier region of space-time.[30] If the boundary represents only a transition to a new kind of physics, then the question arises as to whether that new physics is subject to a BVG boundary.

This is where the extensive general applicability of the BVG proof comes into play, for inasmuch as the proof applies to *any* universe with an average Hubble expansion greater than zero (independent of the physics of that universe), then the BVG proof requires that a past-time boundary be present in any prior state of the universe that is expansive. Ultimately, an absolute boundary to all past expansive states will be reached (which would be a beginning of past time in the universe). There is only one way to avoid this beginning—a prior state that is eternally static (addressed below).

Borde, Vilenkin, and Guth consider some scenarios of prior universal states arising out of quantum gravity and inflation. One such scenario is inspired by string theory:

---

[30] See Borde, Guth, and Vilenkin, "Inflationary Spacetimes", p. 4. See also W.L. Craig and J. Sinclair, "The Kalam Cosmological Argument", in *The Blackwell Companion to Natural Theology*, ed. W.L. Craig and J.P. Moreland (Malden, Mass.: Wiley-Blackwell, 2009), p. 142, n. 41.

Our argument can be straightforwardly extended to cosmology in higher dimensions. For example, in one model, brane worlds are created in collisions of bubbles nucleating in an inflating higher-dimensional bulk space-time. Our analysis implies that the inflating bulk cannot be past-complete [i.e., must have a boundary to past time]. We finally comment on the cyclic Universe model in which a bulk of four spatial dimensions is sandwiched between two three-dimensional branes.... In some versions of the cyclic model the brane space-times are everywhere expanding, so our theorem immediately implies the existence of a past boundary at which boundary conditions must be imposed. In other versions, there are brief periods of contraction, but the net result of each cycle is an expansion.... Thus, as long as $H_{av} > 0$ for a null geodesic when averaged over one cycle, then $H_{av} > 0$ for any number of cycles, and our theorem would imply that the geodesic is incomplete [i.e., must have a boundary to past time].[31]

Notice that the extensive general applicability of the BVG theorem allows it to establish a past-time boundary for quite diverse models where quantum gravity effects play important roles. Notice also that the BVG theorem applies to this hypothesis even though it has a contracting phase, because all that is required for the applicability of the BVG proof is that the *average* Hubble expansion be greater than zero (no matter how small the positive nonzero average might be). Since the above hypothetical condition must have an *average* Hubble expansion greater than zero (amid its many expansions and contractions), it must have a boundary to its past time.

Does the BVG theorem apply also to the Russian-American theoretical physicist Andrei Linde's eternal inflation scenario? According to Borde, Guth, and Vilenkin, it does. Linde originally suggested that each bubble universe begins with a singularity and further suggested that these regional singularities might mitigate the need for a singularity in the whole array of bubble universes.[32] Craig and Sinclair explain why this does not escape the Borde, Vilenkin, and Guth proof:

[31] Borde, Guth, and Vilenkin, "Inflationary Spacetimes", p. 4.
[32] See Andrei Linde, "The Self-Reproducing Inflationary Universe", in "The Magnificent Cosmos", special issue, *Scientific American*, March 1998, p. 104.

Andre Linde has offered a critique, suggesting that BVG implies that all the individual parts of the universe have a beginning, but perhaps the WHOLE does not. This seems misconstrued, however, since BVG are not claiming that each past inextendible geodesic is related to a regional singularity. Rather, they claim that Linde's universe description contains an internal contradiction. As we look backward along the geodesic, it must extend to the infinite past if the universe is to be past-eternal. But it does not (for the observer comoving with the expansion).[33]

The extensive general applicability of the BVG proof (whose only condition is an average Hubble expansion greater than zero) makes possible exceptions fall within a very narrow range. A possible exception will either (1) have to postulate a universal model with an average Hubble expansion *less* than zero or (2) postulate a universal model where the average Hubble expansion is *equal* to zero (what is termed an "eternally static universe").

Since models postulating an average contraction greater than expansion have proven to be physically unrealistic, physicists have turned to the "eternally static hypothesis" to find a way out of the BVG proof. In several important articles, Vilenkin and his graduate student Audrey Mithani have demonstrated significant *physical* problems with this hypothesis (particularly quantum instabilities that force the static state to break down in a finite time).[34] Additionally, the eternally static hypothesis falls prey to an irresolvable *logical* contradiction. Craig and Sinclair sum up the fundamental (and seemingly insurmountable) problem as follows:

> The asymptotically static hypothesis has the dilemma that it must begin static and then transition to an expansion. Hence, the static phase is metastable, which implies that it is finite in lifetime. The universe begins to exist.[35]

---

[33] Craig and Sinclair, "Kalam Cosmological Argument", p. 169.

[34] An excellent summary of this work can be found in Vilenkin's lecture to the physics community at Cambridge University on the occasion of Stephen Hawking's seventieth birthday. See Lisa Grossman, "Why Physicists Can't Avoid a Creation Event", *NewScientist*, January 11, 2012, http://www.newscientist.com/article/mg21328474.400-why-physicists-cant-avoid-a-creation-event.html.

[35] Craig and Sinclair, "Kalam Cosmological Argument", p. 158.

Craig and Sinclair point to a fundamental contradiction in the eternally static hypothesis. In order for a universe to exist in a static state for an infinite time, it would have to be *perfectly* stable. However, for a universe to move from one state to another—say, from a quantum gravity, for example, string theory state (before the Big Bang), to a state described by the General Theory of Relativity (after the Big Bang)—the quantum gravity state would have to have been *metastable* (not perfectly stable) to accommodate the decay of the first state into the second one. This implies that the hypothesis is contradictory—because the quantum gravity state would have to have been *both perfectly* stable (to last for an eternity) *and not perfectly* stable (metastable) in order to decay into an expansive state at the Big Bang.

In sum, there are three consequences of the Borde-Vilenkin-Guth proof:

1. It applies to all inflating universes and multiverses (including bouncing universes in higher dimensions) that have an average rate of expansion greater than zero.
2. It does not matter what the physics of a given universe or multiverse might be, so long as the average Hubble expansion is greater than zero (because every universe or multiverse must have an upper limit to velocity).
3. Since there is only one physical condition required for the proof to work, and it functions independently of all other physical conditions of any given universe or multiverse, it will be very difficult to disprove.

At this point, it seems as if physics is coming very close to proving an absolute beginning of physical reality itself—whether physical reality is simply our universe, or perhaps a multiverse, or a universe in the higher-dimensional space of string theory, or a static quantum cosmological state. If no physically realistic exception can be found to this proof (and to the problems of an eternally static universe), it would indicate the probability of a beginning of physical reality itself. Vilenkin agrees with this assessment and said in 2006:

> It is said that an argument is what convinces reasonable men and a proof [e.g., the BVG Proof] is what it takes to convince even an

unreasonable man. With the proof now in place, cosmologists can no longer hide behind the possibility of a past-eternal universe.... There is no escape, they have to face the problem of a cosmic beginning.[36]

This takes us to the threshold of metaphysics. Before moving in that direction, we will want to first consider another vastly applicable datum that also indicates the likelihood of a beginning of physical reality—entropy.

IV. Entropy and the Beginning of Our Universe

Entropy is a technical concept that measures the degree of "disorder" or disorganization of a system. For purely probabilistic reasons, systems left to their own devices ("isolated systems") tend to evolve in a way that keeps the level of disorganization (entropy) constant or increases it. Almost never does the entropy of an isolated system decrease. Systems do not spontaneously get more organized. To make a system more ordered takes something coming in from outside and expending energy (I can make the coffee in a cup hotter than its surroundings, for instance, by using a "heat pump"—the opposite of a refrigerator—to pump thermal energy from the cooler air into the hotter coffee. But that would require the expenditure of energy to run the heat pump).

The famous second law of thermodynamics says that in isolated systems, entropy always increases or stays the same and never goes down. That is why some processes are irreversible. If a process changes the entropy, then it can only go one way—the way that entropy (disorganization) increases. That is why dead bodies decompose, but do not recompose! Of course, these are, ultimately, probabilistic statements. Entropy can have random fluctuations downward, but these are usually very tiny decreases, and the larger the decrease in entropy, the more unlikely it is to happen.

This is a universal phenomenon. It is why physicists regard "perpetual motion machines" as impossible. And here is the relevance to the question of whether the universe had a beginning. If the universe did not have a beginning, then it has been around for an infinite time. In a sense, the universe is then itself a "perpetual motion machine",

---

[36] Vilenkin, *Many Worlds in One*, p. 176.

a system that never "runs down" or "wears out", which is a violation of the second law of thermodynamics. This argument against an infinite universe can be broken down into five steps:

1. For a physical system to do work, it needs to have order (disequilibrium) within it.[37] Variations of temperature (or other factors such as pressure or molecular distribution) within a system enable it to do physically useful work.

2. Every time a physical system does work, it loses a small amount of its order (disequilibrium), which means that it is not capable of doing as much work as it could in its previous state. This movement from order to disorder is called "entropy".

3. For statistical reasons alone, entropy (the movement from order to disorder) is irreversible in the long term (though there may be random fluctuations toward lower entropy that do not and cannot last long).

4. If the universe is an isolated[38] physical system (the assumption of the standard Big Bang model), then the universe could not have existed for an infinite amount of time, because if it did, it would be at a state of maximum entropy (maximum equilibrium) today (for the reasons stated in item nos. 1–3 above). It would be a dead universe incapable of any work.

5. But the universe is not at maximum entropy (maximum equilibrium); there are hot stars and cold space, galactic clusters and empty space, and physical systems are continuously working—stars burning, planets forming, and physicists thinking about it.

Therefore, the universe has not existed for an infinite amount of time (and therefore has a beginning).

The evidence of entropy has one important quality in common with that of the Borde-Vilenkin Guth proof, namely, its vast

[37] "Order" generally refers to disequilibrium (such as variation in temperature, or differentiation of molecular distribution, or differentiation of pressure within a physical system). Since all thermodynamic systems tend toward equilibrium (the same temperature or distribution of molecules or pressure within a system), it follows that equilibrium is the most probable state of a system—and is considered the most disordered. In contrast to this, the more disequilibrium there is in a system, the more it is said to be ordered (which is a more improbable state).

[38] "Isolated" here refers to a system acting on its own. There is no engine or refrigerator or heating element outside of the physical system that can introduce additional order (disequilibrium) within the system.

applicability (seemingly to every physical system). It was stated earlier that the second law of thermodynamics (entropy) is valid for statistical reasons alone. Therefore, it is applicable to a multiplicity of physical scenarios—and is theoretically applicable to virtually every physical system. Why? Because disequilibrium (order) is so much more improbable than equilibrium (disorder), and every physical system will tend toward its most probable outcome—that is, toward disorder (equilibrium). Einstein was so certain of this that he declared,

> A law is more impressive the greater the simplicity of its premises, the more different are the kinds of things it relates, and the more extended its range of applicability. [Entropy] is the only physical theory of universal content, *which I am convinced, that within the framework of applicability of its basic concepts will never be overthrown.*[39]

There has been no shortage of attempts to elude this consequence of the second law of thermodynamics (entropy). Several physicists have suggested that entropy might be lowered in a universal collapse ("a big crunch") or in a bouncing universe scenario. Both of these suggestions have been virtually ruled out by the research of Roger Penrose,[40] Sean Carroll,[41] and Thomas Banks and Willy

---

[39] Gerald Holton and Yehuda Elkana, *Albert Einstein: Historical and Cultural Perspectives* (Princeton: Princeton University Press, 1997), p. 227 (emphasis mine).

[40] As will be discussed below (Section V), Roger Penrose shows the virtual impossibility of low entropy at a bounce, because the odds against it are $10^{10^{123}}$ to 1 against its occurrence (the odds of a monkey typing Macbeth by random tapping of the keys in one try—this is a virtual impossibility). See Roger Penrose, *The Emperor's New Mind* (Oxford: Oxford University Press, 1989), pp. 343–44.

[41] According to Sean Carroll, a well-known cosmologist, the low entropy of our universe at the Big Bang invalidates an eternal bouncing universe hypothesis; it even makes a single bounce to be exceedingly improbable:

> Bojowald uses some ideas from Loop Quantum Gravity to try to resolve the initial singularity and follow the quantum state of the universe past the [Big] Bang back into a pre-existing universe. If you try to invent a cosmology in which you straightforwardly replace the singular Big Bang by a smooth Big Bounce continuation into a previous space-time, you have one of two choices: either the entropy continues to decrease as we travel backwards in time through the Bang, or it changes direction and begins to increase. Sadly, neither makes any sense. If you are imagining that the arrow of time is continuous as you travel back through the Bounce, then you are positing a very strange universe indeed on the other side. It's one in which the infinite past has an

Fischler.[42] They also show that entropy makes virtually every form of the bouncing universe hypothesis untenable.[43] Though physicists are still hypothesizing new scenarios to elude a beginning of the universe from entropy, they are becoming more and more fantastic and further and further removed from the domain of observable evidence and the discipline of physics.

---

extremely tiny entropy, which increases only very slightly as the universe collapses, so that it can come out the other side in our observed low-entropy state. That requires the state at t = minus infinity state of the universe to be infinitely finely tuned, for no apparent reason (the same holds true for the Steinhardt-Turok cyclic universe). On the other hand, if you imagine that the arrow of time reverses direction at the Bounce, you've moved your extremely-finely-tuned-for-no-good-reason condition to the Bounce itself. In models where the Big Bang is really the beginning of the universe, one could in principle imagine that some unknown law of physics makes the boundary conditions there very special, and explains the low entropy (a possibility that Roger Penrose, for example, has taken seriously). But if it's not a boundary, why are the conditions there [at the Bounce] so special? (Sean Carroll, "Against Bounces", *Discover Magazine*, July 2, 2007, p. 1)

[42] Banks and Fischler believe that a universal collapse will lead to a "black crunch" (maximum entropy) from which a low entropy bounce would be virtually impossible ($10^{10^{123}}$ to 1 against, according to Roger Penrose). (See below Section VI.) In fact, things are probably even worse for models in which the Big Bang was a bounce preceded by a phase in which the universe was collapsing. It has been argued by Banks and Fischler (particle physicists) that during such a collapse the rapidly changing space-time would have excited and amplified random "quantum fluctuations" in such a way that entropy would have been driven to very *large* values, rather than small ones. This makes it even more difficult to account for the fantastically low entropy just after the Big Bang. In Banks' words,

I have a problem with ALL cyclic cosmologies.... The collapsing phase of these models always have a time-dependent Hamiltonian for the quantum field fluctuations around the classical background. Furthermore the classical backgrounds are becoming singular. This means that the field theories will be excited to higher and higher energy states.... High energy states in field theory have the ergodic property—they thermalize rapidly, in the sense that the system explores all of its states. Willy Fischler and I proposed that in this situation you would again tend to *maximize the entropy*. We called this a black crunch and suggested the equation of state of matter would again tend toward p = ρ. It seems silly to imagine that, even if this is followed by a re-expansion, that one would start that expansion with a low entropy initial state, or that one had any control over the initial state at all. (Private communication from Thomas Banks to James Sinclair, October 12, 2007, in Craig and Sinclair, "Kalam Cosmological Argument", p. 156; also, see T. Banks, "Entropy and Initial Conditions in Cosmology", January 16, 2007, http://arxiv.org/pdf/hep-th/0701146v1.pdf)

[43] See the previous three footnotes.

V. From Physics to Metaphysics

The discussion in the two foregoing sections shows that the preponderance of cosmological evidence favors a beginning, not only of *our* universe, but also of other expanding universes, multiverses, universes in the higher-dimensional space of string theory, and static universes. The need for a beginning of all these scenarios suggests (but does not prove) the need for a beginning of physical reality itself. This beginning may mark the point at which physical reality *came into existence*. Before examining this metaphysical claim, it may be helpful to review the need for a beginning in the four hypothetical scenarios that allow physical reality to exist prior to the Big Bang:

1. Every multiverse hypothesis must be inflationary, subjecting it to the Borde-Vilenkin-Guth proof, which entails a beginning in the finite past.
2. Bouncing universe hypotheses fall prey to four major problems:
   a. They are subject to the Borde-Vilenkin-Guth proof (because their average Hubble expansion is greater than zero),
   b. Carroll's requirement of "infinite fine-tuning for no apparent reason" in eternally bouncing universes (making them virtually impossible),
   c. Banks' and Fischler's prediction that a single collapse will lead to a black crunch (maximum entropy), and
   d. the probable flat geometry and preponderance of dark energy in our universe disallows a universal collapse (and therefore, a bounce).
3. The eternally static hypothesis falls prey to quantum instabilities according to Vilenkin and Mithani. It also appears to be intrinsically contradictory—*both* perfectly stable and not perfectly stable prior to the Big Bang.
4. The expanding and bouncing forms of the higher dimensional space hypothesis are subject to the Borde-Vilenkin-Guth proof, which entails a beginning in a finite past time.

Currently there are no physically realistic alternatives to this evidence for a beginning.[44] As will be seen below, this evidence may

---

[44]Since the Borde-Vilenkin-Guth theorem rules out all expanding universes (or multiverses), and the entropy evidence rules out an eternal universe and all bouncing universes, and

well point to an *absolute* beginning of *physical* reality—to a point prior to which physical reality (that is, physical energy, physical space and time, and physical laws) was nonexistent. If an *absolute beginning* of physical reality can be established, it implies the existence of a causative power (a Creator) beyond physical reality itself. This conclusion requires not only physical evidence, but metaphysical evidence. The argument runs as follows:

1. There is strong evidence suggesting a beginning of physical reality (prior to which physical reality was literally nothing) from contemporary physics.
2. From nothing, only nothing comes—the most fundamental claim of Parmenides, that a state of nothing (absolute nonexistence) can only produce nothing; it can*not* produce or do something (a priori true).
3. If nothing can only produce nothing, then "prior"[45] to the absolute beginning of physical reality (when physical reality was nothing), physical reality could *not* have moved *itself* from nothing to something (because as nothing, it could not produce or *do* anything).

Therefore, there is strong evidence suggesting that the universe came from *something* that is *not* physical reality (i.e., *beyond* physical reality). This is commonly referred to as "a transcendent cause of physical reality"—in short, "a Creator".

This encounter with "nothing" brings us into the domain of metaphysics, which many physicists have unwittingly entered because of

---

the static universe hypothesis is intrinsically contradictory and highly improbable in light of quantum instabilities, the only recourse left seems to be that of postulating "backward time" prior to the Big Bang (see Anthony Aguirre and Steven Gratton, "Steady-State Eternal Inflation", *Physical Review D* 65, no. 8 [March 2002]: 083507). Most physicists have unhesitatingly declared this hypothesis to be physically unrealistic because it enables physically unrealistic phenomena to occur, such as the sound of the clap coming before the clap.

[45] Please note: use of "prior" here is *merely linguistic*—that is, it is a way of making a linguistic reference without implying existence. When we use the phrase "prior to which there is nothing physical", it includes physical time, which would be the condition necessary for a *real* prior state. Obviously, we are saying that there is *no* physical time and, therefore, no "prior" prior to the beginning.

Similarly, the term "nothing" must also be *merely linguistic*, for it cannot refer to something *real*, but only to the *absence* of everything real. All words do not have to have ontological referents; they can have merely linguistic or conceptual referents that can refer to a merely conceptual condition (such as "prior to a beginning" or "nothing").

the strong evidence for a beginning of physical reality. For example, Stephen Hawking has recently claimed that spontaneous creation can occur from *nothing* because of the law of gravitation: "Because there is a law such as gravity, the Universe can and will create itself from nothing.... Spontaneous creation is the reason there is something rather than nothing, why the Universe exists, why we exist."[46] Hawking has been criticized for this because of several problems, such as "sneaking" something into nothing, equivocating on the term "nothing", or postulating an unacknowledged transphysical mentative state that allows laws (without physical reality) to generate the whole of physical reality (e.g., a law of gravitation without a physical universe). If we are to avoid these confusions, we should follow the example of Parmenides, and allow "nothing" to be nothing (the complete absence of reality). This means not putting any content into "nothing", such as continuity, dimensionality, or orientability (as might be found in a spatial manifold), and not confusing "nothing" with physical laws without a physical universe (entailing an unacknowledged transphysical mind or mentative state). Anything else argues the most fundamental of contradictions.

This last point requires close attention, because Stephen Hawking is not the only physicist who advocates that there was *something physical* prior to an absolute beginning of physical reality (whether physical reality is considered to be only our universe, a multiverse, a universe in the higher-dimensional space of string theory, or some other hypothetical exotic form). Interestingly, physicists who advocate for this position admit that prior to a fundamental or absolute beginning, physical reality was "nothing". But then the logical and metaphysical problems begin, because they have to explain how *something* (e.g., the universe or a multiverse) can come from *nothing*.

These claims fall into three groups—all of which advocate that "something seemingly physical occurred at or prior to the beginning of physical reality."

    1. Something physical like a false vacuum fluctuation of a quantum field (which could be confused with "nothing") existed before or at the beginning and generated the whole of physical reality.

---

[46] Hawking and Mlodinow, *Grand Design*, p. 180.

2. Something physical like "quantum tunneling from nothing" (which seems to come from nothing) generates the conditions for physical reality at the beginning.

3. Something seemingly "physical", like the law of gravitation—existing apart from a physical universe with physical energy and time—existed before the absolute beginning and spontaneously generated the whole of physical reality (i.e., the Hawking-Mlodinow proposal).

Let us discuss each of these views of nothing in turn.

Let's consider the first proposal—"nothing viewed as a false vacuum". Something physical, such as a false vacuum of a quantum field, is *not* nothing, because the quantum condition through which the false vacuum occurs is *something*. This can be compared to my bank account. Just because it has a zero balance does not mean that the bank account and the bank do not exist. Thus, this proposal suggests only that "the beginning" is not absolute (since *something physical* precedes it in time).

Since there is yet another *physical condition* existing prior to the beginning, we must now ask whether that condition was eternal into the past or whether *it* had a beginning. A false vacuum is metastable, and, therefore, *temporary*, and cannot go eternally back into the past, which means it too must have a beginning. This provokes the further question: Was physical reality *nothing*—nonexistent—prior to *that* beginning? If *that* beginning was preceded by nothing (the absence of physical reality), then there would be a need for a transcendent Creator of physical reality (for the reasons mentioned above). However, if it is proposed that still another *physical* condition (such as another false vacuum—or something else) existed prior to *that* beginning, then we would have to ask again whether that "physical condition" was merely a temporary condition (like a false vacuum), or some other condition that could be eternal into the past. If it is a condition that could be eternal into the past, then we would have to ask whether it was subject to the above three parameters of physical time—namely, an expansive condition subject to the Borde-Vilenkin-Guth proof and the second law of thermodynamics (entropy) and the intrinsic contradiction of an "eternally static condition giving rise to the Big Bang".

We can continue to "play this game" until we finally arrive at a beginning prior to which there is *nothing physical* (a complete absence of physical reality). When we do, it will require a "transcendent Creator beyond physical reality" to create the whole of physical reality. In sum, the proposal "that a physical reality or condition (like a false vacuum) precedes a beginning" will have to ultimately be resolved by an *absolute* beginning without a prior physical condition.[47]

Now let us turn to the second hypothetical proposal to explain how something can come from nothing—"quantum tunneling from nothing" (at or before the beginning). Though the idea of tunneling from *nothing* seems to bridge the gap from "nothing" to something, it is really not an improvement over the previous proposal. From a logical vantage point, "nothing" cannot mean "the absence of reality" in this proposal, because that claim would be patently absurd. To say that tunneling occurred from the complete absence of reality is the same as saying that something (i.e., tunneling) can come from nothing. Some proponents might object that they didn't mean "the absence of reality" by "nothing", but instead something physical, like a "false vacuum", from which tunneling could occur. But as the reader may have already surmised, this simply brings us back to the first proposal mentioned above, which, as we saw, will ultimately be resolved by a transcendent Creator (if those "physical conditions at or before beginnings" are either temporary or subject to the three parameters of physical time, which currently seems likely). Recall that if there is something *physical* prior to or at the beginning (like a false vacuum), we must ask whether it too must have a beginning (i.e., whether it too is only temporary or subject to the three parameters of physical time). If so, we would ask whether this beginning was preceded by "the absence of physical reality" or yet another physical condition (e.g., another false vacuum). If this physical condition also is either temporary or subject to the three parameters of physical time, then it too will require a beginning. Since other

---

[47] I have used a *logical* argument (using the three *physical* parameters of physical time) to show that a transcendent creation cannot be avoided by postulating a physical condition or reality at or before the beginning. William Lane Craig has provided an argument on the basis of *physics* alone that is quite cogent; see William Craig, "Vilenkin's Cosmic Vision: A Review Essay of *Many Worlds in One: The Search for Other Universes*", *Philosophia Christi* 11 (2009): 232–38.

proposed "physical conditions at or prior to a beginning" are likely to be either temporary or subject to the three parameters of physical time, it is also likely that we will eventually arrive at a beginning that is not preceded by something physical (i.e., the absence of physical reality), which will require a transcendent positive power outside of physical time.[48]

We may now proceed to the third proposal for explaining how something can come from nothing, namely, that of Hawking and Mlodinow. As noted above, this proposal does not suggest that something *physical* (such as a false vacuum or tunneling) occurred at or before the beginning. No doubt Hawking and Mlodinow recognized the logical and physical problems of those proposals and decided to identify "nothing" with something that looks physical but is *not* physical: the law of gravity. This is a more ingenious proposal than the first two, because it avoids the problems of having physical conditions at or prior to the beginning of *physical* reality. However, it takes them into the *trans*physical (the *meta*physical)[49] domain. Think about it: What is the ontological status of a "physical" law without physical energy and physical space and time (a physical universe)? Clearly, it cannot be *physical*. If lawlike principles are to be physical, they must inhere in physical reality (physical energy, space, and time). If they do not, then their existence is purely *intelligible*—an internally consistent equation with the *potential* to determine physical reality, but *not actually* determining physical reality. So what is a *purely* intelligible reality like? It must exist as the *content* of an act of thinking or understanding—that is, as an *idea*.

Though Plato (in his early and middle period) believed that there could be purely intelligible realities—like separated ideas—without an act of thinking, he seems to have adjusted this view (particularly in the *Timaeus*[50]). Subsequent philosophers since the time of

---

[48] Again I have argued against "tunneling from nothing" on *logical* grounds (using data from physics, including the temporary status of metastable conditions and the three parameters of physical time). William Lane Craig has provided a cogent argument against it on purely physical grounds; see ibid., pp. 236–37.

[49] "Transphysical" (Latin) and "metaphysical" (Greek) refer to the same condition—being *beyond* the physical domain.

[50] See Plato, *Timaeus*, in *The Collected Dialogues of Plato*, trans. Benjamin Jowett, ed. Edith Hamilton and Huntington Cairns (Princeton, N.J.: Princeton University Press, 1961), pp. 1161–166.

Aristotle recognized that ideas are ontologically subordinate to an act of thinking—for the latter is the condition necessary for the former. If this is correct, then purely intelligible realities imply the existence of a transphysical act of thinking (i.e., a Creator).[51]

Though the Hawking-Mlodinow proposal avoids the problems of physical conditions existing at or prior to the beginning of physical reality, it seems to argue to either something like Platonic separated ideas (without the condition necessary for their existence) or the existence of a transphysical act of thinking (i.e., God)!

Curiously, Stephen Hawking seems to have realized in an earlier period of his life that purely intelligible realities are not *physical* until they are embedded in physical energy and physical space and time. This provokes the question that he rightly asks about a transphysical Creator: "Even if there is only one possible unified theory, it is *just* a set of rules and equations. What is it that breathes fire into the equations and makes a universe for them to describe?"[52]

Where does this leave us? If the above evidence of physics is leading toward a beginning of physical reality (prior to which physical reality was completely nonexistent), and if proposals to define "nothing" as physical realities (such as quantum vacuums or quantum tunneling) also point to the same more fundamental beginning (prior to which there is an absence of physical reality), then we are being pushed to the very threshold of metaphysics—pushed toward the need for a transphysical causative power. If proposals like that of Hawking and Mlodinow lead us only to transphysical purely intelligible realities (like the law of gravity) without the necessary condition for their existence, then it seems that physics is pushing us closer and closer to a transphysical act of thinking, which looks remarkably similar to Lonergan's "unique unrestricted act of thinking which is the Creator of everything else" (proved in Chapter 3).

This leads to our final consideration: Are there other physical clues to the intelligence of a Creator?

---

[51] See Lonergan's initial definition of "God" in Chapter 3, Section IV—"a unique unrestricted act of thinking which is the Creator of everything else".

[52] Stephen Hawking, *A Brief History of Time: From the Big Bang to Black Holes* (New York: Bantam, 1988), p. 174 (emphasis mine).

VI. Fine-Tuning "for Life" at the Big Bang: Implications of Supernatural Intelligence

There are several conditions of our universe necessary for the emergence of any life form. Many of these conditions are so improbable that it is not reasonable to expect that they could have occurred by pure chance. For this reason many physicists attribute their occurrence to supernatural design. Some other physicists prefer to believe instead in trillions upon trillions of "other universes" (in a multiverse that is unobserved and likely unobservable). Before discussing which explanation is more probative, we need to explore some specific instances of this highly improbable fine-tuning. We may break the discussion into two parts:

1. The exceedingly high improbability of our low-entropy universe
2. The exceedingly high improbability of the anthropic values of our universe's constants

We will discuss each in turn.

A. The High Improbability of Our Low-Entropy Universe

A low-entropy universe is necessary for the emergence, evolution, and complexification of life forms, because a high-entropy universe would be too run down to allow for such development (see above Section IV). Roger Penrose has calculated the exceedingly small probability of a pure chance occurrence of our low-entropy universe as $10^{10^{123}}$ to 1 against:

> how big was the original phase-space volume $\mathbf{W}$ that the Creator had to aim for in order to provide a universe compatible with the second law of thermodynamics and with what we now observe? It does not much matter whether we take the value $\mathbf{W} = 10^{10^{101}}$ or $\mathbf{W} = 10^{10^{88}}$, given by the galactic black holes or by the background radiation, respectively, or a much smaller (and, in fact, more appropriate) figure

which would have been the *actual* figure at the big bang. Either way, the ratio of **V** to **W** will be closely $\mathbf{V}/\mathbf{W} = 10^{10^{123}}$.[53]

This number is so large that it is difficult to "wrap our minds around". It is a ten raised to an exponent of the following: 1000000000000000 0000000000000000000000000000000000000000000000000000000000 0000000000000000000000000000000000000000000000000000.

If we put this number in nonexponential notation—with every zero being 10 point type—our solar system would not be able to hold it! As mentioned previously, this is about the same odds as a monkey typing Shakespeare's *Macbeth* by random tapping of the keys in a single attempt (virtually impossible). Currently, there is no natural explanation for the occurrence of this exceedingly improbable universal condition, and if none is found, then we are left with the words of Roger Penrose himself: "In order to produce a universe resembling the one in which we live, the *Creator* would have to aim for an absurdly tiny volume of the phase space of possible universes—about $1/10^{10^{123}}$ of the entire volume, for the situation under consideration."[54] What Penrose is saying here is that this occurrence cannot be explained by a random (pure chance) occurrence. Therefore, one will have to make recourse either to a multiverse (composed of bubble universes, each having different initial conditions and values of constants) or, as Penrose implies, a Creator (with a superintellect). We will examine both of these options after the following subsection.

B. The High Improbability of Anthropic Conditions
(Based on Universal Constants)

A universal constant is a number that controls the equations of physics, and the equations of physics, in turn, describe the laws of nature. Therefore, these numbers control the laws of nature (and whether these laws of nature will be hospitable or hostile to any life form). Some examples of constants are the following: the speed of light

[53] Penrose, *Emperor's New Mind*, p. 343.
[54] Ibid.

constant (c = 300,000 km per second), Planck's constant ($\hbar$ = 6.6 × 10^{-34} joule seconds), the gravitational attraction constant (G = 6.67 × 10^{-11}), the strong nuclear force coupling constant (g_s = 15), the weak force constant (g_w = 1.43 × 10^{-62}), the rest mass of the proton (m_p = 1.67 × 10^{-27} kg), the rest mass of an electron (m_e = 9.11 × 10^{-31} kg), and the charge of an electron proton (e = 1.6 × 10^{-19} coulombs). There are several other constants, but the above constants are sufficient to show the fine-tuning of our universe.

Before proceeding to some examples, it should be noted that the constants could have been virtually any value (higher or lower) within a very broad range at the Big Bang. However, the range of values of the constants that will allow for the development of a life form is exceedingly small (given the essential laws of physics and the mass of the universe). This means that the occurrence of *any* life form was exceedingly improbable in our universe.

Notice also that the Big Bang is thought to be a boundary condition to natural causation in our universe, because what preceded the Big Bang was not the universe described by the General Theory of Relativity (with a space-time manifold), but rather what might be called "a quantum cosmological universe" (described perhaps by string theory or by loop quantum gravity). This hypothetical pre–Big Bang configuration would be causally *distinct* from the universe described by the General Theory of Relativity. This makes it very difficult to appeal to some kind of prior *natural* causation to account for the values of our constants and the low entropy of our universe at the Big Bang. It virtually forces physicists to answer the question with either a multiverse or supernatural design (explained below).

We may now proceed to some examples of how the constants' values are fine-tuned for life.

1. If the gravitational constant (G) or weak force constant (g_w) varied from their values by an exceedingly small fraction (higher *or* lower)—one part in 10^{50} (.00000000000000000000000000 0000000000000000000001)—then either the universe would have suffered a catastrophic collapse or would have exploded throughout its expansion. Both of these options would have prevented the emergence and development of *any* life form. Paul Davies describes it as follows:

If G [the gravitational constant], or g_w [the weak force constant], differed from their actual values by even *one part in* 10^{50}, the precise balance against Λ_{bare} [radioactive decay constant] would be upset, and the structure of the universe would be drastically altered.... [I]f Λ were several orders of magnitude greater, the expansion of the universe would be explosive, and it is doubtful if galaxies could ever have formed against such a disruptive force. If Λ were negative, the explosion would be replaced by a catastrophic collapse of the universe. It is truly extraordinary that such dramatic effects would result from changes in the strength of either gravity, or the weak force, of less than one part in 10^{50}.[55]

This cannot be reasonably explained by a single random occurrence.

2. If the strong nuclear force constant were higher than its value (15) by only 2 percent, there would be no hydrogen in the universe (and therefore no nuclear fuel or water, prohibiting the development of a life form). If, on the other hand, the strong nuclear force constant had been 2 percent lower than its value, then no element heavier than hydrogen could have emerged in the universe (helium, carbon, etc.). This would have prevented the development of a life form from the periodic table (specifically carbon-based life forms). Walter Bradley sums up Australian theoretical physicist Brandon Carter's research on this topic by noting:

Brandon Carter in 1970 showed that a 2 percent reduction in the strong force and its associated constant would preclude the formation of nuclei with larger numbers of protons, making the formation of elements heavier than hydrogen impossible. On the other hand, if the strong force and associated constant were just 2 percent greater than it is, then all hydrogen would be converted to helium and heavier elements from the beginning, leaving the universe no water and no long-term fuel for the stars. The absolute value of the strong force constant, and more importantly, its value relative to the electromagnetic force

[55] Paul Davies, *The Accidental Universe* (New York: Cambridge University Press, 1982), p. 107–8.

constant is not "prescribed" by any physical theories, but it is certainly a critical *requirement* for a universe suitable for life.[56]

This "anthropic coincidence" also seems to lie beyond the boundaries of pure chance.

3. If the gravitational constant, electromagnetism, or the "proton mass relative to the electron mass" varied from their values by only a tiny fraction (higher *or* lower), then all stars would be either blue giants or red dwarfs. These kinds of stars would not emit the proper kind of heat and light for a long enough period to allow for the emergence, development, and complexification of life forms. Paul Davies outlines this coincidence as follows:

> What is remarkable is that this typical mass M_* just happens to lie in the narrow range between the blue giants and red dwarfs. This circumstance is in turn a consequence of an apparently accidental relation between the relative strengths of gravity and electromagnetism, as will be shown.... This remarkable relation compares the strength of gravity (on the left) with the strength of electromagnetism, and the ratio of electron to proton mass.... Putting in the numbers, one obtains 5.9×10^{-39} for the left hand, and 2.0×10^{-39} for the right hand side. Nature has evidently picked the values of the fundamental constants in such a way that typical stars lie very close indeed to the boundary of convective instability. The fact that the two sides of the inequality are such enormous numbers, and yet lie so close to one another [10^{-39}], *is truly astonishing.* If gravity were *very* slightly weaker, or electromagnetism *very* slightly stronger, (or the electron slightly less massive relative to the proton), all stars would be *red dwarfs.* A correspondingly tiny change the other way, and they would all be *blue giants.*[57]

Again, this "anthropic coincidence" is inexplicable by a single random occurrence.

[56] Walter L. Bradley, "Designed or Designoid?" *Mere Creation: Science, Faith and Intelligent Design,* ed. William A. Dembski (Downers Grove, Ill.: InterVarsity Press, 1998), p. 39 (emphasis mine). See also R. Breuer, *The Anthropic Principle: Man as the Focal Point of Nature* (Boston: Birkhauser, 1991), p. 183.

[57] Davies, *Accidental Universe,* pp. 71–73 (emphasis mine).

4. Fred Hoyle and William Fowler discovered the exceedingly high improbability of oxygen, carbon, helium, and beryllium having the precise resonance levels to allow for an abundance of carbon necessary for life. He compared the emergence of a single cell within the universe by pure chance to "a tornado sweeping through a junk-yard assembling a Boeing 747 from the materials therein."[58]

He also compared the emergence of a single protein in the universe by pure chance to a solar system full of blind men solving Rubik's Cubes simultaneously.

The "resonance level" anthropic coincidence was so striking that it caused Hoyle to abandon his former atheism and declare:

> A common sense interpretation of the facts suggests that a superintellect has monkeyed with physics, as well as with chemistry and biology, and that there are no blind forces worth speaking about in nature. The numbers one calculates from the facts seem to me so overwhelming as to put this conclusion almost beyond question.[59]

The vast majority of physicists do not attribute these four and other anthropic coincidences (or the low entropy of the universe) at the Big Bang to random occurrence. Neither do they appeal to a prior natural cause (since the low entropy and constant values occur at the Big Bang, a boundary to natural causation). This virtually forces physicists to select one of two transuniversal explanations:

1. A multiverse in which every bubble universe has its own set of constant values, ultimately allowing trillions upon trillions upon trillions of bubble universes with different values of constants to naturalistically produce one highly improbable anthropic universe like our own
2. Supernatural design in which a highly intelligent transphysical Creator selects the values of the constants and produces the low

[58] Adam Marczyk, "Genetic Algorithms and Evolutionary Computation", TalkOrigins Archive, April 23, 2004, http://www.talkorigins.org/faqs/genalg/genalg.html.
[59] Fred Hoyle, "The Universe: Past and Present Reflections", *Engineering and Science* 45, no. 2 (November 1981): 12, http://calteches.library.caltech.edu/527/1/ES45.2.1981.pdf.

entropy of the universe at the Big Bang (similar to Sir Fred Hoyle's "superintellect")

Is the multiverse hypothesis more reasonable and responsible than supernatural intelligence? A combination of three factors implies that it is not. First, the multiverse hypothesis runs contrary to the canon of parsimony (Ockham's razor—the principle devised by William of Ockham that states that the explanation with the least number of assumptions, conditions, and requirements is to be preferred, because nature favors elegance over needless complexity). As Paul Davies notes,

> Another weakness of the anthropic argument is that it seems the very antithesis of Ockham's Razor, according to which the most plausible of a possible set of explanations is that which contains the simplest ideas and least number of assumptions. To invoke an infinity of other universes just to explain one is surely carrying excess baggage to cosmic extremes.... It is hard to see how such a purely theoretical construct can ever be used as an *explanation*, in the scientific sense, of a feature of nature. Of course, one might find it easier to believe in an infinite array of universes than in an infinite Deity, but such a belief must rest on faith rather than observation.[60]

Though the first reason does not invalidate the multiverse hypothesis, it seems to run contrary to nature's elegance and faces problems for being used as a scientific or naturalistic explanation.

The second factor concerns the requirement that every multiverse have a beginning because every multiverse must be inflationary (have an expansion rate greater than zero), making it subject to the Borde-Vilenkin-Guth proof. This means that no multiverse could produce an unlimited number of bubble universes. Again, this factor alone does not invalidate the multiverse as a possible explanation for our highly improbable anthropic universe, because a multiverse could theoretically produce $10^{10^{123}}$ (or more) bubble universes. However, when the above two factors are combined with the third, it raises serious doubts about the adequacy of the multiverse as an explanation of anthropic coincidences.

[60] Paul Davies, *God and the New Physics* (New York: Simon and Schuster, 1983), pp. 173–74.

The third factor concerns fine-tuning in the multiverse itself. Currently, all known multiverse theories have significant fine-tuning requirements. Linde's Chaotic Inflationary Multiverse cannot randomly cough out bubble universes because they would collide and make the bubble universes inhospitable to life; the bubble universes must be spaced out in a slow roll, which requires considerable fine-tuning in the multiverses' initial parameters.[61] Similarly, Susskind's String Theory Landscape requires considerable meta-level fine-tuning to explain its "anthropic tendencies".[62] Currently, no multiverse hypothesis is able to escape the need for such fine-tuning in its initial conditions and parameters.[63]

In view of the above three factors, many physicists consider the supernatural design hypothesis to be just as reasonable and responsible as the multiverse hypothesis for explaining the occurrence of our highly improbable anthropic universe.

VII. Conclusion

The supernatural design hypothesis is corroborated by the evidence for a beginning of physical reality (indicated by the Borde-Vilenkin-Guth proof, the second law of thermodynamics—entropy—and the intrinsic contradiction of an eternally static universe). If this evidence indicates the likelihood of a beginning of physical reality, and such a beginning implies the likelihood of a creation of physical reality by a causative force beyond it, then the real possibility of a supernatural designer (implied by universal fine-tuning at the Big Bang) might reasonably be associated with that Creator. In view of this, it might be more reasonable and responsible to believe in supernatural design than a multiverse.

We must now respond to another criticism of the supernatural design hypothesis proposed by Richard Dawkins in *The God Delusion*. Dawkins' argument runs as follows:

---

[61] See Laila Alabidi and David Lyth, "Inflation Models and Observation", *Journal of Cosmology and Astroparticle Physics* 0605 (2006): 016, doi:10.1088-1475-7516/2006/05016.

[62] See Gordon, "Inflationary Cosmology and the String Multiverse", pp. 100–102.

[63] See ibid., pp. 75–103.

1. A Creator–supernatural designer would have to be more complex than anything it could create.
2. Whatever is more complex is more improbable.
3. Therefore, a Creator–supernatural designer would have to be more improbable than anything it could create.[64]

Dawkins' argument is *not* from physics, but is decidedly metaphysical. To respond to the fallacy in his first premise, we must first formally examine the metaphysical presuppositions of it (which Dawkins himself does not do). This will take us to a Thomistic metaphysical argument for God that will reveal not that a Creator must be *more* complex than what it creates, but rather must be *less complex*—indeed absolutely simple. This has the effect of turning Dawkins' conclusion on its head, because if "more complexity is more improbable", then absolute simplicity (the absence of complexity) must be the most probable of all states of affairs! When Dawkins' fallacy is corrected, he presents us with a strong indication of God—not the invalidation of God. (This will be taken up in Appendix 2.)

For the moment, we can conclude that current physical evidence certainly does not point away from God. Indeed, it comes so close to establishing a beginning of physical reality and an intelligent influence in the setting of our universe's initial conditions and constants that physicists are being pushed to the threshold—and even beyond the threshold—of metaphysics, into the domain of "nothing", purely intelligible realities, and the source of multiversal fine-tuning. This foray into metaphysics is not done out of a sense of curiosity, but out of a desire to avert the implications of transphysical causation; and so it seems that physics has not explained away transphysical causation, but rather is opening the door evermore widely to an intelligent, transtemporal, causative power.

---

[64] See Richard Dawkins, *The God Delusion* (New York: Mariner Books, 2008), pp. 157–58.

Appendix Two

A Thomistic Metaphysical Proof of God: A Response to Richard Dawkins' "Complexity Error"

Introduction

In Appendix 1 we presented Richard Dawkins' assertion that a Creator would have to be more improbable than anything it creates because it would have to be more complex. Evidently this argument turns on the assertion that God is complex. However, since Plato, and more explicitly, Thomas Aquinas, a rationale was developed for precisely the opposite contention, namely, the absolute simplicity (noncomplexity) of God. Perhaps the best way of understanding this is to examine a *full* Thomistic argument for the existence of God.

In the *Summa Theologica* (Part I, Question 2, Article 3), Aquinas gives five "*ways*" to God, for example, the way of the unmoved mover, the way of the uncaused cause, and so on. In these brief presentations, Aquinas shows only the *necessity* of an unmoved mover or an uncaused cause, but does not show their *simplicity*, unrestrictedness, and uniqueness, because he does so elsewhere in the *Summa* (see below). Unfortunately, Dawkins did not recognize this, and so he failed to understand both the validity of the proofs and the simplicity (noncomplexity) of the Creator.[1]

The following eight-step argument represents a basic outline of what Dawkins failed to understand (and present) in his survey of philosophical arguments for God and his dismissal of Thomas Aquinas' proofs in *The God Delusion*.

[1] See Richard Dawkins, *The God Delusion* (New York: Mariner Books, 2008), Chapter 3, particularly pp. 100–103.

I. An Eight-Step Thomistic Metaphysical Proof of God

Definitions

"*Caused cause*". A caused cause is a reality that does not exist through itself—it is dependent on causation for existence and must therefore await causation in order to exist. Without causation, it is merely hypothetical, and literally nothing.

Causes include constituent parts or conditions for something to exist; for example, cells are composed of proteins and amino acids, which in turn are composed of molecules, which in turn are composed of atoms, and so on. This includes structures and organizing components of those constituent parts, such as the particular structures of proteins, amino acids, molecules, and so on. Without these constituent parts, conditions, and organizing structures, the cell would not exist. These causes are called "formal and material causes". Additionally, any element "outside" of a reality necessary for its existence would also be a cause, such as light, water, and nutriment for a cell's metabolism. These are called "efficient causes".

"*Uncaused cause*". An uncaused cause is a reality that does not require any cause to exist. It exists purely through itself without any conditions whatsoever. As will be seen below, it must be a pure act of existing through itself.

Step 1: There Must Exist at Least One Uncaused Cause [2]

Recall (from the above definition) that a caused cause must await causation in order to exist. Now, if the whole of reality were composed only of caused causes (realities that must await causation to exist), then the whole of reality would be awaiting causation to exist,

---

[2] Aristotle first formulated this proof as an "Unmoved Mover" proof in Book 8 of the *Physics* and Book 12 of the *Metaphysics*. See Aristotle, *Aristotle's* Metaphysics, trans. and ed. Hippocrates Apostle (Grinnell, Iowa: Peripatetic Press, 1979), and *Physics*, trans. Hippocrates Apostle (Bloomington, Ind.: Indiana University Press, 1969). The proof was later expanded to the "Uncaused Cause" proof by Thomas Aquinas, and there are many versions of it today (see, for example, Bernard Lonergan, *Insight: A Study of Human Understanding*, in *Collected Works of Bernard Lonergan* 3, ed. Frederick E. Crowe and Robert M. Doran [Toronto: University of Toronto Press, 1992], Chapter 19). Saint Thomas Aquinas discusses this in a variety of different places, but for the most well-known see *Summa Theologica*, Part I, Question 2, Article 3.

in which case the whole of reality would be awaiting existence—in which case the whole of reality would not exist. Therefore, there must be at least one reality that does not have to await causation to exist (which exists through itself alone) and causes the existence of realities awaiting that causation. Without at least one uncaused cause, the whole of reality would be literally nothing.

Further explanation. It does not matter whether one postulates an *infinite* number of caused causes (realities awaiting causation to exist), because an infinite number of hypothesized realities awaiting causation to exist is collectively still awaiting causation to exist—it is literally an infinite amount of nothing, and an infinite amount of nothing is still nothing. Therefore, there must be at least one reality that does not have to await causation to exist—a reality that exists through itself (an uncaused cause)—in order to have *anything* real.

Step 2: An Uncaused Cause Must Be the Pure Act of Existing through Itself[3]

As shown in Step 1, there must be at least one uncaused cause—at least one reality that does not await causation to exist, a reality that exists through itself alone (for if it did not, there would be nothing in the whole of reality). An uncaused cause must have the power to exist through itself, and more than this, that power must be acting— otherwise it would be a power awaiting activation; it would need a cause.

Inasmuch as an uncaused cause would have to be an act of existing through itself *alone*, it must also be a *pure* act of existing through itself. The word "pure" here is important because there cannot be *anything* in the "act of existing through itself" that is different from it. If there were anything other than the "act of existing through itself" in it, that part or dimension of it would *not* exist through itself and would therefore have to be caused. Since an uncaused cause cannot have a part or dimension that needs to be caused, it must be a *pure* "act of existing through itself".

---

[3] This insight is perhaps the crowning achievement of Saint Thomas Aquinas' metaphysics. One excellent articulation of it may be found in *Summa Contra Gentiles, Book One*, trans. Anton C. Pegis (Notre Dame: Notre Dame University Press, 1991), Chapter 16, Paragraph 3.

Step 3: An Uncaused Cause (a Pure Act of Existing through Itself) Must Be Unrestricted[4]

If something were to restrict an act of existing through itself, it would have to be *different* from it, otherwise the restricting factor would be identical with the act of existing through itself—in which case, that restriction would be intrinsic to the act of existing, requiring that every act of existing be so restricted. Why?

Let's take as examples the three most well-known ways in which something can be restricted—spatially, temporally, and a particular way of acting. Let's start with space. If space were not different from the act of existing through itself, then it would be identical with the act of existing, in which case they would be one and the same. This would mean that every act of existing would have to be spatial. But this is clearly not the case because trans-spatial realities can exist—as indicated in our universe by certain quantum effects (see Chapter 6, Section III.C). Moreover, spatiality is ontologically subordinate to existence—that is, existence is the condition necessary for space but not vice versa. Therefore, existence need not be spatial (which would have to have been the case if spatiality were *not different* from the act of existing through itself).

The same thing holds true for temporality. If temporality were not different from an act of existing through itself, then it would be identical with the act of existing—they would be one and the same thing, in which case every act of existing would have to be temporal. However, temporality is ontologically subordinate to the act of existing, because existence is a condition necessary for time—but not vice versa. Therefore, the act of existing need not be temporal (which would have to have been the case if temporality were *not different* from the act of existing through itself). (This is explained more fully below in Step 8.)

The same thing holds true for a particular way of acting (say, the way of acting as a proton or an electron). If the way of acting like an

---

[4] This crucial insight is first developed by Saint Thomas in his early metaphysical work *De Ente et Essentia* (*On Being and Essence*), particularly Chapters 4 and 5 (see Thomas Aquinas, *On Being and Essence*, trans. Armand Maurer, 2nd. rev. ed. [Toronto: Pontifical Institute of Mediaeval Studies, 1968]). For Thomas' view of "infinity" (in the sense of "unrestricted existence"), see *Summa Contra Gentiles*, Book 1, Chapter 43, Paragraphs 1 and 3.

electron were not different from an act of existing through itself, then it would be identical with an act of existing, which means that every act of existing would have to be the way of acting like an electron. But this does not have to be the case—as is clear from the existence of protons and neutrons, and so on. Moreover, particular ways of existing (like that of an electron) are ontologically subordinate to the act of existing. Again we see that existence is the condition necessary for any particular way of acting—but not vice versa. Therefore, existence need not be *any* particular way of acting (which would have to have been the case if *any* particular way of acting were *not different* from the act of existing through itself).

It really does not matter what kind of restriction one hypothesizes— if that restriction is not *different* from a pure act of existing through itself, then every act of existing would necessarily be identical with it. But this clearly does not have to be the case. An act of existing need not be limited to any way of existing, place of existing, time of existing, or *any* other conceivable restriction to existence.

Now, let us return to the proof. If all restrictions must be different from an act of existing through itself, then those restrictions are *not* the act of existing through itself, which means that they do not exist through themselves and therefore must be caused. Since all restrictions to the act of existing through itself must be caused, a *pure* act of existing through itself (a pure *uncaused* cause) cannot have any restrictions to it. It must be completely unrestricted.

One last clarification. The term "unrestricted" refers to the absence of restriction within the act of existing through itself. It does not refer to an infinite spatial manifold or temporal manifold, which are distinct from a pure act of existing through itself. Infinite extension (space) and distension (time) imply the *presence* of space and time (that continues forever). However, "unrestricted" applied to a pure act of existing through itself indicates "the *absence* of spatial, temporal, and other restrictions in the act of existing through itself".

Though it is virtually impossible to visualize what a nonspatial and nontemporal act of existence through itself would be like, we must acknowledge that a pure act of existing through itself must be the most fundamental kind of reality—because all restrictions to the act of existing through itself must be caused, making them *less* fundamental than an uncaused cause.

Step 4: A Pure Unrestricted Act of Existing through Itself Must Be Unique (One and Only One)[5]

The basic proof may be set out in three premises:

1. If there is to be multiplicity among realities, there must be a difference between those realities.
2. If there is to be differences among realities, at least one of those realities must be restricted.
3. But there can be no restriction in the pure act of existing through itself (from Step 3 above).

Therefore, there cannot be more than one pure act of existing through itself (*modus tollens*).

Explanation of the Proof

The first premise is true a priori, because if there is no difference of any kind between two realities, they must be the self-same reality. Let us postulate two realities: X_1 and X_2. Now, let us suppose there is no difference between them—no difference as to space-time point, no difference in power or activity, no difference of qualities or characteristics, no difference of any kind whatsoever. What are they? Obviously, they are the same reality, and as such "they" are only one.

The second premise is also true a priori. Think about it. If there is a difference between say X_1 and X_2 (so there can be a multiplicity of them), then one of them will have to be something or have something or be somewhere or be in some other dimension that the other one is *not*. Let's suppose that X_1 has something that X_2 does not have. This means that X_2 is restricted or limited because it lacks this quality or characteristic. Similarly, if one postulates that X_1 *is* something that X_2 is not, then X_2 would again have to be limited (as manifest by its lack of that "something"). The same would hold true if X_1 were somewhere that X_2 was not, and if X_1 were in another dimension that X_2 was not. In short, every differentiating factor will entail a restriction of at least one of the differentiated realities.

---

[5] For Aquinas' proof of this, see *Summa Contra Gentiles*, Book 1, Chapter 42, Paragraph 3.

The third premise has already been proved in Step 3 above ("but there can be no restriction in a pure act of existing through itself"); therefore, there cannot be a difference between two (hypothetical) pure acts of existing through themselves (*modus tollens*), meaning that there cannot be a multiplicity of pure acts of existing through themselves (*modus tollens*).

Let's see how this works. Suppose that there are two pure acts of existing through themselves; then by the first premise, there will have to be some difference between pure Act of Existing$_1$ and pure Act of Existing$_2$. Recall that if there are no differences whatsoever between them, then they would be the self-same reality (one reality). Now if there is a difference between them, then one of them will have to have something, be something, be somewhere, or be in another dimension that the other one is not; in other words, at least one of them will have to be *restricted*. If one of the pure acts of existing through itself is restricted as to what it is (its way of existing), or where it is (its space-time point or its dimension), then it could not be unrestricted. As was shown in Step 3 above, a pure act of existing through itself must be completely unrestricted (otherwise there would be something in it that did not exist through itself—which would have to be caused). In sum, every hypothetical "act of existing through itself" would have to have some kind of restriction that could not exist through itself and would therefore have to be caused. This second pure act of existence therefore could not really be a *pure* act of existing through itself (a completely uncaused cause).

Therefore, there can only be one pure act of existing through itself (only one uncaused cause).

Step 5: The One Pure Act of Existing through Itself Must Be the Ultimate Cause (Creator) of All Else That Is[6]

This is derived from a two-step argument:

1. As shown above, an uncaused cause must be a pure unrestricted act of existing through itself, and there can only be one pure

[6] For Aquinas' discussion of this, see *Summa Theologica*, Part I, Question 44, Article 1.

unrestricted act of existing through itself, meaning that there can only be one uncaused cause in all reality.
2. If there can only be one uncaused cause in all reality, then the rest of reality must be caused (brought into existence).

Therefore, the one uncaused cause must be the ultimate cause of the existence of everything in reality besides itself. This is what is meant by the term "Creator".

Step 6: The Pure Unrestricted Act of Existing through Itself Must Be Absolutely Simple (the Absence of Complexity)[7]

Basic Argument

The basic argument is as follows:

1. Complexity entails parts.
2. Parts entail restriction.
3. But there can be no restriction in the pure act of existing through itself.

Therefore, there can be no parts and no complexity in the pure act of existing through itself (*modus tollens*).

Explanation

The first and second premises are true a priori. Anything that is complex must have parts constituting a greater whole. For example, atoms are constituted by protons and electrons; molecules are composed of atoms; cells are composed of molecules; complex organisms are composed of multiple cells and cellular structure, and so on. Notice that each of these parts is restricted as to its place, duration, and way of acting. Now if there are parts constituting a greater whole, the parts must be more restricted than the whole (by definition), and therefore the parts must have restrictions as to their time, space, or way

---

[7] Aquinas articulated this in many different ways and works. A particularly clear one may be found in *Summa Theologica*, Part I, Question 3, Article 7.

of existing. For example, protons must be more restricted in space and way of acting than atoms, and atoms must be more restricted in space and way of acting than molecules, and molecules must be more restricted in space and way of acting than cells, and so on.

The proof of the third premise ("there can be no restriction in the pure act of existing through itself") was given in Step 3 above.

Therefore, by *modus tollens*, if there can be no restrictions in the pure act of existing through itself, then there can be no parts in the pure act of existing through itself, and if no parts, then no complexity. It must be absolutely simple.

This stands in direct contradistinction to Dawkins' assertion that a Creator must be more complex than what it creates. As shown above, the Creator—the unique unrestricted act of existing through itself—cannot have parts and therefore must be completely simple and devoid of complexity. Dawkins' failure to look more deeply into the metaphysical underpinnings of the five ways led to what I would call his fundamental "complexity error". Instead of grasping the necessity for the one creative power to be absolutely simple, he confused creative power with complexity. Nothing could further from the truth.

Step 7: The One Unrestricted Act of Existing through Itself is Transtemporal[8]

In Step 3 above, we showed that the pure act of existing through itself could not be restricted by temporality, because temporality must

---

[8] Saint Augustine wrestled with this in Book 11 of *The Confessions*, coming to the conclusion that God is "an eternal now", and that he was not before time, because he was not in time (and that there was no time before time); see particularly Book 11, Chapter 13, paragraph 16 (Augustine, *Confessions*, trans. Henry Chadwick [New York: Oxford University, 1991]). Of course, he meant this *analogously*, because the best any of us can do is a negative judgment, an act of existing that is not subject to a temporal manifold. Aquinas follows Augustine in the timelessness of God (as "eternal now") and goes further, attempting to explain how such a timeless reality could understand "all time" of created realities that are conditioned by and progressing in time. He uses *analogies* to discuss this (such as seeing the progression of time from on high in a single vision *or* being at the center of a circle and observing all equidistant points at once), but we cannot think that he believed these analogies to represent *God's* reality, for they would imply that God's reality is conditioned by space and geometry, and also imply "eternalism" in which the past, present, and future coexist (a theory to which Aquinas did not subscribe). See *Compendium Theologiae* 133; *De Veritate* 11, 12, resp.; and *Summa*

be different from the pure act of existing through itself, and if it is different, it does not exist through itself and must therefore be caused. We noted further that temporality had to be different from the pure act of existing through itself, because temporality (a noncontemporaneous continuum of "earlier-later"[9]) is ontologically subordinate to the act of existing through itself, because existence is the condition necessary for temporality, but not vice versa. This showed that existence need *not* be temporal (which would have to have been the case if temporality were *not different* from the act of existing through itself). We concluded from this that if temporality is different from the pure act of existing through itself, the *pure* act of existing through itself is not restricted by temporality—for if it were, there would be a part of it that is not "the act of existing through itself", which would have to be caused (a contradiction).

The idea of a reality being nontemporal or transtemporal is difficult to imagine. But Henri Bergson provides an analogy to help us understand it. If time is a continuum of earlier and later, then it must be held together by something like "elementary memory" or "elementary consciousness", otherwise all time would be reduced to a dimensionless instant. Why? Because without it, the earlier part of the continuum would pass away as a later part becomes present. In order for time to be more than a dimensionless instant, the earlier part of the continuum must be retained when the later part becomes present. For Bergson, elementary memory or consciousness (in the universe) retains these earlier moments and, as such, is the unifying substrate of the temporal continuum.

This gives rise to an interesting question: Can this elementary act of memory or consciousness be a unifying substrate without itself

---

Theologica, Part I, Question 10. So we are back to the negative judgment that God is *not* conditioned by time, and that the whole of temporal reality (such as our universe and any other temporal reality beyond it) exists as a single *transtemporal* "thought" in God's unrestricted act of thinking (see Step 7 below). For a contemporary understanding of time and transtemporality (in light of Bergson and others), see Robert J. Spitzer, "Definitions of Real Time and Ultimate Reality", *Ultimate Reality and Meaning: Interdisciplinary Studies in the Philosophy of Understanding* 23, no. 3 (2000): 260–67; see also Robert J. Spitzer, *New Proofs for the Existence of God: Contributions of Contemporary Physics and Philosophy* (Grand Rapids, Mich.: Eerdmans, 2010), pp. 183–96; see also Henri Bergson, *Duration and Simultaneity*, trans. Leon Jacobson (Indianapolis: Bobbs-Merrill, 1965).

[9] For an ontological explanation of time, see Spitzer, *New Proofs for the Existence of God*, pp. 187–97, and Spitzer, "Definitions of Real Time and Ultimate Reality", pp. 260–67.

being subject to time (an earlier-later continuum)? There is no reason why this unifying substrate would have to be "inside" the temporal continuum it unifies any more than *my* act of consciousness must be subject to its contents. My consciousness does not have to become square in order to unify four inscribed right angles with equal sides, and it need not be subject to an earlier-later condition when it unifies an ever-growing number line. Consciousness is capable of unifying spatial and temporal manifolds without itself being subject to them. To deny this is to reduce a more fundamental reality to a less fundamental one.

In Step 8, it will be shown that the pure unrestricted act of existing through itself is an unrestricted act of mentation (thinking). As such, it need not be subject to the "earlier-later continuum" it unifies. The whole of time can be unified in a timeless reflective act.

We must acknowledge at the outset that a timeless act of mentation is impossible to visualize because, as many philosophers have noted, our experience and imagination are conditioned by space and time. So how can we conceive of something we cannot imagine (picture think)? We can only do this by a kind of *via negativa*—that is, by a conceptual process that avoids the temporalizing dimension of the imagination (picture thinking). We will have to avoid trying to "get a picture of it" and rest content with a negative judgment, namely, that there exists the pure unrestricted act of existing through itself that does *not* exist through a temporal manifold or a spatial manifold, or anything else that is not itself. This pure act of existing must therefore be beyond any universe and any spatio-temporal reality, making it unimaginable. Nothing more can be said without distorting this reality through the conditions of our spatial and temporal imagination.

Step 8: The Pure Unrestricted Act of Existing through Itself Is an Unrestricted Act of Mentation (Thinking)[10]

What is thinking? A detailed explanation of this is given in Chapter 3 of this volume; so a brief synopsis will suffice here.

---

[10] Aquinas' views here are expressed by Bernard Lonergan; see Bernard Lonergan, *Verbum: Word and Idea in Aquinas*, in *Collected Works of Bernard J. F. Lonergan* 2, ed. Frederick E. Crowe (Toronto: University of Toronto Press, 1994), pp. 191–228. Aquinas first shows

1. Thinking (in contrast to imagining or picture thinking) is the grasp of relationships among realities—qualitative relationships, causal relationships, quantitative relationships, logical relationships, temporal relationships, spatial relationships, and any other intelligible relationship responding to the questions *what, where, why, when, how*, as well as the questions, how many? and, how frequently?

2. The ability to grasp relationships presumes an underlying unity through which the differences among realities can be related. For example, a map can unify diverse geographical locations so that they can be seen *in relation* to one another. A clock provides a unity for different times so that they may be seen in relationship to one another. There must be some underlying unity to bring together causes and effects in causal relationships. The same holds true for the questions of what, how, or how many, and so on. We might summarize by saying that thinking is a unifying act that sets differing realities or ideas into relationship with one another. Therefore, thinking goes beyond imagination (picture thinking that is limited to mere identification of individual things). When realities or ideas are set into relationship with one another, we can detect similarities and differences, quantities and causes, relative location and time, and we can even detect relationships among relationships.

3. As noted in Steps 3 and 7 above, the pure act of existing through itself has no spatial, temporal, or other intrinsic restrictions. Therefore, there is nothing to prevent it from being in a perfectly transparent and reflective relationship to itself.

This can be analogically understood by our own act of self-consciousness in which the same act of consciousness is both "experienced" and "experiencer" simultaneously. This does not imply that our thinking has distinct parts, but rather that the one indivisible act

---

the spiritual nature of self-consciousness and thought in mankind (captured by Chapters 1 through 4 in ibid.) and then proceeds to use this as an analogy of God's completely simple, unrestricted act of self-consciousness (in Chapter 5 of ibid.—"*Imago Dei*"). The spiritual nature of man's intellection is also captured by Lonergan's "notion of being" in Lonergan, *Insight*, pp. 380–81 (see the reference below).

of consciousness has *relational* differences "within"[11] itself. (This is explained in detail in Chapter 6, Section III.C.)

Let us return now to the pure unrestricted act of existing through itself. Inasmuch as it is perfectly self-transparent (because it has no intrinsic spatial, temporal, or other restrictions), it can be perfectly present to itself as "experiencer" and "experienced". This means it is perfectly self-conscious (in a fundamental unity without parts). The absence of spatial, temporal, and all other restrictions makes the one act of existing through itself perfectly self-transparent, perfectly self-relational, and, therefore, perfectly present to itself and perfectly self-conscious. This completely simple, self-transparent reality can generate the whole domain of restricted intelligibility. Consider the following:

1. Embedded in this self-consciousness is an awareness of the *difference* between itself as experiencer and experienced, and so there is not only an awareness of self, but an awareness of relational *differences* within itself. Inasmuch as "self" and "difference" are grasped, so also are all other ideas. The self can grasp not only itself, but what is different from itself (e.g., restriction and change). By grasping "self", "difference", "restriction", and "change", it grasps the whole range of finite intelligibility. Plato shows how this is done in his remarkable late dialogue *The Sophist*.[12]

2. Notice that this unrestricted act of mentation is not like a brain or anything material or restricted. It is identical with the pure unrestricted act of existing through itself, because the complete absence of restriction in this acting power enables it to be present to itself, and differentiate itself from what it is not—the whole range of restricted intelligibility.

---

[11] The term "within" here has no spatial connotation for obvious reasons; it refers only to the relational difference between "experiencing" and "being experienced" in a single act of consciousness.

[12] In *The Sophist*, Plato recognized how the entire domain of restricted intelligibility could be generated and explained through the interrelationship of six fundamental ideas (three diads): being and nonbeing, sameness and difference, and motion and rest. See Plato, *The Sophist*, in *The Collected Dialogues of Plato*, trans. F.M. Cornford, ed. Edith Hamilton and Huntington Cairns (Princeton, N.J.: Princeton University Press, 1961), pp. 978–1028 (236d–264b).

We cannot visualize it or imagine it; we can only *understand* that there must exist the one unrestricted act of existence through itself, and that it must be a perfect unity in relation to itself, and therefore perfectly self-conscious and perfectly conscious of everything that could be different from it (the whole domain of restricted intelligibility). Bernard Lonergan comes to a similar conclusion in his work *Insight: A Study of Human Understanding* and calls the first cause "an unrestricted act of understanding—understanding trans-spatial itself"[13] (see Chapter 3, Sections IV and V). Inasmuch as the pure unrestricted act of existing through itself is an unrestricted act of thinking, its awareness of all finite intelligibility allows for the creation of finite being.

The Problems in the Materialistic Bias

Dawkins (and some other scientists) has a difficult time understanding how an absolutely simple reality can think, but if one takes thinking out of a materialistic context (e.g., a brain or a machine) and views it instead from the vantage point of a "completely unifying acting power", the problem vanishes. As we have seen above, the "pure act of existing through itself" is the most fundamental acting power—the "acting power of all acting powers", the condition necessary for the possibility of everything else. This most fundamental acting power must be unrestricted—for the reasons mentioned above in Step 3—and so there is no restriction, either internally or externally to its capacity to act. It is capable of doing absolutely everything that is not contradictory.

Since it has no intrinsic restrictions, it can be in perfect relationship to itself—like our self-consciousness, which can be in two relative positions with respect to itself simultaneously. As such, it is perfectly self-conscious and perfectly conscious of what is not itself (i.e., the whole range of *restricted* intelligibility)—so it is at once perfect self-consciousness and a perfect act of thinking.

In short, a pure act of existing through itself must be unrestricted, and if unrestricted, then unique and absolutely simple, and

---

[13] Lonergan, *Insight*, pp. 657–708.

if absolutely simple, then absolutely self-transparent, and if absolutely self-transparent, then perfectly self-conscious, and if perfectly self-conscious, then a perfect act of thinking—or as Lonergan would call it, "An unrestricted act of understanding—understanding itself."

We sometimes think of the most powerful and sophisticated reality as being the most *complex*, but this approach is the result of a *materialistic* bias, which prevents its adherents from finding an adequate solution to the question of the *ultimate* ground and source of intelligibility and reality. Most materialists give up the quest for this ultimate ground and content themselves with partially explanatory restricted theories. We can do better than this by lifting our perspective out of the materialistic bias, which associates the most simple reality with the most simple *physical* realities—the most basic *restricted* realities. This can be accomplished by starting our inquiry anew. Instead of beginning with the most simple *physical and restricted* realities, we will want to begin with the most *fundamental* reality, the one that must be the condition necessary for the possibility of everything else— namely, an uncaused cause that can exist through itself. By doing this, we can resolve the "complexity error" as well as the problem of how the simplest reality can be an unrestricted and creative act of self-consciousness and thinking. Without this change of perspective, physicists and philosophers will chain themselves to their materialistic assumptions, which will force them to "build" an absolutely fundamental ground and source of reality out of a multitude of intrinsically restricted realities—an impossible and futile endeavor. They will be constrained, like those in Plato's cave, to count, aggregate, and study mere shadows cast on the wall of a cave by an *unseen* light, which is reality itself.

Conclusion to the Proof

Therefore, there must exist a unique pure unrestricted act of existing through itself that is an absolutely simple, timeless, self-conscious pure act of mentation and the Creator of all else that exists. This entity may be termed "God".

To deny this reality has two untenable consequences: either we must deny the existence of at least one uncaused cause, which means denying the existence of everything in reality (because without an uncaused cause, everything in reality would still be awaiting causation to exist—from Step 1 above), *or* we must affirm that restrictions to a pure act of existing through itself are *not* different from an act of existing through itself, which is contradictory (see Step 3 above). If we affirm the untenability of these two consequences, then all the other proven attributes of an uncaused cause will follow by means of simple noncontradictory proofs. This enables us to affirm the existence of God as defined above.

II. A Response to Richard Dawkins' "Complexity Error"

As noted above in Appendix 1, Dawkins' core argument in *The God Delusion* may be summarized as follows:

1. A designer must always be more complex than what it designs.
2. Whatever is more complex is more improbable.
3. Therefore, a designer must be more improbable than what it designs.[14]

There can be little doubt that Dawkins' second premise ("whatever is more complex is more improbable") is true, because the more complex a reality is, the more parts there are to order or organize. Since order or organization is more improbable than disorder, it follows that the more parts there are to order, the more improbable the ordering will be.

However, Dawkins' *first* premise is highly contestable and ignores twenty-four hundred years of philosophical history[15] going back to Plato and Aristotle, and proceeding to Augustine and Aquinas (including the metaphysical proof given above) and to contemporary

---

[14]See Dawkins, *God Delusion*, pp. 157–58.

[15]Dawkins makes a perfunctory criticism of Aquinas' proofs for the existence of God (see ibid., pp. 100–103) but regrettably does not understand these proofs in any meaningful way. If he had, he would not have constructed a virtual "straw man" version of them, while missing the solution to one of the greatest metaphysical problems—the connection between an uncaused cause, absolute simplicity, and the nature of mentation (thinking).

philosophers such as Etienne Gilson, Josef Pieper, Bernard Loner-gan, Karl Rahner, and their followers. These philosophers contend (in conformity with the above metaphysical proof) that an uncaused cause (a Creator and designer) must be *absolutely simple* (a complete absence of complexity) instead of more complex. Ironically, this means by Dawkins' second premise ("whatever is more complex is more improbable") that an absolutely simple Creator or designer would have to be the most probable reality of all. Thus, Dawkins' argument serves only to *affirm*—not to deny—the existence of a Creator if an uncaused cause must be absolutely simple (as proven above).

Dawkins' argument reveals another weakness in his philosophical viewpoint: he interprets thinking in a *materialistic* way. This may conform to his biological background, but it again ignores twenty-four hundred years of philosophical reflection (summarized in the above metaphysical proof—Steps 3, 6, and 8). In brief, if an uncaused cause must be unrestricted and absolutely simple (Steps 3 and 6, respectively), then it can be in perfect relationship to itself (like an act of self-consciousness) where there is no differentiation of *parts*, but only differences in *relationships* within its self-reflective act. This position was intimated first by Plato and carried to fruition by Boethius, Augustine, and Aquinas in their treatises on the Trinity. Bernard Lonergan[16] and Karl Rahner[17] articulate it in more contemporary terms and concepts.

If Step 8 of the metaphysical argument is correct, then the pure unrestricted act of existing through itself—which must be unrestricted and absolutely simple—must also be an unrestricted act of thinking (generating the whole range of all possible relationships through its perfect and unrestricted relationship to itself). This means that the perfect act of thinking comes not from complexity, but from *absolute simplicity*. To deny this is to subordinate a more fundamental reality (complete self-transparency intrinsic to unrestricted power) to a less fundamental one (a complex reality that has restrictions)—see the comment on materialistic bias above in Step 8.

A brain or a computer cannot generate a completely self-transparent act of thinking, because they are restricted in their activities and

---

[16] See Lonergan, *Insight*, Chapter 19.
[17] See Karl Rahner, *Spirit in the World* (London: Bloomsbury Academic, 1994).

operations and in their physical structures and laws, including quantum activities, structures, and laws. No amount of complexity of restricted parts will ever be able to generate an unrestricted act of mentation, because in their totality they will always be restricted.[18]

In *The God Delusion*, Dawkins shows little understanding of how an unrestricted act of existing can be self-transparent, self-relational, self-conscious, and, therefore, capable of thinking and creating. He assumes that the more comprehensive the act of thinking, the more complex a reality must be. However, this is true only for materialistic conceptions of thinking, which are based on assembling restricted "building blocks" or material parts, like those found in brains and computers (see the comment on materialistic bias above in Step 8). It does not include *nonmaterialistic* views of thinking that are based on self-relationship within an unrestricted, absolutely simple power (i.e., the pure act of existing through itself).

Though nonmaterialistic views of thinking were developed by ancient and medieval philosophers, the materialistic reductionism (which arose out of some interpretations of natural science) closed man's imagination to this possibility until Gödel's theorem and the quantum revolution perforce reopened it.[19] Bernard Lonergan and other contemporary philosophers combine the ancient and medieval insight into absolute simplicity with the Gödelian and quantum revolutions, and so their assessment of mind is important for resolving

---

[18] I develop this position in much more detail in Robert J. Spitzer, "Why Is Human Self-Consciousness Different from Artificial Intelligence and Animal Consciousness?" *Ultimate Reality and Meaning: Interdisciplinary Studies in the Philosophy of Understanding* 33, nos. 1–2 (2010): 5–27.

[19] Göedel's Theorem gave the first modern clue to the nonmechanistic and nonalgorithmic dimension of man's consciousness (see Kurt Gödel, "Über formal unentscheidbare Sätze der Principia Mathematica undverwandter Systeme I", *Monatshefte für Mathematik und Physik* 38 [1931]: 173–98). Later John Lucas and Roger Penrose combined this insight with developments in quantum theory (see John Lucas, "Minds, Machines, and Gödel", *Philosophy* 36 [1961]: 120; Roger Penrose, *The Emperor's New Mind* [Oxford: Oxford University Press, 1989]; and Roger Penrose, *Shadows of the Mind* [Oxford: Oxford University Press, 1994], pp. 7–59). Stephen Barr has an excellent summary of Gödel, quantum theory, and the transphysical dimension of human intelligence (see Stephen M. Barr, *Modern Physics and Ancient Faith* [Notre Dame: University of Notre Dame Press, 2003], p. 214ff.). A detailed explanation of the contributions of Göedel and quantum theory may be found in Chapter 3, Section V.C, and Chapter 6, Sections I.B and III.C. See also the explanation of the transphysical notion of thinking in light of Lonergan's notion of being, quantum theory, and Gödel's theorem in Spitzer, "Why Is Human Self-Consciousness Different?", pp. 5–27.

contemporary paradoxes in artificial intelligence and the unexplained creativity of human intelligence.[20]

In my view, Dawkins' materialistic view of thinking and his denial of an intelligent Creator arise out of his unawareness of three pillars of physical and metaphysical thought:

1. The necessity of an uncaused cause that must exist through itself alone (and must therefore be a pure act of existing through itself)
2. The necessity that a pure act of existing through itself be unrestricted and unique
3. The necessity that this unique uncaused cause be absolutely simple, perfectly self-transparent, perfectly self-relational, perfectly self-conscious, and a perfect act of thinking

Thus Dawkins' materialistic view of thinking is out of step with current developments in the philosophy of mathematics (from the time of Gödel to today) and quantum theory. These developments reflect the veracity of the "simplicity of a pure act of mentation" proposed many centuries earlier by Aquinas and his predecessors.[21]

III. Conclusion: Combining the Physical and Metaphysical Evidence

In Appendixes 1 and 2 we have discussed four kinds of evidence for the existence of an intelligent Creator:

---

[20] See Lonergan's assessment of "The Notion of Being", in *Insight*:

> The notion of being penetrates *all* cognitional contents. It is the supreme heuristic notion. *Prior* to every content, it is the notion of the *to-be-known* through that content. As each content emerges, the "to-be-known through that content" passes without residue into the "known through that content." Some blank in *universal anticipation* is filled in, not merely to end that element of anticipation, but also to make the filler a part of the anticipated. Hence, *prior* to all answers, the notion of being is the notion of the *totality* to be known through all answers. (pp. 380–81; emphasis mine)

A detailed explanation of Lonergan's notion of being is given in Chapter 3 (Sections V.A and V.B).

[21] See Spitzer, "Why Is Human Self-Consciousness Different?", pp. 5–27.

1. Space-time geometry proofs for a beginning of physical reality (implying a causative power transcending physical reality—Appendix 1, Section III)
2. The evidence from entropy for a beginning of our universe supporting the above conclusion of a causative power transcending physical reality (Appendix 1, Section IV)
3. The fine-tuning of the initial conditions and constants of the universe at the Big Bang (implying supernatural intelligence—Appendix 1, Section VI)
4. A logical-metaphysical proof for the existence of a unique unrestricted pure act of existing through itself that is an unrestricted act of thinking and the Creator of all else that is (Appendix 2)

Each of these four kinds of evidence has probative force in its own right (independently of the others). But when they are combined, they become complementary because they corroborate each other while emphasizing different dimensions of the one transcendent intelligent Creator.

John Henry Newman termed such a network of complementary evidence an "informal inference",[22] that is, reaching a conclusion by considering the accumulation of converging antecedently probable data sets. As explained in the introduction to this volume, Newman held that truth claims did not have to be grounded in an infallible source of evidence or in a strictly formal deduction. They could be grounded in the convergence (complementarity and corroboration) of a multiplicity of *probabilistic* evidential bases. In so doing, certitude would not be grounded in one base alone, but in a multiplicity of likely or probable evidential *bases*. Thus, even if one (or more) of these bases undergoes modification, the certitude intrinsic to the convergence remains intact (though it may be lessened).

Our conclusion, then, is that both physical and philosophical evidence lead to the high probability of a unique, unrestricted, intelligent Creator. Space-time geometry proofs and entropy give *physical and scientific* evidence for a transcendent power creating our universe (and even a hypothetical multiverse or universe in the higher-dimensional

---

[22] See John Henry Newman, *An Essay in Aid of a Grammar of Assent* (Notre Dame, Ind.: University of Notre Dame Press, 1992), pp. 259–342 (Chapter 8).

space of string theory). The evidence of the fine-tuning of initial conditions and constants of our universe complements the evidence of a creation by providing *physical* and *scientific* evidence of intelligence. In combination, they support the existence of a highly intelligent transcendent power that is a Creator of physical reality.

The above Thomistic metaphysical argument for a unique unrestricted act of thinking gives logical-metaphysical evidence for an intelligent Creator and so corroborates the evidence of physics. Yet, it goes far beyond this by showing the uniqueness, unrestrictedness, and absolute simplicity of an uncaused cause. It also shows that this Being must be transphysical (transtemporal and trans-spatial), and in the absence of any restrictions, must be completely self-transparent and self-relational, making it perfectly self-conscious and capable of grasping everything different from itself (the entire realm of finite intelligibility).

BIBLIOGRAPHY

Aguirre, Anthony, and Steven Gratton. "Steady-State Eternal Inflation". *Physical Review D* 65, no. 8 (March 2002): 083507.

Alabidi, Laila, and David Lyth. "Inflation Models and Observation". *Journal of Cosmology and Astroparticle Physics* 0605 (2006): 016. doi:10.1088-1475-7516/2006/05016.

Alexander, Eben. "The Science of Heaven". *Newsweek*, November 18, 2012.

Aquinas, Thomas. *On Being and Essence*. Translated by Armand Maurer. 2nd rev. ed. Toronto, Canada: Pontifical Institute of Mediaeval Studies, 1968.

———. *Summa Contra Gentiles, Book One*. Translated by Anton C. Pegis. Notre Dame: Notre Dame University Press, 1991.

———. *The Summa Theologica of St. Thomas Aquinas*. Vol. 1. Translated by Fathers of the English Dominican Province. New York: Benziger Brothers, 1947.

Aristotle. *Aristotle's* Metaphysics. Translated and edited by Hippocrates Apostle. Grinnell, Iowa: Peripatetic Press, 1979.

———. *Aristotle's* On the Soul. Translated and edited by Hippocrates Apostle. Grinnell, Iowa: Peripatetic Press, 1981.

Armstrong, David. *The Nature of Mind and Other Essays*. Ithaca, N.Y.: Cornell University Press, 1980.

Augustine. *Confessions*. Translated by Henry Chadwick. New York: Oxford University Press, 1991.

Baker, David J. "Measurement Outcomes and Probability in Everettian Quantum Mechanics". *Studies in History and Philosophy of Science Part B: Studies In History and Philosophy of Modern Physics* 38, no. 1 (2007): 153–69.

Banks, T. "Entropy and Initial Conditions in Cosmology", January 16, 2007. http://arxiv.org/pdf/hep-th/0701146v1.pdf.

Barr, Stephen M. *Modern Physics and Ancient Faith*. Notre Dame: University of Notre Dame Press, 2003.

Basford, T. K. *Near-Death Experiences: An Annotated Bibliography.* New York: Garland, 1990.

Beauregard, Mario. *Brain Wars: The Scientific Battle over the Existence of the Mind and the Proof That Will Change the Way We Live.* New York: HarperOne, 2012.

———. "Near Death, Explained". *Salon*, April 21, 2012. http://www.salon.com/2012/04/21/near_death_explained.

Beauregard, Mario, and Denyse O'Leary. *The Spiritual Brain: A Neuroscientist's Case for the Existence of the Soul.* New York: HarperOne, 2008.

Beck, Friedrich. "Synaptic Quantum Tunneling in Brain Activity". *NeuroQuantology* 6, no. 2 (2008): 140–51.

Beck, Friedrich, and John C. Eccles. "Quantum Aspects of Brain Activity and the Role of Consciousness". *Proceedings of the National Academy of Sciences—USA* 89 (1992): 11357–61.

———. "Quantum Processes in the Brain: A Scientific Basis of Consciousness". In Naoyuki Oasaka, *Neural Basis of Consciousness*, pp. 141–65. Philadelphia: John Benjamins, 2003.

Bennett, Jonathan. *Rationality: An Essay Towards an Analysis.* 1964. Reprint, Indianapolis: Hackett, 1989.

Bergson, Henri. *Duration and Simultaneity.* Translated by Leon Jacobson. Indianapolis: Bobbs-Merrill, 1965.

Bermúdez, José L. *Thinking without Words.* Oxford: Oxford University Press, 2003.

Blacher, R. S. "To Sleep, Perchance to Dream ...". *Journal of the American Medical Association* 242, no. 21 (November 23, 1979): 2291.

Blackmore, Susan. *Dying to Live: Science and the Near-Death Experience.* London: Grafton, 1993.

Boekraad, Adrian, and Henry Tristram, eds. *The Argument from Conscience to the Existence of God according to J. H. Newman* [with an unpublished manuscript by Newman entitled "Proof of Theism"]. London: Mill Hill, 1961.

Borde, Arvind, Alan Guth, and Alexander Vilenkin. "Inflationary Spacetimes Are Not Past-Complete". *Physical Review Letters* 90, no. 15 (2003): 151301-1–151301-4.

Borde, Arvind, and Alexander Vilenkin. "Eternal Inflation and Initial Singularity". *Physical Review Letters* 72, no. 21 (1994): 3305–8.

———. "Violation of the Weak Energy Condition in Inflating Spacetimes". *Physical Review D* 56 (1997): 717–23.

Borjigin, Jimo. "Surge of Neurophysiological Coherence and Connectivity in the Dying Brain". *Proceedings of the National Academy of Sciences* 110, no. 5 (August 27, 2013): 14432–37.

Bradley, Walter L. "Designed or Designoid?" In *Mere Creation: Science, Faith and Intelligent Design*, edited by William A. Dembski, pp. 33–50. Downers Grove, Ill.: InterVarsity Press, 1998.

Breuer, R. *The Anthropic Principle: Man as the Focal Point of Nature*. Boston: Birkhauser, 1991.

Brown, Cindy Gunther, Stephen Mory, Rebecca Williams, and Michael McClymond. "Study of the Therapeutic Effects of Proximal Intercessory Prayer (STEPP) on Auditory and Visual Impairments in Rural Mozambique". *Southern Medical Journal* 103(9) (September 2010): 864–69.

Campbell, Joseph. *The Hero with a Thousand Faces*. Princeton: Princeton University Press, 1949.

Carroll, Sean. "Against Bounces". *Discover Magazine*, July 2, 2007. http://blogs.discovermagazine.com/cosmicvariance/2007/07/02/against-bounces/.

Carruthers, Peter. "Meta-Cognition in Animals: A Skeptical Look". *Mind and Language* 23 (2009): 58–59.

———. *Phenomenal Consciousness: A Naturalistic Theory*. Cambridge: Cambridge University Press, 2000.

Carter, Christopher. *Science and the Near-Death Experience: How Consciousness Survives Death*. Rochester, Vt.: Inner Traditions, 2010.

Chalmers, David. *The Character of Consciousness (Philosophy of Mind)*. London: Oxford University Press, 2010.

———. *The Conscious Mind: In Search of a Fundamental Theory*. London: Oxford University Press, 1997.

———. "Facing Up to the Problem of Consciousness". *Journal of Consciousness Studies* 2, no. 3 (1995): 200–219.

Chomsky, Noam. "The Case against B. F. Skinner". *The New York Review of Books*, December 30, 1971.

———. Interview by Matt Aames Cucchiaro, "On the Myth of Ape Language", 2007. http://www.chomsky.info/interviews/2007----.htm.

———. "A Review of B. F. Skinner's *Verbal Behavior*". In *Readings in the Psychology of Language*, edited by Leon A. Jakobovits and Murray S. Miron. Englewood Cliffs, N.J.: Prentice Hall, 1967.

Churchland, Patricia Smith. *Brain-Wise: Studies in Neurophilosophy*. Cambridge, Mass.: MIT Press, 2002.

Clark, Kim. "Clinical Interventions with Near-Death Experiencers". In *The Near-Death Experience: Problems, Prospects, Prospectives*, edited by B. Greyson and C. P. Flynn, pp. 242–48. Springfield, Ill.: Charles C. Thomas, 1984.

Coles, Robert. *The Spiritual Life of Children*. New York: Mariner Books, 1991.

Cook, E. W., B. Greyson, and I. Stevenson. "Do Any Near-Death Experiences Provide Evidence for the Survival of Human Personality After Death? Relevant Features and Illustrative Case Reports". *Journal of Scientific Exploration* 12 (1998): 377–406.

Coreth, Emerich. *Metaphysics*. Translated by Joseph Donceel. New York: Herder and Herder, 1968.

Cornwall, Marie, and Stan L. Albrecht, Perry H. Cunningham, and Brian L. Pitcher. "The Dimensions of Religiosity: A Conceptual Model with an Empirical Test". *Review of Religious Research* 27, no. 3 (March 1986): 226–44.

Craig, William. "Vilenkin's Cosmic Vision: A Review Essay of *Many Worlds in One: The Search for Other Universes*". *Philosophia Christi* 11 (2009): 232–38.

Craig, W. L., and J. Sinclair. "The Kalam Cosmological Argument". In *The Blackwell Companion to Natural Theology*, edited by W. L. Craig and J. P. Moreland, pp. 101–201. Malden, Mass.: Wiley-Blackwell, 2009.

Davidson, Donald. "The Emergence of Thought". *Erkenntnis* 51 (1997): 7–17.

———. "Thought and Talk". In *Inquiries into Truth and Interpretation*, pp. 155–79. Oxford: Clarendon Press, 1984.

Davies, Paul. *The Accidental Universe*. New York: Cambridge University Press, 1982.

———. *God and the New Physics*. New York: Simon and Schuster, 1983.

Dawkins, Richard. *The God Delusion*. New York: Mariner Books, 2008.

Dervic, Kanita, and Maria A. Oquendo, Michael F. Grunebaum, Steve Ellis, Ainsley Burke, and J. John Mann. "Religious Affiliation and Suicide Attempt". *American Journal of Psychiatry* 161, no. 12 (December 2004): 2303–8. http://ajp.psychiatryonline.org /article.aspx?articleid=177228.

Dine, Michael. "Is There a String Theory Landscape: Some Cautionary Remarks". February 17, 2004. http://arxiv.org/pdf/hep -th/0402101v2.pdf.

Eccles, Sir John. *Evolution of the Brain: Creation of the Self.* London, UK: Routledge, 1989.

————. *Facing Reality: Philosophical Adventures by a Brain Scientist.* Heidelberg: Heidelberg Science Library, 1970.

————, ed. *Mind and Brain: The Many-Faceted Problems.* St. Paul Minnesota: Paragon Books, 1983.

————. "A Unitary Hypothesis of Mind—Brain Interaction in the Cerebral Cortex". *Proceedings of the Royal Society—Biological Sciences B* 240 (1990): 433–51.

Eddington, Sir Arthur. *The Nature of the Physical World.* Cambridge: Cambridge University Press, 1928.

Eliade, Mircea. *Encyclopedia of Religion.* 16 vols. New York: Macmillan, 1986.

————. *The Myth of the Eternal Return: Or, Cosmos and History.* Princeton: Princeton University Press, 1971.

————. *Myths, Dreams, and Mysteries.* New York: Harper and Row, 1975.

————. *Patterns in Comparative Religion.* Nebraska: University of Nebraska Press, 1996.

————. *The Sacred and the Profane: The Nature of Religion.* New York: Harcourt Brace Jovanovich, 1987.

Everett, Hugh. "Relative State Formulation of Quantum Mechanics". *Reviews of Modern Physics* 29 (1957): 454–62.

Fararo, Thomas J., and John Skvoretz. "Action and Institution, Network and Function: The Cybernetic Concept of Social Structure". *Sociological Forum* 1, no. 2 (March 1, 1986): 219–50.

Fenwick, P., and E. Fenwick. *The Truth in the Light: An Investigation of Over 300 Near-Death Experiences.* New York: Berkley Books, 1995.

Fry, Roger. "Retrospect". In *Vision and Design*, edited by J. B. Bullen, pp. 199–212. Mineola, N.Y.: Dover Publications, 1998.

Gallup, George, Jr., and William Proctor. *Adventures in Immortality.* New York: McGraw-Hill, 1982.

Gallup, Gordon, Jr., J.R. Anderson, and D.J. Shillito. "The Mirror Test". In *The Cognitive Animal*, edited by M. Bekoff, C. Allen, and G. Burghardt, pp. 325–34. Cambridge, Mass.: MIT Press, 2002.

Gardner, Allen, Beatrix Gardner, and Thomas Van Cantfort. *Teaching Sign Language to Chimpanzees*. New York: State University of New York Press, 1989.

Gerver, Joseph. "The Past as Backward Movies of the Future". *Physics Today* 24, no. 4 (1971): 46–47.

Gil, Roger, E.M. Arroyo-Anllo, P. Ingrand, M. Gil, J.P. Neau, C. Ornon, and V. Bonnaud. "Self-Consciousness and Alzheimer's Disease". *Acta Neurologica Scandinavica* 104, no. 5 (2001): 296–300.

Gödel, Kurt. "Über formal unentscheidbare Sätze der Principia Mathematica undverwandter Systeme I". *Monatshefte für Mathematik und Physik* 38 (1931): 173–98.

Gordon, Bruce. "Inflationary Cosmology and the String Multiverse". In *New Proofs for the Existence of God: Contributions of Contemporary Physics and Philosophy*, by Robert J. Spitzer, pp. 75–103. Grand Rapids: Eerdmans, 2010.

Greenfield-Boyce, Nell. "Galaxy Quest: Just How Many Earth-Like Planets Are Out There?" NPR. November 5, 2013. www.npr.org /2013/11/05/242991030/galaxy-quest-just-how-many-earth-like -planets-are-out-there.

Greyson, Bruce. "Seeing Dead People Not Known to Have Died: 'Peak in Darien' Experiences". American Anthropological Association, November 21, 2010. http://onlinelibrary.wiley.com/doi /10.1111/j.1548-1409.2010.01064.x/abstract.

Greyson, B., and C.P. Flynn, eds. *The Near-Death Experience: Problems, Prospects, Perspectives*. Springfield, Ill.: Charles C. Thomas, 1984.

Groeschel, Benedict. *Spiritual Passages: The Psychology of Spiritual Development*. New York: Crossroads Publishing, 1984.

Grossman, Lisa. "Why Physicists Can't Avoid a Creation Event". *NewScientist*, January 11, 2012. http://www.newscientist.com /article/mg21328474.400-why-physicists-cant-avoid-a-creation-event.html.

Guth, Alan H. "Eternal Inflation". Paper presented at *Cosmic Questions*, National Museum of Natural History, Washington, D.C., April 14–16, 1999, pp. 1–15.

Habermas, Gary R. "Mapping the Recent Trend toward the Bodily Resurrection Appearances of Jesus in Light of Other Prominent

Critical Positions". In *The Resurrection of Jesus: John Dominic Crossan and N. T. Wright in Dialogue*, edited by Robert B. Stewart. Minneapolis: Fortress, 2006.

Hameroff, Stuart. "Quantum Computation in Brain Microtubules? The Penrose-Hameroff 'Orch OR' Model of Consciousness". In *Philosophical Transactions Royal Society London (A)* 356 (1998): 1869–96.

Hameroff, Stuart, and Roger Penrose. "Orchestrated Reduction of Quantum Coherence in Brain Microtubules: A Model for Consciousness". In *Toward a Science of Consciousness—The First Tucson Discussions and Debates*, edited by S. R. Hameroff, A. Kaszniak, and A. C. Scott, pp. 507–40. Cambridge, Mass.: MIT Press, 1996. Also published in *Mathematics and Computers in Simulation* 40 (1996): 453–80.

Hawking, Stephen. *A Brief History of Time: From the Big Bang to Black Holes*. New York: Bantam, 1988.

———. "Theoretical Advances in General Relativity". In *Some Strangeness in the Proportion*, edited by H. Woolf, pp. 145–55. Reading, Mass.: Addison-Wesley, 1980.

Hawking, Stephen, and Leonard Mlodinow. *The Grand Design*. New York: Random House, 2010.

Hawking, Stephen, and Roger Penrose. "The Singularities of Gravitational Collapse and Cosmology". *Proc. Roy. Soc. Lond. A* 314 (1970): 529–48.

Heiler, Friedrich. "The History of Religions as a Preparation for the Cooperation of Religions." In *The History of Religions*, edited by Mircea Eliade and J. Kitagawa, pp. 142–53. Chicago, Ill.: Chicago University Press, 1959.

Hermanns, William. *Einstein and the Poet: In Search of the Cosmic Man*. Wellesley, Mass.: Branden Books, 1983.

Holden, Janice. *Handbook of Near Death Experiences: Thirty Years of Investigation*. Westport, Conn.: Praeger Press, 2009.

———. "More Things in Heaven and Earth: A Response to Near-Death Experiences with Hallucinatory Features". *Journal of Near-Death Studies* 26, no. 1 (Fall 2007): 33–42.

Holton, Gerald, and Yehuda Elkana. *Albert Einstein: Historical and Cultural Perspectives*. Princeton: Princeton University Press, 1997.

Hosinski, Thomas. "Process, Insight, and Empirical Method: An Argument for the Compatibility of the Philosophies of Alfred

North Whitehead and Bernard J. F. Lonergan and Its Implications for Foundational Theology". Ph.D. dissertation, University of Chicago Divinity School, 1983. http://www.anthonyflood.com/hosinski12.htm.

Hoyle, Fred. "The Universe: Past and Present Reflections". *Engineering and Science* 45, no. 2 (November 1981): 8–12. http://calteches.library.caltech.edu/527/1/ES45.2.1981.pdf.

Husserl, Edmund. *The Crisis of European Sciences and Transcendental Philosophy*. Translated by D. Carr. Evanston, Ill.: Northwestern University Press, 1970.

———. *Erste Philosophie II*. Husserliana VIII. Den Haag: Martinus Nijhoff, 1959.

James, William. *The Varieties of Religious Experience*. New York: Modern Library, 1929.

John of the Cross. "The Living Flame of Love". In *The Collected Works of St. John of the Cross*. Translated by Kieran Kavanaugh and Otilio Rodriguez. Washington, D.C.: ICS Publications, 1979.

Jung, Carl. *The Archetypes and the Collective Unconscious*. In *Collected Works of C. G. Jung*. Vol. 9, pt. 1, translated by R. F. C. Hull. Princeton: Princeton University Press, 1981.

Kant, Immanuel. *Critique of Pure Reason*. Translated by Norman Kemp Smith. New York: St. Martin's Press, 1965.

———. *Kant's Critique of Practical Reason and Other Works on the Theory of Ethics*. Translated by T. K. Abbott. New York: Barnes and Noble, 2004.

———. *Opus Postumum*. Vol. 21. Berlin Critical Edition. Berlin: Georg Reimer, 1960.

Kelly, Emily. "Near-Death Experiences with Reports of Meeting Deceased People". *Death Studies* 25 (2001): 229–49. http://www.medicine.virginia.edu/clinical/departments/psychiatry/sections/cspp/dops/emily-kelly-pdfs/KEL13%20NDEwithReports%20of%20Meeting%20Deceased%20People.pdf/view.

Kelly, E. W., B. Greyson, and I. Stevenson. "Can Experiences Near Death Furnish Evidence of Life After Death?" *Omega: Journal of Death and Dying* 40 (2000): 39–45.

Kelly, Edward, Adam Crabtree, and E. W. Crabtree. *Irreducible Mind: Toward a Psychology for the 21st Century*. Lanham, Md.: Rowman & Littlefield, 2007.

Lemaître, Georges. *The Primeval Atom*. New York: University Press, 1943.

——. *Surprised by Joy: The Shape of My Early Life*. New York: Harcourt, Brace, Jovanovich, 1966.

Linde, Andrei. "The Self-Reproducing Inflationary Universe". In "The Magnificent Cosmos", special issue, *Scientific American*, March 1998, pp. 98–104.

Livio, Mario. "Mystery of the Missing Text Solved". Comment. *Nature* 479 (November 10, 2011): 171–73. http://www.fisica .ufmg.br/~dsoares/cosmos/11/mario-livio.pdf.

Lonergan, Bernard. *Insight: A Study of Human Understanding*. In *Collected Works of Bernard Lonergan* 3, edited by Frederick E. Crowe and Robert M. Doran. Toronto: University of Toronto Press, 1992.

——. *Method in Theology*. New York: Herder and Herder, 1972.

——. *Verbum: Word and Idea in Aquinas*. Vol. 2 of *Collected Works of Bernard J. F. Lonergan*, edited by Frederick E. Crowe. Toronto: University of Toronto Press, 1994.

Long, Jeffery. *Evidence of the Afterlife*. New York: HarperOne, 2010.

Lotz, Johannes B. "Beauty". In *Philosophical Dictionary*, translated and edited by Kenneth Baker. Spokane, Wash.: Gonzaga University Press, 1972.

Lucas, John R. "Mechanism: A Rejoinder". *Philosophy* 45 (1970): 149–51.

——. "Mind, Machines and Gödel: A Retrospect". Paper presented at the Turing Conference, Brighton, UK, April 6, 1990.

——. "Minds, Machines, and Gödel". *Philosophy* 36 (1961): 149–51.

Lycan, William. *Consciousness and Experience*. Cambridge: MIT Press, 1996.

Marczyk, Adam. "Genetic Algorithms and Evolutionary Computation". TalkOrigins Archive, April 23, 2004. http://www.talkorigins .org/faqs/genalg/genalg.html.

Matthew, Dale and Connie Clark. *The Faith Factor: Proof of the Healing Power of Prayer*. New York: Viking Books, 1998.

McLerran, Dan. "Chimps, Humans Share a Key Evolutionary Development, Study Says". *Popular Archaeology* 3 (August 11, 2011). http://popular-archaeology.com/issue/june-2011/article/chimps -humans-share-a-key-evolutionary-development-study-says.

Merleau-Ponty, Maurice. *Phénoménologie de la perception*. Paris: Éditions Gallimard, 1945. Translated by C. Smith as *Phenomenology of Perception* (London: Routledge and Kegan Paul, 1962).

Moody, Raymond A. *Life After Life*. New York: Harper Collins, 1975.

———. *The Light Beyond*. New York: Bantam Books, 1988.

———. *Reunions: Visionary Encounters with Departed Loved Ones*. New York: Random House, 1993.

Morse, Melvin. *Closer to the Light: Learning from the Near-Death Experiences of Children*. New York: Random House, 1990.

Moser, Paul. "Rationality without Surprise: Davidson on Rational Belief". *Dialectica* 37 (1983): 221–26.

Nagel, Thomas. *Mind and Cosmos*. London: Oxford University Press, 2012.

———. "What Is It Like to Be a Bat?" *Philosophical Review* 83 (1974): 435–50.

NASA. APPEL [Academy of Program/Project and Engineering Leadership] News Staff. "This Month in NASA History: WMAP Began to Transform Cosmology". June 25, 2014. http://appel.nasa.gov/2014/06/25/this-month-in-nasa-history-wmap-began-to-transform-cosmology/.

———. "COBE: Cosmic Background Explorer". Accessed February 23, 2015. http://lambda.gsfc.nasa.gov/product/cobe/.

———. "Planck Mission Brings Universe into Sharp Focus". March 21, 2013. www.nasa.gov/mission_pages/planck/news/planck20130321.html.

Newman, John Henry. *An Essay in Aid of a Grammar of Assent*. Notre Dame, Ind.: University of Notre Dame Press, 1992.

———. *An Essay in Aid of a Grammar of Assent*. Worcester, Mass.: Assumption Press, 2013.

———. *Sermons Preached on Various Occasions*. London: Longmans, Green, 1908.

Nuland, S.B. *How We Die: Reflections on Life's Final Chapter*. Norwalk, Conn.: Hastings House, 1994.

Otto, Rudolf. *The Idea of the Holy: An Inquiry into the Non-Rational Factor in the Idea of the Divine and Its Relation to the Rational*. New York: Oxford University Press, 1958.

Parboteeah, K. Praveen, Martin Hoegl, and John B. Cullen. "Ethics and Religion: An Empirical Test of a Multidimensional Model". *Journal of Business Ethics* 80, no. 2 (June 1, 2008): 387–98.

Parnia, Sam, et al. "AWARE—AWAreness during REsuscitation—A Prospective Study". *Journal of Resuscitation*, October 6, 2014, pp. 1799–805. http://www.resuscitationjournal.com/article/S0300-9572%2814%2900739-4/fulltext.

Parnia, Sam, and Josh Young. *Erasing Death: The Science That Is Rewriting the Boundaries between Life and Death*. New York: HarperOne, 2014.

Pearce, Joseph. *Tolkien Man and Myth*. San Francisco, Ignatius Press, 2001.

Penrose, Roger. "Beyond the Doubting of a Shadow". *Psyche* 2, no. 23 (1996): 89–129.

―――. *The Emperor's New Mind*. Oxford: Oxford University Press, 1989.

―――. *Shadows of the Mind*. Oxford: Oxford University Press, 1994.

Penrose, Roger, and S. R. Hameroff. "What 'Gaps'? Reply to Grush and Churchland". *Journal of Consciousness Studies* 2, no. 2 (1995): 99–112.

Penzias, Arno A., and Robert W. Wilson. "A Measurement of Excess Antenna Temperature at $408°$ Mc/s". *Astrophysical Journal* 142 (1965): 419–21.

Pew Research Center. "The Global Religious Landscape". December 18, 2012. http://www.pewforum.org/2012/12/18/global-religious-landscape-exec.

Piaget, Jean. *The Child's Conception of Physical Causality*. New York: Harcourt Brace, 1930.

―――. *The Essential Piaget*. Edited by Howard E. Gruber and J. Jacques Voneche. London: Routledge and Kegan Paul, 1977.

Plato. *The Collected Dialogues of Plato*. Edited by Edith Hamilton and Huntington Cairns. Princeton, N.J.: Princeton University Press, 1961.

―――. *Republic*. Translated by Paul Shorey. In *The Collected Dialogues of Plato*, Book VII, edited by Edith Hamilton and Huntington Cairns, pp. 747–51. Princeton, N.J.: Princeton University Press, 1961.

————. *Sophist*. Translated by F. M. Cornford. In *The Collected Dialogues of Plato*, edited by Edith Hamilton and Huntington Cairns, pp. 957–1017. Princeton, N.J.: Princeton University Press, 1961.

————. *Symposium and Phaedrus*. Translated by Benjamin Jowett. New York: Classic Books America, 2009.

————. *Timaeus*. Translated by Benjamin Jowett. In *The Collected Dialogues of Plato*, edited by Edith Hamilton and Huntington Cairns, pp. 1151–211. Princeton, N.J.: Princeton University Press, 1961.

Polanyi, Michael. *Being and Knowing*. London: Routledge and Kegan Paul, 1969.

————. "Life's Irreducible Structure". *Science* 160, no. 3834 (June 21, 1968): 1308–12.

————. *Personal Knowledge: Towards a Post-Critical Philosophy*. Chicago: University of Chicago Press, 1974.

————. *The Tacit Dimension*. Chicago: University of Chicago Press, 2009.

————. "Transcendence and Self-Transcendence". *Soundings* 53, no. 1 (1970): 88–94.

Popper, Karl, and John Eccles. *The Self and Its Brain: An Argument for Interactionism*. New York: Routledge, 1984.

Rahner, Karl. *Foundations of Christian Faith*. New York: Crossroad Publishing, 1982.

————. *Spirit in the World*. New York: Herder and Herder, 1968.

————. *Spirit in the World*. London: Bloomsbury Academic, 1994.

Ring, Kenneth. *Life at Death: A Scientific Investigation of the Near-Death Experience*. New York: Coward, McCann and Geoghegan, 1980.

Ring, Kenneth, Sharon Cooper, and Charles Tart. *Mindsight: Near-Death and Out-of-Body Experiences in the Blind*. Palo Alto, Calif.: William James Center for Consciousness Studies at the Institute of Transpersonal Psychology, 1999.

Ring, Kenneth, and Evelyn Elsaesser Valarino. *Lessons from the Light: What We Can Learn from the Near-Death Experience*. New York: Insight Books, 2006.

Roberts, G., and J. Owen. "The Near-Death Experience". *British Journal of Psychiatry* 153 (1988): 607–17.

Rodin, E. "The Reality of Death Experiences: A Personal Perspective". *Journal of Nervous and Mental Disease* 168 (1980): 259–63.

Russell, Peter. "The Anomaly of Consciousness". Science and Non-duality. June 6, 2014. http:// www.scienceandnonduality.com/the -anomaly-of-consciousness.

———. *From Science to God: A Physicist's Journey into the Mystery of Consciousness.* Novato, Calif.: New World Library, 2004.

Sabom, M.B. *Recollections of Death: A Medical Investigation.* New York: Harper and Row, 1982.

Searle, John. "Animal Minds". *Midwest Studies in Philosophy* 19 (1994): 206–19.

———. *Intentionality.* New York: Cambridge University Press, 1983.

———. *Rationality in Action.* Cambridge, Mass.: MIT Press, 2001.

———. *The Rediscovery of the Mind.* Cambridge, Mass.: Bradford/ MIT, 1991.

Singh, Simon. "Even Einstein Had His Off Days". Opinion, *New York Times,* January 2, 2005. http://www.nytimes.com/2005/01/02 /opinion/02singh.html?_r=0.

Spitzer, Robert J. "Definitions of Real Time and Ultimate Reality". *Ultimate Reality and Meaning: Interdisciplinary Studies in the Philosophy of Understanding* 23, no. 3 (2000): 260–67.

———. *Indications of Creation in Contemporary Big Bang Cosmology.* Vol. 10 of *Philosophy in Science.* Tucson: Pachart Publishing, 2003.

———. *New Proofs for the Existence of God: Contributions of Contemporary Physics and Philosophy.* Grand Rapids, Mich.: Eerdmans, 2010.

———. "Why Is Human Self-Consciousness Different from Artificial Intelligence and Animal Consciousness?". *Ultimate Reality and Meaning: Interdisciplinary Studies in the Philosophy of Understanding* 33, nos. 1–2 (2010): 5–27.

Stapp, Henry. "The Basis Problem in Many-World Theories". *Canadian Journal of Physics* 80 (2002): 1043–52.

———. *Mindful Universe: Quantum Mechanics and the Participating Observer.* New York: Springer Publications, 2007.

———. "Reply to a Critic: Mind Efforts, Quantum Zeno Effect and Environmental Decoherence". *NeuroQuantology* 10, no. 4 (2012): 601–5.

Stein, Edith. *On the Problem of Empathy.* Translated by Waltraut Stein. Washington, D.C.: Institute of Carmelite Studies Publications, 1989.

Stewart, Robert B., ed. *The Resurrection of Jesus: John Dominic Crossan and N. T. Wright in Dialogue.* Minneapolis, Minn.: Fortress Press, 2006.

Tanqueray, Adolphe. *The Spiritual Life: A Treatise on Ascetical and Mystical Theology.* Rockford, Ill.: Tan Books and Publishers, 2013.

Teresa of Avila. *The Book of Her Life.* In *The Collected Works of St. Teresa of Avila.* Vol. 1, translated by Kieran Kavanaugh and Otilio Rodriguez. Washington, D.C.: ICS Publications, 1976.

Terrace, Herbert S., L. A. Petitto, R. J. Sanders, and T. G. Bever. "Can an Ape Create a Sentence?" *Science* 206, no. 4421 (November 23, 1979): 891–902. http://www.sciencemag.org/content/206/4421/891.

Tittle, Charles R., and Michael R. Welch. "Religiosity and Deviance: Toward a Contingency Theory of Constraining Effects". *Social Forces* 61, no. 3 (March 1983): 653–82.

Topper, David. *How Einstein Created Relativity Out of Physics and Astronomy.* New York: Springer, 2013.

Tulving, Endel. "Episodic Memory and Autonoesis: Uniquely Human?" In *The Missing Link in Cognition: Origins of Self-Reflective Consciousness,* edited by Herbert Terrace and Janet Metcalfe, pp. 3–56. New York: Oxford University Press, 2005.

Turner, Jonathan H. *The Institutional Order.* New York: Addison-Wesley Educational Publishers, 1997.

Underhill, Evelyn. *Mysticism: A Study in the Nature and Development of Spiritual Consciousness.* New York: Renaissance Classics, 2012.

Van Lommel, Pim. *Consciousness beyond Life.* New York: HarperOne, 2010.

Van Lommel, Pim, and Ruud van Wees, Vincent Meyers, and Ingrid Elfferich. "Near-Death Experience in Survivors of Cardiac Arrest: A Prospective Study in the Netherlands". *The Lancet* 358, no. 9298 (2001): 2039–45.

Vilenkin, Alexander. *Many Worlds in One: The Search for Other Universes.* New York: Hill and Wang, 2006.

Von Balthasar, Hans Urs. *The Glory of the Lord: A Theological Aesthetics.* Translated by Erasmo Leiva-Merikakis. Vol. 1, *Seeing the Form.* Edinburgh: T and T Clark, 1982.

Von Neumann, John. *Mathematical Foundations of Quantum Mechanics.* Translated by Robert Beyer. Princeton: Princeton University Press, 1996.

Watson, J.N. "Mind and Brain". In *Mind and Brain: The Many-Faceted Problems*, edited by Sir John Eccles, pp. 315–25. St. Paul Minn.: Paragon, 1983.

Weaver, Gary R., and Bradley R. Agle. "Religiosity and Ethical Behavior in Organizations: A Symbolic Interactionist Perspective". *Academy of Management Review* 27, no. 1 (January 2002): 77–97.

Wright, N. T. *The Resurrection of the Son of God*. Minneapolis, Minn.: Fortress Press, 2003.

Zaleski, C. *Otherworld Journeys: Accounts of Near-Death Experience in Medieval and Modern Times*. Oxford: Oxford University Press, 1987.

NAME INDEX

SUBJECT INDEX